AF564665

The Vaiśeshika Aphorisms of Kaṇāda

The Vaiśeshika system forms one of the most important among six orthodox schools of early Indian Philosophy. The founder of this school was Kaṇāda or Ulūka and the philosophy was termed as Vaiśeshika because in it has been discussed *viśesha* as a category of knowledge.

The *Vaiśeshika-sūtra* of Kaṇāda, the first systematic work propounding this philosophy, is divided into ten *adhyāyas* or books, each book consisting of two *āhnikas* or lessons. The present English translation of the original Sanskrit text is being published along with the commentary on the text by Śaṅkara Miśra and Jaya-Nārāyaṇa. Tarkapañchānana elaborating and explaining the concepts basic to the subject.

Being the basic work on this important school of Indian philosophy, the present translation is indispensable alike for the students and teachers of Indian philosophy.

The Vaiśeshika Aphorisms of Kaṇāda

With comments from the Upaskāra of Śankara Misra and the Vivritti of Jaya-Nārāyaṇa Tarkapañchānana

Translated by
Archibald Edward Gough

Dev Publishers & Distributors
New Delhi

Published by:
Dev Publishers & Distributors
Second Floor, Prakashdeep,
22, Delhi Medical Association Road,
Darya Ganj,
New Delhi - 110 002
Phone : +91-11-43572647
e-mail: devbooks@hotmail.com
www.devbooks.co.in

ISBN 978-93-81406-31-1
This edition 2014

© 2014, **Dev Publishers & Distributors**

Copyright reserved. Subject to the exceptions provided by the law, no part of this publication may be reproduced and/or published in print, by photocopying, on microfilm or in any other way without the written consent of the copyright-holder(s); the same applies to whole or partial adaptations. The publisher retains the sole right to collect from third parties fees in respect of copying and/or take legal or other action for this purpose.

Printed in India

Contents

Preface

The following pages will, it is trusted, facilitate to Sanskrit students the perusal of the original text, and to general readers an estimate, of one of the schools of Indian thought. Such interest as they may claim, will be historical, as a picture of a low stage of metaphysical culture. The system must be judged from its proper place in the history of philosophy; not hastily condemned from a modern point of view. The Indian cosmologies, imperfect in analysis, and hasty in synthesis, may be compared to the pre-Socratic schemes among the Greeks. In India, the Socratic reform in method has been wanting, and speculation has lapsed into a fruitless scholasticism. By these systems, however, it is that Indian thinkers are formed, and we may well remember that in mental discipline "speculation is higher than speculative truth," and that where philosophers "have not realized truth, they, have always determined exertion."[1]

The technical terms employed in translation are necessarily rather suggestive than reproductive of the original. The artificial groupings, or (to use Locke's expression) mixed modes, of European and of Indian thought, intersect and overlap, rather than coincide with, one another. The reader should bear this in mind, that he may avoid the misleading associations of an English terminology.

A brief indication of the conceptions dominant in the Vaiśeshika system, may be useful to the uninitiated. These are the transition of souls from everlasting through new embodiments and new spheres of being; therein reaping in pleasures and pains the fruits of merits and demerits ever reproduced as seed by plant and plant by seed; the atomic aggregates which make up the object world, eternally disintegrated and redintegrated by

1 See Sir W. Hamilton's Discussions, pp. 40–42.

the efficacy of works, with or without—for it is questioned—the intervention of a creator spirit. Thus in bondage to sensuous experience, painful at the best, the soul must wait its release until, the uderstanding purified by good works, it attains to knowledge of the modes of being. This knowledge disengages the soul from its appetent and active functions, and merges it in the absolute.

English readers will find abundant information, for further guidance, in Colebrooke's *Essays on the Religion and Philosophy of the Hindūs,* the Rev. K.M. Banerjea's *Dialogues on Hindū Philosophy,* Dr. Fitzedward Hall's *Rational Refutation of Hindū Philosophy* translated from the Hindī of the Rev. Nehemiah Nīlakaṇtha, Professor Max Müller's Essay on Indian Logic appended to Abp. Thomson's Laws of Thought, and the articles on the "Vaiśeshika and other Indian philosophies" in *Chambers's Encyclopaedia,* Those who read Sanskrit will find a useful epitome of the Vaiśeshika doctrines in the *Tattva-padārtha-sāra* the work of an illustrious pandit of the present day, Jayanārāyaṇa-Tarkapañchānana late professor of Hindū Philosophy in the Government Sanskrit College Calcutta, the author of the Vivṛtti from which many of the comments in the following pages are reproduced.

The translation of the Vaiśeshika Aphorisms is reprinted from the 'Pandit,' a monthly publication of the Benares Sanskrit College. It was undertaken at the instance of Mr. R.T.H. Griffith, the learned principal of the Benares College, as supplementary, in however imperfect a manner, to the text-books of the other Indian systems translated by the late Dr. Jas. Ballantyne. The text followed is that of Dr. Röer and Pandit Jayanārāyaṇa Tarkapañchānana published in the Bibliotheca Indica.

Its re-appearance is due to Dr. E.J. Lazarus, proprietor of the Benares Medical Hall Press, to whom Indian literature is already largely indebted for similar encouragement.

Benares College

Book I

FIRST DAILYLESSON

Introduction[1]

All students who wish to shun the multitude of pains engendered in this world by birth, old age, death, and the like, learn from revelation, tradition, the epies, the Purāṇas, and other sources, that the means of escaping them is investigation of the real nature of soul. Now, certain disciples who had in the prescribed manner studied the Vedas and their subordinate sciences, unenvious, and attentive hearers, in quest of knowledge reverentially approached the great and holy sage Kaṇāda. The sage full of compassion taught them the system of the ten sections. Enunciation, definition, investigation [of the adequacy of definitions],—such is the threefold method of this system. Division is only a particular kind of enuniation; hence there is no addition [to be made]. Although description of the categories is the chief object of this treatise, yet from the importance of merit as the instrumental cause of real knowledge of the categories, he in the first place promises a description of that. *Vivṛti.*[1]

अथातो धर्मं व्याख्यास्यामः।। 1।।

Aph. 1. Now, then, we will explain [what] merit [is].

" 'Now,' means after being requested by his disciples. 'Then,' since pupils quick in hearing etc., and unenvious have approached. Or

[1] इह खलु जन्मजरामरणादिजनिततापकलापं जिहासवः सर्व एवान्तेवासिनस्तद्धानिदानमात्मतत्त्व-दर्शनमाकर्णयन्ति श्रुतिस्मृतीतिहासपुराणादिषु। अथ केचिदन्तेवासिनो विधिवदधीतवेदवेदाङ्गां अनसूयकाः सम्पन्नश्रवणा मननार्थं भगवन्तं कणादमहर्षि विधिवदुपसेदुः। ततः परमकारुणिकः स मुनिर्दशाध्यायीतन्त्रं तानुपदिदेश। उद्देशो लक्षणं परीक्षा चेति त्रिविधा ऽस्य शास्त्रस्य प्रवृत्तिः विभागस्तु विशेषोद्देश एवेति नाधिक्यम्। यद्यप्यत्र तन्त्रे पदार्थनिरूपणस्यैव प्राचुर्यं तथापि पदार्थतत्त्वज्ञाननिदानतया धर्मस्यैव प्राधान्यात् तन्निरूपणमेव प्रथमं प्रतिजानीते।।

else the word 'Now' *(atha)* has an auspicious sense. Thus, it is said. "The syllable *Om* and the word *atha,* these two cleft of old the throat of Brahmā and issued forth; therefore both are of happy omen.[1]" *Upaskāra.*

यतो ऽभ्युदयनिःश्रेयससिद्धिः स धर्मः।। 2।।

Merit defined

Aph. 2. Merit is that from which (results) attainment of elevation and of the highest good.

It might be objected that because merit is not productive of any result, a description of it is useless. Hence, he states its characteristic, shewing that to merit belongs the attainment of the highest object of man. Exaltation is paradise; the highest good is emancipation; that cause from which [results] the attainment—production—, of these is merit : and therefore it is fitting that merit should be explained, inasmuch as, by reason of its effecting the highest object of man which consists of paradise and liberation [of the soul], it is to be acquired by those who are desirous of enjoyment and of emancipation.[2] V.

Exaltation is knowledge of the truth; the highest good is final cessation of pain; that from which both [result] is merit. The highest good is [attained] by means of exaltation. If this be the meaning, the compound [*abhyudaya-nihśreyasa*] has an ellipse of a central member or is a Tat-purusha ablatively dependent, and merit is implied to be characterized by Cessation ([of pain]; but if merit to be attained by practices such as devout meditation, etc., and [synonymous with] the result of good actions done is a former state of being, then the compound is regular in form.[3] U.

[1]अथेति शिष्याकाङ्क्षानन्तर्यमाह।.अत इति। यतः श्रवणादिपटवो ऽनसूयकाश्चान्तेवासिन उपसेदुरित्यर्थः। यद्वा अथशब्दो मङ्गलार्थः। तदुक्तम्।

ओङ्कारश्चाथशब्दश्च द्वावेतो ब्रह्मणः पुरा।
कण्ठं भित्त्वा विनिर्यातौ तेन माङ्गलिकावुभौ।। इति।।

[2]ननु धर्मस्याकिञ्चित्करत्वेन तन्निरूपणं व्यर्थमतो धर्मस्य परमपुरुषार्थसाधनत्वं दर्शयन् तल्लक्षणमाह। अभ्युदयः स्वर्गः निःधेयसं मोक्षस्तयोः सिद्धिरुत्पत्तिर्यतः कारणात् स धर्मः तथा च स्वर्गापवर्गरूपपरम-पुरुषार्थसाधनतया बुभुक्षूणां मुमुक्षूणाञ्चोपादेयत्वाद्धर्मस्य व्याख्यानं युक्तमेव।।

[3]अभ्युदयस्तत्त्वज्ञानं निःश्रेयसमात्यन्तिकी दुःखनिवृत्तिः तदुभयं यतः स धर्मः अभ्युदयद्वारकं निःश्रेयसमिति मध्यपदलोपी समासः पञ्चमीतत्पुरुषो वा स च धर्मो निवृत्तिलक्षणो वक्ष्यते यदि तु निदिध्यासनादियोग-साध्यो धर्मो ऽदृष्टभव तदा विधिरूपः।।

[*Note:* Exaltation according to the Upaskāra means either knowledge of the truth (*tattva-jñāna*) or the result of good works done in a former birth *(adṛshṭa)*. If it signifies knowledge of the truth, the aphorism must be translated, 'That is merit from which [results] the highest good by means of exaltation.' If the result of actions done in a former life be intended by exaltation, the aphorism is to be rendered as above.]

The attainment of paradise by merit is with visible means, while the attainment of liberation is by means of knowledge of the truth; consequently, there is a distinction.[1] V.

He proceeds to remove the doubt. What proof is there of (the existance of) merit and of its being the means of attaining to knowledge of the truth, etc. If you say, the Veda, we reply not so, for the authority of that is doubted, and accordingly an aphorism of Aksha-charana says, That (Veda) is unauthoritative being vitiated by falsity, self-contradictoriness, and repetition.[2] V

तद्वचनादाम्नायस्य प्रामाण्यम्।। 3।।

The Veda authoritative

Aph. 3. Authoritativeness belongs to revelation because it is declaration of that.

The word that *(tat)* signifies God though he has not been previously mentioned, it being inferred from his being universally known, just as in the aphorism of Gautama, 'That is unauthoritative being vitiated by falsity, self-contradictoriness, and repetition,' by the word 'That' the Veda is signified though not previously mentioned. Accordingly authori-tativeness belongs to revelation— the Veda—, because it was declared by him—revealed by God. Or else 'That' signifies the contiguous [zword] merit, and accordingly authoritativeness belongs to revelation— the Veda— because it declares—expounds— merit: for whatever statement sets forth a matter of certain knowledge is an authority.[3] U.

[1]धर्मस्य स्वर्गसाधनता साक्षादेव अपवर्गसाधनता तु तत्त्वाज्ञानद्वारेति विशेषः।।

[2]ननु धर्मे तस्य तत्त्वाज्ञानादिसाधनत्वे च किं मानं वेद एव मानमिति चेत् न तत्प्रामाण्यस्यापि सन्दिग्धत्वात् तथा चाक्षचरणसूत्रं तदप्रामाण्यमनृतव्याघातपुनरुक्तदो प्रेभ्य इतीत्याशङ्कां निरस्यति।।

[3]तदित्यनुप्रक्रान्तमपि प्रसिद्धिसिद्धतयेश्वरं परामृशति यथा तदप्रामाण्यनृत व्याघातपुनरुक्तदोषेभ्य इति गौतमीयसूत्रे तच्छब्देनानुपक्रान्तोऽपि वेदः परामृश्यते। तथा च तद्वचनात् तेनेश्वरेण प्रणयनादाम्नायस्य वेदस्य प्रामाण्यं यद्वा तदिति सन्निहितं धर्ममेव परामृशति तथा च धर्मस्य वचनात् प्रतिपादनात् आम्रायस्य वेदस्य प्रमाण्यं यद्धि वाक्यं प्रमाणिकमर्थं प्रतिपादयति तत्प्रमाणमेव यत इत्यर्थः।।

By the word 'That' expressive of something already known God is signified, though not previously mentioned. And, accordingly, the sense is that the authoritativeness of the Veda must necessarily be admitted since it was declared by an everlasting, all-wise, and all holy Spirit.[2] V

धर्मविशेषप्रसूताद् द्रव्यगुणकर्मसामान्यविशेषसमवायानां पदार्थानां साधर्म्यवैधर्म्याभ्यां तत्त्वज्ञानान्निःश्रेयसम्।। 4।।

Means of attaining the highest good

Aph. 4. The high good (results) from knowledge of the truth which springs from particular merit (and is obtained) by means of the similarity and dissimilarity of the categories, substance, attribute, action, generality, particularity, and inhesion.

Such knowledge of the truth depends upon the Vaiśeshika system, hence even causation of the highest good belongs to that [system]. Between the system and the highest good the connection of relation of cause to effect, between the system and knowledge of the truth the connection of relation of agency to the agent, between the highest good and knowledge of the truth the connection of relation of effect to cause, between the categories substance, etc. and the system the connection of relation of matter expounded to exposition, is understood to exist. It is from knowledge of these connections that in this world, seekers of the highest good apply themselves to this system. The highest good is final cessation of pain. Finality of cessation of pain is non-simultaneity with antecedent non-existence [potential existence] of pain in the common substratum, or simultaneity with subsequent nonexistence [destruction] of all particular qualities of soul which are produced at the same time and have a common substratum. Or emancipation [of the soul] is potential existence of pain terminated by cessation of all particular qualities [of the soul]. In the second aphorism of Gautama it is stated that on the successive removal of pain, birth, activity, faults (i.e., desires and aversions) and false knowledge, and on their consequent non-existence emancipation ensues. Here the argument from non-existence of cause to non-existence of effect proves emancipation to be characterised by antecedent non-existence of pain, for with respect to the removal of activity, consequent upon the removal of vice, the removal

[1] ईश्वरस्याप्रक्रान्तत्वेऽपि प्रसिद्धार्थकेन तच्छब्देन परामर्शो भवत्येव तथाच नित्य सर्वज्ञनिर्दोषपुरुषप्रणीतत्वात् वेदस्य प्रामाण्यमवश्यमेवाभ्युग्रेयमित्यर्थः।।

of birth on the removal of activity and the removal of pain on the removal of birth. Such removal is not subsequent non-existence but non-production, and non-production is antecedent non-existence. From knowledge of the truth which springs from particular merit,—such is the special character of that [knowledge], and accordingly particular merit is merit differentiated by finality; but if by knowledge of the truth the [Vaiśeshika] system be intended (the truth being known by means of that system), then particular merit must be explained as characterized by the ordinance and grace of God, for it is a tradition that the great saint Kaṇāda revealed the system in consequence of having obtained the ordinance and grace of God.[1] U.

Particular merit is particular good works done either in this life or in a former state of existence. By special good works, knowledge of the truth is produced by means of the similarity and dissimilarity of substance and the other categories. Next meditation on the soul is produced; next by means of meditation a [mental] presentation of the soul is produced; and after that, by means of destruction of false knowledge etc., emancipation ensures. In this place, there is mention of six categories spoken of as existing, but in reality non-existence is also implied by the sage as another category. Accordingly, there is no discrepancy in such aphorisms as the following in the second daily lesson, 'From non-existence of cause is non-existence of effect,' and in the ninth book, [An effect has non antecedent existence] because of the non-existence of ascription to it of actions and attributes.[2] V.

[1] एतादृशं तत्त्वज्ञानं वैशेषिकशास्त्राधीनमिति तस्याति निःश्रेयसहेतुत्वं दण्डापूपायित्म शास्त्रनिः-श्रेयसयोर्हेतुहेतुमद्भावः शास्त्रतत्त्वज्ञानयोर्व्यापारव्यापारिभावः निःश्रेय सतत्त्वज्ञानयोः कार्यकारणभावः द्रव्यादिपदार्थशास्त्रयोः प्रतिपाद्यप्रतिपादकभावः सम्बन्धो ऽवगम्यते एतेषाञ्च सम्बन्धानां ज्ञानान्निःश्रेयसार्थिनामिह शास्त्रे प्रवृत्तिः। निःश्रेय समात्यन्तकी दुःखनिवृत्तिः। दुःखनिवृत्तेश्चात्यन्तिकत्वं समानाधि-करणदुःखप्रागभावासमानकालीनत्वं युगपदुत्पन्नसमानाधिकरणसर्वात्मविशेषगुणाध्वंसमानकालीनत्वं वा। अशेषविषेषगुणध्वंसावधिकदुःखप्रागभावो वा मुक्तिः। गौतमीयद्वितीयसूत्रे दुःखजन्मप्रवृत्तिदोष-मिथ्याज्ञानानमुत्तरोत्तरापाये तदनन्तराभावादपवर्ग इत्यत्र कारणाभावात् कार्याभावाभिधानं दुःखप्रागभावरूपामेव मुक्तिं दृढयति नहि दोषापाये प्रवृत्त्यपायः प्रवृत्त्यपाये जन्मापायः जन्मापाये दुःखापाय इत्यपायो ध्वंसः किन्त्वनुत्पत्तिः सा च प्रागभाव एव। धर्मविशेषप्रसूतादिति तत्त्वज्ञानादित्यस्य विशेषणं तत्र धर्मविशेषो निवृत्तिलक्षणो धर्मः यदि तु तत्त्वं ज्ञायते ऽनेनेति तत्त्वज्ञानं शास्त्रमुच्यते तदा धर्मविशेष ईश्वनियोगप्रसादरूपो वक्तव्यः श्रूथते हीश्वरनियोगप्रसादावधिगम्य कणादो महर्षिः शास्त्रं प्रणीतवानिति।।

[2] धर्मविशेषः ऐहिको जन्तान्मारीयो वा सुकृतविशेषः। सुकृतविशेषेण द्रव्यादिपदार्थानां साधर्म्यावैधर्म्याभ्यां तत्त्वज्ञानं जायते तत श्रात्ममननं अनन्तरं निदिध्यासनेनात्मसाक्षात्कारो जायते तदनन्तरं मिथ्याज्ञानादिनाशक्रमेणा मोक्षो भवतीत्यर्थः। अत्र षट्पदार्थकीर्त्तनं भावाभिप्रायेण वस्तुतो ऽभावो ऽपि पदार्थान्तरतया मुनेरभिप्रेतः।

पृथिव्यापस्तेजो वायुराकाशं कालो दिगात्मा मन इति द्रव्याणि।। 5।।

Division of substance

Aph. 5. Earth, water, light, air, ether, time, space, soul, and the internal organ, —are the substances.

The particle *iti* is expressive of limitation, therefore the meaning is that there are nine substances, neither more nor less. If it be objected, What is the use of the particular *iti* when the exclusion of a lesser or greater number [of substances] is effected by the mere force of the division? This is to be determined,that it is because the particle *iti* is employed to indicate the logical subject in the construction of the aphorism, and only in order to elucidate the purport of the division since gold, etc., and God are included in this [enumeration], and since it is explained [in V. 2, 19] that darkness, suspected [by some] of being additional, is a non-existence. The construction without the use of compound words is to shew the importance of all [the substances]; and the author of the aphorisms himself will point out their definitions when treating of their dissimilarities.[1] U.

Note—Cp., the *Muktāvalī* on Bhāṣā-pariccheda 3.[3] If it be objected. There is a tenth substance, darkness; why is it not enumerated? for it is cognized by preception; and substantiality belongs to it because it is possessed of colour and action; and, because devoid of odour, it is not earth; and, because it possesses dark colour, it is not water, etc.; and the eye deprived of light is the organ [used] in perceiving it. We reply that it is not so, because it is illogical to imagine another substance, when it is necessarily produced by non-existence of light. The notion that it is possessed of colour is erroneous. The notion that it possesses action is also an error occasioned by the departure of light. It will be declared how it is that gold is included in light.

Darkness was affirmed to be a substance by the Sāṅkhyas; gold by the Mīmāṁsakas.

अत एव द्वितीयाह्निके कारणाभावात् कार्याभाव इति सूत्रस्य नवमाध्याये क्रियागुणव्यपदेशाभावात् इत्यादि सूत्राणाञ्च नासङ्गतिः।

[1] इतिकारो ऽवधारणार्थः तेन नवैव द्रव्याणि नाधिकानि न न्यूनानीत्यर्थः। ननु विभागबलादेव न्यूनाधिक-सङ्ख्यासव्यवच्छेदसिद्धौ किमितिकारेणेति चेत् उद्देशमात्रपरतया ऽपि सूत्रसम्भवे विभागतात्पर्यस्फोरणार्थ-मेवेतिकाराभिधानात् सुवर्णादीनामीश्वरस्य चात्रैवान्तर्भावात् अन्धकारस्य चाधिकत्वेनाशङ्क्यमानस्याभावत्वव्युत्पाद-नादेतदध्यवसेयम्। असमासकरणं तु सर्वेषां प्राधान्यप्रदर्शनाय लक्षणमेतेषांतु वैधर्म्यावसरे सूत्रकृदेव दर्शयिष्यति।।

The construction without the use of compound words is designed to show that all the substances, independently of one another, produce particular effects, or is intended to teach that they all equally produce effects which inhere in them. Among these nine divisions of substance, ether, time, and space do not form any class since they have only a single existence, but the rest form classes.[1] V.

रूपरसगन्धस्पर्शाः सङ्ख्याः परिमाणानि पृथक्त्वं संयोगविभागौ परत्वापरत्वे बुद्धयः सुखदुःखे इच्छाद्वषौ प्रयत्नाश्च गुणाः।। 6।।

Qualities enumerated

Aph. 6. Colour, taste, smell and touch, numbers, extensions, individuality, conjunction and disjunction, priority and posteriority, intellections, pleasure and pain, desire and aversion, and volitions are qualities.

By the particle *cha,* he implies in addition to these gravity, fluidity, viscidity, self-restitution, merit, demerit, and sound; for those being well-known to be qualities are not expressly mentioned. He will explain in the proper place from their characteristic and form that these are qualities. The compound 'colour, taste, smell, and touch,' is intended to point out that there is no common substratum of synchronous colours, tastes, smells, and touches. Numbers and extensions are not made a compound word and are named in the plural number, the design being to indicate that contemporaneous numbers and extensions have a common substratum. Although the common substratum of unity is not another unity, and the common substratum of greatness and length, in not another greatness and length, yet duality, etc. are the common substratum of each other, and in greatness, length, etc., is a common substratum for two heterogeneous extensions. Although individuality is the common substratum for the individuality of two, etc., and should accordingly be specified in the plural like numbers, yet the singular is

[1] ननु दशमं द्रव्यं तमः कुतो नोक्तं। तद्धि प्रत्यक्षेण गृह्यते। तस्य च रूपवत्त्वात् कर्मवत्त्वाच्च द्रव्यत्वम्। तच्च गन्धशून्यत्वात् न पृथिवी। नोलरूपवत्त्वाच्च न जलादि कम्। तत्प्रत्यक्षे चालोकनिरपेक्षं चक्षुः करणमिति चेत्। न। आवश्यकतेजो ऽमावेनो पपत्तौ द्रव्यान्तरकल्पनाया अन्यायत्वात्। रूपवत्ताप्रतीतिस्तु भ्रमरूपा। कर्मवत्त्वप्रती तिरपिआलोकापसारणौपाधिकी भान्तिरेव। स्वर्णस्य यथा तेजस्यन्तर्भावस्तथा वक्ष्यते।।

[1] असमासकरणं तु सर्वेषामितरनैरपेक्ष्येण कार्यविशेषोत्पादकताप्रदर्शनार्थं स्वसमवे तकार्यजनने सर्वेषां तुल्यताज्ञापनार्थं वा। अत्र नवसु द्रव्यविभाजकेषु गगनत्वकालत्व दित्तवानामेकैकमात्रवृत्तित्वान्न जातित्वं शेषाणां पुनर जातित्त्वमेवेति।।

employed to indicate its difference from numbers, on account of its being characterized by the implying of limitation. Conjunction and disjunction are expressed by [one word in] the dual to indicate that, though two, they are produced by one action [or motion]. Priority and posteriority are expressed in the dual to imply that they are relative to one another, and to imply that they are indifferently properties of space and time. The plural intellections is intended to expel the doctrine of the Sāṅkhyas that intellection is one only, on the grounds of their division into knowledge, etc. The dual term pleasure and pain is used to establish [the doctrine] that they, though two, produce one effect to be distinguished as fruition, that they indifferently bring to pass the consequences of actions done in a former state, and that even pleasure must be accounted as pain. Desire and aversion are in the dual to indicate that both are causes of activity. The plural form of volitions implies that they are the cause of merit from ten kinds of lawful and prohibited objects, and the cause of sin from ten kinds of objects. Or else colour, taste, smell, and touch are mentioned in a compound word to teach that they are the cause of the relation between the elements and the organs of sense, or else to establish the effects which are produced by heat. There is a contrariety in number which consists of duality, plurality, etc.:—it is to imply the denial of this that [number] is mentioned in the plural. Individuality is enumerated separately to denote that it is manifold by reason of the plurality of numbers, and to imply that its difference from number consists in revealing the knowledge of a limit. In the case of extension, the plural is used to deny that there is any contrariety between length, breadth, etc. Conjunction and disjunction are in the dual to denote their mutual opposition.[1] U.

[1] चकारेण गुरुत्वद्रवत्वस्नेहसंस्कारधर्माधर्मशब्दान् समुच्चनोति ते हि प्रसिद्धगुणभावा एवेति कण्ठतो नोक्ताः। गुणात्वञ्चामीषां यथास्थानं लक्षणतः स्वरूपतश्च वक्ष्यति रूपरसगन्धस्पर्शानां समानकालीनरूप-रसगन्धस्पर्शसामानाधिकरण्यं नास्तीति सूचनार्थं समासः संख्यापरिमाणयोस्तु समानकालीनसंख्यापरिमाण-सामानाधिकरण्यसूचनायासमासो बहुवचननिर्देशश्च यद्यप्येकत्वसमानाधिकरणं नैकत्वान्तरं न वा महत्त्वदीर्घत्वसमानाधिकरणं महत्त्वदीर्घत्वान्तरं तथापि द्वित्वादीनामन्योन्यं सामानाधिकरण्यं महत्त्वदीर्घत्वादीनाञ्च विजातीयपरिमाणयोः सामानाधिकरण्यमस्त्येव। पृथत्तवञ्च यद्यपि द्विपृथत्तवादिसमानाधिरणं तेन संख्या-वद्बहुत्वेनैव निर्देष्टुमर्हति तथाप्यवधिव्यङ्ग्ययत्वलक्षणं संख्यातो वैधर्म्यं सूचयितुमेकवचननिर्देशः। संयोगविभागयोर्द्वयौरप्येककर्मजन्यत्वसूचनाय द्विवचनं परत्वापरत्वयोरन्योन्याश्रयनिरूप्यतया दिक्काललिङ्गत्वावशेषसूचनाय च द्विवचनं बुद्धीनां विद्यादिभेदेन सांख्याभिमतैकमात्रबुद्धिनिराकरणसूचनाय बहुवचनं सुखदुःखयोर्द्वयोरपि भोगत्वावच्छेदौककार्यजनकत्वमविशेषेण चादृष्टोन्नायकत्वं सुखस्यापि दुःखेनापि भावनञ्च ख्यापयितुं द्विवचनं इन्छाद्वेषयोर्द्वयोरपि प्रवृत्तिं प्रति कारणत्वसूचनाय द्विवचनं प्रयत्नानां

उत्क्षेपणमवक्षेपणमाकुञ्चनं प्रसारणं गमनमिति कर्माणि।। 7।।

Enumeration of action

Aph. 7. Throwing upwards, throwing downwards, contracting, expanding, and going are the actions.

Actions by reason of their production by substances and by qualities, and from their inhesion in substances possessed of colour, are known by perception. Accordingly after the enumeration of substances and qualities [Kaṇāda] declared the enunciation and division of actions.[1] U.

Iti as before expresses limitation. Action as a class is cognized by perception, so also are throwing upwards, etc., according to the author of the Muktāvalī. Going is a particular class comprising revolution, evacuation, dropping, flaming upwards, bending up and down, etc.[2] V.

सदनित्यं द्रव्यवत् कार्यं कारणं सामान्यविशेषवदिति द्रव्यगुणकर्मणामविशेषः।। 8।।

Common element in substance, quality, and action

Aph. 8. Existence, transitoriness, inhesion in substance, effect, cause, and possession of generality and particularity are the common element of substances, qualities, and actions.

After *iti,* the word *pratyaya* is to be supplied. The general is existence, the particular is substantiality. The notion 'existence,' etc., is applicable to quality and action as well as to substance, in this there is no particularity. Therefore, existence, opposition to subsequent non-existence [or to destruction], the possession of substance as a coinherent [or material] cause, opposition to antecedent non-

विहितनिषिद्धगोचराणां दशविधानां पुण्यहेतुत्वं दशविधानाञ्च पापहेतुत्वमभिसन्धाय बहुवचनमित्युन्नेयम्। यद्वा रूपरसगन्धस्पर्शानां भौतिकेन्द्रियव्यवस्थाहेतुत्वज्ञापनार्थं पाकजप्रक्रियाव्यवस्थापनार्थं वा ते समस्योक्ताः संख्यायां द्वित्वबहुत्वादौ विप्रतिपत्तिरिति तच्चिराकरणसूचनार्थं बहुत्वेनाभिधानं पृथत्तवे तु संख्या बहुत्वेनैवास्यापि बहुत्वमिति सूचनाय विधिज्ञानव्यञ्जनीयत्वं संख्यातो वैधर्म्यमिति सूचनायच पृथगभिधानं परिमाणे तु दीर्घत्वह्रस्वत्वादिविप्रतिपत्तिनिरासाय बहुवचनं संयोगविभागयोरन्योन्यविरोधज्ञापनाय द्विवचनं।।

[1]कर्मणां द्रव्यजन्यतया गुणजन्यतया च रूपवद्द्रव्यसमवायाच्च प्रत्यक्षतेति द्रव्यगुणाभिधानानन्तरं कर्मोद्देशविभागावाह।।

[2] इतिः पूर्ववदवधारणपरः। कर्मत्वजातिः ग्रत्यक्षसिद्धा एवमुत्क्षेपणत्वादिकमपीति मुक्तावलीकारः। गमनत्वञ्च जातिविशेषो भ्रमणरेचनस्यन्दनोद्ध्र्वज्वलननमनोन्नमनामनादिष्वपि।।

existence, causality, and the constituting of a class contained under existence, is that which is similar in substances, qualities, and actions. Although transitoriness, inhesion in substance, effect, and cause, are not comprehended in an eternal substance or quality, or causality in an atom, yet it is here meant that transitoriness is a condition of such members of the categories as exist in virtue of a being opposed to subsequent non-existence, inhesion in substance is a condition of such members of the categories as exist in virtue of substance as their coinherent cause; the being an effect is a condition of such members of the categories as exist in virtue of being opposed to antecedent non-existence; and causality is a condition of such members of the categories as exist as coinherent or non-coinherent causes.[1] V.

द्रव्यगुणयोः सजातीयारम्भकत्वं साधर्म्यम्।। ९।।

Common element in substances and qualities

Aph. 9. The common property of substance and quality is that they originate things of the same class.

Terrene atoms originate a terrene aggregate of two atoms; blue colour and the like in an atom produce blue colour and the like in an aggregate of two atoms. Such is the origination by substance and quality of things of the same class. Although this cannot be predicated of ether, etc., and of simple substances, and of the qualities of these, yet the meaning is that there is a similarity in the conditions of the divisions of the categories existing by reason of the origination of homogeneous things.[2] V.

[1] इतीत्यनन्तरं प्रत्यय इत्यध्याहार्यं सामान्यं तद्विशेषो द्रव्यत्वादि तद्वत्। सदित्यादिप्रत्ययो यथा द्रव्ये तथा गुणकर्मणोरपि तत्र न कश्चिद्विशेषः। तथा च सत्तावत्त्वं ध्वंसप्रतियोगित्वं द्रव्यसमवायिकारणत्वं प्रागभावप्रतियोगित्वं कारणत्वं सत्ताव्याप्यजातिमत्त्वञ्च द्रव्यगुणकर्मणां साधर्म्यमिति भावः। यद्यप्यनित्यत्वादित्रिकं नित्ये द्रव्ये गुणे चाव्याप्तं कारणत्वञ्च पारिमाण्डल्यादौ तथापि ध्वंसग्रतियोगिभाव-वृत्तिपदार्थविभाजकोपाधिमत्त्वं द्रव्यवत्त्वं प्रागभावप्रतियोगिभाववृत्तिपदार्थविभाजकोपाधिमत्त्वं कार्यत्वं समवाय्यसमवाय्यन्यतरकारणवृत्तिपदार्थविभाजकोपाधिमत्त्वं कारणत्वं द्रव्यादीनां साधर्म्यमित्यत्र तात्पर्यम्।।

[2] पार्थिवाः परमाणवः पार्थिवद्व्यणुकमारभन्ते परमाणुनीलरूपादिकञ्च द्व्यणुकादिगतं नीलरूपादिकमारभते इति द्रव्यगुणयोः सजातीयारम्भकत्वं यद्यपि गगनादावन्त्यावयविनि तद्‌गुणो चाव्याप्तिस्तथापि सजातीयारम्भकवृत्तिपदार्थविभाजकोपाधिमत्त्वस्य साधर्म्मत्वे तात्पर्यम्।।

Cp. *Muktāvalī* on Bhāshā-parichchheda 14.[1] That which is of atomic dimension is not the cause of anything, for that would originate an extension in substance originated by its own substratum [the atom]. But this is impossible, for one extension is productive of another extension exceeding that which belongs to things of its own class, as from a great thing a greater is originated; and so consequently that which would be produced from an atom, would be smaller than an atom the same is to be understood to be the case with respect to infinitely great extension, and generality transcending sense, and particularity.

द्रव्याणि द्रव्यान्तरमारभन्ते गुणाश्च गुणान्तरम्।। 10।।

Explanation of the foregoing aphorism.

Aph. 10. Substances originate another substance, and qualities another quality.

He elucidates what was said before. The sense is obvious.[2] V.

कर्म कर्मसाध्यं न विद्यते।। 11।।

Actions do not originate actions

Aph. 11. An action cannot be effected by an action.

The meaning is that there is no proof that one action can be effected by another, as there is that substances and qualities are originated by things of the same class. It is here intended to be said that if one action produced another, it would produce it after being itself produced, as in the case of sound. Now, as the former action produced a disjunction from conjunct substances, from what would the second action produce a disjunction? For disjunction is preceded by conjunction, and there is not another conjunction produced in the same substratum; but if [by the subsequent action] there is no production of disjunction, the definition of action is violated.[3] U.

[1] अणुपरिमाणं न तु कस्यापि कारणम्। तद्धि स्वाश्रयारब्धद्रव्यपरिमाणारम्भकं भवेत्। तच्च न सम्भवति। परिमाणस्य स्वसमानजातीयोत्कष्टपरिमाणजनकत्वात्। महदारब्धस्य महत्तरत्ववत्। अणुजन्यस्याणुतरत्वप्रसङ्गाच्च। एवं परममहत्परिमाणमतीन्द्रियसामान्यं विशेषाश्चेति बोध्यम्।।

[2] पूर्वोक्तमेव स्पष्टयति। सुगमम्।।

[3] सजातीयारब्धद्रव्यगुणयोरिव कर्मसाध्ये कर्मणि प्रमाणं नास्तीत्यर्थः। इदमत्राकूतम्। कर्म यदि कर्म जनयेत् स्वोत्पत्त्यनन्तरमेव जनयेत् शष्दवत्। तथा च पूर्वकर्मणैव यावत् संयोगिद्रव्येभ्यो विभागे जनिते द्वितीयं कर्म येन सह विभागं जनयेत् विभागस्य संयोगपूर्वकत्वात् संयोगान्तरस्य च तत्राधिकरणे ऽनुत्पन्नत्वात् विभागाजनने तु कर्मलक्षणक्षतेः।।

The characteristic of action is that it is the immediate cause of conjunction and disjunction.

न द्रव्यं कार्यं कारणञ्च बधति।। 12।।

Difference of substances, qualities, and actions

Aph. 12. A substance is not destroyed either by its effect or by its cause.

The meaning is that between two substances which have entered into the relation of effect and cause there is not the relation of destroyer and destroyed, inasmuch as the destruction of a substance is due to the destruction of its substratum, and the destruction of its originative conjunction.[1] U.

उभयथा गुणाः।। 13।।

Continued

Aph. 13. Qualities [are destroyed] in both [the above] manners.

[Qualities] are destroyed by their effects, and are destroyed by their causes. First sounds, etc., [in a series] are destroyed by their effects, but the last is destroyed by its cause, for the last sound but one destroys the last.[2] U.

कार्यविरोधि कर्म।। 14।।

Continued

Aph. 14. An action is opposed to its effect.

He declares that an action is destroyed by its own effect. The sense is that an action is subject to opposition, i.e., destruction, wrought by its effect which consists of a subsequent cojunction.[3] V.

क्रियागुणवत् समवायिकारणमिति द्रव्यलक्षणम्।। 15।।

Characteristic of substance

[1] कार्यकारणभावापन्नयोर्द्रव्ययोर्वध्यघातकभावो नास्तीत्यर्थः। आश्रयनाशारम्भकसंयोगनाशाभ्यामेव द्रव्यनाशादिति भावः।

[2] कार्यवध्याः कारणवध्याश्चेत्यर्थः। आद्यशब्दादीनां कार्यवध्यत्वं चरमस्य तु कारणवध्यत्वमुपान्त्येन शब्देन अन्त्यस्य नाशात्।।

[3] स्वकार्यमेव कर्मणो नाशकमित्याह। कार्येणोत्तरसंयोगरूपेण कृतो यो विरोधो नाशस्तद्वत् कर्मेत्यर्थः।।

Aph. 15. The definition of substance is that it is possessed of actions and qualities, and is a coinherent cause.

'Possessed of actions and qualities because actions and qualities exist in it. In this place, the word characteristic (*lakshaṇa)* denotes a sign and a particular distinctive property excluding objects of the same and of different classes, according to the force of the etymology. It is discerned (*lakshyate*) by means of this. Accordingly be means of action it is discerned that such and such a thing is a substance, and by the possession of qualities substance is discerned as excluded from things of the same and of different classes. The five categories, quality, etc., [quality, action, generality, particularity, and inhesions] belong to the same class by reason of the notion of existence, while non-existence is of a different class. Substance, then is different from quality, etc., because it possesses qualities. That which is not different from quality, etc., does not possess qualities, as quality, etc., And although there is not possession of qualities in a compound substance during its first moment, yet opposition to absolute non-existence of qualities is meant to be stated, for absolute non-existence of qualities is opposed also to antecedent and subsequent non-existence of qualities. In like manner, the being a coinherent cause is a characteristic of the category substance, distinguishing it from the [other] six categories.[1] U.

द्रव्याश्रय्यगुणवान् संयोगविभागेष्वकारणमनपेक्ष इति गुणलक्षणम्।। 16।।

Characteristic of quality

Aph. 16. That it has substance as a substratum, that it is without qualities and that it is not a cause of conjunctions and disjunctions being unconcerned with them, is the difinition of quality.

Having substance as a substratum, because its character is to inhere is substance. But this would apply to substanccs also, accordingly its is

[1] क्रियाश्च गुणाश्च विद्यन्ते ऽस्मिन्निति क्रियागुणवत् अत्र लक्षणशब्दश्चिन्हवचनः सामानासमानजातीयव्यवच्छेदकव्यतिरेकिलिङ्गविशेषवचनश्च लक्ष्यते ऽनेनेति व्युत्पत्तिबलात् तत्र क्रियया कर्मणा द्रव्यमिदमिति लक्ष्यते गुणवत्त्वेन च समानासमानजातीयेभ्यो व्यावृत्तं द्रव्यं लक्ष्यते तत्र समानजातीया भावत्वेन गुणादयः पञ्च असमानजातीयस्त्वभावः तेन द्रव्यं गुणादिभ्यो भिन्नं गुणवत्त्वात् यन्न गुणदिभ्यो भिद्यते तन्न गुणवत् यथा गुणादीति। गुणवत्त्वं यद्यप्याद्यक्षणे ऽवयविनि नास्ति तथापि गुणात्यन्ताभावविरोधिमत्त्वं विविक्षितं गुणप्रागभावप्रध्वंसयोरपि गुणात्यन्ताभावविरोधित्वात् एवं समवायिकारणत्वमपि षट्पदार्थभेदकमेव द्रव्यपदार्थस्य लक्षणम्।।

said to be without qualities. But this is predicable also of action, therefore it is stated not to be a cause of conjunctions and disjunctions.[1] U.

एकद्रव्यमगुणं संयोगविभागेष्वनपेक्षकारणमिति कर्म लक्षणम्।। 17।।

Characteristic of action

Aph. 17. That it abides in one substance, is without qualities, and is the absolute cause of conjunctions and disjunctions, is the definition of action.

That which has one substance for its substratum abides in one substance. No action has more than one substratum, as compound substances and conjunctions and other qualities, have more than one substratum.[2] V.

द्रव्यगुणकर्मणां द्रव्यं कारणं सामान्यम्।। 18।।

Similarity of the first three categories

Aph. 18 Substance is the common cause of substance, quality and actions.

The meaning is that substance, quality and action exist in one substance as their coinherent cause. A common property of the three is their forming a class existing in substance as a coinherent cause.[3] U

तथा गुणः।। 19।।

Continued

Aph. 19. Likewise quality (is the common cause of substances, qualities and actions).

A common property of the three is their forming a class existing in quality as a non-coinherent cause. Of substances the non-coinherent cause is conjunction. Of qualities which are effects such as colour, taste,

[1] द्रव्यमाश्रयितुं शीलमस्येति द्रव्याश्रयी एतच्च अव्येऽपि गतमत आह अगुणवानिति तथापि कर्मण्यतिव्याप्तिरित्यत आह संयोगविभागेष्वकारणम्।।

[2] एकं द्रव्यमाश्रयो यस्य तदेकद्रव्यं संयोगादिगुणाश्चानेकाश्रिताः तथा किमपि कर्म नानेकाश्रितम्।।

[3] एकास्मिन्नेव द्रव्ये समवायिकारणे द्रव्यगुणकर्माणि वर्तन्ते इत्यर्थः द्रव्यसमवायिकारणकवृत्तिर्जातिमत्त्वं त्रयाणां साधर्म्यम्।।

smell, touch, number, extension, individuality etc., the non-inherent cause is homogeneous causative qualities. Of the qualities of the soul such as intellections etc., the non-inherent cause is conjunction with the internal organ. The non-coinherent cause of the qualities of terrene atoms is conjunction with fire. The non-coinherent cause of actions is slight contact with fire, a blow, gravity, fluidity, self-restitution, conjunction with soul influenced by actions done in a former state, conjunction with soul exerting volition, etc. Sometimes even a single quality originates the three, substance, quality, and action, as, for instance, conjunction with a ball of cotton possessed of impetus produces action [i.e., motion] in another ball of cotton, and originates a substance consisting of an aggregate of two balls of cotton and the extension of that aggregate. Sometimes a single quality originates a substance and a quality, e.g., conjunction which may be described as aggregation independent of impetus, with a ball of cotton, originates a substance consisting of an aggregate of two balls of cotton and the extension of that substance.[1] U.

संयोगविभागवेगानां कर्म समानम्।। 20।।

Effects of action

Aph. 20. Action is the common [cause] of conjunctions disjunctions, and impetus.

The action [motion] which is produced in a bow etc., produces disjunction of the arrow from the bow, and conjunction elsewhere, and impetus in the arrow. V.

न द्रव्याणां कर्म।। 21।।

Dissimilarity between action and substance.

Aph. 21 Action is not [a cause] of substances.

[1] गुणासमवायिकारणकवृत्तिजातिमस्वं त्रितयसाधर्म्यं द्रव्याणां संयोगो ऽसमवायिकारणं कार्यगुणानां रूपरसगन्धस्पर्शसंख्यापरिमाणापृथक्त्वादीनां सजातीयकारणगुणासमवायिकारणकत्वं बुद्ध्यादीनामात्मगुणानां मनःसंयोगासमवायिकारणकत्वं पार्थिवपरमाणुगुणानामग्निसंयोगासमवायिकारणकत्वं कर्मणां तु वह्न्यादिनोदनाभिघातगुरुत्वद्रवत्वसंस्कारादृष्टवदात्मसंयोगप्रयत्नवदात्मसंयोगाद्यसमवायिकारणकत्वं यथायथं स्वयमूहनीयम्। क्वचिदेकस्यापि गुणस्य त्रयाणां द्रव्यगुणकर्मणामारम्भकत्वं वेगवत्तूलपिण्डसंयोगस्तूलपिण्डान्तरे कर्म करोति द्वितूलकञ्च द्रव्यमारभते तत्परिमाणञ्च। क्वचिदेको गुणो द्रव्यगुणावारभते यथा तूलपिण्डसंयोग एव वेगानपेक्षप्रचयाख्यो द्वितूलकं द्रव्यं तत्परिमाणञ्चारभते।

व्यतिरेकात्।। 22।।

Continued

Aph. 22. Because it is excluded [from them].

Because it is—excluded—because of the non-existence of action at the time of the production of substance. The action which produces an originative conjunction of constituent parts is destroyed at the time of the production of the substance [constituted by those parts] subsequent to conjunction, for conjunction is destructive to disjunction. Nor can it be maintained that action, though non-existent at the time of its effect, from having existed the previous moment is the cause [of the substance so constituted]. For after the destruction of a large piece of cloth there is non-existence of action in the constituent parts at the moment previous to the production of fragments of cloth. In reality action is not the cause even of a substance depending on an originative conjunction produced by action, for it is to be considered that [the substance] is produced otherwise, [viz.,] by conjunction.[1] V.

द्रव्याणां द्रव्यं कार्यं सामान्यम्।। 23।।

Continued

Aph. 23. Substance is the common effect of substances.

Having stated that many things may originate one, [Kaṇāda] now declares that one product may be originated by many. Of substances, i.e., of two more substances. Thus by two threads a piece of cloth consisting of two threads, and similarly by many threads, one piece of cloth, is originated. If it be objected that cloth may be seen which is made of one thread, in which the woof and the warp are made of one and the same thread, we reply that it is not so, for there can be no cloth produced in this case, there being no non-coinherent cause, for there can be no conjunction of a single object.[2] U.

[1] व्यतिरेकात् द्रव्योत्पर्त्तिसमये कर्मणो ऽभावात् यत् कर्मावयवारम्भकसंयोगं जनयति संयोगस्य तन्नाशकत्वेन संयोगोत्तरं द्रव्योत्पत्तिकाले तस्य नाशात् न च कर्मणः कार्यकाले ऽसत्त्वे ऽपि तत्पूर्वक्षणवृत्तित्वात् कारणत्वं निराबाधमिति वाच्यं महापटनाशानन्तरं खण्डपटाद्युत्पत्तेः पूर्वक्षणे ऽपि तदवयवेषु कर्मणो ऽभावात् वस्तुतः कर्म जनिता रम्भकसंगाधांनद्रव्ये ऽपि न कर्म कारणं संयोगोऽन्यथासिद्धत्वादिति ध्येयम्।।

[2] बहूनामेकस्यारम्भकत्वमुक्त्वा इदानीमेकस्मिन् कार्ये बहूनामारम्भकत्वमाह। द्रव्ये च द्रव्याणि चेति द्रव्याणि तेषां द्रव्याणां। तत्र द्वाभ्यां तन्तुभ्यां द्वितन्तुकः पटो बहुभिरपि तन्तुभिरेकः पट आरभ्यते। नन्वेकतन्तुको ऽपि पटो दृश्यते यत्रैकेनैव तन्तुना तानप्रतितन्त्रौ भवत इति चेन्न तत्रैकस्य संयोगाभावेनासमवायिकारणाभावात् पटानुत्पत्तेः।।

गुणवैधर्म्याश्च कर्मणां कर्म।। 24।।

Continued

Aph. 24. Action because of its dissimilarity from quality is not [an effect] of actions.

It has been stated that the similarity between substance and quality is that they originate things of the same class. Also this has been denied of actions, in the aphorism 'An action is not effected by another action'. This is here repeated.[1] U.

द्वित्वप्रभृतयः संख्याः पृथक्त्वसंयोगविभागाश्च।। 25।।

Aph. 25. Numbers from duality upwards, individuality, conjunction, and disjunction [are originated by more than one substance].

He states that certain qualities also are originated by more than one substance. Here the word individuality means the individuality of two or more objects. Accordingly the sense is that numbers, from duality to the highest, individuality of two or more objects, conjunctions, and disjunctions are originated by more than one substance.[2] V.

असमवायात् सामान्यकार्यं कर्म न विद्यते।। 26।।

Aph. 26. Action is not the common effect [of several substances] because it does not inhere [in more than one substance].

Action is not a common effect originated by more than one, because it does not inhere in two or more. It is established by experience that action is different in different substances.[3]

संयोगानां द्रव्यम्।। 27।।

Aph. 27 Substance is the effect of conjunctions.

[1] द्रव्यगुणयोः सजातीयारम्भकत्वं साधर्म्यमुक्तं तत्र कर्म कर्मसाध्यं न विद्यते इति सूत्रे कर्मणां कर्मजनकत्वं प्रतिषिद्धमेव तदिहानूद्यते इति भावः।।

[2] केषाञ्चित् गुणानामप्यनेकद्रव्यारब्धत्वमित्याह। अत्र पृथत्कपदं द्विपृथक्त्वादिपरं तथा च द्वित्वादिपरार्द्धपर्यन्ताः संख्या द्विपृथक्त्वादीनि संयोगविभागाश्च अनेकद्रव्यारब्धा इत्यर्थः।।

[3] असमवायात् द्वयोर्बहुषु च समवायेन कर्मणो ऽभावात् सामान्यकार्यम् अनेकारब्धंकर्म न विद्यते नास्तीत्यर्थः तथा च प्रतिद्रव्यं भिन्नं भिन्नं कर्म अनुभवसिद्धम्।।

One substance consisting of a piece of cloth etc, is the effect of many conjunctions of threads etc.[1] U.

This is to be understood with the exception of the conjunctions of impalpable substances, of those of final wholes, and of those of heterogeneous substances.[2] V.

रूपाणां रूपम्।। 28।।

Aph. 28. A colour is the effect of colours (more than one).

The word colour in both places implies also taste, smell, touch, viscidity, intrinsic fluidity, unity, individuality of units, extension, velocity, elasticity and gravity. One colour etc., then, as a complex whole is produced by many colours etc., having become its coinherent cause.[3] V.

गुरुत्वप्रयत्नसंयोगानामुत्क्षेपणम्।। 29।।

Aph. 29. Throwing upwards (is the effect) of gravity, volition, and conjunction.

Here gravity existing in the hand, a clod of earth etc., is the instrumental cause; conjunction with soul possessing volitions is the non-coinherent cause of the throwing upwards of the hand; the throwing out of the hand is the non-coinherent cause of the throwing upwards of the clod. Here also the term throwing upwards is applicable to throwing downwards etc.[4] U.

Gravity in that which is to be thrown upward, volition in the thrower, and expulsion of the thrown from the hand,—these are the three causes of throwing upwards. Hence in the case of action also the existence of more than one cause must be admitted.[5] V.

संयोगविभागाश्च कर्मणाम्।। 30।।

[1] बहूनां तन्त्वादिसंयोगानां पठादिरूपमेकं द्रव्यं कार्यमित्यर्थः।

[2] निःस्पर्शानां द्रव्याणाम् अन्त्यावयविनां विजातीयद्रव्याणाञ्च ये संयोगास्तान् विहायेति द्रष्टव्यम्।।

[3] रूपपदे रसगन्धस्पर्शस्नेहसांसिद्धिकद्रवत्वैकत्वैकपृथक्त्वपरिमाणवेगस्थितिस्थापकगुरुत्वाना-मप्युपलक्षके तथा च समवायिकारणगतैर्बहुभी रुपादिभिरवयविगतमेकं जायते इत्यर्थः।।

[4] अत्र गुरुत्वस्य हस्तलोष्टादिवर्तिनो निमित्तकारणत्वं प्रयत्नवदात्मसंगयोस्य समवायिकारणत्वं हस्तनिष्ठोत्क्षेपणस्य तु हस्तनोदनमसममवायिकारणम् अत्राप्युत्क्षेपणपदमवक्षेपणादावपि लाक्षणिकम्।।

[5] उत्क्षेप्यस्य गुरुत्वम् उत्क्षेप्तुः प्रयत्नः उत्क्षेप्यहस्तनोदनञ्च एते त्रय एवोत्क्षपणहेतवः अतः कर्मण्यप्यनेककारणाकत्वं निराबाधमिति भावः।

Aph. 30. Conjunctions and disjunctions (are the effects) of actions.

It might be asked, By means of what property is there an inference of supersensual objects such as the courses of the sun, the moon, etc., as there is in inference of fire and other causes from smoke and other effects, for an action has no effects? He therefore recalls to mind the previously mentioned effects of actions. The word 'and' implies in addition to conjunctions and disjunctions impetus and elasticity.[1] V.

कारणसामान्ये द्रव्यकर्मणां कर्माकारणमुक्तम्।। 31।।

Aph. 31. In (treating of) causes in general action is said not be a cause of substances and actions.

By the term 'causes in general,' the section treating thereof is indicated; therefore in the section treating of causes in general the non-causality of action with regard to substance and action is affirmed, but it is not meant that action is in no way a cause so that aphorism, conjunctions and disjunctions (are the effects) of actions, should be set aside.[2] U.

[1] ननु यथा धूमादिरूपकार्येण वह्न्यादिकारणानामनुमानं तथा ऽतीन्द्रिकर्मणां सूर्यादिगतीनां केन लिङ्गेनानुमानं कर्मणः कार्याभावादित्यतः पूर्वोक्तानि कर्मकार्याणि स्मारयति।।

[2] कारणसामान्यपदेन तत्प्रकरणमुपलक्ष्यते तेन कारणसामान्याभिधानप्रकरणे द्रव्यकर्मणी प्रति कर्मणो ऽकारणत्वमुक्तं न तु सर्वथाप्यकारणमेव कर्मेति विवक्षितं येन संयोगविभागाश्च कर्मणामिति सूत्रं व्याहन्येतेति भावः।

SECOND DAILY LESSON

कारणाभावात् कार्याभावः।। 1।।

Causation

Aph. 1. From non-existence of cause is non-existence of effect.

It may be said, In the foregoing daily lesson similarity between the categories, substance, quality, and action, as constituted by the notion of effect and the notion of cause, has been explained. How is this possible? for while the relation between effect and cause is not demonstrated it is like talking about the horn of a hare. To obviate this Kaṇāda establishes the realation between effect and cause.[1] V.

For it is seen that even when earth, a potter's wheel, water a potter, thread etc., are brought together, from non-existence of a potter's staff there is non-existence of the pot; and though earth water etc., be brought together, from non-existence of a seed there is non-existence of a shoot. This relation between the potter's staff and the pot, and between the seed and the shoot, is impossible without the relation of cause and effect; for otherwise there would be non-existence of the pot also in the case of non-existence of a loom, and non-existence of the shoot even in the case of non-existence of a fragment of stone etc. Moreover it is observed that a pot, a piece of cloth, and the like exist only from time to time. This too would be impossible without the relation between cause and effect; for the temporary existence of things which are, which consists in their being at one time and not being at another, is impossible without connexion with a cause. For in this case (were there no connexion with a cause), a thing might be or not be, but could not be from time to time, since an existing thing is not non-existent, nor does it come into existence without a cause, nor does it come into existence fortuitously, nor does it come into

[1] ननु पूर्वाह्निके कार्यत्वघटितं कारणत्वघटितञ्च साधर्म्यमुक्तं तत्कथं सङ्गच्छते कार्यकारणभावस्यासिद्धत्वेन शशविषाणसमानत्वादित्यतः कार्यकारणभावमेव व्यवस्थापयति।

existence from anything unreal such as the horn of a hare, but from a really existing assignable determinant such as a staff or a loom, as is seen in effects such as a pot or a piece of cloth. Now the limit or determinant is the cause. Moreover were there no relation of cause and effect there would no activity or inactivity, for in such a case the universe would be desireless, since without a knowledge of the means of attaining that which is desired there would be no such thing as activity, and without the knowledge of the means of avoiding that which is undesired there would be no such thing as inactivity.[1] U.

न तु कार्याभावात् कारणाभावः।। 2।।

Continued

Aph. 2. But there is not from non-existence of effect nonexistence of cause.

If there were not a restriction in the relation between cause and effect, it would follow also that if the effect should not exist, the cause would not exist. The rule is not that non-existence of effect results in non-existence of cause, but that non-existence of cause results in non-existence of effect. Therefore the practical application of this introductory section of two aphorisms is that persons desirous of emancipation are concerened in non-existence of birth for the sake of non-existence of pain, in non-existence of activity for the sake of non-existence of birth, in non-existence of faults for the sake of non-existence of activity, in the cessation of false knowledge for the sake of non-existence of faults, and in forming a mental presentation of the soul for the sake of cessation of false knowledge.[2] U.

[1] दृश्यते हि मृच्चक्रसलिलकुलालसूत्रादौ समवहिते ऽपि दण्डाभावाघ्दटाभावः भूसलिलादौ समवहिते ऽपि बीजाभावादङ्कुराभावः स च दण्डघटयोर्बीजाङ्कुरयोर्वा कार्यकारणभावमन्तरेणानुपन्नः। अन्यथा वेमाद्यभावे ऽपि घटाभावः शिलाशकलाद्यभावे ऽप्यङ्कुराभावः स्यात् किञ्च घटपटादीनां कादाचित्कत्वमुभूयते तदपि हेतुफलभावमनतरेणानुन्नं न हि किञ्चित्कालासत्त्वे सति किञ्चित्कालसत्त्वरूपं कादाचित्कत्वं भावानां कारणापेक्षामन्तरेण सम्भवति तदा हि स्यादेव न स्यादेववा न तु कदाचित् स्यात् न हि भावो न भवत्येव नाप्यहेतोर्भवति नाप्यकस्मादेव भवति न वा निरूपाख्यादेव शशविषाणादेर्भवति किन्तु दण्डवेमादेः सोपाख्यस्यावधेर्घटपटादौ कार्ये दर्शनादवधिस्तु कारणमेव एवं कार्यकारणभावाभावे प्रवृत्तिनिवृत्ती न स्यातां तथा च निरीहं जगज्जायेत न हीञ्चसाधनताज्ञानमन्तरेण प्रवृत्तिरनिष्टसाधनताज्ञानमन्तरेण निवृतिः।

[2] यदि कार्यकारणाभावनियमो न भवति तदा कार्याभावादपि कारणाभावः स्यात् कार्याभावः कारणाभावप्रत्यतन्त्रं कारणाभावस्तु कार्यभावं प्रति तन्त्र तेन दुःखाभावार्थं जन्माभावे जन्माभावार्थं

सामान्य विशेष इति बुद्धपेक्षम्।। 3।।

Generality and particularity

Aph. 3. Generality and particularity both depend upon intellection.

After the enunciation and definition of the first three categories he now states the definition of the category generality formerly enunciated. Generality is twofold, highest and not highest. The highest is being, the not-highest is substantiality etc., contained under being. The distinguishing property of generality and particularity is intellection. Extensive intellection is that of generality, exclusive intellection is that of particularity.[1]

Generality is the highest, and particularity the not highest generality. Accordingly there are two kinds of generality. That is dependent upon intellection which has intellection for its characteristic. Generality then, is twofold, highest and not highest. The highest generality is being, the not-highest generality is substantiality etc. The distinguishing property of the highest and not highest kinds of generality is intellection, the intellection of extensiveness being the characteristic of generality i.e., of highest generality, and the intellection of non-extensiveness the chracteristic of particularity (i.e., of not highest generality). Extensiveness is existence in many places, non-extensiveness is existence in few places. Being, therefore, is the highest, because it exists in more places than any other universal, and the classes substantiality etc., are not-highest because they exist in fewer places than the notion of earth etc., so that, generality or the highest and particularity or the not highest universals are not absolute but relative to intellection. The following hindrances to universality are enumerated by the Nyāya teachers, 'Indivisibility of the individual, identity, confusion, infinite regression, loss of form, and absence of connection are the aggregete of things preventing universality.' Thus the notion of ether in not a class because

प्रवृत्याभावे तदर्थञ्च दोषाभावे तदर्थं मिथ्याज्ञाननिवृत्तये तदर्थञ्चात्मसाक्षात्काराय मुमुक्षूणां प्रवृतिः प्रयोजनमौपोद्घातिकस्याप्यस्य द्विसूत्रप्रकरणस्य।।

[2] पदार्थत्रयोद्देशलक्षणानन्तरमिदानीमुद्दिष्टस्य सामान्यपदार्थस्य लक्षणमाह। सामान्यं द्विविधं परमपरञ्च तत्र परं सत्ता श्रपरं सत्ताव्याप्यं तत्र द्रव्यत्वादि सामान्यस्य तद्विशेषस्य च लक्षणां बुद्धिरेव। अनुवृत्तबुद्धिसामान्यस्य व्यावृत्तबुद्धिर्विशेषस्य।।

it exists only as one individual. The notions of a pitcher and a water-pot are not two universals, because there are neither more nor less individuals under either. The notions of matter and form are not one universal, because of the confusion pervading the one individual by reason of two common substrata of absoulte mutual non-existence. Generality is not a universal, for if so there would be a regress to infinity. The notion of particularity is prevented from being a universal by loss of form, for particularity is naturally exclusive. . . . The notion of co-inhesion is not a class, because of the non existence of connection by co-inhesion, for from the assumption that co-inhesion inheres in anything else a regression to infinity would follow. [1]V.

Cp. the Muktāvalī on Bhāshā-parichchheda, 8.[2] The Characteristic of generality is co-inhesion in more than one, together with eternity. It is said, 'Together with eternity,' because co-inhesion in more than one belongs also to conjunction etc. It is said 'In more than one,' because co-inhesion together with eternity belongs also to ether, to exstension, and the like.[2]

भावो ऽनुवृत्तेरेव हेतुत्वत् सामान्यमेव।। 4।।

Existence is universal

Aph. 4. Existence is general only, for it is a cause of extensive intellection.

Existence—being—[is general] because it is a cause of extensive intellection—of the notion of existing in many places, the word only

[1] सामान्यं परं विशेषः अपरं सामान्यम् इति द्वयं बुद्ध्यपेक्षं बुद्धिरपेक्षालक्षणं यस्य तत् तथा च सामान्यं द्विविधं परमपरञ्च तत्र परसामान्यं सत्ता द्रव्यत्वादिकन्त्वपरसामान्यं तत्र सामान्यविशेषयोः परापरयोर्लक्षणं बुद्धिरेव अनुवृत्तत्वबुद्धिः सामान्यस्य व्यावृत्तत्वबुद्धिर्विशेषस्य लक्षणम् अधिकदेशवृत्तित्वं व्यावृत्तत्वमल्पदेशवृत्तित्वं तथा च सत्तायाः सर्वसामान्यापेक्षया ऽधिकदेशवृतित्वात् परत्वमेव द्रव्यत्वादिजातेस्तु सत्ता पेक्षया न्यूनदेशवृत्तित्वादपरत्वं पृथिवीत्वाद्यपेक्षया ऽधिकदेशवृत्तित्वात् परत्वमपीति परत्वरूपं सामान्यत्वम् अपरत्वरूपं विशेषत्वञ्च न नियतं किन्तु बुद्धपेक्षमिति। जातिबाधका उक्ता न्यायाचार्यैः व्यक्तेरभेदस्तुल्यत्वं सङ्करो ऽथानवस्थितिः। रूपहानिरसम्बन्धो जातिबाधकसङ्ग्रह इति। तत्रैकव्यक्तिकत्वादाकाशत्वं न जातिः अन्यूनानातिरिक्तव्यक्तिकत्वाद् घटत्वं कलसत्वञ्च न जातिद्वयं परस्परात्यन्ताभावसमानाधिकरणयोरेकव्यक्तिसमावेशेन सङ्करेण भूतत्वं मूर्तत्वञ्च न जातिः अनवस्थाभयात् सामान्यत्वं न जातिः विशेषत्वं व्यावृत्तस्वभावस्य रूपहानिर्विशेषत्वजातिबाधिका समावायसम्बन्धभावात् समवायत्वं न जातिः समवाये समवायान्तरस्वीकारे ऽनवस्थाप्रसङ्गात्।।

[2] सामान्यमिति। तल्लक्षन्तु नित्यत्वे सत्यनेकसमवेतत्वम्। अनेकसमवेतत्वं संयोगादीनामप्यस्त्यत उक्तम्। नित्यत्वे सतीति। नित्यत्वे सति समवेतत्वं गगणापरिमाणदीनामप्यस्त्यत उक्तम् अनेकेति।।

(*eva*) excludes the notion of existence in few places.[1] V.

द्रव्यत्वं गुणत्वं कर्मत्वञ्च सामान्यानि विशेषाश्च।। 5।।

Aph. 5. The essences of substance, quality, and action, are general and particular.

The particle 'and' (*cha*) implies in addition the notions of earth etc., the classes contained in substance; the notions of colour etc. the classes contained in quality; and the notions of throwing upwards etc. the classes contained in action.[2] U.

अन्यत्रान्त्येभ्यो विशेषेभ्यः।। 6।।

Aph. 6. With the exception of the ultimate particulars.

The words general and particular [in the preceding aphorism] are to be understood with the exception of those particulars that are said to exist as eternal substances. According to the teachers [of this system] they are ultimate, beause they exist in the end or conclusion [of the division of a compound substance], and there is [then] nothing further which causes non-extensive conception. According to the authors of the Vṛtti they are ultimate because they exist at the end or conclusion of production and destruction, and are ultimate particlars because they exist in eternal substances. For those particulars only are causes of non-extensive conception, and are not at the same time general in their character.[3] U.

सदिति यतो द्रव्यगुणकर्मसु सा सत्ता।। 7।।

Aph. 7. That is existence from which [there arises the conviction] with respect to substances, qualities, and actions, that they are existent.

[1] भाव सत्ता अनुवृत्तिरधिकदेशवृत्तित्वबुद्धेर्हेतुत्वात् एवकारेणाल्पदेशवृत्तित्वबुद्धिव्यवच्छेदः।

[2] चकारः पृथिवीत्वादीनि द्रव्यगतजातीः रूपत्वादीनि गुणगतजातीः उत्क्षेपण त्वादीनि कर्मगतजातीः समुच्चिनोति।।

[3] अन्त्या विशेषा नित्यद्रव्यवृत्तयो ये ऽभिहिताः तान वर्जयित्वा सामान्यविशेषाभिधानमित्यर्थः। अन्ते ऽबसाने भवन्तीत्यन्त्या यतो न व्यावर्तकान्तरमस्तीत्याचार्याः उत्पादविनाशयोरन्ते ऽवसाने भवन्तीत्यन्त्या नित्यद्रव्याणि तेषु भवन्तीत्यन्त्या विशेषा इति वृत्तिकृतः। ते हि विशेषा एव व्यावृत्तिबुद्धिहेतवो न तु सामान्यरूपा अपीति।।

द्रव्यगुणकर्मभ्यो ऽर्थान्तरं सत्ता।। 8।।

Existence is not identical with substance etc.

Aph. 8. Existence is something different from substances, qualities, and actions.

It might be said, Existence is not apprehended by means of its being something distinct from substance, quality, and action. Therefore existence is one or other of those three. For whatever is different from anything else is apprehended by means of its difference from it, as a water-pot [by means of its difference] from a piece of cloth, whereas existence is not apprehended by means of its difference from them. Consequently it is identical with them. For this reason [Kaṇāda] proclaimed [the above aphorism.] substance etc., is not extensive, existence is extensive. Accordingly its difference from them may be established by the consideration of their opposite properties characterised by extensiveness and non-extensiveness.[1] U.

गुणकर्मसु च भावान्न कर्म न गुणः।। 9।।

Continued

Aph. 9. Existence is neither an action nor a quality because it exists in qualities and actions.

When it is said neither an action nor a quality the proposition negatively implies that neither is it a substance. For an action does not exist in actions, nor a quality in qualities nor a substance in quality or action. But existence is in quality and action. Existence, then, is different from them, for it differs in property from substance, quality, and action.[2] U.

सामान्यविशेषाभावेन च।। 10।।

Continued

Aph. 10. And by reason of the non-existence [in existence] of generality and particularity

[1] ननु द्रव्यगुणाकर्मभ्यः पृथग्भावेन सत्ता नानुभूयते ऽतो द्रव्याद्यन्यतममेव सत्ता यतो हि यद्भिन्नं भवति तत्ततो भेदेनानुभूयते यथा घटः पटात् न च सत्ता तेभ्यो भेदेनानुभूयत इति तदात्मिकैवेत्यत आह।। द्रव्यादयो ऽननुगताः सत्ता चानुगता। तथा च अनुगतत्वाननुगतत्वलक्षणाविरुद्धधर्माध्यासेन तेभ्यो भेदस्य सिद्धत्वात्।।

[2] न गुणो न कर्मेति वक्तव्ये व्यत्ययेनाभिधानं न द्रव्यत्वमित्यपि सूचयति न हि कर्म कर्मसु वर्त्तते न वा गुणो गुणेषु न वा द्रव्यं गुणे कर्मणि वा सत्ता तु गुणे कर्मणि च वर्तते तेन द्रव्यगुणकर्मवैधर्म्यात् तेभ्यो भिन्नैव सत्ता।।

Substance etc. have been previously stated to be general and particular. Therefore from the non-existence in it of substance etc., existence is not identical with substance etc.[1] V.

अनेकद्रव्यवत्त्वेन द्रव्यत्वमुक्तम्।। 11।।

The essence of substance not identical with substance etc

Aph. 11. The essence of substance is explained by means of its inherence in many substances.

He states that the universal in substance [or substantiality] also is not identical with substance etc., [i.e., with substances, qualities, and actions]. Inherence in many substances is inferred from connexion with co-inhesion, and eternity from generality. Accordingly substantiality as well as existenee, is explained to be different from substance, etc., on the grounds of its co-inhesion in many substances and of its eternity.[2] V.

सामान्यविशेषाभावेन च।। 12।।

Continued

Aph. 12. And by reason of the non existence [in the essence of substance] of generality and particularity.

If substantiality as a universal were a class identical with substance etc., the general and particular entities of earth, water, light, and the like would exist in that class.[3] U.

The universal in substance is not identical with substance etc., because of the non-existence [in that essence] of the essence of substance, quality, action, earth, water, light, and the like.[4] V.

तथा गुणेषु भावाद्गुणत्वमुक्तम्।। 13।।

The notion of quality

[1] सामान्यविशेषाः पूर्वोक्ताः द्रव्यत्वादयः तथा च द्रव्यत्वाद्यभावात् सत्ता न दव्यात्मिकेत्यर्थः।।

[2] द्रव्यत्वमपि न द्रव्याद्यात्मकमित्याह। अनेकद्रव्यवत्त्वं समवेतत्वसम्बन्धेन नित्यत्वन्तु सामान्यत्वादेव प्राप्तं तथा च द्रव्यत्वमनेकद्रव्यसमवेतत्वेन नित्यत्वेन च द्रव्याविभिन्नतया सत्तावदेव व्याख्यातमित्यर्थः।

[3] यदि द्रव्यत्वजार्तिव्याद्यात्मिकैव स्यात् यदा तस्यां पृथिवीत्वजलत्वतेजस्त्वादयः समान्यविशेषाः स्युरित्यर्थः।।

[4] द्रव्यत्वगुणत्वकर्मत्वपृथिवीत्वजलत्वंतेजस्त्वाद्यभावात् द्रव्यत्वं न द्रव्याद्यात्मकमित्यर्थः।।

Aph. 13. In like manner the universal in quality is explained from its existence in qualities.

He explains the universal in quality. The universal in quality, like existence, is declared to be distinct from substances, qualities, and actions on ccount of its existence or co-inhesion inqualities only.[1] U.

सामान्यविशेषाभावेन च।। 14।।

Aph. 14. Also by the non-existence [in it] of generality and particularity.

He states another distinction. If the universal in quality were not something over and above substances, qualities, and actious, it would then be apprehended as constituting a class contained under one or other of the universals, substance, quality, or action.[2] U.

कर्मसु भावात् कर्मत्वमुक्तम्।। 15।।

The essence of action.

Aph. 15. The essence of action is explained from its existence in actions.

He states the distinction of the universal in action from substances, qualities, and actions. The essence of action is also explained, like existence, to be another class distinct from substances, qualities, and actions, on account of its existence or co-inhesion in action only.[3] U.

सामान्यविशेषाभावेन च।। 16।।

Aph. 16. Also by the non-existence [in it] of generality particularity.

If the essence of action were identical with substances etc., the generality and particularity of substances etc., would inhere in it. It is to be understood that these four aphorisms alike in form [viz. 10, 12, 14, 16] are stated in one section to explain the distinction from

[1] गुणात्वमाह। नृणेष्टेव भावात् समवायात् गुणात्वं द्रव्यकर्मभ्यो भिन्नं सत्तावदेवोक्तमित्यर्थः।।

[2] भेदकान्तरनाह। यदि द्रव्यगुणाकर्मभ्यो गुणात्वमतिरिक्तं न भवेत्तदा द्रव्यत्वगुणत्वकर्मत्वत-दवान्तरजातिमत्तया उपलभ्येतेत्यर्थः।।

[3] दव्यगुणाकर्मभ्यो भेदकं कर्मत्वस्याह। कर्मत्वेन भावान् समवायात् कर्मत्वमपि जात्यन्तरं द्रव्यगुणकर्मभ्यो भिन्नमुक्तं सत्तावदित्यर्थः।

substances, qualities, and actions, of the four universals existence, substantiality the universal in quality and the universal in action.[1] U.

सदिति लिङ्गाविशेषाद्विशेषलिङ्गाभावाच्चैकोभा वः।। 17।।

Existence is one

Aph 17. Because of the non-particularity of the property of being, and of the non-existence of a particular property therein there is [only] one existence.

A conception in the form of being or the applicability of that word is the property of existence. This conception is common, without distinction, in regard to substances, qualities, and actions. Hence existence or being abides in them as only one. For otherwise either being would not exist, or they would not exist, for existence is in the same number of individuals as substance etc. Because of the non-existence of a property or ground of inference in particularity or distinction, there is no distinction. For there is no particular property in existence, like the particular property or distinction of extension of length and shortness in the case of the inference, 'That is the selfsame lamp.'[2] U.

[1] कर्मत्वं यदि द्रव्याद्यात्मकं भवेत्तदा द्रव्यत्वादिसामान्यविशेषस्तत्र समवेयादित्यर्थः। सेयमेकाकारा चतुःसूत्री सत्ताद्रव्यत्वगुणत्वकर्मत्वानां चतसृणां जातीनां व्यगुणाकर्मभेदप्रतिपादनाय एकप्रकरणेनोक्तेत्यवधेयम्।।

[2] सत्ता एकैव तेषु वर्तते अन्यथा द्रव्यत्वादिभिस्तुल्यवयक्तिकतया सत्ता वा न स्यात् तानि वा न स्युः विशेषलिङ्गाभावाच्चेतिं विशेषो भेदस्तत्र यल्लिङ्गमनुमानं तदभावाच्च न भेद इत्यर्थः। भवति हि स एवायं दीप इत्यनुगमस्तत्र यथा विशेषलिङ्गं दीर्घह्रस्वत्वादिपरिमाणभेदस्तथात्र विशेषलिङ्गं नास्तीति भावः।

Book II

FIRST DAILYLESSON

रूपरसगन्धस्पर्शवती पृथिवी।। 1।।

Qualities of earth

Aph. 1. Earth is possessed of colour, taste, smell and touch.

The colour of the earth is of many kinds, blue, yellow etc. Hence the characteristic of possessing universality contained under the universality of substance and being the general substratum of blue colour. So also there is in the earth taste of various kinds, pungent, astringent etc. Hence the characteristic of possessing a universality contained under the universal existence and being the general substratum of pungent taste. In like manner by the substitution of the words 'astringent' etc., other characteristics are to be inferred. Smell is of two kinds, fragrant and unfragrant. Hence the characteristic of possessing a universality contained under the universal substantiality and being the general substratum of smell. Thus too it will be seen that the notion of substance is a substratum of classes which are substrata not general of qualities which are substrata general or not general of odour. It must not be objected that as smell and taste are not observed in a stone etc., both these qualities are not invariably present. For even though smell and taste accidentally be not observed in it, they are observed in its ashes. The self-same particles which were originally constituent of the stones are also originally constituent of its ashes. Therefore the presence of these attributes is not merely occasional. If it be asked How then is a breeze fragrant, and water mixed with Kāravella [a kind of gourd] bitter? This is no objection, for the taste and smell of those are conditions produced by the earth. There is a touch in the earth, neither hot nor cold, but temperate. Hence the characteristic of possessing a universality contained under the universal substance and being the general substratum of the feeling of temperate warmth. Themperate warmth may be clearly explained by another description, that it is the touch of the earth; another description is clearer, viz., that it is a species of touch residing in the flowers of the Śirīśa, Lavaṅgī etc.[1] U.

रूपरसस्पर्शवत्य आपो द्रवाः स्निग्धाः।। 2।।

Qualities of water

Aph. 2. Water is possessed of colour, teste, and touch, and is fluid and viscid.

In water the colour is white, the taste sweet, the touch cold, the fluidity natural. Thus in the aphorism on water by the enumeration of five qualities, five characteristics of water are implied by the sage. The characteristics of water are that it is a class preceptibly contained under the universal substance and existing in possession of colour not the general substratum of bright and white but the general substratum of blue colour. It is a class perceptibly contained under the universal substance existing as something sweet and not existing as something bitter. It is possessed of cold touch, of intrinsic fluidity and of viscidity. If there is no natural fluidity in ice, hail, etc., it must be understood that they belong to a class included under the universal substance and existing in the possession of intrinsic fluidity. The observation of blue colour in the sea, the water of the Kālindī (Yamunā) etc., is an illusion produced by the conditions of the substratum, for when it is tossed into the air it is perceived to be white. Though no taste be perceived in water, yet after eating astringent substances such as yellow myrobalan, sweetness is observed in water, for it is distinguished by that [taste]. The hot touch which appears in water through conjunction with the sun's rays etc., belongs properly to the sun's rays etc. Though it might

[1] रूपं नीलपीताद्यनेकप्रकारं पृथिव्या एव। तथा च नीलरूपसमानाधिकरणद्रव्यत्वव्याप्यजातिमत्त्वं लक्षणम् एव रसः कटुकषायद्यनेकप्रकारकः पृथिव्यामेव तथा च कटुरससमानाधिकरणद्रव्यत्वव्याप्यजातिमत्त्वं लक्षणम् एवं कषायादिपदप्रक्षेपेण लक्षणान्यूहनीयानि। गन्धो द्विविधः सुरभिरसुभिश्च तथा च गन्धसमाना- धिकरणद्रव्यत्वव्याप्यजातिमत्त्वं लक्षणं तथा गन्धसमानाधिकरणगन्धासमानाधिकरणगुणासमानाधिकरणजात्यधिकरणद्रव्यत्वं द्रष्टव्यम्। न च पाषाणादौ गन्धरसयोरननुभवात् तत्राव्यापकमिदमुभयमपीति वाच्यं तत्रायाततो गन्धरसयोरननुभवेऽपि तदीयभस्मसु तदुपलम्भात् य एवावयवाः पाषाणारम्भकास्त एव तद्भस्मारम्भका अपीति नाव्याप्तिः कथं तर्हि सुरभिः समीरणः तिक्तं कारवेल्लजलमिति प्रतीतिरिति चेन्न पार्थिवोपाधिकत्वात् तयोर्गन्धरसयोः स्पर्शोऽग्र्यनुष्णाशीतः पाकजः पृथिव्यामेव तथा च पाकजस्पर्शसमानाधिकरणद्रव्यत्वव्याप्यजातिमत्त्वं लक्षणम् पाकजत्वञ्च विशेषान्तरव्यङ्ग्यं पृथिवीस्पर्श एव विशेषान्तरञ्च शिरीशलवङ्गीकुसुमादौ स्पर्शविशेषे स्फुटतरम्।।

be asked, inasmuch as fluidity is not perceived in ice, hail etc., how it is possible that it should be contained in water, yet when the ice, hail etc., are melted with heat, it is proved sensibly to be water. The author of the Muktāvalī maintains that its fludity is not derived from conjunction with celestial light, but the appearance of solidity is in those cases an illusion. But some contend that through conjunction with celestial light there are produced in ice etc., successively from aqueous atoms an aggregate of two atoms, an aggregate of three atoms and so forth, and that such aggregates of two or more atoms are destitute of fluidity, and solid, and that accordingly the appearance of solidity is not an illusion. There is also viscidity in water, and that of clarified butter and the like is the viscidity of the water which is one of the ingredients. It is through the excess of this that clarified butter etc., is highly inflammable. That kind of conjunction which is called agglomeration, and which consists in meal, sand etc., becoming globular, is caused by viscidity accompanied with fluidity. Were it caused by fluidity alone, it would be produced from the fluidity of glass, gold etc. Nor is it produced by viscidity alone, for then it would follow that it would be produced also by thickened clarified butter etc.[1] V.

तेजो रूपस्पर्शवत्।। 3।।

Qualities of light

Aph. 3. Light has colour and touch.

[1]जले रूपं शुक्लं रसो मधुरः स्पर्शः शीतः द्रव्यत्वं सांसिद्धिकं तथा च जलसूत्रे पञ्चानां गुणानामुपादानात् पञ्चैव जललक्षणानि मुनेरभिप्रेतानि। तथा च नीलसमानाधिकरणभास्वरशुक्लासमानाधिकरणरूपवद्वृत्तिद्रव्यत्वसाक्षाद्व्याप्यजातिमत्त्वं तिक्तावृत्तिमधुरवृत्तिद्रव्यत्वसाक्षाद्व्याप्यजातिमत्त्वं शीतस्पर्शवत्त्वं सांसिद्धिकद्रवत्ववत्त्वं स्नेहवत्त्वमित्येतानि लक्षणानि जलस्येति भावः। हिमकरकादौ यदि न सांसिद्धिकद्रवत्वं तदा सांसिद्धिकद्रवत्ववद्वृत्तिद्रव्यत्वव्याप्यजातिमत्त्वं विवक्षणीयम्। लवणोदकालिन्दीजलादौ या नीलोपलब्धिः सा आश्रयौपाधिकी भ्रान्तिरेव वियति बिक्षेपे तस्यैव धवलिमोपलब्धेः यद्यपि जले कोऽपि रसो नानुभूयते तथापि हरीतक्यादिकषायद्रव्यभक्षणानन्तरं जलमाधुर्यमनुभूयत एव तस्य तद्व्यञ्जकत्वात्। सूर्यकरादिसंयोगाज्जले यदुष्णस्पर्शः प्रतीयते सोऽपि सूर्यकरादेरेव यद्यपि हिमकरकादौ द्रवत्वं नानुभूयते इति मतं तस्य जले ऽन्तर्भावः सम्भवति तथापि उष्मणा विलीने तत्र जलत्वं प्रत्यक्षसिद्धमेव दिव्यतेजःसंयोगात्तु तत्र द्रवत्वप्रतिरोधः काठिन्यप्रतीतिस्तु तत्र भ्रान्तिरेवेति मुक्तावलीकारः। केचित्तु दिव्यतेजःसंयोगात् जलपरमाणुभ्यां द्व्यणुकं तैश्च त्रसरेण्वादिकं क्रमेण हिमादौ जायते तादृशद्व्यणुकादिकञ्च द्रवत्वरहितं कठिनमेवेति हिमादौ काठिन्यप्रतीतिर्न भ्रान्तिरित्याहुः। स्नेहस्तु जलएव घृतादावपि तदुपस्तम्भकजलस्यैव स्नेहः तत्प्रकर्षाच्च घृतादेर्दहनानुकूलत्वं सक्तुसिकतादौ पिण्डीभावरूपः सङ्ग्रहनामकः संयोगविशेषो द्रवत्वसहितस्नेहकारित एव द्रवत्वमात्रकारितत्वे काचकाञ्चनद्रवत्वादिव तदुत्पत्तेर्नापि स्नेहमात्रकारितः घनीभूतघृतादिभिरपि तदुत्पत्तिप्रसङ्गात्।।

Light [or heat] is possessed of luminous colour and hot touch. If it be objected, Luminousness is the giving of light to other bodies, and such colour is not found in heat or in such light as in exists in gold, in a frying-pan, or in water. White colour is nowhere found in these, nor is a hot feel found in moonlight or gold. How then is this so? We reply that it may be inferred that luminous colour exists in heat etc., because they are light. It it be said, Luminosity is not proved to exist in these by their own colour, we reply that it is inferred from their possessing a hot feel. If it be asked, How is the luminosity [proved to exist in gold?] We reply that it will be explained that it is because it is inferred to be light from its being a distinctive substratum of fluidity which is produced, but not destroyed, by the closest conjunction with fire ; and that the existence of light in a frying-pan etc., is inferred from the possession of heat to the touch. For light is of four kinds : that in which colour and touch predominate, as sunlight; that in which colour predominates and touch does not, as moonlight;that in which neither colour nor touch predominates, as the eye; that in which colour does not, but touch does, predominate, as the hot season, and light as existing in water, a frying-pan, and the like.[1] U.

With respect to the relation between light and heat, cp. *Muktāvalī* on Bhāshā-parichchheda, v 40. Heat is a particular class existing in touch, and is known by perception. So also light is a particular class which is the inherent cause of the feeling of generated heat. It is not to be maintained that the possession [by light] of a hot feel cannot be predicated of the rays of the moon etc.; for heat exists there too, but is not recognised because it is overpowered by the touch of the water which they contain. In like manner it is not recognised in the brilliance of a gem, because it is overpowered by an earthy feel; nor in the eye etc., because it does not there predominate.[2]

[1] रूपं भास्वरं स्पर्शश्चोष्णस्तद्वत्तेज इत्यर्थः। ननु भास्वरत्वं प्रकाशकत्वं तादृशंञ्च रूपं नोष्मणि न वा चामीकरस्थे भर्ज्जनकपालस्थे वारिस्थे वा तेजसि। शुल्कञ्च रूपमुक्तेषु न क्वापि उष्णश्च स्पर्शो न चान्द्रे न वा चामीकरे तत् कथमेतदिति चेन्न उष्मादेत तेजस्वित्वेन भास्वररूपानुमानात्। तेजस्त्वमेव तत्र स्वरूपासिद्धमिति चेन्न उष्णस्पर्शवत्त्वेन तदनुमानात् चामीकरें कथमिति चेत् तत्र भास्वरस्वभावे ऽपि अत्यन्तानलसंयोगेनानुच्छिद्यमानजन्यद्रवत्वाधिकरणत्वेन व्यतिरेकिणा तेजस्यानुमानादिति वक्ष्यमाणत्वात् भर्ज्जनकपालादिनिष्ठे चोष्णस्पर्शवत्त्वेन तेजस्यानुमानात्। चतुर्विधं हि तेजः किञ्चिदुद्भूतरूपस्पर्शे यथा तौरादि किञ्चिदुद्भूतरूपस्पर्शं यथा नयनम् किञ्चिदनुद्भूतस्पर्शं यथा निदाघं वारिभर्जनकपालादिगतञ्च तेजः।।

[2] उष्णत्वं स्पर्शनिष्ठो जातिविशेषः प्रत्यक्षसिद्धम्। इत्थञ्च जन्योष्णस्पर्शसमवायिकारणतावच्छेदकं तेजस्त्वं जातिविशेषः। न चोष्णस्पर्शवत्त्वं चन्द्रकिरणादावव्याप्तमिति वाच्यम्। तत्रापि औष्णस्य सत्त्वात्। किन्तु तदन्तःपातिजलस्पर्शेनाभिभवाच्चक्षुरादौ चानुद्भूतत्वादवग्रहः।।

स्पर्शवान् वायुः।। 4।।

Quality of air

Aph. 4. Air is possessed of touch.

We are hear to understand a touch that is neither temperate, nor hot, nor cold. A touch of a different class belonging to the air is understood. The possession of such a heterogeneous touch is the characteristic of air, and the heterogeneity of the touch of the air is known by perception.[1] V.

त आकाशे न विद्यन्ते।। 5।।

Ether

Aph. 5. Those [qualities] do not exist in ether.

Those [qualities] colour, taste, smell, and touch do not exist in either. The appearance in ether of whiteness like that of co-agulated milk, is an illusion caused by the whiteness of the rays of the sun. The appearance also of blueness in the sky is an illusion occasioned by the blueness of the sapphire peak situated on the south side of mount Meru. Some maintain that this appearance is occasioned by the blueness of the pupil of the eye, from the eye's falling upon its own pupil after travelling to a distance and returning. This is not the case, for those whose eyes are tawny have the same perception.[2] V.

सर्पिर्जतुमधूच्छिष्टानामग्निसंयोगाद्द्रवत्वमद्भिः सामान्यम्।। 6।।

Aph. 6. The fluidity, through conjunction with fire, of clarified butter, lac, and wax, is common to them and water.

The fluidity which belongs to clarified butter etc., is due to a special cause, the conjunction of them with fire and is not intrinsic. Such intrinsic fluidity is the characteristic of water. Only fluidity is common to earth and water, not natural fluidity. Hence there is not too much asserted.[3] U.

[2] अत्र स्पर्शो ऽपाकजो ऽनुष्णाशीतो ग्राह्यः तेन वायवीयो विजातीयस्पर्शो लभ्यते तथा च तादृशविजातीयस्पर्शत्वमेव वायुलक्षणं वैजात्यं तु वायुस्पर्शे प्रत्यक्षसिद्धमिति।।

[3] ते रूपरसगन्धस्पर्शाः आकाशे न सन्तीत्यर्थः। दधिधवलिमाशसिति प्रतीतिस्तु सूर्यकरधवलिमौपाधिकी भ्रान्तिरेव नीलं नभ इति प्रतीतिरपि सुमेरोर्दक्षिणादिगवस्थित स्येन्द्रनीलमयंशिखरस्य नीलमविषयिणी भ्रान्तिरेव केचितु सुदूरगतस्य परावर्तमानस्प च क्षुषः स्वगोलकस्थकनीनिकापतनात् तद्गतनीलरूपविषयिशी तादृशप्रतीति-रित्याहुत्च पिङ्गलसारनयनानामपि तथोपलम्भादिति सङ्ेप।।

[3] सर्पिरादीनां यद्द्रवत्वमस्ति तदग्निसंयोगान्निमित्तात् नतु सांसिद्धिकं तादृशञ्चापां लक्षणं द्रवत्वमात्रन्तु पृथिव्या अद्भिः सामान्यं न तु सांसिद्धिकं द्रवत्वमपीति नातिव्याप्तिरित्यर्थः।।

The fluidity of clarified butter etc., which is due to a special cause, is like the intrinsic fluidity existing in water, because the class constituted by the universal fluidity exists in both, but there is in clarified butter etc., no possession of natural fluidity. Fluid in the aphorism on water (II.1.2.) has the special meaning of natural fluidity. Accordingly there is no discrepancy.[1] V.

त्रपुसीसलोहरजतसुवर्णानांमग्निसंयोगाद्द्रवत्त्वमद्भिः सामान्यम्।। 7।।

Aph. 7. The fluidity, through conjunction with fire, of tin, lead, iron, silver, and gold, is common to them with water.

By the use of the plural number of the word gold, white copper, copper, brass, quicksilver, etc., are implied, The explanation of this aphorism is to be understood as similar to that of the former.[2] V.

विषाणी ककुद्मान् प्रान्तबालधिः
सास्नावान् इति गोत्वे दृष्टं लिङ्गम्।। 8।।

Aph. 8. That she has horns, a hump, a tail hairy at the extremity, and a dewlap is the received mark of being a cow.

As in case of the universal cow the marks of possessing horns etc., are generally received or universally assumed means of proof; so with respect to air the mark of touch etc., is also the means of proof. This is the inner meaning of this and the following aphorism. In the former of these aphorisms in the mention of the cow's having horns the verb 'to be' is implied. Accordingly a particular kind of horn, not common to the buffalo, is understood, and this is a mark of being a cow, as also is the possession of a hump. That it has a tail hairy at the extremity,— according to the derivation 'the hair is situated at the extremity in this,' a peculiarity of the body, constituted by the tail, is asserted. That is a particular cow with a tail hairy at the extremity, whose tail is hairy and particularly so at the extremity. With respect to the tail of the sheep etc., there is not hairiness at the extremity, for the whole tail is hairy.

[1] घृतादीनां यन्नैमित्तिकं द्रवत्वं तज्जलगतसांसिद्धिकद्रवत्वतुल्यं द्रवत्वत्वजातेरुभयत्र सत्त्वात् सांसिद्धिकद्रवत्वं तु घृतादिषु नास्ति जलसूत्रोक्तद्रवपदं सांसिद्धिकद्रवत्वविशिष्टपरमिति नासङ्गतिरति भावः।।

[2] सुवर्णानामिति बहुवचनेन कांस्यताम्रपित्तलपारदादीनामप्युपग्रहः। व्याख्यानञ्चास्य सूत्रस्य पूर्ववदेव बोध्यम्।।

As there is nothing remarkable, on account of pendulousness etc., in the tail of the buffalo etc., a peculiarity in the tail is a mark of being a cow. The dewlap is a particular formation in the neck, the possession of which is a mark of the class cow. By the word *'iti'* is pointed out the distinctive attribute of being an object commonly known by the possession of horns etc. The practical cognition is, This is a cow because it possesses horns, a hump, a particular kind of tail, or a dewlap, as was the case with particular cows formerly observed.[1] V.

As with respect to the universal cow, the horns etc. are properties [marks] recognised as predicable of the whole class [known to prevade it]; so also the properties [marks] of air and the other five supersensible substances [viz., ether, space, time, soul, and the internal organ] recognised generally, come to be a means of proof.[2] U.

स्पर्शश्च वायोः।। 9।।

Existence of air proved

Aph. 9. Also touch is [a mark] of air.

Having stated the validity of [this form of] inference which effects the requirements of common life, he proves by it the existence of air. The word mark is to be supplied. The particle and implies also sound, wafting, and agitating. The sense of the aphorism is, therefore, that the existence of the air is inferred from a heterogenous touch, from the rustling of leaves etc., from the wafting aloft of grass, cotton, etc., and from the agitation of branches etc.[3] V.

[1] यथा गात्वे विषाणित्वादीनि लिङ्गानि सामान्यतो दृष्टानि लोकसिद्धानि प्रमाणानि तथा अतीन्द्रिये वायौ स्पर्शादीनि लिङ्गान्यपि प्रमाणानीति सूत्रद्वयनिगूढार्थः। तत्र प्रथमसूत्रे विषाणीति प्रशंसायामस्त्यर्थः प्रत्ययः तेन च महिषादिव्यावृत्तो विषाणविशेषो लभ्यते स च गोत्वे लिङ्गम् एवं ककुद्वत्तापि। प्रान्ते बालधिरिति अन्ते बाला आधीयन्ते ऽस्मिन्निति व्युत्पत्त्या पुच्छरूपाङ्गविशेष उच्यते प्रकृष्टे ऽन्ते बालधिर्यस्य स प्रान्ते बालधिर्गोपिण्डः मेषादिपुच्छे तु सामस्त्येन बालमयत्वान्नान्ते बालधित्वं महिषादिपुच्छे प्रलम्बत्वादिरूपप्रकर्षाभावात् पुच्छविशेषो गोत्वे लिङ्गम् सास्ना गलकम्बलं तद्वत्ता गोत्वे लिङ्गम् बिषाणीत्यादिव्यादिव्यवहारविषयतावच्छेदकम् इति शब्देन परामृश्यते तत्रायं प्रयोगः अयं गौर्विषाणविशेषवत्त्वात् ककुद्वत्त्वात् पुच्छविशेषवत्त्वात् सास्नावत्त्वाद्वा पूर्वानुभूतगोपिण्डवदिति।।

[2] यथा गोत्वं प्रति विषाणादीनि लिङ्गानि गृहीतव्याप्तिकानि तथा ऽतीन्द्रियवाय्वादिद्रव्यपञ्चकलिङ्गान्यपि सामान्यतो दृष्टानि प्रमाणभावमासादयन्तीति भावः।

[3] एवं लोकयात्रानिर्वाहकस्यानुमानस्य प्रामाण्यमुक्त्वा ऽनुमानेन वायुं साधयति। लिङ्गमित्यनुषज्यते चकारः शब्दधृतिकम्पान समुच्चिनोति तथा च विजातीयस्पर्शेन पर्णादिशब्देन नभसि तृणतूलादीनां धृत्या शाखादीनां कम्पेन च वायुरनुमीयते इति भावः।।

न च दृष्टानां स्पर्श इत्यदृष्टलिङ्गो वायुः ।। 10 ।।

Its properties invisible

Aph. 10. And it is not the touch which belongs to visible things, therefore air has an invisible mark.

This touch which is made the ground of inference, does not belong to earth, water, and light which are visible, for it is unaccompanied with colour. Accordingly, since it must be inferred that this touch has some substratum, air has an invisible mark or a mark that is observed generally, and is ascertained to exist from the force of the properties of the ground of the inference.[1] U.

That touch from which, as being its substratum, air is inferred [to exist], does not belong to visible things, viz., earth water, and light. For this reason air has an invisible mark. It has, as being a substratum, a mark which is not visible, wherefore the resultant sense is that air has for its mark a touch which does not exist in visible things.[2] V.

अद्रव्यवत्त्वेन द्रव्यम् ।। 11 ।।

Air a substance

Aph. 11. It is a substance because of its not inhering in any substance.

That of which a substance is the substratum is said to inhere in that substance; that of which a substance is not the substratum does not inhere in a substance. The sense is that air is not inherent in any substance. Accordingly the substance air has, like ether, an atomic characteristic. For all other categories inhere in substance, and inherence belongs to all except the eternal substances; for according to this explanation, since a combination of two atoms is originated by primary atoms, the material cause of the origin of a large integrate whole is a succession of combinations of two or more atoms.[3] U.

[1] अयं स्पर्शो यः पक्षः क्रियते स दृष्टानां पृथिव्यप्तेजसां न भवति रूपासहचरत्वात् तथा वायं स्पर्शः क्वचिदाश्रियत इत्यनुमेयमित्यदृष्टलिङ्गः सामान्यतो दृष्टलिङ्गोऽपि वायुः पक्षधर्मताबलादायात इत्यर्थः।।

[2] येन स्पर्शेन वायुरधिकरणत्या ऽनुमीयते स स्पर्शो न दृष्टानां पृथिव्यप्तेजसाम् इति हेतोः वायुरदृष्टलिङ्गः नास्ति दृष्टमधिकरणतया यस्य ताद्दृशं लिङ्गं यस्य स दृष्टावृत्तिस्पर्शलिङ्गको वायुरिति फलितार्थः।।

[3] द्रव्यमाश्रयभूतमस्यास्तीति द्रव्यवत् न द्रव्यवत् अद्रव्यवत् द्रव्यानाश्रितमित्यर्थः तथा चाकाशवत् परमाणुलक्षणो वायुर्द्रव्यम् अन्येषां पदार्थानां द्रव्याश्रितत्वात् आश्रितत्वञ्चान्यत्र नित्यद्रव्येभ्य इत्यभिधानात् परमाणुभ्यां द्व्यणुकारम्भात् द्व्यणुकादिप्रक्रमेणावर्धावनौ महत आरम्भस्योपादनीयत्वादिति।।

क्रियावत्त्वाद्गुणवत्त्वाच्च।। 12।।

Continued

Aph. 12. Also [air is a substance] from its possessing actions and qualities.

The words The aerial atom is a substance are to be supplied. It must be admitted that there exist in the primary atom the possession of qualities such as conjunction originative of combinations of two atoms etc., and the possession of action in conformity with those qualities. This is not a doubtful and undemonstrated assertion, but the means of establishing the existence of primary atoms are a mote in a sunbeam and the like, which mote is composed of parts because it is a substance that may be seen with the eye, like a waterpot. The portions of a mote are like a half-jar [both integrate and integrant] since they are small portions composed also themselves of parts. Therefore as in earth etc. there is a primary atom, so it must be allowed equally in the case of the air, since there are in each case similar series of portions and combinations of portions.[1] V.

अद्रव्यवत्त्वेन नित्यत्वमुक्तम्।। 13।।

Air an eternal substance

Aph. 13. [Air] is said to be eternal because it does not inhere in any substance.

Air in its primary atomic character is to be supplied. A substance is destroyed by the destruction of either its co-inherent or its non-coinherent cause. A primary atom, not being composed of parts, has neither such cause. Therefore, there being nothing to destroy it, it is not liable to destructioin. The being composed of parts is a condition of which the cause is the possession of actions and qualities.[2] U.

Of the primary aerial atom, is to be supplied. That which has no substance as its co-inherent cause, is said to differ in that respect from that which has a substance as its co-inherent cause.[3] V.

[1] वायवीयपरमाणुद्रव्यमिति शेषः। द्व्यणुकारम्भकसंसोगादिरूपगुणवत्त्वं तदनुकूलक्रियावत्त्वञ्च परमाणाव-वश्यमङ्गीकार्यमिति न सन्दिग्धसिद्धो हेतुः परमाणुसिद्धिप्रकारस्तु त्रसरेणुः सावयवश्चाक्षुषद्रव्यत्वाद् घटवत् त्रसरेणोरवयवाः सावयवा महदवयवत्वात् कपालवदित्यादिः एवञ्च पृथिव्यादौ यथा परमाणुस्तथा वायुस्थेले ऽपि निराबाध एव अवयवावयविपरम्परायास्तुल्यत्वादिति।।

[2] परमाणुलक्षणवायोरिति शेषः द्रव्यं हि समवायिकारणासमवायिकारणान्मतरनाशान्नश्यति परमाणोस्तु निरवयवतया नैतदुभयमस्ति तथाच विनाशकाभावान्न विनश्यति क्रियावत्त्वे गुणवत्त्वे च हेतो मावयवत्वमुपाधिः।।

[3] वायुपरमाणोरिति शेषः नास्ति द्रव्यं समवायिकारणतया यस्य तद्द्रव्यं द्रव्यसमवायिकारणकभिन्नं तत्त्वेनेत्यर्थः।।

वायोर्वायुसम्मूर्च्छनं नानात्वलिङ्गम्।। 14।।

Aph. 14. The concurrence of air with air is a mark of its multiplicity.

Concurrence of wind with wind, or conflict of winds, is a kind of conjunction. This conjunction is the meeting two winds of equal velocity. but coming in different directions and different in their action [or motion.] It is inferred from the flying upwards of grass, cotton etc. For the upward motion and concurrence of two winds is invisible. But it is inferred that the visible action characterised by the flying upward of visible grass etc., is produced by either a blow or impulse of substance possessing touch and velocity. The upward motion of the two winds, the character of which is to move horizontally, being impossible unless they repel each other, proves a mutual repulse.[1] U.

वायुसन्निकर्षे प्रत्यक्षाभावाद्दृष्ट लिङ्गं न विद्यते।। 15।।

Aph. 15. Inasmuch as in the contact with air there is no act of perception there exists [in it] no visible mark.

For where there is a visible mark there is a perception of pervasion [universal concomitance] as of fire by smoke; but in the present case of contact, with air, perception of pervasion of air is impossible because air transcends sense. Accordingly there is no mark in air universally concomitant and cognised by perception, and air has therefore an invisible mark.[2] V.

सामान्यतो दृष्टाच्चाविशेषः।। 16।।

Aph. 16. And inasmuch as its existence is known by general inference it is not a particular.

Not particular means devoid of particularity, not particularised by particularity, and particular is the particular class included in the

[1] वायुसम्मूच्छनमिति वाय्वोर्वायूनां वा सम्मूर्च्छनं संयोगविशेषः। स च समानवेगयोर्विरूद्धदिक्क्रिययोः सन्निपातः। स च तृणतूलकादेरूर्ध्वगमनेनानुमीयते वाय्योरूर्ध्वगमनस्य सन्निपातस्य चातीन्द्रियत्वात् तृणादीनान्तु प्रत्यक्षाणा-मूर्ध्वगमनलक्षणायाः क्रियायाः प्रत्यक्षायाः स्पर्शवद्वेगवदद्रव्याभिघातनोदनान्यतरजन्यत्वमनुमीयते तथा हि तिर्यग्गमनस्वभावस्य वायोरूर्ध्वगमनं परस्परप्रतीघातमन्तरेणानुपपद्यमानं परस्परप्रतीघातं साधयति।।

[2] दृष्टं लिङ्गं हि यत्र व्याप्तेः प्रत्यक्षं भवति यथा वह्नेर्धूमः प्रकृते तु वायुसन्निकर्षेऽपि वायुव्याप्तिप्रत्यक्षं न सम्भवति वायोरतीन्द्रियत्वात् तथा च प्रत्यक्षगृहीतव्याप्तिकं लिङ्गं वायौ नास्तीत्यदृष्टलिङ्गो वायुरिति सुष्ठूक्तमेवेत्यर्थः।।

universal substance, i.e., the universal of air. And by inferring from the notion of touch that the touch which is experienced must have some substratum, as also that it cannot be one of the other [substances], the notion of its inhesion in a substance other than the eight substances being established, air is proved to be a substance other than the eight substances, with respect to the subject which determines that which is to be proved. By general inference means from a mark different from the relation of cause and effect, or from a mark other than that of invariable sequence. In the Nyāya Aphorisms it is taught that inference is of three kinds, from the antecedent, from the subsequent, and that which is drawn generally That which is from antecedence, [or progressive inference] has for its mark a cause, or an invariable sequence. That which is from subsequence, [or regressive inference] has an effect for its mark, or the incompatibility of other causes. That which is general has for its mark something distinct from cause and effect, or is from concomitance and incompatibility.[1] V.

तस्मादागमिकम् ।। 17 ।।

Aph. 17. It is therefore declared by revelation.

Since the existence of air is not inferred by means of a class having for its form the aerial, the name air is given by revelation, proclaimed by the Veda.[2] V.

सञ्ज्ञाकर्म त्वस्मद्विशिष्टानां लिङ्गम् ।। 18 ।।

The existence of God

Aph. 18. But word and work are the mark of those beings who are distinguished from ourselves.

The word but implies the exclusion of the marks of touch etc. A word is a name; a work an effect such as the earth etc. Both of these are

[1] अविशेषः विशेषरहितः विशेषाविशेषित इति यावत् विशेषश्च द्रव्यत्वव्याप्यजातिविशेषो वायुत्वं तथा चानुभूयमानः स्पर्शः क्वचिदाश्रितः स्पर्शत्वादित्यनुमानेन इतरबाधसहकृतेन स्पर्शे अष्टद्रव्यातिरिक्तद्रव्याश्रितत्वसिद्धौ अष्टद्रव्यातिरिक्तद्रव्यत्वेन वायुरपि साध्यतावच्छेदककोटौ सिध्यतीति भावः सामान्यतो दृष्टादिति कार्यकारणभिन्नलिङ्गात् अन्वयव्यतिरेकिलिङ्गाद्वेत्यर्थः। न्यायसूत्रे पूर्ववत् शेषवत् सामान्यतो दृष्टमिति त्रिविधमनुमानमुक्तं तत्र पूर्ववत् कारणलिङ्गकं केवलान्वयि वा शेषवत् कार्यलिङ्गकं केवलव्यतिरेकि वा सामान्यतो दृष्टं कार्यकारणभिन्नलिङ्गकम् अन्वयव्यतिरेकि वा इत्यर्थः।।

[2] यस्माद्वायुत्वस्वरूपजातिप्रकारेण वायोर्नानुमितिः तस्माद्वायुरिति नामआगमिकं वेदप्रसिद्धम्।।

a mark of the existence of God and the great sages who are more excellent than ourselves.[1] U.

The word but expresses a division of the sections, and implies that the section treating of the Deity is now commenced A word is a name such as air, a boar, barley, a reed, and the like; a work is an effect, as the earth, a blade of grass etc. These are both marks inferring the existence of God and the great sages. who are distinguished from ourselves, who are able to produce this and that effect, and are possessed of omniscience and omnipotence. Or the particle but may express the exclusion of other marks. According to this when the existence of God and the great sages is proved, the authority of the Veda, Smṛti, etc., must be acknowledged, because they were promulgated by them. Although this has been stated before, it is repeated for the sake of confirming it and of stating the [mode of] inferring the existence of God, etc.[2] V.

प्रत्यक्षप्रवृत्तत्वात् संज्ञाकर्मणः।। 19।।

Aph. 19. Because words and works are known by perception to be produced.

In this place also by the aggregative, copulative compound word and work, existence as a single object is denoted, with the purpose of implying that the framer of names and the maker of the work are indivisible. He of whose perception paradise, requitative efficacy etc., are objects, wills to frame the terms paradise, unforseen results, etc. As when the bodies of Chaitra, Maitra and others are objects of perception to a father and others, the names Chaitra, Maitra, etc, are given; so the giving of names to a water-pot, a piece of cloth, etc., is dependent on the will of God. Whatever word God wills to be the name of anything is applicable to it, in the same manner that every herb that is touched by the edge of an ichneumon's teeth is an antidote to the venom of a snake. Therefore a name of this kind is a mark inferential of those

[1] तु शब्दः स्पर्शादिलिङ्गव्यवच्छेदार्थः संज्ञा नाम कर्म कार्यं क्षित्यादि तदुभयमस्मद्विशिष्टानाम् ईश्वरमहर्षीणां सत्त्वे ऽपि लिङ्गम्।।

[2] तु शब्दः प्रकरणविच्छेदार्थः इदानीमीश्वरप्रकरणारब्धमिति भावः। संज्ञा नाम वायुवराहयववेतसादि कर्म कार्यं क्षित्यङ्कुरादि एतदुभयमस्मद्विशिष्टानाम् अस्मत्तो विशिष्टानां तत्तत्कार्यसमर्थानां सर्वज्ञैश्वर्यसम्पन्नानाम् ईश्वरमहर्षीणां लिङ्गमनुमापकं तुकारो लिङ्गान्तरव्यवच्छेदार्थो वा तथा चेश्वरमहर्षिसिद्धौ तत्प्रणीतत्वेन वेदस्मृत्यादेः प्रामाण्यमवश्यमङ्गीकार्यमिति यद्यपीदं पूर्वमुक्तं तथापि दाढर्यार्थमीश्वराद्यनुमानकथामार्थञ्च पुनर्वचनम्।।

beings which are distinguished from ourselves and others. The names also of Maitra and the like, which are given by a father to a son are virtually given by God by means of such precepts as, Let a father on the twelfth day give a name to his child. Thus it is established that a name is a mark of the existence of God. In like manner a work being a product is a mark of the being of a God, for the earth etc., being effects, must have a maker, as is the case with a waterpot.[1] U.

It may be asked, How is the omniscience of the maker of words and works proved? Accordingly it is stated.... A name is produced on perceiving the thing named, and an effect is produced on perceiving the material cause. A father and others on seeing the body of a son etc., give it a name such as Chaitra or Maitra; and in like manner a potter and others on seeing a piece of earthenware, etc., make a water-pot etc. So it is concluded from the nature of the case that the framer of all applicable names and the maker of the earth etc., which are effects, must be omniscient, for he must know by perception all such things named, and the material causes of earth, etc.[2] V.

निष्क्रमणं प्रवेशनमित्याकाशस्य लिङ्गम्।। 20।।

The existence of ether

Aph. 20. Egress and ingress,— such is the mark of the existence of ether.

Here the word such, expressive of a class, includes also throwing upwards, etc. It is a doctrine of the Sāṅkhyas that the motion of tangible bodies, i.e., their egress and ingress, being impossible without the existence of ether which is a unoccupied, enables us to infer that there

[1] अत्रापि संज्ञा च कर्म चेति समाहारद्वन्द्वादेकवद्भावः संज्ञाकर्तुर्जगत्कर्तुश्चाभेदसूचनार्थः।।

तथाहि यस्य स्वर्गापूर्वादयः प्रत्यक्षाः स एव तत्र स्वर्गापूर्वादिसंज्ञाः कर्तुमीष्टे प्रत्यक्षे चैत्रमैत्रादिसंज्ञानिवेशनवत् एवञ्च घटपटादिसंज्ञानिवेशनमपि ईश्वरसङ्केताधीनमेव यः शब्दो यत्रेश्वरेण सङ्केतितः स तत्र साधुः यथा या काचिदोष-धिर्नकुलदंष्ट्राग्रस्पृष्टा सा सर्वा ऽपि सर्पविषं हन्तीत्येतादृशी संज्ञा अस्मदादिविशिष्टानां लिङ्गमनुमापकं या ऽपि मैत्रादिसंज्ञा पित्रा पुत्रे क्रियते सा ऽपि द्वादशे ऽहनि पिता नाम कुर्यात् इत्यादि विधिना नूनमीश्वरप्रयुक्तैव तथा च सिद्धं संज्ञाया ईश्वरलिङ्गत्वम् एवं कर्मापि कार्यमपीश्वरे लिङ्गं तथा हि क्षित्यादिकं सकर्तृकं कार्यत्वात् घटवत्।।

[2] ननु सर्वज्ञत्वं संज्ञाकर्मकर्तुः कुतः सिद्धमित्य आह। संज्ञायाः संज्ञिप्रत्यक्षसाध्यत्वम् कार्यस्य तूपादानप्रत्यक्ष-साध्यत्वं पित्रादिना हि पुत्रादिशरीरं दृष्ट्वैव तत्र चैत्रमैत्रादिसंज्ञा निवेश्यन्ते एवं कुलालादयो ऽपि कपालादिकं दृष्ट्वैव घटादिकं कुर्वन्ति अतो निखिलसाधुसंज्ञाकर्तुस्तादृशसंज्ञिप्रत्यक्षस्य क्षित्यादिकार्यकर्तुस्तदुपादानप्रत्यक्षस्य चावश्यकत्वात् सर्वज्ञत्वमर्थवशसम्पन्नमेव।।

is another substance called ether.[1] V.

तदलिङ्गमेकद्रव्यत्वात् कर्मणः ।। 21 ।।

Aph. 21. That is not a mark [of the existence of ether,] for an action inheres in one substance only.

This opinion of the Sānkhyas is rejected. That egress, etc., is not a mark, is not a mark of existence of ether. Since action has one solid substance as its site, action which inheres only in that which is solid cannot warrant an inference of the existence of ether as underlying it. For an effect which is inherent implies a co-inherent [or material] cause, and there is not between ether and action the relation of inherence and subsistence.[2] V.

कारणान्तरानुक्लृप्तिवैधर्म्याच्च ।। 22 ।।

Aph. 22. Also because the properties [of ether] differ from the mark of another cause.

It might be urged that egress, ingress, etc., infer the existence of ether as being its non-coinherent cause. Hence this statement is made. [Egress and ingress are not a mark of the existence of ether] because its properties differ from the mark of another cause, viz., of a non-coinherent cause.[3] U.

Agreement (anuklṛpti) is an abstract term formed by a primary (kṛt) affix. The meaning is, therefore, that since there exists in either a difference of properties, in consequence of its being a substance, from quality and action which are another universally acknowledged cause, viz., the non-coinherent cause, therefore egress etc., connot infer the existence of ether as being its non-inherent cause.[4] V.

[1] अत्र प्रकारार्थकेतिशब्देनोत्क्षेपणादेरपि ग्रहणं स्पर्शवतां सञ्चारो निष्क्रमणं प्रवेशनञ्च शून्यात्मकाकाशं विना ऽनुपपद्यमानमाकाशनामकं द्रव्यान्तरमनुमापयतीति सांख्यमतम्।।

[2] तदेतन्मतं निरस्यति। तत् निष्क्रमणादिकम् अलिङ्गम् आकाशस्य लिङ्गं न भवति कर्मणः क्रियाया एकं मूर्तं द्रव्यमाश्रयो यस्य तत्त्वात् तथा च मूर्तमात्रसमवेतं कर्म न समवायितयाकाशानुमानसमर्थं हि समवेतकार्यं समवायिकारणमाक्षिपति न चाकाशकर्मणोः समवायिसमवेतभाव इत्यर्थः।

[3] ननु चासमवायिकारणतयैवाकाशमनुमापयिष्यति निष्क्रमणप्रवेशनादीत्यत आह कारणान्तरस्य असमवायिकारणस्य या ऽनुक्लृप्तिर्लक्षणं तद्वैधर्म्यादित्यर्थः।।

[4] अनुक्लृप्तिरिति कृद्विहितो भाव इति न्यायात् अनुक्लृप्तं वादिप्रतिवाद्युभयसम्मतं यत् कारणान्तरम् असमवायिकारणं गुणः कर्म च तद्वैधर्म्यात् द्रव्यत्वरूपतद्वैधर्म्यस्याकाशे सत्त्वात् नासमवायिकारणतयाकाशमनुमापयितुं निष्क्रमणादिकं शक्नोतीत्यर्थः।।

संयोगादभावः कर्मणः।। 23।।

Aph. 23. Non-existence of action results from conjunction.

It is stated that action does not infer the existence of ether as its instrumental cause. Since after conjunction there is non-existence, i.e., non-production, of action, ether is not in relation to action an instru-mental cause. The sense is that since it is observed that action (or motion) does not come into being in fruits, leaves, etc., after their conjunction with the ground, the instrumenttal cause of motion is the non-existence of a particular kind of conjunction, etc., and not ether, for the negation of ether does not involve the negation of action, ether being universally diffused.[1] V

कारणगुणपूर्वकः कार्यगुणो दृष्टः।। 24।।

Aph. 24. The quality of an effect is observed to be pre-existent in the quality of the cause.

The way is prepared for the statement that it is sound that necessitates the inference of the existence of ether. The particular quality of an effect is observed to pre-exist in the cause, as the colour of a water-pot. etc., in portions of the water-pot etc. Accordingly the particular quality or sound which is apprehended by the organ of hearing, having no prior existence as the quality of a cause, is not the quality of an effect, but of an eternal substance. Thus it is proved that ether, as being that in which sound exists, in an eternal substance.[2]V.

कार्यान्तराप्रादुर्भावाच्च शब्दः स्पर्शवतामगुणः।। 25।।

Aph. 25. Sound is not a quality of tangible things, since there appears no other effect.

It might be urged that sound is observed in a lute, flute, tabour,

[1] निमित्तकारणतया ऽपि नाकाशानुमापकं कर्मेत्याह। यतः संयोगात् संयोगानन्तरं कर्मणो ऽभावः अनुत्पादः अत आकाशं न कर्मणि निमित्तकारणमित्यर्थः।। अयं भावः फलपत्रादीनां भूम्यादिसंयोगानन्तरं कर्मानुत्पत्तिदर्शनात् संयोगविशेषाभावादिकमेव कर्मणि निमित्तकारणं न त्वाकाशं तद्व्यतिरेकेण कर्मव्यतिरेकस्यासिद्धेस्तस्य व्यापकत्वादिति भावः।।

[2] शब्द एव आकाशानुमापक इत्यभिधातुं भूमिकामारचयति। कार्यस्य यो विशेषगुणः स कारणगुणपूर्वक एव दृष्टः यथा घटरूपादिः कपालरूपादिपूर्वकः तथा च शब्दरूपो यो विशेषगुणः श्रोत्रेन्द्रियेणोपलभ्यते तस्य कारणगुणपूर्वकत्वाभावात् न कार्यगुणत्वं किन्तु नित्यद्रव्यस्यैव गुणः शब्द इति शब्दाधारतया नित्यद्रव्यसिद्धिरित्यर्थः।।

conch shell, drum etc., which are effects, and that consequently it exists previously as a quality of their cause. Hence this statement is made. Let this be so, then as colour, taste, etc., are observed in threads, in the portions of a pot. etc., and as other homogeneous colour, taste; etc., are perceived in a piece of cloth, a water-pot, etc., so a sound homogeneous with that which is observed in the integrant parts of a lute, flute, tabour etc., will be found in the integrate whole, in the lute, flute, tabour, etc. But this is not the case. On the contrary it is seen that a lute etc., has its origin in integrant parts destitute of sound, whereas it does not appear that a piece of cloth, a water-pot, etc., have their origin in threads and pieces of earthenware destitute of colour. Moreover if sound were a particular quality of tangible things, a relation of high and higher and low and lower tones would not be observed; for colours etc., existing in a single complex substance are not perceived to be various in degree; therefore sound is not a particular quality of tangible things.[1] U.

परत्र समवायात् प्रत्यक्षत्वाच्च नात्मगुणो न मनोगुणः।। 26।।

Aph. 26. Since it inheres in something else and is known by perception, sound is neither a quality of the soul nor a quality of the internal organ.

If sound were a quality of the soul there would be such cognitions as I am played by the breath or by the hand, I am sounding; as there are such cognitions as I am happy, I will, I know, I wish etc. But this is not the case, whereas it appears to all that a conch shell is played with the breath, and a lute with the hand. Moreover sound is not a quality of the soul, becaues it is, like colour, apprehended by an external organ. So too if sound were a particular quality belonging to the soul, it would be, like pain, etc., perceived by a deaf man. It is therefore fairly stated that it must inhere in something else. The reason that it is not a quality of the internal organ is stated to be that it is known by perception. The

[1] ननु वीणावेणुमृमदङ्गशङ्खपटहादौ कार्ये शब्द उपलभ्यते तथा च तत्कारणगुणपूर्वकः स्यादत आह। भवेदेवं यथा तन्तुकपालादिषु रूपरेसाद्यनुभूयते तत्सजातीयञ्च रूपरसाद्यन्तरं पटघटादावुपलभ्यते तथा वीणावेणुमृदङ्गाद्यवयवेषु यः शब्द उपलब्धस्तत्सजातीयश्चेत् वीणावेणामृदङ्गाद्यवयवविन्युपलभ्यते न चैवम् प्रत्युत निःशब्दैरेवावयववीणाद्यारम्भदर्शनात् नीरूपैस्तु तन्तुकपालादिभिः पटघटाद्यारम्भस्यादर्शनात् किञ्च यदि शब्दः स्पर्शवतां विशेषगुणः स्यान् तदा तत्र तारतारतरमन्दमृदतरादिभावो नानुभूयेत न ह्येकावयव्याश्रिता रूपादयो विचित्र्येणानुभूयन्ते तस्मान्न स्पर्शवद्विशेषगुणः शब्दः।।

reason that the words soul and internal organ are not, as they might have been, made into one compound word (ātma-manase), is that they may both with equal propriety be said to be known by perception. For the same reason it is implied that sound is a quality of sapace and time.[1] U.

परिशेषाल्लिङ्गमाकाशस्य।। 27।।

Aph. 27. It remains that sound is a mark of ether.

Sound is to be supplied. Sound must exist in something, because it is a quality, like colour, etc. Thus it is proved by a general inference that there is another substance over and above the eight substances [earth, water, light, air, time, space, the soul, and the internal organ.] Sound is a quality because, like colour etc., it constitutes a class known by one external organ. It will be proved hereafter from its inhering without continuity in an eternal substance, that, like knowledge, it is not eternal. The substance proved by the residuary method is eternal, since there is no proof of its being formed of parts, and universally diffused, inasmuch as sound is perceived everywhere.[2] U.

द्रव्यत्वनित्यत्वे वायुना व्याख्याते।। 28।।

Ether and eternal substance

Aph. 28. The substantiality and eternity of ether are explained by air.

To prove by analogy that the substance that was sound for its mark is a substance and eternal, it is stated that as air is eternal because it does not inhere in any substance, so also is ether, and that as air is a substance because it has qualities, so also is ether.[3] U.

[1] शब्दी यद्यात्मनुणः स्यात् तदा ऽहं सुखी यते जाने इच्छामीत्यादिवत् अहं पूर्ये अहं वाद्ये अहं शब्दवानित्यादिधीः स्यात् न त्वेवमस्ति किन्तु शङ्खः पूर्यते वीणा वाद्यते इति प्रतियन्ति लौकिकाः। किञ्च शब्दो नात्मगुणः बाह्येन्द्रियग्राह्यत्वात् रूपादिवत् अपिच शब्दो यद्यात्मयोग्यविशेषगुणः स्याद्बधिरेणाप्युपलभ्येत दुःखादिवत् तस्मात् सुष्ठूक्तं परत्र समवायादिति अमनोगुणत्वे हेतुमाह प्रत्यक्षत्वादिति नात्ममनसोर्गुण इति समासे कर्तव्ये यदसमासकरणं तेन तुल्यन्यायतया प्रत्यक्षत्वादित्यनेनैव हेतुना दिक्कालयोरपि गुणत्वं शब्दस्य प्रतिषिद्धमिति सूचितम्।।

[2] अब्द इति शेषः। अत्रापि शब्दः क्वचिदाश्रितौ गुणत्वात् रूपादिवदिति सामान्यतोदृष्टादृष्टद्रव्यातिरिक्तद्रव्यसिद्धिः। गुणश्चायं बाह्यैकेन्द्रियग्राह्यजातीयत्वात् रूपादिवत् अनित्यत्वे सति विभुसमवेतत्वात् ज्ञानादिवत् अनित्यत्वञ्च साधयिष्यते। परिशेषसिद्धस्य द्रव्यस्यावयवकल्पनायां प्रमाणाभावनित्यत्वं सर्वत्र शब्दोपलब्धेर्विभुत्वम्।।

[3] शब्दलिङ्गस्य द्रव्यस्य द्रव्यत्वनित्यत्वे अतिदेशेन साधयन्नाह। श्रद्रव्यत्वाद्यथा वायोर्नित्यत्वं तथाकाशस्यापि गुणवत्त्वाद्यथा वायोर्द्रव्यत्वं तथाकाशस्यापीत्यर्थः।।

As the primary aerial atom is eternal because it does not in here in any substance, and because it has qualities, so also is ether.[1] V.

तत्त्वं भावेन॥ 29॥

Ether a unit

Aph. 29. Its unity is explained by existence.

As being or existence is one, so also is ether only one.[2] U.

शब्दलिङ्गाविशेषाद्विशेषलिङ्गाभावाच्च॥ 30॥

Aph. 30. Also because sound, its mark, is not particular, and because there does not exist a particular mark of ether.

The unity of ether is established is to be understood. It being ascertained that it is an eternal substance, and that all sounds have that one only substratum, it follows that the hypothesis of another substratum would be superflous. Moreover in the conception of ether sound is regarded as its mark, and this mark is not particular, and there is no other mark establishing its particularity or establishing its divisibility. It will be stated hereafter that though knowledge etc. are a non-particular mark of souls, yet there is a proof of the plurality of souls in another mark which is difference of condition.[3] U.

As plurality of souls is proved by the consideration that in one soul at one time an effect is produced in the form of pleasure, and in another soul an effect is produced in the form of pain, and so there is a difference in two effects of soul, pleasure and pain; so is it established, by the absence of proof to the contrary, and by the simplicity of the hypothesis, that ether is not manifold but exists as a unit; inasmuch as there is no particularity in sound, which is the mark of ether, by which the multiplicity of ether might be proved, there being no other mark demonstrative of the multiplicity of ether.[4] V.

1 यथा वायुपरमाणोरद्रव्यत्वेन नित्यत्वं गुणवत्त्वेन च द्रव्यत्वं तथाकाशस्यापीत्यर्थः।

2 भावः सत्ता सा यथैका तथाकाशमप्येकमेवेत्यर्थः॥

3 तत्त्वमाकाशस्य सिद्धमित्यर्थः वैभवे सति सर्वेषां शब्दानां तदैकाश्रयतयैवोपयत्तावाश्रयान्तरकल्पनायां कल्पनागौरवप्रसङ्गः अन्यदपि यदाकाशं कल्पनीयं तत्रापि शब्द एव लिङ्गं तच्चावशिष्टं न च विशेषसाधकं भेदसाधकं लिङ्गान्तरमस्ति आत्मनां यद्यपि ज्ञानादिकमविशिष्टमेव लिङ्गं तथापि व्यवस्थातो लिङ्गान्तरादात्मनानात्वसिद्धिरिति वक्ष्यते॥

4 यथा कुत्रचिदात्मनि कदाचित् सुखरूपमेव कार्यं जायते तदैवान्यस्मिन्नात्मनि दुःखरूपमेव कार्यं जायते इत्यात्मकार्ययोः

तदनुविधानादेकपृथक्त्वञ्चेति।। 31।।

Individuality of ether

Aph. 31. In conformity with this is its individual unity.

The individual unity of ether is proved by its unity, from the consideration of the universal presence of the attribute individual unity wherever unity exists.[1] V.

The proof of its individual unity is that individual unity necessarily follows unity. The purticle *iti* indicates the completion of the daily lesson. The scope of this section is to state the characteristics of particular substances which possess, qualities and are not objects of the cognition of the internal organ. Therefore the characteristics of earth, water, light, ether, and in connection with them that of the divine soul, are stated in this daily lesson. Accordingly the earth has been said to be possessed of fourteen qualities. These qualities are colour, taste, smell, touch, number, extension, individuality, conjunction, disjunction, highest and not highest generality, gravity, fluidity, and self-restitution. Exactly the same number of qualities, with the exception of small, and with the addition of viscidity, belong to water. These same qualities with the exception of taste, small, viscidity, and gravity, belong to light; and with the exception of smell, taste, colour, gravity, viscidity and fluidity, to air. With the addition of sound, number and the four following qualities [extension, individuality, conjunction and disjunction,] belong to ether. Only number and the four following qualities belong to time and space. Number and the four following qualities, accompanied with highest and not highest generality, and impetus, belong to the internal organ. Number and the four following qualities, and knowledge, desire, and volition belong to God.[2]

सुखदुःखयोर्वैलक्षण्यादात्मनानात्वं तथाकाशे शब्दरूपलिङ्गस्य न कश्चिद्विशेषो येनाकाशनानात्वं सिध्यति न वाकाशनानात्वसाधकं लिङ्गान्तरमस्ति तथा च प्रमाणाभावात् लाघवाच्चाकाशस्य न नानात्वं किन्त्वेकव्यक्तित्वमित्यर्थः।।

[1] यत्र यत्र एकत्वं तत्रैवैकपृथत्तवमिति व्याप्तेराकाशस्यैकत्वेनैव एकपृथक्त्वसिद्धिरिति।।

[2] नियमेनैकपृथक्त्वमेकत्वमनुविधत्ते इत्येकपृथक्त्वसिद्धिः इति आह्निकपरिसमाप्तौ मानसप्रत्यक्षा-विषयविशेषगुणवद्द्रव्यलक्षणमाह्निकार्थः। तेन पृथिव्यप्तेजोवाय्वाकाशानां द्रसङ्गत ईश्वरात्मनश्च लक्षणमस्मिन्नाह्निके तेन चतुर्दशगुणवती पृथिवी ते च गुणा रूपरसगन्धस्पर्शसंख्यापरिमाणपृथक्त्वसंयोगविभागपरत्वा-परत्वगुरुत्वद्रवत्वसंस्काराः। तावन्त एव गन्धमपास्य स्नेहेन सहापाम्। एत एव रसगन्धस्नेहगुरुत्वान्यपास्य तेजसः। गन्धरसरूपगुरुत्वस्नेहद्रवत्वान्यपास्य वायोः। शब्देन सह संख्यादिपञ्चगुणवत्त्वमाकाशस्य संख्यादिपञ्चकमात्रं दिक्कालयोः। परत्वापरत्ववेगसहितं संख्यादिपञ्चकं मनसः। संख्यादिपञ्चकं ज्ञानेच्छाप्रयत्नाश्चेश्वरस्य।।

SECOND DAILYLESSON

पुष्पवस्त्रयोः सति सन्निकर्षे गुणान्तराप्रादुर्भावो वस्त्रे गन्धाभावलिङ्गम्।। 1।।

Natural and communicated qualities

Aph. 1. A flower and a garment being brought into contact, the non-appearance in the garment of another quality is a mark of the non-existence of smell in the garment.

With the purpose of investigating smell etc., the characteristics of the elements, it is now established that smell etc., are natural and communicated. Colour, taste, smell, and touch being natural where they are produced in the order of qualities proceeding from causes, become in such cases characteristics, but not in other cases. For the fragrance experienced in a breeze, or the cold experienced on the surface of a stone, or the warmth experienced in water, is not a characteristic. Therefore it is said, A flower and a garment being brought into contact, or when a garment is brought into contact with a golden ketakī (Pandanus Odoratissimus) flower, the fragrance of the golden ketakī which is then experienced does not belong to the garment; for it is not produced from the garment in the order of a quality proceeding from a cause, but is communicated through contiguity with the golden ketakī flower. For the non-existence of smell in the ketakī is not a mark of the non-eisitence of smell in the garment. What then is the mark? It is said to be the non-appearance of smell from another attribute i.e., its non-appearance or non-production from a quality which is a cause. Form if the smell which is smelt in the garment be natural, it will be perceived before the contact with the ketakī, in the threads which are its constituent parts. This is not the case and therefore the smell in question does not inhere in the garment, inasmuch as the particular quality is not produced by the qualities of the integrant parts, as is the case in cold and hot touch and the like.[1] U.

[1] इदानीं भूतानां लक्षणानि गन्धादीनि परीचिक्षिषुर्गन्धादीनां स्वाभाविकत्वमौपाधिकत्वञ्च व्यवस्थापयन्नाह। रूपरसगन्धस्पर्शा यत्र कारणगुणप्रक्रमेणोत्पद्यन्ते तत्र स्वाभाविकाः सन्तो लक्षणतामुपयान्ति नान्यथा न हि समीरणे उपलभ्यमानं सौरभं शिलातले उपलभ्यमानं शैत्यं जले उपलभ्यमानमौष्ण्यं वा लक्षणं भवति तदेतदाह

व्यवस्थितः पृथिव्यां गन्धः।। 2।।

Smell the characteristic of earth

Aph. 2. Smell is established as the mark of earth.

The characteristic of earth is stated to be its natural smell. Smell discriminated by its disjunction from and junction with other things, and by its excluding things of similar and dissimilar classes, is established as the characteristic of earth. For the earth indeed has smell and only the earth has smell. It is therefore established that smell, which excludes earth from water and the next seven substances which are of the same class, and from quality and the four following categories which are of a different class, is natural to earth.[1] U.

एतेनोष्णता व्याख्याता।। 3।।

Analogously heat is the characteristic of light

Aph. 3. By this heat is explained.

It is stated that the method of establishing that smell is a natural quality may be analogously applied to heat as the characteristic of light (or fire). This analogy is to be regarded as holding good with respect to cold etc., as characteristics of water etc.[2] U.

It is stated that the characteristic of light [or fire] which consists of a hot feel is, like the characteristic of earth, not universally predicable of water, etc.[3] V.

पुव्यवस्त्रयोरिति न हि कनककेतकीकुसुमसन्निकृष्टे वाससि कनककेतकीसौरभमुपलभ्यमानं वाससः। न हि वाससः कारणगुणप्रक्रमेण तदुत्पन्नम् किं तर्हि कनककेतकीसन्निधानादौपाधिकं न हि वस्त्रे गन्धाभावे केतकीगन्धाभावो लिङ्गम्। किं लिङ्गमत उक्तं गुणान्तराप्रादुर्भाव इति गुणान्तरात् कारणगुणात् अप्रादुर्भावो ऽनुत्पत्तिः यदि हि वस्त्रे यो गन्ध उपलभ्यते स तस्य स्वाभाविकः स्यात्तदा तदवयवेषु तन्तुषु केतकीसन्निकर्षात् पूर्वं तत्र वस्त्रे चोपलभ्येत न चैवमित्यर्थः तथा च विवादाध्यासितो गन्धो न वस्त्रसमवेतः तदवयवगुणजन्यविशेषगुणत्वात् शीतोष्णस्पर्शादिवत्।।

[1] स्वाभाविकं गन्धं पृथिव्यां लक्षणमाह। पृथिव्यां व्यवस्थितो ऽयोगान्ययोगाभ्यां परिच्छिन्नः समानासमानजातीयव्यावर्तकतया गन्धो लक्षणमित्यर्थः भवति हि पृथिवी गन्धवत्येव पृथिव्येव गन्धवतीति तदेवं समानजातीयेभ्यो जलाद्यष्ठभ्यो ऽसमानजातीयेभ्यो गुणादिपञ्चभ्यो व्यावर्तकः स्वाभाविकः पृथिव्यां गन्ध इति व्यवस्थितम्।।

[2] गन्धस्य स्वाभाविकत्वव्यवस्थापनप्रकारमुष्णातायां तेजोलक्षणेप्यतिदिशन्नाह। अब्रादिलक्षणे शैत्यादावप्ययमतिदेशो द्रष्टव्यः।।

[3] पृथिवीलक्षणस्येव उष्णस्पर्शवत्त्वरूपतेजोलक्षणस्यापि न जलादावतिव्याप्तिरित्याह।।

तेजस उष्णता।। 4।।

Aph. 4. Heat is [the characteristic] of light.

The characteristic of light is examined. It is meant that natural heat is the Characteristic of light. Colour also, white and luminous, is implied.[1] U.

Heat belongs to light alone not to any thing else. Therefore the characteristic of light cannot be universally affirmed of any thing else.[2] V.

अप्सु शीतता।। 5।।

Cold the characteristic of water

Aph. 5. Cold is [the characteristic] of water.

Natural cold is the characteristic of water. Therefore it cannot be also universally affirmed of the surface of stone, sandalwood, etc. By cold also its colour and taste are characterised, and viscidity and natural fluidity are also implied.[3] U.

Cold belongs to water, not to any thing else. Therefore the characteristic of light cannot be universally affirmed also of the surface of stone etc., inasmuch as its appearance there is communicated [i.e. not natural.][4] V.

अपरस्मिन्नपरं युगपत् चिरं क्षिप्रमितिकाललिङ्गानि।। 6।।

Existence of time as a substance proved

Aph. 6. The notions of posteriority in relation to posteriority of simultaneity, of slowness, and quickness are marks of the existence of time.

The particle *iti* implying a kind of notion has relation to each individual word, so that the meaning is that the conception of posteriority, the conception of simultaneity, the conception of slowness, and the conception of quickness, are marks of the existence of time. By

[1] तेजोलक्षणं परीक्षते। स्वाभाविक्युष्णता तेजोलक्षणमित्यर्थः रूपमेव शुक्लभास्वरमुपलक्ष्यते।।

[2] तेजस एव उष्णता नान्येषामिति तेजोलक्षणस्य नातिव्यांप्तिरिति भावः।।

[3] स्वाभाविकी शीतता अपां लक्षणमित्यर्थः। तथा च शिलातलश्रीखण्डादौ नातिव्याप्तिरिति भावः। शीततया रूपरसावप्युक्तलक्षणौ स्नेहं सांसिद्धिकद्रवत्वञ्चोयलक्षयति।।

[4] अप्सु शीतता नान्यत्रेति न जललक्षणस्य शिलातन्नादावतिव्याप्तिस्तत्र शैत्यप्रतीतेरौपाधिकत्वादिति भावः।

posteriority in relation to posteriority we are to understand also priority in relation to priority. The sense is therefore as follows:—if in relation to an old man, between whose birth and the present time there is an interval of many revolutions of the sun, we make a youth the term of relation, a notion of priority is evolved, and this must have some non-coinherent cause. In like manner if the old man be made the term of comparison with reference to the youth, we shall find that a notion of posteriority is evolved. Simultaneously means at the same time, during the same revolutions of the sun, or during the same time other than a revolution of the sun, with reference to such judgments as, 'They are bron at the same time', 'They stand at the same time,' 'They make something at the same time.' Revolutions of the sun which have not yet taken place are not thus determinant nor are those revolutions actually presented. The substance then, which determines such particular notions, because otherwise they could not be produced, is time.[1] U.

द्रव्यत्वनित्यत्वे वायुना व्याख्याते।। 7।।

Time an eternal substance

Aph. 7. Its substantiality and eternity are explained by air.

As the primary aerial atom is a substance because it possesses qualities, and eternal because it is a substance not inhering in any other substance (cp., II.I, 12 & 13), so also is time.[2] U.

Time is, like the primary aerial atom, a substance because a subject in which qualities exist, and eternal because it has no parts.[3] V.

तत्त्वं भावेन।। 8।।

Unity of time

Aph. 8. Its unity is explained by existence.

[1] इतिकारो ज्ञानप्रकारपरः प्रत्येकमभिसम्बध्यते तथा चापरमिति प्रत्ययो युगप्रदिति प्रत्ययः चिरमिति प्रत्ययः क्षिप्रमिति प्रत्ययः काललिङ्गानीत्यर्थः। अपरस्मिन्नपरमित्यनेन परस्मिन् परमित्यपि द्रष्टव्यं तेनायमर्थः बहुतरतपनपरिस्पन्दनान्तरितजन्मनि स्थविरे युवानमवधिं कृत्वा परत्वमुत्पद्यते तच्च परत्वमसम-वायिकारणसापेक्षम्। एवं स्थविरमवधिं कृत्वा यूनि अपरत्वोत्पत्तिर्निरूपणीया। युगपदिति युगपज्जायन्ते युगपत् तिष्ठन्ति युगपत् कुर्वन्ति इत्यादिप्रत्ययानाञ्च एकस्मिन् काले एकस्यां सूर्यगतौ एकस्मिन् सूर्यगत्यवच्छिन्नकाले इत्यर्थः न चाप्राप्ता एव सूर्यगतयोविशेषणतामनुभजन्ति न च स्वरूप प्रत्यासन्ना एव ताः तस्मादेतादृशविशिष्टप्रत्ययान्यवानुपपत्त्या विशेषणप्रापकं यद्द्रव्यं स कालः।।

[2] यथा वायुपरमाणोर्गुणवत्त्वाद्द्रवत्वम् अद्रव्यद्रव्यत्वाच्च नित्यत्वं तथा काल स्यापीत्यर्थः।।

[3] वायुपरमाणोरिव कालस्यापि गुणाश्रयत्त्वाद्द्रव्यत्वं निरवयवत्त्वान्नित्यत्वमित्यर्थः।।

The sense is that time, like existence, is one because the conception of quickness etc., which are the marks of its existence, are in every case not particular, and because there exists no particular mark like that of the plurality of souls (cp., II. 1, 30). It may be objected, Time is manifold according to its division into moments, aggregates of two moments, hours, watches, days, days and nights, lunar fortnights, months, seasons, half years, years, etc., how then can it be one? This is no valid objection, for the appearance of a division is caused by an accident. It is to be understood that as one and the same crystal, by accidentally reflecting the colour of a China rose, tāpinja (Xanthochymus Pictorius) etc., appears to be divided, so also time though one only appears, by reason of division marking the course of the sun, etc., and the division marking the effects of such and such cause, to be divided. It may be objected, Yet time is threefold according to the division into, past, future, and present, for it is said in the Veda, The three times return, the three times are unaccomplished, etc. This is no valid objection, for the ordinary conception of time as threefold rests upon the distinguishing of things as antecedently non-existent or potentially existent, and subsequently non-existent i.e., as having ceased to exist. For the time occupied by a thing existent is its present, the time occupied by its antecedent non-existence is its future, and the time distinguished by its destruction or subsequent non-existence is its past; so that the ordinary conception of time as threefold rests upon trinal nature of the distinction.[1] U.

नित्येष्वभावादनित्येषु भावात् कारणे कालाख्येति।। ९।।

Time a cause of non-eternal substances

Aph. 9. The term *time* is applicable to a cause, inasmuch as it exists not in eternal and exists in not eternal things.

The term *time* is applicable to a cause, the cause of all things

[1] चिरादिप्रत्ययानां काललिङ्गानां सर्वत्राविशेषादनेकत्वे ऽप्यात्मनामिव विशेषलिङ्गाभावात् सत्तावदेकत्वं कालस्येत्यर्थः। नन्वेवं क्षणलवमुहूर्तयामदिवसाहोरात्रपक्षमासर्त्वयनसंवत्सरादिभेदेन भूयांसः कालास्तत् कथमेक इति चेन्न भेदमानस्य उपाधिनबिन्धत्वात् तथा एक एव स्फटिकमणिर्जवातापिञ्जाद्युपाध्युपरागेण भिन्न इव भासते तथैक एव कालः सूर्यस्पन्दाद्यवच्छेदभेदेन तत्त्वकार्यावच्छेदभेदेन च भिन्न इव भासते इत्यभ्युपगमात्।।
ननु तथाप्यतीतानागतवर्तमानभेदेन कालत्रयमस्तु श्रूयते हि त्रैकाल्यमुपावर्तते त्रैकाल्यासिद्धिः इत्यादीतिचेन्न वस्तुतत्प्रागभावतत्प्रध्वंसावच्छेदेन त्रैकाल्यव्यवहारात् येन हि वस्तुना यः कालो ऽवच्छिद्यते स तस्य वर्तमानः यत्प्रागभावेन यः कालो ऽवच्छिद्यते स तस्य भविष्यत्कालः यत् प्रध्वंसेन यः कालो ऽवच्छिद्यते स तस्यातीतकालः तथा चावच्छेदकत्रित्वाधीनः कालत्रित्वव्यवहारः।।

produced. The reason is stated to be that it does not exist in things eternal, and exists in things not eternal. For since with regard to eternal substances such as ether, there is no such notion as produced simultaneously, produced slowly, produced quickly, produced now, produced during the day, produced at night whereas notions of simultaneity and the like do exist with regard to substances not eternal such as a water-pot, a piece of cloth, etc., time is proved by an inclusive and an exclusive (i.e., by an affirmative and a negative) argument to be a cause. It should be understood that time is the efficient cause of all things produced, not only in virtue of such notions as simultaneity, but also in virtue of the terms hibernal, vernal, pluvial, etc., as applied to flowers fruits, etc.[1] U.

इत इदमिति यतस्तद्दिश्यं लिङ्गम्।। 10।।

Existence of space proved

Aph. 10. The mark pertaining to space is that whence the knowledge arises that one thing is remote or not remote from another.

Pertaining to space—belonging to space, causing us to infer the existence of space. For that substance is space from which, with reference to two bodies in a determinate position and existing simultaneously, there springs the knowledge that one is which there is there the conjunction with more numerous conjunct objects, is more remote than one in which there is conjunction with less numerous conjunct object, and that that body in which there are less numerous conjunctions of conjunct objects is more remote than body in which there are more numerous conjunctions of conjunct objects. For unless such a substance exist there is nothing to account for the two bodies having more or less numerous conjunctions with conjunct objects. Unless this be accounted for, there can exist no such thing as the conception of each body so characterised; and without such a notion a highest and not highest [generic and specific] form of generality is impossible; but if that

[1] कारणे सर्वोत्पत्तिमत्कारणे काल इत्याख्या। हेतुमाह नित्येष्वभावात् अनित्येषु भावादिति नित्येषु आकाशादिषु युगपज्जातः चिरं जातः क्षिप्रं जातः इदानीं जातः दिवा जातः रात्रौ जात इत्यादिप्रत्ययस्याभावात् अनित्येषु घटपटादिषु यौगपद्यादिप्रत्ययाानां भावात् अन्वयव्यतिरेकाभ्यां कारणं काल इत्यर्थः न केवलं यौगपद्यादिप्रत्ययानां भावात् अन्वयव्यतिरेकाभ्यां कारणं काल इत्यर्थः न केवलं यौगपद्यादिप्रत्ययबलात् कालस्य सर्वोत्पत्तिमन्निमित्तकारणत्वम् अपि तु पुष्पफलादीनां हैमन्तिकवासन्तिकप्रावृषेण्यादिसंज्ञाबलादेतदध्यवसेयम्।।

were impossible there would not be, as there actually are, cognitions speculative and practical characterised by such generality.[1] U.

The words near or remote are to be supplied after one thing from another. The mark, then, of space is the conception of local contiguity or remoteness, according to which we know that one thing is far from, or near to, another. Space, therefore, like time, is proved to exist inasmuch as it is that in which conjunction takes place, and the not inherent cause of local propinquity or remoteness. Space moreover, though one, being divided according to difference of concomitants gives rise to the common distinction of east etc. The quarter adjacent to this concomitant i.e., to the mountain behind which the sun rises, is the east. That which is remote from this mountain is the west. The region adjacent to mount Meru is the north. That which is remote from mount Meru is the south. That which is adjacent to the mountain behind which the sun rises, and remote from mount Meru, is the southeast. The region remote from Meru, and remote from the mountain behind which the sun rises, is the south-west. That which is adjacent to Meru, and remote from the mountain behind which the sun rises, is the north-west. That which is adjacent to Meru and adjacent to the mountain behind which the sun rises, is the north-east. That in which the conjunction takes place which is produced by the conjunction of soul with requitative efficacy and by the rites of fire is above; that in which the conjunction caused by falling takes place is below.[2] V.

[1] दिश इदं दिश्यं दिगनुमापकम् इतो ऽल्पतरसंयुक्तसंयोगाश्रयादिदं बहुतरसंयुक्तसंयोगाधिकरणं परम् इतश्त संयुक्तसंयोगभूयस्त्वाधिकरणादिदं संयुक्तसंयोगाल्पीयस्त्वाधिकरणमपरमिति नियतदिग्देशयोः समानकालयोः पिण्डयोर्यतो द्रव्याद्भवति सा दिगित्यर्थः। न हि ताद्वशं द्रव्यमन्तरेण भूयसां संयुक्तसंयोगानाल्पीयसां वा पिण्डयोरुपनायकमन्यदस्ति न च तदुपनयमन्तरेण तत्तद्विशिष्टबुद्धिः न च तामन्तरेण परत्वापरत्वयोरूरुत्पत्तिः न च तदुत्पत्तिं विना तद्विशिष्टप्रत्ययव्यवहारौ।।

[2] इत इदमिति परमपरं वेति शेषः तथा चास्मादिदं दूरम् अस्मादिदमन्तिकमिति दैशिकपरत्वबुद्धिर्यतस्तादृशं दिग्लिङ्गं तथा च कालवत् दैशिकपरत्वापरत्वासमवायिकारणसंयोगाश्रयतया दिक् सिध्यति सा च एकापि उपाधिभेदात् प्राच्यादिव्यवहारं उपाधिश्च तदीयोदयगिरिसन्निहिता या दिक सा तदीयप्राची तदीयोदयगिरिव्यवहिता तु तदीयप्रतीची तदीयसुमेरुसन्निहिता या दिक् सा तदीयोदीची एवं सुमेरुव्यवहिता आवाची उदयगिरिसन्निहिता सुमेरुव्यवहिता आग्नेयी सुमेरुव्यवहितोदयगिरिव्यवहिता च नैर्ऋती सुमेरुसन्निहिता उदयगिरिव्यवहिता च वायवी सुमेरुसन्निहिता उदयगिरिसन्निहिता च ऐशानी श्रदृष्टवदात्मसंयोगजन्याग्निक्रियाजन्यसंयोगाश्रयः ऊर्ध्वम् पतनजन्यसंयोगाश्रयः अधः।

द्रव्यत्वनित्यत्वे वायुना व्याख्याते।। 11।।

Space an eternal substance

Aph. 11. The substantiality and eternity [of space] are explained by air.

It is a substance because possessed of attributes, and eternal because it has no substratum [cf., II. 2. 7.][1] U.

तत्त्वं भावेन।। 12।।

Aph. 12. Its unity [is explained] by existence.

The unity of space, like that of existence, is proved by its having a not particular mark, and by the non-existence in it of a particular mark. From this its individual unity may be inferred [cf., II. 1.31][2] U.

कार्यविशेषेण नानात्वम्।। 13।।

Aph. 13. Its diversity is [caused to be conceived] by the difference of its effects.

It is explained why, whereas space is one only, there is the practical assurance of east, etc. Its diversity, the common diverse conceptions of east etc., is caused by the difference of its effects, the accidental qualities of produced bodies. But in reality space is one only.[3] V.

आदित्यसंयोगाद्भूतपूर्वाद्भविष्यतो भूताच्च प्राची।। 14।।

Aph. 14. [Space is regarded as] east because of a past, future, or present conjunction of the sun.

The east [*prāchi*] is so called because the sun moves [*aṇchati*] forward [*prāk*] there. Accordingly the space in which conjunction first takes place of the sun in its course from east to west of Meru, whether such conjunction be past, future, or present, is east. Mention is here made of these three divisions of time, which rest upon the division of human observation. One man has the practical assurance—that this is the east, because the conjunction of the sun in the orient first took place

[1] गुणवत्त्वाद् द्रव्यत्वम् अनाश्रितत्वाच्च नित्यत्वमित्यर्थः।।

[2] दिग्लिङ्गाविशेषाद्विशेषलिङ्गाभावाच्च सत्तावदेकत्वं तदनुविधानादेकपृथक्त्वम्।।

[3] दिश एकत्वे ऽपि प्राच्यादिव्यवहारमुपपादयति। कार्यविशेषेण जन्यमूर्तरूपोपाधिना जानात्वं प्राच्यादिनानाव्यवहारः वस्तुत एकैव दिगित्यर्थः।।

yesterday. Another has the notion of the east from observing that the conjunction of the sun in the orient will first take place tomorrow. Another has the notion of the east from observing that there is a present conjunction of the sun now taking place in that quarter.[1] U.

तथा दक्षिणा प्रतीची उदीची च।। 15।।

Aph. 15. So likewise [space is regarded as] south, west and north.

In like manner the practical assurance of the south arises from past, future, or present conjunction of the sun with the mountains, etc., in the southern quarter. So also the notion of west and north may be analogously accounted for.[2] U.

एतेन दिगन्तरालानि व्याख्यातानि।। 16।।

Aph. 16. By this [similiarly] the intermediate divisions of space are explained.

The notion of the south-east quarter arises from combining the characteristics of the eastern and southern quarters. So also the south-west, and north-east may be inferred. It is explained at length in the Kaṇāda-rahasya that space is that by which, as an eternal substance, these and other conjunctions of the sun are manifested.[3] U.

सामान्यप्रत्यक्षाद्विशेषाप्रत्यक्षाद्विशेषस्मृतेश्च संशयः।। 17।।

Nature of doubt

Aph. 17. Doubt [arises] from perception of a general, non perception of a particular, and remembrance of particularity.

Doubt arises from perception or knowledge of a general i.e. of a

[1] प्राक् अस्यां सविता अञ्चतीति प्राची तथा च यस्यां दिशि मेरुप्रदक्षिणक्रमेण भ्रमत आदित्यस्य प्रथमं संयोगो भूतपूर्वो भविष्यन् वा भवन् वा दिक् प्राची अत्र पुरुषाभिसन्धिभेदमाश्रित्य कालत्रयोपवर्णनं भवति हि कस्यचित् पूर्वेद्युः प्रातरस्यांदिशि आदित्यसंयोगः प्रथमं वृत्त इतीयं प्राचीति प्राचीव्यवहारः कस्यचिदपरेद्युरस्यां आदित्यसंयोगः प्रथमं भावीत्यभिसन्धाय प्राचीव्यवहारः कस्यचिदिदानीं अस्यां आदित्यसंयोगो भवन्नस्तीत्यभि-सन्धाय प्राचीव्यवहारः।।

[2] तद्वदेव दक्षिणदिग्वर्तिनगादिना सहादित्यसंयोगाद्भूतपूर्वाद्भविष्यतो भूताद्वा दक्षिणाव्यवहारः एवं प्रतीच्युदीच्योरपि व्यवहार उन्नेयः।।

[3] प्राचीदक्षिणयोर्दिशोर्लक्षणसाङ्कर्येण दक्षिणपूर्वा दिगिति व्यवहारः एवं दक्षिणः पश्चिमा पश्चिमोत्तरा उत्तरपूर्वेत्यू-र्ध्वम् एते चादित्यसंयोगा येन विभुना द्रव्येणोपनीयन्ते सा दिगिति कणादरहस्ये व्युत्पादितं विस्तरतः।।

common property, from non-perception or ignorance of a particular included in one of two alternatives, and from remembrance or knowledge of two alternatives. With reference to doubt therefore, the cause is knowledge of a common property, absence of certainty as to something comprised in one of two alternatives, and knowledge of two alternatives. The word 'and' implies the addition of knowledge of a non-general propoerty, and of opposed propositions, which are mentioned in the Nyāya Aphorisms.[1] V.

दृष्टश्च दृष्टवत्।। 18।।

Aph. 18. That which is seen, and that which was formerly seen [are causes of doubt.]

Doubt is twofold, that which has an external, and that which has an internal object. That again which has an external object relates to something of which the properties are perceived, or to something of which the properties are unperceived. That which relates to something of which the properties are perceived, is such as when on seeing a determinate object and having tallness as an attribute, the doubt arises whether the object be a post or a man. That which relates to an object the properties of which are not perceived, is such as when on seeing merely the horns belonging to a cow, gayal, or other animal in a forest where it is concealed by the intervention of bushes, etc., the doubt arises whether it be a cow or a gayal. But in the latter case the doubt really relates to the quality of the horn, whether the horn belong to a cow or to a gayal, and consequently the statement of this distinction is due merely to a refinement of language. The general [i.e., common property] which is the cause of doubt, gives rise to doubt either when observed in several objects or in one. The first statement is therefore explained in this aphorism. Height perceived in [in the former case] the cause of the doubt. The height, that is to say, which is perceived in a present object, and which belonged equally to a post and to a man previously seen is the cause of the doubt.[2] U.

[3] सामान्यस्य साधारणधर्मस्य प्रत्यक्षात् ज्ञानात् विशेषस्य एककोटिव्याप्यस्य अप्रत्यक्षात् अज्ञानात् विशेषस्य कोटिद्वयस्य स्मृतेर्ज्ञानात् संशयो भवतीति शेषः। तथा च संशयं प्रति साधारणधर्मज्ञानम् एककोटिव्याप्यनिश्चयाभावः कोटिद्वयज्ञानञ्च हेतुरित्यर्थः चकारात् न्यायसूत्रोक्तयाः असाधारणधर्मज्ञानप्रतिवाक्यज्ञानयोः सङ्ग्रहः।।

[2] द्विविधः संशयो बन्हिर्विषयको ऽन्तर्विषयकश्च बहिर्विषयको ऽपि दृश्यमानधर्मिको दृश्यमानधमिकश्च तत्र दृश्यमानधर्मिको यथा ऊर्ध्वत्वविशिष्टस्य धर्मिणे दर्शनात् अयं स्थाणुः पुरुषो वेति अदृश्यमानधर्मिको यथा अरण्ये भाटाद्यन्तरिते गोगवयादिपिण्डे विषाणमात्रदर्शनात् अयं गौर्गवयो वेति वस्तुतस्तत्रापि विषाणा-धर्मिक एव सन्देहो विषाणमिदं गोसम्बन्धि गवयसम्बन्धि वेति विवक्षणामात्रात्तु द्वैविध्याभिधानम् यत्

यथादृष्टमयथादृष्टत्वाच्च।। 19।।

Aph. 19. That which is perceived in a certain way [is a cause of doubt] because it is [at another time] perceived not in that way.

That which is seen in a certain way, gives rise to doubt by reason of its being perceived not in that way. For instance Chaitra being seen in a certain manner, with hair, is at another time seen not in that manner, but without hair. When in the course of time Chaitra is seen with his head covered with his garments, a doubt arises wheather this Chaitra have hair or no. In this case the being Chaitra is a common property which gives rise to doubt, and this common property is seen in one object. The cause of the doubt therefore is seen in one undivided object.[1] U.

It is stated that a property may exist under two alternative conditions in one object. For if Chaitra, be seen with his head muffed up, a doubt arises whether he have hair or no, and the cause of this doubt is the knowledge of the notion Chaitra, accompanied by the notion of hair or of the absence of hair.[2] V.

विद्या ऽविद्यातश्च संशयः।। 20।।

Aph. 20. Doubt also [arises] from knowledge and want of knowledge.

Internal doubt is produced by knowledge and the want of knowledge. For instance, an astronomer predicts truly, and predicts untruly, eclipses, of the moon etc. Accordingly a doubt arises in his mind as to his knowledge, whether it be correct, or not. Or knowledge is sometimes science, and sometimes not science, wanting demonstration; and consequently a doubt arises with respect to something, whether, inasmuch as it is known, it exists or not.[3] U.

सामान्यसंशयहेतुस्तुदनेकत्र दृष्टं संशायकम् चैकत्र धर्मिणि वा दृष्टं संशयहेतुरित्यत्र प्रथमां विधामाह। दृष्टमूर्धत्वं संशयहेतुः तेन दृष्टाभ्यां स्थाणुपुरुषाभ्यां तुल्यं वर्तते पुरोवर्तते यदूर्ध्वत्वं तद्दृष्टं संशयहेतुरित्यर्थः।।

[1] अयथादृष्टत्वाद्धेतोर्यथादृष्टमपि संशायकं यथा चैत्रो यथाद्दृष्टः केशवान् कालान्तरे अयथादृष्टः केशविनाकृतो दृष्ट इत्यर्थः। क्रमेण तत्रैव चैत्रे वस्त्रावृत्तमस्तके दृष्टे सति भवति संशयश्चैत्रोऽयं सकेशो निष्केशो वेति तत्र हि चैत्रत्वं समानो धर्मः संशायकः चैकत्रैव दृष्ट इत्यभिन्न एव धर्मिणि दृष्टः संशयहेतुः।।

[2] एकत्र कोटिद्वयसहचरितं धर्ममाह। भवति हि प्रावृत्तशिरसि चैत्रे अयं केशवान् निष्केशो वेत्यादिसंशयः तत्कारणञ्च केशतदभावसहचरितचैत्रत्वज्ञानम्।।

[3] आन्तरसंशयो हि विद्या ऽविद्याभ्यां भवति यथा मौहूर्तिकः सम्यगादिशति चन्द्रोपरागादि असम्यगपि तत्र स्वज्ञाने संशयो ऽस्य जायते सम्यगादिष्टमसंयग्वेति यद्वा ज्ञानं हि क्वचिद्विद्या क्वच्चिदविद्या अप्रमा भवति तथा च ज्ञायमानत्वात् सदिदमसा द्वेति संशयो जायते।।

श्रोत्रग्रहणो यो ऽर्थः स शब्दः।। 21।।

Aph. 21. The object which is apprehended by hearing is sound.

It is now established by means of a definition that sound is possessed of properties. It is apprehended by hearing, that is, is an object of ordinary perception produced in the organ of hearing. The notion of sound, being of the same kind, is an object, and is therefore a class. The full definition, then, of sound is that it is a class included in the notion of a quality which exists as the object of common perception produced in the organ of hearing.[1] V.

तुल्यजातीयेष्वर्थान्तरभूतेषु विशेषस्य उभयथा दृष्टत्वात्।। 22।।

Doubt with respect to sound answered

Aph. 22. Since the particular [class of sound] is perceived both in things homogeneous and in things heterogeneous [a doubt arises with respect to it.]

'A doubt arises with respect to sound' is to be supplied, and by 'sound' must also be understood the notion or class of sound and the notion of its being apprehended by the organ of hearing. Since, then, the exclusion of particularity or difference of sound is perceived in things homogeneous, i.e., in the twenty-three qualities, and in things heterogeneous, i.e., in substances and actions, sound gives rise to a doubt respecting itself, whether it be a quality, a substance, or an action.[2] U.

Some have maintained that, inasmuch as there exist names and notions of low and loud sounds, sound is a substance. The refutation of this opinion is here commenced. Since there is perceived no particularity in the nature of sound apprehended in sound, both in the twenty-three things homogeneous, i.e., in the qualities, colour, etc., and in things heterogenous i.e.,in substances and actions, which are distinguished by belonging to the class substance and other classes, 'a

[1] इदानीं शब्दं धर्मिणं लक्षणमुखेन व्यवस्थापयति। श्रोत्रेण गृह्यते ऽसौ श्रवणेयिन्द्रजन्यलौकिकप्रत्यक्षविषय इत्यर्थः। शब्दत्वादेरपि तादृशत्वादर्थः इति जातिमान् इति तदर्थस्तथा च श्रवणेन्द्रियजन्यलौकिक-प्रत्यक्षविषयवृत्तिगुणत्वव्याप्यजातिमत्त्वमेव शब्दलक्षणं पर्यवसितम्।।

[2] शब्दे संशय इति शेषः। शब्दे शब्दत्वं श्रोत्रग्राह्यत्वं चोपलभ्यते तच्च तुल्यजातीयेषु त्रवोविंशतौ गुणेषु अर्थान्तरभूतेषु द्रव्येषु कर्मसु च विशेषस्य व्यावृत्तेः उभयथा उभयत्र दर्शनात् शब्दो किं गुणो द्रव्यं कर्म वेति संशयं जनयति।।

doubt arises'—for these words are to be supplied—whether sound be a substance or no. The knowledge of the existence in the nature of sound of particularity, in the form of exclusion from that of which both alternatives are distinguished, gives rise to such a doubt.[1] V.

एकद्रव्यत्वान्न द्रव्यम्।। 23।।

Aph. 23. Since it inheres in one substance only, [sound] is not a substance.

That of which one substance is the substratum, inheres in one substance only. Inasmuch, therefore, as no substance has only one cause of inhesion, sound, since it differs in properties from substance, is not a substance.[2] U.

The opinion that sound is a substance is here rejected. Sound is not a substance, for it inheres in one substance, i.e., resides in one only; whereas it is well known that no substance abides in one other substance only.[3] V.

नापि कर्माचाक्षुषत्वात्।। 24।।

Aph. 24. Now is it an action, for it is invisible.

Sound is not an action, for the perception of which sound is the object is not visual, i.e., is produced by some other external organ than the eye. The class sound, therefore, does not belong to action, because like the class taste etc. it exists as a class not included in things visually perceived.[4] U.

[1] केचित्तु सूक्ष्मः शब्दः महाञ्छब्द इत्यादिव्यवहाराणद्द्रव्यमेव शब्द इत्याहुस्तन्मतं निराकर्तुमारभते। शब्दे गृह्यमाणस्य शब्दत्वादेर्विशेषस्य तुल्यजातीयेषु रूपादिषु त्रयोविंशतौ गुणेषु अर्थान्तरेषु द्रव्येषु कर्मसु च उभयया उभयत्र द्रव्यत्वादिमत्तया निश्चितेषु तदभाववत्तया निश्चितेषु च अदृष्टत्वात् शब्दो द्रव्यं न वेति संशय इति पूरणीयं तथा च निश्चितोभयकोटिमद्व्यावृत्तत्वरूपासाधारण्यस्य शब्दत्वादौ सत्त्वात् तज्ज्ञानं तादृशसंशयं जनयतीति भावः।।

[2] एकं द्रव्यं समवायि यस्य तदेकद्रव्यं द्रव्यञ्च किमप्यकद्रव्यसमवायिकारणकं न भवतीति द्रव्यवैधर्म्यन्नायं शब्दो द्रव्यमित्यर्थः।।

[3] इदानीं शब्दस्य द्रव्यत्वं निरस्यति। शब्दो न द्रव्यम् एकद्रव्यत्वात् एकमात्राश्रितत्वात् न ह्येकमात्राश्रितत्वं किमपि द्रव्यं प्रसिद्धम्।।

[4] प्रत्ययस्य शब्दविषयकस्याचाक्षुषत्वात् चक्षुर्भिन्नबहिरिन्द्रियजन्यत्वादित्यर्थः तथा च शब्दत्वं न कर्मवृत्तिचाक्षुषप्रत्यक्षावृत्तिजातित्वात् रसत्वादिवदिति भावः।।

गुणस्य सतो ऽपवर्गः कर्मभिः साधर्म्यम्।। 25।।

Aph. 25. The transiency of [sound] which is a quality, is a property common also to actions.

It may be objected that sound is an action, since like throwing upwards etc. it comes rapidly to an end. The answer is as follows:— Transiency is rapid destruction. This in the class quality is dependent, like qualities [such as pleasure and pain, and the like], on rapid occurrence of being and ceasing to be. It is, therefore, only a property common also to actions, but not the whole essence of action. Rapid destruction, which you advance as an argument, is found in other instances besides action, as is shown by the conception of duality by pleasure and pain, etc.[1] U.

सतो लिङ्गाभावात्।। 26।।

Aph. 26. Since there is no mark of [sound as] existing [before utterance, it does not so exist.]

Meeting the objection :—Let it be allowed that sound is a quality; yet it is not a mark of the existence of ether; for it would justify the inference of the existence of ether, only if it were an effect of ether; whereas it is eternal, its occasionally not being observed being due to the non-existence of something to make it known, it is stated:If sound existed previously to its utterance, there would be a mark or another proof of it as an existing thing. There is no proof of sound in the case of its not being heard. It is not therefore manifested as pre-existent.[2] U.

The doctrine of the Mīmāṁsakas that sound is not produced, but eternal but that it sometimes unperceived because there is nothing to make it known is rejected. Because there is no mark of sound as existing, means because there exists no proof establishing the eternity of sound.[3] V.

[1] ननु शब्दः कर्म आशुतरविनाशित्वात् उत्क्षेपणादिवदिति चेदत्राह। अपवर्गः आशुनाशः स च गुणत्वे ऽपि द्वित्वादिवदाशुभाविनाशकसन्निपाताधीन इति कर्मभिः साधर्म्यमात्रमस्य न तु कर्मत्वमेव त्वदुक्तहेतोराशुतरविनाशित्वस्य द्वित्वज्ञानसुखदुःखादिभिरनेकान्तिकत्वमिति भावः।।

[2] ननु सिध्यतु शब्दो गुणस्तथापि नासावाकाशलिङ्गम् आकाशं हि तदा ऽनुमाप येत् यदि तस्य कार्यं स्यात् किन्तु नित्य एवायं कदाचिदनुपलम्भस्तु व्यञ्जकाभावः प्रयुक्त इत्याशङ्क्याह। यदि हि उच्चारणात् प्रागूर्ध्वं शब्दः सन् स्यात् तदा सतो ऽस्य लिङ्गं प्रमाणान्तरं स्यात् न चाश्रवणदशायां शब्दसत्त्वे प्रमाणमस्ति तस्मात् कार्य एवायं न व्यङ्ग्य इति।।

[3] शब्दो न जन्यते किन्तु नित्य एव सः कदाचिदप्रत्यक्षन्तु तस्य व्यञ्जकवैधुर्यादिति मीमांसकमतं निरस्यति।। सतो नित्यस्य शब्दस्य लिङ्गाभावात् शब्दनित्यतासाधकप्रमाणाभावादिति फलितार्थः।।

नित्यवैधर्म्यात्।। 27।।

Aph. 27. Since [sound] differs from the eternal [it does not exist previously to utterance.]

A difference is perceived between sound and the eternal. For it is inferred by what is spoken, that Chaitra, Maitra and others exist even when concealed, because Chaitra speaks; but it is never inferred from that which is made known, as a waterpot and the like, that that which makes known, such as a lamp and the like, exists. Therefore sound is produced, but is not made known as previously existent.[1] U.

After the statement of the absence of a proof, a proof of the contrary is stated. Sound is not eternal because it differs from the eternal, i. e. because it ceases to be: for that it ceases to be is established by the evidence of sense.[2] V.

अनित्यश्चायं कारणतः।। 28।।

Aph. 28. It is not eternal, for it has a cause.

Because its production from a cause is observed, is to be supplied. For a sound is observed becoming manifest by the conjunction of a drum and drumstick, and the like. It is, therefore, not eternal, because it is produced. Or 'for it has cause' implies that the reason is that it possesses a cause.[3] U.

Sound is not eternal, because it has a cause. For eternal things have no causes.[4] V.

न चासिद्धं विकारात्।। 29।।

Aph. 29. This is not unproved by change.

It must not be argued that there is no proof that sound has a cause, since, inasmuch as it is loud or soft, a change is perceived. For a loud or soft sound is perceived in consequence of the hardness or softness of

[1] नित्येन सहास्य शब्दस्य वैधर्म्यमुपलभ्यते यतश्चैत्रो वक्तीत्यत्रावृतो ऽपि चैत्रमैत्रादिवचनेनानुमीयते न च व्यञ्जकः प्रदीपादिर्व्यङ्ग्येन घटादिना क्वचिदनुमीयते तस्माज्जन्य एवायं न व्यङ्ग्य इति भावः।।

[2] साधकाभावमुक्त्वा बाधकमप्याह। नित्यवैधर्म्यात् विनाशित्वात् शब्दो न नित्यस्तन्नाशस्य प्रत्यक्षसिद्धत्वादिति भावः।।

[3] कारणत उत्प्रत्तेर्दृष्टत्वादिति शेषः उपलभ्यते हि भेरीदण्डसंयोगादिभ्यः प्रादुर्भवन शब्दः तथा चोत्पत्तिमत्त्वादनित्यो ऽयमिति यद्वा कारणत इति कारणवत्त्वहेतुमुपलक्षयति।।

[4] शब्दे ऽनित्यः कारणतः कारणवत्त्वादिति यावत् न हि नित्यानि कारणवन्ति भवन्ति इत्यर्थः।।

the beating of a drum with a drumstick, and the like. But the loudness etc., of that which is manifested, is not dependent on the loudness etc., of that which makes known. From its cause or change, therefore, it is inferred that it is produced, not that its existence is made known.[1] U.

That sound has a cause is not disproved by its change or existence as loud, soft, etc. For in the absence of hardness or softness in the beating of a drum with a drumstick and the like, there could not be observed to exist loudness or softness of sound. It is impossible that loudness, softness, etc., should exist in sound as a consequence of the loudness, softness, etc., of that which manifests it. It must therefore be admitted even by an opponent that sound is produced from a cause, this cause being the beating etc., of a drum with a drumstick, etc.[2] V.

अभिव्यक्तौ दोषात्।। 30।।

Aph. 30. Since in its manifestation there would be a defect [sound is not manifested.].

If sound were manifested, an unalterable relation of evolvement and evolute in things co-extensive and apprehended by the same sense would be wrongly conceived to exist. But no such unalterable relation is observed to exist among such objects. If this be not assented to, it will follow that when one letter. (as *ka*) is manifested, all letters will be manifested. The objection that an unalterable relation of that which manifests and that which is manifested is observed to exist between the existent, a man, and a Brahman, which are co-extensive, and are manifested according to their diverse natures, places, and origins is invalid. For they are not co-extensive, for the extension of the human and the Brāhmanical, is not so great as that of the existent.[3] U.

[1] शब्दस्य कारणवत्त्वमसिद्धमिति न वाच्यं तीव्रमन्दादिभावेन विकारस्य दर्शनात् भेरीदण्डाभिघातस्य तीव्रतया तीव्रस्य मन्दतया मन्दस्य शब्दोपलम्भात् न ह्यभिव्यञ्जा कतीव्रत्वाद्याधीनो ऽभिव्यङ्ग्यतीव्रत्वादिः तथा च कारणतो विकारादनुमीयते जन्यो ऽयं न त्वभिव्यङ्ग्य इति।।

[2] शब्दस्य कारणवत्त्वं नासिद्धं विकारात् तीव्रमन्दादिभावात् न हि भेरीदण्डाद्यभिघातस्य तीव्रमन्दादित्वाभावे शब्दस्य तीव्रमन्दादिभावः केनचिदुपभ्यते नाप्यभिव्यञ्जकस्य तीव्रमन्दादिभावेन शब्दे तीव्रमन्दादिभावो भवितुमर्हति अतो भेरीदण्डाद्यभिघातादिरकारणजन्यत्वं शब्दस्याकामेनापि वाच्यमिति नासिद्धिरिति भावः।।

[3] शब्दस्याभिव्यक्तौ समानदेशानां समानेन्द्रियग्राह्याणां प्रतिनियतव्यञ्जकव्यङ्ग्यत्वं दोषः स्यात् न च तादृशानां प्रतिनियतव्यञ्जकव्यङ्ग्यत्वं कच्चिददृष्टम् अत्र यदि तदा न स्वीक्रियेत तदा ककाराभिव्यक्तौ सर्ववर्णाभिव्यक्ति-प्रसङ्गः। ननु समानदेशानामपि सत्त्वनरत्वब्राह्मणत्वानां स्वरूपभेदसंस्थानयोनिव्यङ्ग्यानां प्रतिनियतव्यञ्जक-व्यङ्ग्ययत्वं दृष्टमेवेति चेन्न तेषां समानदेशत्वाभावात् न हि यावत् देशः सत्त्वस्य तावानेव नरत्वस्य ब्राह्मणत्वस्य वा।

संयोगाद्विभागाच्च शब्दाच्च शब्दनिष्पत्तिः।। 31।।

Aph. 31. Sound is produced by conjunction, disjunction and [other] sound.

By conjunction—by the conjunction of a drum and drumstick, and the like. By disjunction—in a bamboo when being split, for in this case conjunction is not the cause of the first sound, for no such conjunction exists; and consequently disjunction of the two pieces of bamboo is the efficient cause, and the non-coinherent [or extrinsic or immaterial] cause is the disjunction between the piece split off and the ether. When sound is produced at a distance on a lute etc., it is propagated by continual reproduction till arriving at that space in ether which is limited by the outer ear, it is perceived. Sound therefore is produced also from sound.[1] U.

लिङ्गाच्चानित्यः शब्दः।। 32।।

Aph. 32. Sound is not eternal, because of its mark.

Articulate sound is not eternal, because, though constituting a class, it is apprehended by the organ of hearing, as in the case of a ḷute etc.[2] U.

द्वयोस्तु प्रवृत्त्योरभावात्।। 33।।

Objections of the Mṣmāṁsakas

Aph. 33. But [were sound quickly destructible] the activities of two would not exist.

The objection of a Mīmāṁsaka is stated. Of two—of teacher, and pupil,—the activities—the activity of the teacher in teaching and of the pupil in learning—would not exist, would follow to be non-existent. Since such expressions as The teacher teaches his pupils the Vedas, and The teacher gives his pupils the Veda, are recognised to be identical

[1] संयोगात् भेरीदण्डादिसंयोगात् विभागात् वंशे पाट्यमाने तत्र संयोगस्तावन्नाद्यस्य शब्दस्य कारणं तदभावात् तस्मात् वंशदलद्वयविभागो निमित्तकारणं दलाकाशविभागश्चासमवायिकारणम्। यत्र च दूरे वीणदावुत्पन्नः शब्दः तत्र सन्तानक्रमेण उत्पद्यमानः शब्दः कर्णशष्कुव्यल्यच्छिन्नमाकाशदेशमासादयन् गृह्यते तेन शब्दादपि शब्दनिष्पत्तिरिति।।

[2] वर्णात्मकः शब्दोऽनित्यः जातिमत्त्वे सति श्रोत्रगाह्यत्वात् वीणादिध्वनिवदित्यर्थः।।

in sense, teaching is nothing else than giving. As, therefore, if sound were rapidly destructible it would be impossible to give and receive it, there would exist no activity in relation to teaching and learning, the permanency of sound must, therefore, be admitted. It also follows from the absence of a proof of destruction of sound, no destroying agent being observed. The eternity of sound is also established by the argument. It has so long existed, who shall destroy it after this?[1] V.

प्रथमाशब्दात् ।। 34 ।।

Aph. 34. From the word 'first' [it follows that sound is eternal].

The eternity of sound must be admitted, Inasmuch as in the Vedic text, "He thrice recited the first, and thrice the last," it is affirmed that the first and last texts recited at the adding of fuel to the sacred fire were thrice pronounced; for to pronounce them thrice would be impossible, unless sound were eternal. Therefore its eternity is established according to the argument previously employed.[2] V.

सम्प्रतिपत्तिभावाच्च ।। 35 ।।

Aph. 35. Also from the existence of recognition.

The permanence of sound necessarily follows from the existence of recognition or recollection. Such recognitions as that Maitra is reading the same verse as Chaitra read, or that this is the same letter *ka,* would be impossible unless sound were permanent.[3] V.

सन्दिग्धा सति बहुत्वे ।। 36 ।।

Mīmāṁsaka's objections answered

[1] मीमांसकः प्रत्यवतिष्टते। द्वयोर्गुरुशिष्ययोः प्रवत्त्योः गुरोरध्यापने प्रवृत्तिः शिष्यस्य तु अध्ययने तयोरभावात् अभावप्रसङ्गात् गुरुः शिष्यान् वेदमध्यापयति शिष्येभ्यो वेदं ददाति इत्यादिवाक्यानामेकार्थत्वानुभवेन अध्यापनं दानमेव तथा च शब्दस्याशुविनाशित्वे तस्य दानप्रतिग्रहयोरसम्भवत्वात् अध्यापने अध्ययने च प्रवत्तिर्न स्यात् अतः शब्दस्यावश्यं स्थैर्थं स्वीकार्यं नाशकानुपलब्धेश्च तन्नाशे प्रमाणाभावात् तावत् कालं स्थिरञ्चैनं कः पश्चान्नाशयिष्यति इति न्यायेन नित्यतैव फलितेति भावः।।

[2] शब्दस्यावश्यं नित्यत्वमुपेयम् त्रिः प्रथमामन्वाह त्रिरुक्तमामन्वाह इति श्रुतौ प्रथमोत्तमयोः सामिधेन्योः त्रिरुच्चारणस्य विहितत्वात् न हि स्थैर्यमन्तरेण त्रिरुच्चारणं सम्भवतीति पूर्वोक्तन्यायेन नित्यतायाः सिद्धेरित्यर्थः।।

[3] शब्दस्यावश्यं स्थैर्यं सम्प्रतिपत्तेः प्रत्यभिज्ञाया भावात् सत्त्वात् यः श्लोकश्चैत्रेण पठितस्तमेव मैत्रः पठति स एवायं इत्यादि प्रत्यभिज्ञाशब्दस्य स्थिरतामन्तरेणानुपपन्नेति भावः।।

Aph. 36. A plurality existing, [these arguments] are doubtful.

A plurality, diversity, and non-permanency existing in the particular motions of the limbs in dancing and the like, teaching, learning, and recognition are observed to exist in regard to them. Therfore teaching etc., the arguments or middle terms for the permanence of sound are doubtful, that is, undistributed. For otherwise from such observations as "He learns dancing" "He dances thrice" "Maitra is performing the same dance as was performed by Chaitra," permanence would be proved similarly of all these actions.[1] V.

संख्याभावः सामान्यतः।। 37।।

Aph. 37. The existence [in sound] of number, [results] from generality.

It may be said, "There are fifty letters, texts of eight and texts of three syllables, and the anushtubh metre of eight syllables. How, if letters be not eternal, can they be infinite according to diversity of utterance?" The reply is as follows: "The existence of number i.e., of the number fifty and the like, results from universality, from the letters *ka, ga* etc., existing as classes. Though there be an infinity of the letters *ka* etc., the things belonging to the class *ka, ga,* etc., exist as fifty or three or eight, just as substance, quality etc. exist as nine or twenty-four in virtue of a division of that which is included in the class."[2] U.

[1] नृत्यादीनामङ्गक्रियाविशेषाणां बहुत्वे ऽपि नानात्वे ऽपि अस्थैर्ये ऽपीति यावत् सति अध्यापनाभ्यास-प्रत्यभिज्ञानां दर्शनात् अध्यापनाद्याः स्थैर्यं साध्ये सन्दिग्धाः अनैकान्तिकाः नृत्यमधीते त्रिर्नृत्यते यदेव नृत्यं चैत्रेण कृतं मैत्रस्तदेव करोतीत्यनुभवस्य सर्वसिद्धत्वादित्यर्थः।।

[2] ननु पञ्चाशद्वर्णा अष्टाक्षरो मन्त्रः त्र्यक्षरो मन्त्रः अष्टाक्षरो ऽनुष्टुबित्यादिसंख्या कथं वर्णनामनित्यत्वे उच्चारणभेदेनानन्त्यसम्भवादित्यत आह। संख्यायाः पञ्चाशदादिसंख्याया भावः सद्भावः सामान्यतः कत्वगत्वादिजातित इत्यर्थः ककारादीनामानन्त्ये ऽपि कत्वगत्वाद्यवच्छिन्नानपञ्चाशत्त्वं त्रित्वमष्टत्वं वा द्रव्यगुणादीनामान्तर्गणिकभेदेन नवचतुर्विंशतित्वादिवदित्यर्थः।।

Book III

FIRST DAILY LESSON

प्रसिद्धा इन्द्रियार्थाः।। 1।।

Aph. 1. The objects of sense are universally known.

Having in the second book completed his investigation of external substances, the author according to the order of enunciation now proceeds to lay the foundation for an inquiry respecting the soul. The objects of sense, smells, tastes, colours, feels and sounds are cognisable by the several exterior organs of sense. That object which is apprehended by the organ of hearing is sound. It having been shown that sound is universally known, it is in like manner demonstrated that objects from odour to touch [i.e., smells, tastes, colours, touches] are universally known. Thus the objects, which is apprehended by the olfactory organ is odour; the object which is apprehended by the organ of taste is savour; the object which is apprehended by the eye alone is colour; the object which is apprehended by the organ of touch alone is feel. By the word object there is everywhere intended an actual subject of attributes, and therefore there is in the above aphorism no excess of predication which would apply also to the idea of smell and to the non-existence of smell. It is therefore to be understood that the nature of smell is that of a species included under the genus quality and existing as something apprehended by olfactory organ, and so also with regard to taste, etc. Consequently there is not wanting a subaudition of supersensual odour etc.[1] U.

[1] तदेवं द्वितीयाध्याये बहिर्द्रव्यपरीक्षामुपपाद्य, उद्देशक्रमादिदानीमात्मपरीक्षायै पीठमारचयितुमाह। इन्द्रयाणामर्था गन्धरूपरसस्पर्शशब्दा बाह्यैकैकेन्द्रियग्राह्याः तत्र श्रोत्रग्रहणो यो ऽर्थः स शब्द इति शब्दप्रसिद्धौ दर्शितायामर्थाद्-गन्धादौ स्पर्शपर्यन्ते प्रसिद्धिदर्शितेत्यर्थः तथाहि घ्राणग्रहणो यो ऽर्थः स गन्धः रसनग्रहणो यो ऽर्थः स रसः चक्षुर्मात्रग्रहणो यो ऽर्थः तद्रूपम् त्वगिन्द्रियमात्रग्रहणेः यो ऽर्थः स स्पर्शः सर्वत्र चार्थ शब्देन धर्मीभावेभूत उच्यते तेन गन्धात्वादौ गन्धद्यभावे च नातिव्याप्तिः तदेवं घ्राणग्रहणवृत्तिगुणत्वावान्तरजातिमत्त्वं गन्धत्वं एवं रसादावपि वाच्यं तेन नातीन्द्रियगन्धाद्यनुपग्रहः।।

The objects of the senses are colour, taste, smell, touch and sound. 'Universally known' means 'objects of assurance given in perception.' That immediate presentation to the mind which has for its objects colour etc. is allowed by all.[1] V.

इन्द्रियार्थप्रसिद्धिरिन्द्रियार्थेभ्यो ऽर्थान्तरस्य हेतुः।। 2।।

Aph. 2. The universal cognition of the objects of sense is an argument for [the existence of] another object than the objects of sense.

The application of the doctrine of universal cognition of objects of sense to the inquiry respecting the soul is here explained. By an 'argument' is meant a 'mark of the existance' of another object, which other object is the soul; a mark of the existence of the soul which is an object other than the senses and their objects, than colour etc., and the substrata of colour etc., though it is implied here that knowledge is the mark of the existence of the soul; yet inasmuch as there being a universal cognition of the objects of sense, the immediate presentation to the mind of colour etc., being more commonly knwon, the mark or evidence of there being a soul, is described as constituted by that universal cognition. This universal cognition must inhere in something; either as an effect as a water-pot, or as an attribute, or as an action. Since it is an action in the same manner as cutting is an action, it must be produced by an instrument. The instrument of universal cognition is sense, and that, being an instrument, must be employed by an agent, as an axe and the like are employed. Now, that in which this universal cognition resides and which employs for its instruments the olfactory and other organs is the soul.[2] U.

सो ऽनप्रदेशः।। 3।।

Aph. 3. That is an invalid argument [which affirms that sensible

[1] इन्द्रियार्थाः रूपरसगन्धस्पर्शशब्दाः प्रसिद्धाः प्रत्यक्षनिश्चयविषया इत्यर्थः तथापि रूपादिविषयकः साक्षात्कारः सर्वसिद्ध इति भावः।।

[2] इन्द्रियार्थप्रसिद्धेरात्मपरीक्षायामुपयोगमाह। हेतुर्लिङ्गमर्थान्तरस्य आत्मन इन्द्रियार्थेभ्य इति इन्द्रियेभ्यो अर्थेभ्यश्च रूपादिभ्यस्तद्वद्भ्यश्च यदर्थान्तरमात्मा तस्य लिङ्गमित्यर्थः। यद्यपि ज्ञानमेव लिङ्गमिह मिस विवक्षितं तथापीन्द्रियप्रसिद्धे रूपादिसाक्षात्कारस्य प्रसिद्धतरतया तादूप्येणैव लिङ्गत्वमुक्तं तथाहि प्रसिद्धिः क्वचिदाश्रिता कार्यत्वात् घटवत् गुणत्वाद्वा क्रियात्वाद्वा सा च प्रसिद्धिः करणजन्या क्रियात्वात् छिदिक्रियावत् यच्च प्रसिद्धेः करणं तदिन्द्रियं तच्च कर्तृप्रयोज्यं करणत्वात् वास्यादिवत् तथा यत्रेयं प्रसिद्धिराश्रिता यः घ्राणादीनां करणानां प्रयोक्ता स आत्मा।।

cognition is an attribute either of the body or of the senses].

In anticipation of the objection :—"Let the body or the organs of sense be that in which cognition resides; for, these being both more manifestly related to cognition that their negations are, why should we imagine any other cognising subject? For consciousness is an attribute of the body being, like its colour, etc., one of its effects; and the same may be said to be the case with regard to the organs of sense as attributes,"—it is stated that this is an invalid argument i.e., the appearance of an argument, inasmuch as, the middle term being undistributed, it is as uncertain that cognition is the effect of the body or the senses, as that knowledge of an object is generated by the lamp [by the light of which it is seen].[1] U.

That— the argument to establish the existence of cognition in the body—is a fallacious argument—the mere appearance of an argument. For a water-pot, a piece of cloth and the like do not in virtue of being effects of the body reside in the body. It cannot be proved that cognition exists in the body, for this would be a violation of the argument just stated.[2] V.

कारणाज्ञानात्।। 4।।

Aph. 4. Because there is unconsciousness in the causes.

It is meant that cognition cannot reside in the body or in the organs of sense because of the unconsciousness or absence of consciousness in the causes, or constituent parts, of the body, such as the hands, feet, etc. It is observed that the particular qualities of earth and the other substances are determined by the previous qualities of the cause of the substances. In like manner if there existed consciousness in the causes of the body, it might possibly exist also in the body itself. But this is not the case. Should it be urged that consciousness must also exist in the constitutive portions of the body, it may be denied on the ground of the want of unanimity which would ensue, for unanimity is never observed

[1] ननु शरीरमिन्द्रियाणि वा प्रसिद्धेराश्रयो ऽस्तु प्रसिद्धं प्रति तदुभयान्वयव्यतिरेकयोःस्फुटतग्त्वात किं तदन्याश्रयकल्पनया तथाहि चैतन्यं शरीरगुणः तत्कार्यत्वात् तद्रूपादिवत् एवमिन्द्रियगुणत्वे ऽपि वाच्यमित्याशङ्क्याह। अपदेशो हेतुः तदाभासो ऽनपदेशः तथा च तत्कार्यत्वं प्रदीपजन्यादावनैकान्तिकत्वादनपदेश इत्यर्थः।।

[2] सः देहवृत्तित्वसाधको हेतुः अनपदेशः हेत्वाभासः देहकार्यत्वस्य घटपटादे सत्त्वेन तत्र देहाश्रितत्वाभावात् उक्तहेतोर्व्यभिचारान्न प्रसिद्धेर्देहवृत्तित्वसिद्धिरित्यर्थः।

between many sentient beings, [whereas it is observed in the actions of the body]. Moreover were the hand for instance cut off, there would be no recollection of that which was experienced at the amputation according to the maxim, One does not remember that which is experienced by another. Again when the body perished there would, as a consequence, be no fruition of the results of injuries and the like done therein, for Maitra does not experience the results of the evil done by Chaitra; and actions would accordingly be lost, and there would come to pass event not determined by former acts.[1] U.

कार्येषु ज्ञानात्।। 5।।

Aph. 5. Because there would be consciousness in the effects.

Anticipating the objection that consciousness exists in a minute degree in the causes of the body, and is manifest in the body, and that there is not therefore the absence of a prior existence of the quality in the causes, nor the impossibility of unanimity, it is stated that if consciousness existed in the atoms which are the primary causes of the body, it would exist also in the water-pots and like products or effects which derive their origin from it; and also consciousness would exist in products such as water-pots and the like, because the particular attributes of the earth pervade all terrestrial existence. But consciousness is not observed to exist in these products.[2] U.

अज्ञानाच्च।। 6।।

Aph. 6. And because it is not known [that any minute degree of consciousness exists in products of matter].

In anticipation of the objection that consciousness may exist in an

[1] शरीरकारणानां करचरणादीनां तदवयवानां वा अज्ञानात् ज्ञानशून्यत्वादित्यर्थः पृथिव्यादिविशेषगुणानां हि कारणगुणपूर्वकता दृष्टा तथा च शरीरकारणेषु यदि ज्ञानं स्यात्तदा शरीरे ऽपि सम्भाव्येत न चैवम् नन्वस्तु शरीरकारणेष्वपि चैतन्यमिति चेन्न ऐकमत्याभावप्रसङ्गात् न हि बहूनां चेतनानामैकमत्यं दृष्टम् करावच्छेदेनानुभूतस्यकरच्छेदे ऽस्मरणप्रसङ्गात् ततो नान्यदृष्टं स्मरत्यन्य इति किञ्च शरीरनाशे तत्कृतहिंसादि फलानुपभोप्रसङ्गात् न हि चैत्रेण कृतस्य पापस्य फलं मैत्रो भुङ्क्ते ततश्च कृतहानिरकृताभ्यागमश्च स्यात्।।

[2] ननु शरीरकारणेषु सूक्ष्ममात्रया ज्ञानमस्ति शरीरे तु स्फुटमतो ना ऽकारणगुण पूर्वकता न चैकमत्यानुपपत्तिरिस्याशङ्क्याह। यदि तु शरीरमूलकारणेषु परमाणुषु चैतन्यं स्यात् तदा तदारब्धेषु कार्येषु घटादिष्वपि स्यात् किञ्च पार्थिवविशेषगुणानां सर्वपार्थिववृत्तिताया व्याप्तेः कार्येष्वपि घटादिषु चैतन्यं स्यान्न च तत्र चैतन्यमुपलभ्यते इत्यर्थः।।

inappreciable degree in water-pots and other material products, it is stated that inasmuch as it is not known by any kind of evidence, there is no consciousness in a water-jar and the like. Otherwise it might have to be admitted that a hare has horns, if we are to allow what is unwarranted by any form of evidence. For by no kind of evidence is it known that there exists consciousness in a water-jar and the like.[1] U.

'It is not known,' means 'because there is no form of evidence conveying the notion of consciousness as existing in the various products.' The word 'and' implies that such an hypothesis is unnecessary. It is more fitting to conceive some one other substance as the subject of consciousness than to imagine a varied consciousness existing in various portions of matter.[2] V.

अन्यदेव हेतुरित्यनपदेशः।। 7।।

Aph. 7. The means of proof is something else [than has been suppos-ed] :— this is not a valid argument.

It may be urged : It has been affirmed that a ruling soul is inferred from the organ of hearing and other instruments. This is not a legitimate inference, for the auditory and other organs are neither identical with, nor produced by, the soul; and unless one of these alternatives be admitted, there is no proof of any inseparable co-existence of these organs and the soul; and unless there be such inseparable co-existence, there can be no valid inference of this kind. To this it is replied that the means of proof can but be something else than that which is to be proved.It cannot be identical with that which has to be proved, for were it is so it would follow that there would be no difference between the means of proof and the thing proved. A means of proof constituted by identity with that which is to be proved, is no means of proof,—is invalid as an argument.[3] U.

[1] ननु घटादावपि सूक्ष्ममात्रया चैतन्यमस्त्येवेत्याशङ्क्याह। सर्वैः प्रमाणैरज्ञानात् कुम्भादौ न चैतन्यमित्यर्थः सर्वप्रमाणगोचरस्याप्यभ्युपगमे शशविषाणा देप्यभ्युपगमप्रसङ्गः न हि घटादौ चैतन्यं केनापि प्रमाणेन ज्ञायत इति।।

[2] अज्ञानात् केनापि प्रमाणेन तत्तत्कार्यगतज्ञानस्याज्ञानाजननात् तथा च निष्प्रमाणकत्वान्न तत्तत्कार्येषु ज्ञानमित्यर्थः चकारो गौरवं समुच्चिनोति तथा च नानावयवेषु नानाचैतन्यकल्पनापेक्षया चैतन्यधारतया एकं द्रव्यान्तरमेत कल्पयितुमुचितमितिभावः।।

[3] ननु श्रोत्रादिभिः करणैरधिष्ठाता अनुमीयते इत्युक्तं तदुक्तं न हि श्रोत्रादिभिरात्मनस्तादात्म्यं तदुत्पत्तिर्वा न च ताभ्यामन्तरेणा ऽविनाभावसिद्धिः न चाविनाभावमन्तरेणा ऽनुमितिरित्यत आह। हेतुः साध्यादन्य एव भवति न तु साध्यात्मा साध्याविशेषप्रसङ्गात् तस्मात्तादात्म्यघटितो हेतुरहेतुरनपदेश इत्यर्थः।।

अर्थान्तरं ह्यर्थान्तरस्या ऽनपदेशः।। ८।।

Aph. 8. One thing cannot be an argument [of the existence of another thing with which it is wholly unconnected].

It might be asked by an objector how quality not produced by that which is to be proved can warrant any inference; for were this the case smoke etc., might prove the existence of an ass etc., or as well as that of fire. It is therefore stated that one thing or kind of substance, cannot be an argument for the existence of another thing or another kind of substance. Thus smoke, etc., if the existence of ass is to be proved, would be fallaciously adduced as a means of proof, being void of invariable concomitance with asses, etc. But with reference to fire etc. it would not be so, for in that case there would exist a concomitance. In the present case there must be a cocomitance, there is not merely an accidental relation.[1] V.

संयोगिसमवाय्येकार्थसमवायिविरोधि च।। ९।।

Aph. 9. The conjunct, the inherent, the co-inherent in one thing, and the contradictory [are means of proof].

Such form of proof as: The body has skin because of its corporeality, is that of conjunction. For skin is described as a natural integument of matter capable of growth and decay, and is neither a cause nor an effect of the body, but merely produced together with the body and invariably conjoined with it. In like manner the form of proof from inhesion is such as: Ether possesses extension, because of its substantiality, like a water-pot, etc. Here extension which has to be proved is established by substantiality a property essential to ether. Or another example would be:—The divisibility of extension must somewhere cease; therefore the atomic, as a degree of extension is proved; whence it is inferred that atoms exist in which the atomic inheres. The inference from sound, of ether, and from knowledge etc., of soul, is not given as an inference of cause from effect.[2] U.

[1] ननु साध्यादनुत्पन्नस्य गुणत्वस्य कथमनुमापकत्वम् तथा सति धूमादिना वह्न्यादेरिव रासभादेरप्यनुमानापत्तेरित्यत आह। हि हेतौ यतो ऽर्थान्तरं वस्त्वन्तरम् अर्थान्तरस्य ननु वस्त्वन्तरस्य अनपदेशः अहेतुः रासभादेर्व्याप्तिशून्यो हि धूमादिः रासभादौ साध्यो हेत्वाभासः वह्न्यादौ तद्वाप्यत्वस्य तत्र सत्त्वात् प्रकृते तु व्याप्तिसत्त्वान्नागमकत्वमिति भावः।।

[2] शरीरं त्वग्वत् शरीरत्वादित्ययं हेतुः संयोगी वृद्धिक्षयवदद्रव्यसहजावरणं हि त्वगित्युच्यते तच्च न शरीरस्य कार्यं कारणं वा किन्तु सहोत्पत्तिकमात्रं नियतसंयोगवत्। एवं समवायि यथाकाशं परिमाणुवदद्रव्यत्वात्

The conjunct means the means of proof connected with conjunction. Is a means of the proof is to be supplied after each term of the aphorism? That which is connected by conjunction i.e., the mark of the existence of that which is dependent on conjunction, is included in the conjunction. Otherwise how could there be such inferences as that in a particular place there are charioteers, because there are chariots excellently driven there? Here the relation determining the conclusion is the confiection by conjunction with the conjunct. In like manner the inherent is a mark of the existence of that in wtich it inheres. Else how in the case of seeing a mere portion of an animal etc., could it be inferred from such determinate part that the whole is an animal etc.? Nor can it be argued that there being in the case of conjunction of the sight with that portion, a conjunction with the whole object, it is difficult to prove that such an inference as this is not a mere perception; for it is possible only where there is a desire to infer. Since, therefore, a chariot and the like are not effects or products of a charioteer, etc., and are different from the charioteer etc., but invariably accompanied by the charioteer etc., the being invariably accompanied by an object, i.e., the being inferrible from it, is not astricted to the case of identity with or production by that object.[1] V.

कार्यं कार्यान्तरस्य।। 10।।

Aph. 10. One effect is [a mark of the existence] of another effect.

An effect, colour for instance, is a mark of the existence of another effect, such as touch. It is implied also that that which is not an effect, the unity of ether, is a mark of the existence of the individual unity of ether which is not an effect, and so in the case of infinite magnitude.[2] U.

घटादिवदिति अत्र परिमाणं साध्य द्रव्यत्वेनाकाशसमवायिना धर्मेण साध्यते यद्वा परिमाणतारतम्यं क्वचिद्विश्रान्तमित्यनेनाऽणुत्वं परिमाणविशेषः सिद्धः तेन तदाश्रयः परमाणुरनुमीयते शब्दादिना त्वाकाशस्य ज्ञानादिना त्वात्मनो ऽनुमानं कार्येणैव कारणानुमानमिति नोदाहृतम्।।

[1] संयोगि संयोगानुयोगि लिङ्गमिति सर्वशेषः। तथा च संयोगानुयोगि संयोगप्रतियोगिनो लिङ्गं व्याप्यं कथमन्यथा अयं देशः सारथिमान् विलक्षणगतिमद्रथादित्यादामनुमितिः साध्यतावच्छेदकसम्बन्धश्चात्र स्वसंयुक्तसयोगः एवं समवाय्यपि समवेतस्य लिङ्गं। कथमन्यथा पश्वाद्यवयवमात्रदर्शनदशायां विशिष्टावयवेना ऽवयविनः यत्रवादेरनुमितिः न चावयवचक्षुःसंयोगदशायामवयबिन्यपि संयोगसत्त्वात् तस्वापि प्रत्यक्षं दुर्वारमिति वाच्यं तथापि सिषाधयिषया तादृशानुमानसम्भवात् तथा सारथ्यादिभिन्नस्य सारथ्याद्यकार्यस्य च रथादेः सारथ्यादेर्व्याप्यत्वात् व्याप्यत्वं न तादात्म्यतदुत्पत्तिनियतमिति भावः।।

[2] कार्यं रूपं कार्यान्तरस्य स्पर्शस्य लिङ्गम्। उपलक्षणञ्चैतत् अकार्यमप्याकाशैकत्वम् आकाशैकपृथक्त्वे लिङ्गम् एवं परममहत्त्वे।।

An effect or product of the earth, such as smell, is a mark of the existence—for these words are to be supplied—of another effect such as taste. Co-inhesion in one object is juxtaposition constituted by in-co-existence. In like manner invariable taste etc, should be regarded as a mark of the existence of invariable colour etc. Since, therefore, there is in smell etc., an invarible concomitance with taste, etc. which is not indifferent from or produced by smell, it is proved that invariable concomitance is not astricted to the cases of indentity and causality.[1] V.

विरोध्यभूतं भूतस्य।। 11।।

Aph. 11. A non-existent contradictory [is a mark] of the existent.

The contradictory mark of co-existence or middle term is exemplified. Rain which has not fallen, is a mark of there having been no conjunction of air and clouds. In like manner the recitation of a sacred text is preventive of a tumour etc., and accordingly there not having existed a tumour etc., is a mark of there having been a recitation of a sacred text.[2] U.

It is exemplified how the contradictory may be employed as a middle term. The non-existent, or non-adjacent or in other words non-adjacency of the contradictory is a mark—for these words are to be supplied—of the existent, of that which has come into or remains in existence. The illation assumes the following form. This wood is combustible when conjoined with fire, because gems etc., (said to have the power of extinguishing fire) do not co-exist, as in the case of other substances reduced to ashes. This district contains unintimidated snakes, for though there are snakes there are no ichneumons, as there are in certain other countries where there are venomous serpents.[3] V.

भूतमभूतस्य।। 12।।

[1] कार्यं पृथिव्याः कार्यं गन्धादिकं कार्यान्तरस्य रसादेर्लिङ्गमिति शेषः एकार्थसमवायः समवायघटित-सामानाधिकरण्यम् एवं नित्यरसादिकमपि नित्यरूपादेर्लिङ्गं द्रष्टव्यम् तथा च गन्धादे रसाद्यभेदस्य रसादिजन्यत्वस्य चा ऽभावात् व्याप्तेस्तदुभयनैयत्यं बाधितमेवेति भावः।।

[2] विरोधिलिङ्गमुदाहरति। अभूतं वर्षं भूतस्य वाय्वभ्रसंयोगस्य लिङ्गमेवं स्फोटादेर्विरोधी मन्त्रपाठः तथा चाभूतमनुत्पन्नं स्फोटादि भूतस्य मन्त्रपाठस्य लिङ्गम्।।

[3] विरोधिनो व्याप्यत्वमुदाहरति। अभूतम् असन्निहितं विरोधि विरोध्यसन्निधानमिति यावत् भूतस्य जातस्य स्थितस्य वा विरोधिनो लिङ्गमिति शेषः अयमनुमानप्रकारः अयं काष्ठो दाहवान् वह्निसंयुक्तत्वे सति मण्याद्यसन्निधानात् भस्मीभूतवस्त्वन्तरवत् अयं देशो निर्भयाहिमान् अहिमत्त्वे सति नकुलशून्यत्वात् तादृशनिश्चितदेशान्तरवदित्यर्थः।।

Aph. 12. That which has been [is a mark] of that which has not been.

Another contradictory argument is exemplified. A tumour etc. which has been, is a mark of the recitation of a sacred text which has not been; so also conjunction which has existed between wind and clouds, is a mark that there has not been rain; there having been a fire is a mark that there has not been extinction of fire by means of gems etc. Similar instances may be inferred.[1] U.

That which has been, that which has come into or remains in existence, is a mark that there has not been its contradictory; a mark, in other words, of the non-adjacency of its opposite. For examples : This wood is not co-existent with gems etc., for it burns. This district has no ichneumons, for it has unintimidated snakes; and so forth.[2] V.

भूतो भूतस्य।। 13।।

Aph. 13. That which has been [is a mark of something repugnant] which has been.

Another mark of concomitance or middle term is exemplified. There is sometimes inference from an existing opposite to an existing opposite, as when on seeing a snake swelling with anger it is inferred that there is an ichneumon behind a bush. In this case the snake excited is in existence, and the ichneumon hidden by the bush is in existence. There is therefore an existent object as the mark of an existent object. On the other hand, rain cannot exist at the same time as conjunction of clouds and wind, nor can tumours etc. co-exist with recitation of sacred texts.[3] U.

प्रसिद्धिपूर्वकत्वादपदेशस्य।। 14।।

Aph. 14. [These forms of inference are valid] because the mark is preceded by knowledge [of invariable concomitance.]

[1] विरोधिलिङ्गस्योदाहरणान्तरमाह। भूतं स्फोटादिकम् अभूतस्य मन्त्रपाठस्य लिङ्गम् एवंभूतो वाय्वभ्रसंयोगो ऽभूतस्य वर्षस्य लिङ्गम् एवंभूतो दाहो ऽभूतस्य मण्यादिसमवधानस्य लिङ्गमेवमन्यदापूह्यम्।।

[2] भूतमुत्पन्नं स्थितं वा अभूतस्य विरोधिनो विरोध्यसन्निधानस्य लिङ्गमित्यर्थः यथायं काष्ठो मण्याद्यसन्निहितो दाहवत्त्वात् अयं देशो नकुलशून्यः भीतिरहिताहिमत्त्वात्।।

[3] लिङ्गान्तरमुदाहरति। विद्यमानेनैव विरोधिना विद्यमानस्यैव विरोधिनः क्वचिदनुमानं यथा विस्फूर्जन्तमहिं दृष्ट्वा झाटान्तरितस्य नकुलस्य अत्र हि विस्फूर्जन्निहिर्भूतो विद्यमानो नकुलो ऽपि विद्यमान एवेति भवति भूतो भूतस्य लिङ्गमित्यर्थः वर्षवाय्वभ्रसंयोगयोस्तु नैकस्मिन काले विद्यमानता न वा स्फोटमन्त्रपाठयोरिति।।

Knowledge is recollection of invariable concomitance (vyāpti). The mark of this co-existence is the middle term. There is therefore expressed that member of the syllogism which states the argument, or by the subsumption, a middle term characterised by invariable concomitance mentally resuscitated. Therefore the argument, as has been stated, has for its antecedent some general knowledge. In the above instanced inference, then, of the soul as a governing element from its instruments such as the organ of hearing, and of the soul as a substratum from qualities such as knowledge, there is an invariable concomitance; but when you attempted to prove, by the mark of its being an effect of the body, that knowledge is a quality of the body, there was no invariable concomitance.

It may be asked, what is this invariable concomitance? It is not merely a relation of co-extension; for co-extensiveness, or incompatibility with absence of that which is to be predicated in the conclusion, is not recognised where only positive conditions of concomitance are found; for unsusceptibility of incompatibility with that which is to be so predicated may be such an exclusively positive condition of concomitance. Smoke also contains in itself incompatibility with various predications in the conclusion. Nor is it the relation of inseparability, for that is either non-existence of the mark or middle term in the absence of that which is to be proved [viz., the major which has to be proved of the minor]; or existence of the mark argued from the existence of that which is to be predicated in the conclusion. And if you say that a definite relation of condition and conditioned; positive or negative, may be asserted, between smoke and an ass, because smoke sometimes does not exist where an ass does not exist, and exists where an ass exists, we deny it, for such would be the case only it we found any determinate relation.

Nor is it the relation of totality or integrity. If you say that invariable concomitance is the connection of the middle term with the whole of the major term, such connection does not exist in the case of smoke etc., where the concomitant objects are not co-extensive [for though fire exists wherever smoke exists, smoke is said not always to exist where fire exists, not being found in red-hot iron etc.] Let it be connection of the whole middle term with the major, but this is impossible for there does not exist in the whole of the middle term connection with the individuals denoted by major [e.g. all fire does not exist in a hearth, in a cattlestation, a mountain etc., but exists in the whole aggregate of places where smoke exists, as also elsewhere.] Let it be connection of the whole major with the whole middle term. This also it cannot be, for it is impossible that there should be connection between each extensive part of the middle and each extensive part of the major. In the case of the concomitant objects not being co-extensive the definition that invariable concomitance is connection by totality would be unduly restricted.

Nor is it natural conjunction. For the nature of a thing is the thing's proper mode of being or its being in itself. If by the secondary affix be meant its being produced in such and such a place, our definition will be too narrow to apply to invariable concomitance constituted by in-co-existence. If by the secondary affix be meant co-inherence in any thing, the definition will be too narrow to include co-inhesion, for co-inhesion is not co-inherent with anything else. For conjunction neither inheres in, nor is produced by, smokiness the character of the middle term. Nor is it connection as a general predicate. The general predicate is difficult to explain and were it easy, would be difficult to understand. And were it easy to conceive yet there would be a reciprocal inherence or logical see-saw, being based on an induction of what did not pervade the middle term, though pervading the major. Invariable concomitance is not merely connection. For since fallacious connection includes particular place and particular time, knowledge of such connection, even were it an invariable concomitance, would be useless in illation, for we should prescribe only such invariable concomitance as is the object of cognition causative of illation.

Nor is invariable concomitance in-coexistence of the major which is absent only when there is absolute non-existence of that of which the middle is predicated, fire for example being absent where there is an absolute non-existence of things smoky: for volcanic fire can but be non-existent in a kitchen hearth though smoky. For in such an instance as This is conjunct for it is a substance the definition would be unduly restricted, for otherwise absence of conjunction would reside in the same objects as the middle term conjunction. It may be said that invariable concomitance is in-coexistence of the predicate of the conclusion absent where there is absolute non-existence of an appropriate subject repugnant to such absent predicate, absolute non-existence of conjunction not being repugnant to such absent predicate. This we deny, for absolute non-existence of conjunction is repugnent to such absent predicate, for otherwise it will be useless to imagine any kind of distinctive attribute, as it is not imagined that there is any distinctive attribute discriminating between the produced and the non-eternal.

Nor is invariable concomitance the not being a subject of incompatibility with the predicate, since incompatibility with a predicate does not exist in an inference from only positive conditions for such incompatibility means containing that which does not contain the predicate.

Nor is invariable concomitance the possession of a from determined by the same connection as something else, as for instance the fiery is determined by connection with smoke. This is not the case, for the fiery is more extensive [fire existing where there is no smoke, as in a heated lump of iron]. Were it the case there would be observed a wider extension [of the nature of fire] characterised by invariable co-existence [with smoke], there being a wide extension of the nature of smoke [or vapour] inasmuch as there exists smoke [or vapour] pendent on the surface of the sky [cf., Meghadūta, v. 5. where it is said that a cloud is a mass of vapour, light, water, and air.] If a distinction be made for the purpose of excluding such instances, it must be allowed that that which is characterised by invariable concomitance is allowed to be characterised by existence of connection, and there is thus only an identical affirmation.

If the statement that invariable concomitance, consists in compatibility [or the subject's susceptibility of the predicate] has been thus shown to be fallacious, we may here proceed to state that invariable co-existence is a not accidental connection. By being not accidental is meant in-coexistence of the predicate failing; that is, too widely or too narrowly affirmed, only, where the argument fails. Or, in other words, it is in-coexistence of the predicate determined by absolnte non-existence dependent on absolute non-existence of all that which is in-coexistent therewith The meaning of the last two expressions is in-coexistence of the predicate, such in-coexistence being neither more nor less extensive than the argument. In other words, it is an extensiveness as extensive as the predicate. If you object that this is difficult to understand by reason of the relative compound employed, you must look at it and consider it again.

In other words invariable concomitance is in-coexistence of the predicate absent where there is absolute non-existence of that which contains the mark or argument. By absolute non-existence is meant non-existence of that which has as a common characteristic a universal entity such as the fiery, etc. It is therefore no objection to our definition that the smoke of a culinary hearth is compatible with non-existence of the smoke of a mountain, for there never arises the conviction that there is not fire in that which has smoke. Substantiality never has a common substratum with absolute non-existence of connection, for we have the conviction that there is no substance which is not conjunct. Though conjunctions singly are not included, the nature of conjunction in general is so included, and may be predicated universally of substance.

It may be objected that the being not contingent is absence of a concomitant and that it is difficult to describe a concomitant. This we disallow, for an accident [or special condition] is that which does not invariably exist in the mark of concomitance whereas it does invariably exist in that which is to be proved. Accordingly it has been said : A concomitant is accidental in relation to a mark of co-existence, and not accidental in relation to that which is to be proved. It may be objected : This definition does not include an accident which is only not invariably present in that which is to be proved, as in the instance, Air is perceptible, for there exists in it perceptible touch, where the having an appreciable colour is [a concomitant of that which has to be proved, i.e., of the perceptibility of air]; or in the instance. "He is black, for he is the son of Mitrā [a low caste woman] where the production of blackness by cooking herbs [might be a special condition of blackness.] For possession of an appreciable colour is not invariably concomitant with perceptibility, since it does not exist in the perceptibility of soul, quality and action; nor is the being produced by cooking herbs invariably concomitant with blackness, inasmuch as it does not exist in a black crow, cuckoo, cloud, fruit of the roseapple, etc. This objection will not hold. For it was meant that a special condition is invariably present in that which is finally determined as what is to be proved, and not invariably present in the means of proof. That which is finally determined as that which is to be proved, has as a condition the universal presence in it of the conditions which are special. The possession of appreciable colour, in the first instance is universally present in the perceptible qualified by external substantiality, and is a positive and negative condition [of the perceptible; i.e., it may be asserted that wherever there is appreciable colour there is perceptibility, and wherever there is not appreciable colour there is not perceptibility of external substances.] In the second instance we may make a similar inference from its being observed on the authority of the Charaka and the Suśruta [two medical works] that the fact of being produced by eating herbs is an attribute universally present in that which is to be proved, which is determined to be an accidental darkness in men.

It may be said that this is not the meaning of the word concomitant for a concomitant is that of which the attributes appear in some other object, as a China rose etc., [seen reflected] in crystal etc.; as in the universal co-existence of one thing with another, which other thing does not always co-exist with the first [as in the co-existence of fire with smoke which is said to be invariable, while that of smoke with fire is not invariable] the concomitant not being inseparable, does not appear in the argument. This is true. The term concomitant is used in its primary meaning only where there is a mutually implied co-existence, as of fire produced from moist fuel [for wherever there is such fire there is also smoke, and *vice versa*]. In other cases the word is employed in a secondary sense. The secondary sense expresses that which is casual or accidental, according to the rule That is accidental in an object which is accidental to that which is universally present in that object. The evidence of concomitance is accidental in an accident inseparable from that which is to be shewn to be concomitant. Hence from the hypothesis that the evidence of concomitance is accidental to that which is to be proved, and according to the rule that what is not included in what is invariably concomitant with an object is not included in that object, we are led to conclude that there is no proof of such concomitance, or there results the possibility of a contrary argument. For if a concomitant inseparable from the predicate be not in the subject, it is an argument that the predicate is not in the subject. It has accordingly been said : The respondent may bring forward an accident determining another conclusion, inconsistent with the establishment of the thesis maintained by the defendant, such accident being equivalent to a germinal vitiation of the thesis and this may be upheld by arguments adverse to the absence of erroneous and fallacious arguments in its favour.

It may be said that that is a concomitant by the accidentalness of which the argument is accidental in relation to that which is to be proved. But in this definition the third [or instrumental] case is not employed to express instrument, means, form, or definition. Nor is the construction to be completed thus. That is an accident by the accidentalness of which *being known* the argument *is known* to be accidental in relation to that which is to be proved. For this deifinition would not apply to obvious cases of the accidental, not applying to the unknown accidental. A fitting sense is difficult to discover in these words, since it is impossible to express an accident without stating that it is casual or accidental. The being other than the subject, though included in the definition of an accident, is not the difinition of an accident, for it would involve a contradiction. Where there is an uncertain applicability to the subject, as in such a case if it be not uncertain it is not the subject, and since if it be the subject it must be doubtful, there is certainty of doubtful applicability. That which remains to be said, may be sought in the Mayukha.[1] U.

[1] प्रसिद्धिः स्मर्यमाणा व्याप्तिः अपदेशो हेतुवचनं तेन स्मर्यमाणव्याप्तिविशिष्टो हेतुर्हेत्ववयवेनोपनयावयवेन वोच्यते इति भवति प्रसिद्धिपूर्वको ऽपदेश इति तथा च श्रोत्रादिना करणेनाधिष्ठातुः ज्ञानादिना च गुणेन तदाश्रयस्यात्मनो यदनुमानमुक्तं तत्र सर्वत्र व्याप्तिरस्ति त्वया तु शरीरकार्यत्वेन हेतुना ज्ञानस्य यच्छरीरगुणत्वं साधितं तत्र न व्याप्तिरिति भावः ननु केयं व्याप्तिर्न तावदव्यभिचारितसम्बन्धः अव्यभिचारस्य साध्यात्यन्ताभावसामानाधिकरण्यानधिकरणत्वस्य केवलान्वयिन्यप्रसिद्धेः साध्यानधिकरणानधिकरणत्वस्यापि केवलान्वयिसम्भवात् धूमादेरपि यत्किञ्चित्साध्यानधिकरणाधिकरणत्वात्। नाप्यविनाभावः। स हि साध्यं विना ऽभावो वा हेतोः अविना साध्यान्नये सति भावो वा धूमस्यापि क्वचिदासभावे ऽभावात् रासभसत्त्वे सत्त्वाच्च नियतव्यतिरेको नियतश्चान्वयो विवक्षित इति न नियमस्यैव निरूप्यमाणत्वात् नापि कार्त्स्येन सम्बधः स यदि कृत्स्नस्य साध्यस्य साधनसम्बन्धः स विषमव्याप्ते धूमादावपि नास्ति अथ कृत्सस्नय साधनस्य साध्यसम्बन्धः सो ऽप्येकस्य साध्यस्य कृत्स्नसाधने सम्बन्धाभावादनुपपन्नः अथ कृत्स्नस्थयासाध्यस्य कृत्तेन साधनेन सम्बन्धः एतदप्ययुक्तं न हि कृत्स्नन साधनेन कृत्सुद्रस्य साध्यस्य क्वचिदपि सम्बन्धः सम्भवति प्रत्येकमेव साध्यसाधनयोः सम्बन्धात् विषमव्याप्ते चाव्याप्तेः नापि स्वाभाविकः सम्बन्धः स्वभावो हि स्वस्य भावो वा स्वयमेव भावो वा तत्र तज्जन्यत्वञ्चेत्तद्धितार्थः तदा समवायलक्षणायां व्याप्तावव्याप्तेः तदाश्रितत्वञ्चेत्तद्धितार्थः तदापि समवाये ऽव्याप्तिः न हि समवायः क्वचिद्वाश्रितः संयोगस्यापि हेतुधर्मधूमत्वाद्यनाश्रितत्वात् हेतुधर्मधूमत्वाद्यजन्यत्वाच्च नाप्यनौपाधिकः सम्बन्धः उपाधेरेव दुर्वचत्वात् सुवचत्वे ऽपि दुर्ग्रहत्वात् सुग्रहत्वे ऽप्यन्योन्याश्रयत्वात् साध्यव्यापकत्वे सति साधनाव्यापकत्वादेर्व्याप्तिग्रहाधीनग्रहत्वात् नापि सम्बन्धमात्रं व्याप्तिः व्यभिचारिसम्बन्धस्यापि देशविशेषकालविशेषगर्भतया व्याप्तिरूपत्वे ऽपि तज्ज्ञानस्यानुमितावतन्त्रत्वात् अनुमितिकारणीभूतज्ञानविषयव्याप्तेरेव निरूपयितुमुचितत्वात् नापि साधनवन्निष्ठात्यन्ताभावप्रतियोगिसाध्यसामानाधिकरण्यं व्याप्तिः वह्नेरपि धूमवन्निष्टात्यन्ताभावप्रतियोगित्वात न हि धूमवति महानसे पर्वतीयवह्नेर्नात्यन्ताभावः इदं संयोगि द्रव्यत्वादित्यादौ संयोगात्यन्ताभावस्य साधनसमानाधिकरणत्वादव्यापकताप्रसत् प्रतियोगिविरुद्धस्वसमानाधिकरणात्यन्ताभावापतियोगिसाध्यसामानाधिकरण्यं व्याप्तिः संयोगात्यन्ताभावस्यापि प्रतियोगिविरुद्धत्वाभावादति चेन्न संयोगात्यन्ताभावस्यापि प्रतियोगिविरुद्धत्वात् अन्यथा ऽवच्छेदभेदकल्पनावैयर्थ्यात् न हि कृतकत्वानित्यत्वयोर्वृत्त्यर्थकवच्छेदभेदः कल्प्यते नापि साध्यवैयधिकरण्यानधिकरणत्वं केवलान्वयिनि साध्यवैयधिाकरण्याप्रसिद्धेः साध्यानधिकरणाधिकरणत्वं हि तत् नापि यत्सम्बधितावच्छेदकरूपवत्त्वं यस्य तस्य वा व्याप्तिः वह्नित्वस्यापि धूमसम्बन्धितावच्छेदकत्वात् अधिकदेशवृत्तितया तन्न तथेति चेत् व्यापकताच्छेदकस्याधिकदेशवृत्तेरप्यभ्युपगमात् धूमत्वस्यापि गगनतलावलम्बिधूमवृर्त्तियाधिकदेशवृत्तित्वात् अत एव एतद्वारणार्थं विशेषणमति चेत् तर्हि यद्व्याप्यतावच्छेदकं तदेव सम्बन्धितावच्छेदकत्वेनानुमतं तथा चात्माश्रेयः। एवञ्च

आप्रसिद्धो ऽनपदेशो ऽसन् सन्दिग्धश्चानपदेशः।। 15।।

Enumeration of fallacies

Aph. 15. Fallacious arguments are the unobserved, the nonexistent, and the dubious.

For the discrimination of past and future marks of co-existence from fallacious arguments, the author proceeds to commence the section on fallacies. The unobserved is that which is unaccompanied, that with which no universal concomitance has been observed, and the contradictory is that to which there is a repugnant universal concomitance. In this term unobserved are included that of which the

यत् सामानाधिकरण्यावच्छेदकरूपवत्त्वं यस्य तस्य सा व्याप्तिरित्यप्युक्तदोषाक्रान्तमिति चेत् अत्रोच्यते अनौपाधिकः सम्बन्धो व्याप्तिः अनौपाधिकत्वन्तु यावत् स्वव्यभिचारिव्यभिचारिसाध्यसामानाधिकरण्यं यावत्स्वसमानाधिकरणात्यन्ताभावप्रतियोगिप्रतियोगिकात्यन्ताभावसमानाधिकरणसाध्यसामानाधिकरण्यं वा यावत् साधनाव्यापकाव्याप्यसाधसामानानाधिकरण्यमिति निरुक्तिद्वयार्थः यावत्साध्यव्यापकव्यापकत्वं वा बहुव्रीहिणा दुर्ग्रहमिदमिति चेत् अत एव भूयोदर्शनापेक्षा तर्कापेक्षा च। यद्वा साधनसमानाधिकरणात्यन्ताभावाप्रतियोगिसाध्यसामानाधिकरण्यं व्याप्तिः अत्यन्ताभावश्च वह्नित्वादिसामान्यवच्छिन्नप्रतियोगिताको विवक्षितः तेन महानसीयधूमे पर्वतीयवह्न्यत्यन्ताभावसामान्याभिकरण्ये ऽपि न दोषः धूमवति वह्निर्नास्तीति प्रतीतेरनुदयात् द्रव्यत्वन्तु संयोगित्वात्यन्ताभावासमानाधिकरणमेव न हि भवति द्रव्यं न संयोगीति प्रतीतिः संयोगानां प्रत्येकमव्याप्यवृत्तित्वे ऽपि संयोगित्वसामान्यस्य व्याप्यवृत्तित्वात् तस्यव च व्यापकत्वात्। नन्वनौपाधिकत्वमुपाधिविरहः उपाधिरेव दुष्परिकथनीय इति चेन्न साध्यव्यापकत्वे सति साधनाव्यापकस्योपाधित्वात् तदुक्तं साधने सोपाधिः साध्ये निरूपाधिरूपाधिः। ननु केवलसाध्याव्यापकोप्राध्यव्यापकत्वमेतत् तथा वायुः प्रत्यक्षः प्रत्यक्षस्पर्शाश्रयत्वादित्यत्रोद्भूतरूपवत्वम् स श्यामो मित्रातनयत्वादित्यत्र शाकपाकजत्वम् न ह्युद्भूतरूपवत्त्वं प्रत्यक्षव्यापकम् आत्मनि गुणकर्मादौ च प्रत्यक्षे तदभावात् नापि शाकपाकजत्वं श्यामत्वव्यापकं काककोकिलजलदजम्बूफलादौ श्यामे तदभावादिति चेन्न पर्यवसितसाध्यव्यापकत्वं सति साधनाव्यापकत्वस्य तथा विवक्षितत्वात् पर्यवसितञ्च साध्यं यद्धर्मावच्छेदेनोपाधेर्व्यापकत्वमभग्नं तद्धर्माबच्छिन्नं प्रकृते बहिर्द्रव्यत्वावच्छेदेन प्रत्यक्षस्योद्भूतरूपवत्त्वं व्यापकम् अन्वयव्यतिरेकाभ्यां गृहीतम् श्रौत्पत्तिकनरश्यामत्वावच्छिन्नं साध्यं प्रति चरकसुश्रुतादौ शाकपाकजत्वस्य व्यापकत्वावधारणादेवमन्यत्राप्यूह्यम्। ननु नायमुपाधिपदवाच्यः यद्धर्मो ऽन्यत्र भासते स उपाधिः यथा स्फटिकादौ जपाकुसुमादि विषमव्याप्तोपाधौ च व्याप्यत्वाभावात्तद्धर्मस्य साधनाभिमते ऽनवभासनादिति चेत् सत्यं समव्याप्त एवार्द्रेन्धनप्रभववह्निमत्त्वादौ मुख्य उपाधिपदप्रयोगः अन्यत्र तु गौणः गुणः व्यभिचारोन्नायकत्वं यद्धि यद्व्यपकव्यभिचारि तस्य तद्व्यभिचारित्वनियमात् भवति च साध्यव्यापकस्योपाधेर्व्यभिचारिसाधनं अतः साध्यव्यभिचारिति यद्व्यापकाव्याप्यं यत् तत् तदव्याप्यम् इति व्याप्यत्वासिद्धयुन्नायकत्वं वा सत्प्रतिपक्षोत्थापकत्वं वा पक्षे उपाधेः साध्यव्यापकस्याभावात् साध्याभावसाधनात् तदुक्तं वाद्युक्तसाध्यनियमच्युतो ऽपि कथकैरुपाधिरुद्भाव्यः पर्यवसितं नियमयन् दूषकताबीजसाम्यात् इति उन्नीयते चायं बाधव्यभिचारानुकूलतर्काभावप्रतिकूलतर्कैः। यत्तु यद्व्यभिचारित्वेन साधनस्य साध्यव्यभिचारित्वं स उपाधिरिति तत्र तृतीया न करणे न हेतौ न प्रकारे न लक्षणे न तु यद्व्यभिचारित्वेन ज्ञातेन साधनस्य साध्यव्यभिचारित्वं इति ज्ञायते पूरणीयम् अज्ञायमानोपाध्याव्यापनात् स्फुटव्यभिचारिस्थलोपाध्यव्यापनात् योरयतागर्भा तु दुर्निरूपा व्यभिचारोन्नायकत्वमव्यवस्थाप्य उपाध्युद्भावनाशक्यत्वाच्च पक्षेतरत्वन्तु उपाधिलक्षणाक्रान्तमपि

inclusion is unestablished, and the contrary. The non-existent is that which is not in the subject, or that which is not an attribute of the subject. This is sometimes due to the absence of an essential from, and sometimes to the non-existence of uncertainty and the desire of proving that which is to be proved. The dubious is that which gives rise to a doubt as to the two alternative of the existence or non-existence of the predicate in the subject of the question. Doubt arises sometimes from observation of a common attribute, sometimes from observation of a not common attribute, and sometimes from observation that the argument is accompanied by the predicate or the non-existence of the predicate only in respect to such and such a particular subject. The first is general inconclusiveness, the second is particular inconclusiveness, and the third is non-existence.[1] U.

यस्माद्विषाणी तस्मादश्वः।। 16।।

Aph. 16. Because this has horns, therefore it is a horse.

An example is here given of the fallacies of want of proof of inclusion, of contrary arguments, and of went of proof respecting the nature of the argument.[2] U.

Where a hare or the like is the subject, and the being a horse that which is to be proved, and the notion of having horns the argument, in such a case there exist all the five fallacies.[3] V.

यस्माद्विषाणी तस्माद्गौरिति चानैकान्तिकस्योदाहरणम्।। 17।।

Aph. 17. And Because it has horns, therefore it is a cow is an example of the [fallacy of] plurality of consequents [or undistributed middle.]

स्वव्यथात्कत्वाचोपाधिः यथा पक्षे सन्दिग्धानेक्रान्तकत्वम् यदि हि तत्र न सन्देहस्तवा न पक्षता यदि पक्षता तदा सन्देहस्यावश्यकतया सन्दिग्धानैकान्तिकत्वध्रौव्यात् अवशिष्टं मयूखे ऽन्वेष्टव्यम्।।

1 इदानी वृत्तानां वर्तिष्यमाणाञ्च हेतूनां हेत्वाभासाद्विवेकाय हेत्वाभासप्रकरणमारभमाण आह। अप्रसिद्ध इति अव्याप्तो ऽगृहीतव्याप्तिको विपरीतव्याप्तिकश्च विरुद्धः एतेन व्याप्यत्वासिद्धविरुद्धयोः सङ्ग्रहः असन् इति पक्षे ऽसन् अपक्षधर्म इत्यर्थः स व क्वचित् स्वरूपविरहात् क्वचित् सन्देहसिषाधैयिषयोरभावात् सिद्धसाधने सन्दिग्ध इति पक्षे साध्यसदसत्त्वकोटिकसंशयजनकः स च संशयः संमानधर्मदर्शनात् क्वचिद-साधरणधर्मदर्शनात् क्वचित् पक्षे एव हेतोः साध्यतदभावसाहचर्यदर्शनात् आद्यः साधारणानैकान्तिकः द्वितीयस्त्वसाधारणानैकान्तिकः तृतीयो ऽनुपसंहारी।।

2 तत्र व्याप्यत्वासिद्धविरुद्धस्वरूपासिद्धानामुदाहरणमाह।।

3 यत्र शशादिः पक्षः अश्वत्वं साध्यं विषाणित्वं हेतुस्तत्र पञ्चैव हेतुदोषाः सन्ति।

Non-distribution is exemplified. Where takings as the subject a buffalo it is concluded that it is a cow because it has horns, there is general plurality of consequents [or possibilility of more than one conclusion.] Where it is argued that ether is eternal because sound exists in it, there is particular many-sidedness. So also in such examples as Sound is non-eternal because it is sound, there being no condition observed there is particular plurality of consequents. But when, by employment of argumentation to show that there exist no contrary instances, it is proved that the predicate is in the subject, and it is known to exist in parallel, instances there is a valid middle term; for the subject has parallel instances. An argument which is not ascertained to belong to the subject pervaded is the fallacy of the not certainly known or the unproved. This is of three kinds, want of proof regarding the included, want of proof regarding the nature [of the argument or middle term], and want of proof regarding the subject. Of these, want of proof regarding inclusion is where no invariable concomitance has been observed, whether because the concomitance though real has not been observed, or whether there be no concomitance. Hence the divisions of the unproved, such as absence of favourable probable reasonings. And this same fallacy of absence of proof may be divided a thousand ways according to the diversity of impossibility of predicate, impossibility of subject, impossibility of both subject and predicate, uncertainty or impossibility of predicate, uncertainty or impossibility of subject, and uncertainty or impossibility of predicate and subject. In every one of these cases there must arise absence of proof. Now this principle. I mean the argument, is of three kinds according to its division into the purely positive, the positive and negative, and the purely negative. Among these the purely positive is an attribute existing in all subjects of attributes, such as knowableness, nameableness, subjectibility, predicability, destruction of anything containing absolute non-existence of eternal substances and absolute non-existence by cessation of destructible qualities, etc. For there is no such thing as that in which these properties do not exist. The purely positive is therefore that which exists everywhere or that which cannot be absolute non-existence. Though these exist in themselves, that is no objection. It has been said, Validity of reasoning is recourse to existence, not the being different or indifferent. That argument, therefore, is purely positive, that which is to be proved by which is purely positive. Of this the four forms, existence of the subject, existence of similar instances, absence of contrary instances, and absence of contrary but equally susceptive subjects, lead to conviction. Of an argument positive and negative, together with non-existence of contrary instances, there are five forms; of the purely negative, together with the exclusion of existence of similar instances, there are four forms. An apparent argument of fallacy, is, therefore, that which is void of one or other of the forms which determine illative assurance; and similarly fallaciousness is voidness of one or other of the forms which determine illation. Doubt accompanied by assurance of the voidness of one or other of the forms prevents inference, and proves the inconclusiveness of the defendant's argument. Fallaciousness is not incident upon. voidness of one or other of the two arguments, the purely positive and the purely negative, because of the non-existence of that which leads to the conviction of there not being contrary instances in the purely positive, and of there being similar instances in the purely negative. Absence of proof respecting the subjects, respecting the nature of the argument, and partial inconclusiveness, are fallacies by reason of the absence of that form which is existence of the subject. Absence of proof of inclusion, self-contradiction, and general plurality of conse-quents, are fallacies due to the form which is non-existence of contrary instances. Particular diversity of result and non-exclusion are fallacies due to the failure of similar instances. Impossibility [where the predicate does not exist in the subject], and possibility of a contrary subject, are fallacies due to the absence of possibility and of impossibility of contrary subjects. In like manner accidentalness and inapplicability in an argument fail to determine illation, because of the absence of certainty of the non-existence of contrary instances. Absence of favourable, and unfavourable probable argumentation also fail to determine illation, because of the absence of certitude as to the non-existence of contrary instances. In like manner apparent but unreal examples inadequate in regard to that which is to be proved, or in regard to the argument, invalid as being fallacious, are so through the uncertainty of the existence of similar instances. If they are immediately invalid as being examples in appearance only, yet are they so mediately through the arguments on account of the uncertainty of the existence of similar instances. Arguments where neither positiveness nor negativeness can be shown, are concluded by urging the objection that time is insufficient or not to be obtained. Petitio principii, arguing in a circle, and arguments which involve an infinite regression, though they should afford conviction of a universal concomitance being deficient of one or other of the froms or conditions of valid argumentation, i.e., of existence of similar instances or non-existence of contrary instances, involve fallaciousness. The fallacy which gives rise to doubt with respect to the alternatives of the existence or non-existence of the predicate in the subjects, is that of including too much or too little in the enunciation of a sumption . The fallacy which results in certainty of the non-existence of that which is to be proved in the subject, is the contradictory Absence of certain knowledge of what are the attributes of a subject of a genearal proposition, is the unproved. But in the opinion of Kāśyapa the impossible and the existence of contrary but equally valid subjects, are not independent fallacies. Of these the impossible is determined to be included in absence of proof as regards the subject, or plurality of consequents. Therefore it has been said, An impossible or too extensive attribute of the subject as an argument, leads to diverse results. Valid counter-subject also, showing the doubtfulness of the universal concomitance he determines to be included in plurality of consequents. The author of the Vṛtti asserts that the particle and in the aphorism, Fallacious arguments are the unproved, the non-existent and the dubious, implies the addition of the impossible, and possibility of a real cont-radictory subject. He therefore follows the doctrine of Gautama : The five merely apparent arguments are that of which the extension is too great or too small, that which involves a contradiction, that which is identical with the subject, that which is identical with the major term, and that the time of which is the past. But the author's own view of the fallacious appears from such statements as that Kāśyapa declared the self-contradictory, the unproved, and the doubtful to be no arguments, and the particle and in reality serves to connect the aphorism with the preceding aphorisms. Prolixity has been avoided in this note from fear of needlessly encumbering the treatise. Full details may be sought in the Mayūkha.[1] U.

[1] अनैकान्तिकमुदाहरति। यत्र महिषं पक्षयित्वा अयं गौर्विषाणित्वादिति साधयति तत्र साधारणानौकान्तिकता तदा त्वाकाशं नित्यं शब्दाश्रयत्वादिति साधयति तदा ऽस्यासाधरणानैकान्तिकता एवं शब्दो ऽनित्यः शब्दत्वाद्रित्याद्यप्यगृह्यमाणदशायामसाधारणानैकान्तिकमेव यदा तु विपक्षबाधकतर्कावतारात् पक्ष एव साध्यं सिध्येत् तदा सपक्षवृत्तिताज्ञानदशायां सद्धेतुरेव पक्षस्यापि सपक्षत्वात् तत्र व्याप्तपक्षधर्मतया ऽप्रमितो ऽसिद्धः स एव त्रिविधः व्याप्यत्वासिद्धः स्वरूपासिद्धः आश्रयासिद्धश्च तत्रागृहीतव्याप्तिको व्याप्यत्वासिद्धः सत्या एव व्याप्तेरग्रहात् व्याप्तेरभावाच्च उभयथा ऽपि तेनानुकूलतर्काभावादयो ऽसिद्धभेदः स चायमसमर्थ-विशेषणासमर्थविशेष्यासमर्थोभयसन्दिग्धासमर्थविशेषणसन्दिग्धासमर्थविशेष्यसन्दिग्धासमर्थोभयभेदप्रपञ्चेन सहस्त्रधा भिद्यते सर्वत्र नात्र सिद्धिविरह एवोद्भाव्यः। अत्रेदं तत्त्वं हेतुस्तावत् केवलान्वय्यन्वय-

आत्मेन्द्रियार्थसन्निकर्षाद्यन्निष्पद्यते तदन्यत्।। 18।।

The existence of the soul proved

Aph. 18. That which is effectuated from the connection of soul with objects of sense is other [than a fallacious argument].

The result of the distinction drawn between fallacies is now stated. It is by connection of the soul with objects of sense that knowledge is produced; and knowledge, the argument for existence of the soul, is other than the unproved, the contradictory, and plurality of consequents, i.e., it is not an argument in appearance only. Knowledge, then, is in two ways a mark of the existence of the soul; either because kowledge must exist in knowing subject, because it is an effect, like colour, or because it assumes the form of recollection, I who saw am the same as I who am touching. In the former case, that knowledge is an effect is not unproved,

व्यतिरेकिकेवलव्यतिरेकिभेदात् त्रिविधः तत्र सर्वधर्मिगतो धर्मः केवलान्वयी यथा प्रसेवत्वाभिधेयत्व-विशेष्यत्वविशेषणत्वनित्यद्रव्यात्यन्ताभावाश्रयनाशनाश्यगुणादिध्वंसात्यन्ताभावादयः न ह्यस्ति तादृशं किञ्चित् यत्रैते धर्मा न विद्यन्ते तथा च सर्वगतत्वम् अत्यन्ताभावप्रतियोगित्वं वा केवलान्वयित्वं एतेषाञ्च स्वात्मवृत्तित्वे ऽपि न दोषः तदुक्तं प्रमाणं वृतौ न भिन्नाभिन्नते यतः इति केवलान्वयिसाधको हेतुः केवलान्वयी अस्य च पक्षसत्वसपक्षसत्त्वाबाधितत्वासत्प्रतिपक्षितत्वानि चत्वारि रूपाणि गमकत्वौपयिकानि अन्वयव्यतिरेकिणस्तु हेतोर्विपक्षासत्त्वेन सह पञ्च केवलव्यतिरेकिणः सपक्षत्वव्यतिरेकेण चत्वारि तथा च यस्य हेतोर्यावन्ति रूपाणि गमकात्वौपयिकानि तदन्यतररूपहीनः स हेतुराभासः एवञ्च गमकतौपयिकान्यतररूपशून्यत्वं हेत्वाभासत्वं तेनान्यतररूपशून्यत्वस्य निश्चयवत्सन्देहो ऽप्यनुमितिप्रतिबन्धकः वादिहेतोरसाधकतासाधकः न च केवलान्वयिकेवलव्यतिरेकिणोर्हेत्वोरन्यतररूपशून्यतया हेत्वाभासत्वापत्तिः केवलान्वयिनि विपक्षासत्त्वस्य केवलव्यतिरेकिणि सपक्षसत्त्वस्य गमकत्वौषयिकत्वाभावात् एवञ्चाश्रयासिद्धस्वरूपासिद्धभागासिद्धानां पक्षसत्त्वरूपविरहादाभासत्वं व्याप्यत्वासिद्धविसद्धसाधारणानैकान्तिकानां विपक्षासत्त्वरूपवैकल्वात् असाधारणनैकान्तिकानुपसंहारिणोः सपक्षसत्त्ववैकल्यात् बाधितसत्याप्रतिपक्षितयोरबाधितत्वासत्प्रतिपक्षितत्वविरहात् एवं सोपाधित्वाप्रयोजकत्वयोरपि विपक्षासत्त्वनिश्चयाभावादगमकत्वं अनुकूलतर्काभावप्रतिकूलतर्कयोरपि विपक्षासत्त्वनिश्चयविरहात् एवं साध्यविकलसाधनविकलोभयविकलदृष्टान्ताभासानां यदि हेत्वाभासविधया दोषत्वं तदा सपक्षसत्त्वानिश्चयात् यदि स्वातन्त्र्येण दृष्टान्ताभासतया तथापि द्वारं हेतोः सपक्षसत्त्वानिश्चय एव अनुपदर्शितान्वयानुप्रदर्शितव्यातिरेकास्तु न्यूनाप्राप्तनिग्रहस्थानपयवसन्ना एव आत्माश्रयान्योन्या-श्रयचक्रकानवस्थास्तु व्याप्तिनिश्चयं विघटयन्तः सपक्षसत्त्वविपक्षासत्त्वान्यतररूपविकला एव हेत्वाभासतामासादयन्ति तत्र पक्षे साध्यसदसत्त्वकोटिकसंशयजनको हेत्वाभासः सव्यभिचारः पक्षे साध्याभावनिश्चयफलको हेत्वाभासो विरुद्धः व्याप्तिपक्षधर्मताप्रमितिविरहे ऽसिद्धः बाधसत्प्रतिपक्षौ काश्यपे मते न स्वतन्त्रौ तत्र बाध आश्रयासिद्धावनैकान्तिके वा पर्यव्रसति तदुक्तं बाधायामपक्षधर्मो हेतुरनैकान्तिको वा इति सत्प्रतिपक्षो ऽन्यतरत्र व्याप्यादिसंशयमापादयन अनैकान्तिकादावेव पर्यवसति वृत्तिकारस्तु अप्रसिद्धो ऽनपदेशो ऽसन् सन्दिग्धश्चानप्रदेशः इति सूत्रस्थचकारस्य बाधसत्प्रतिपक्षसमुच्चयार्थतामाह तेन सव्यभिचारविरुद्धप्रकरणसमसाध्यसमातीतकालाः पञ्च हेत्वाभासा इति गौतमीयमेव मतमनुधावति परन्तु विमद्धासिद्धसन्दिग्धमलिङ्गं काश्यपो ऽब्रवीत् इत्याद्यभिधानात् सूत्रकारस्वरसो हेत्वाभासत्रित्वे चकारिस्तूक्तसमुच्चयार्थ इति तत्त्वम् ग्रन्थगौरवभयात् प्रपञ्चो न कृतो मयूखे विस्तरो ऽन्वेष्टव्यः।।

knowledge being designated in the text as that which is produced; nor is it contradictory, for there can be no contradiction with regard to what is universally observed; and on the same grounds it is not many-sided. Knowledge, then, mediately through its nature as being an effect or an attribute, is a mark of the existence of the soul. Again recollection being excluded from diverse agents is limited to a single agency.[1] U.

प्रवृत्तिनिवृत्तिश्च प्रत्यगात्मनि दृष्टे परत्र लिङ्गम्।। 19।।

Plurality of souls

Aph. 19. Activity and inactivity observed in one's own soul are the mark of the existence of other souls.

The inference of the existence of soul being explained, the mode in which the existence of other souls is inferred, is now stated. Activity and inactivity generated by desire and aversion are modes of volition. By activity and inactivity bodily functions having for their end attainment of the pleasant and avoidance of the unpleasant, and characterised by muscular action, are produced. Therefore when we see muscular action in the body of another, we infer in the following manner the existence of another soul. This muscular action is generated by volition, being a muscular action like our own muscular action; and this volition is produced by, or exists in soul, being a volition like our own volitions.[2] U.

Though in going and other actions activity only, and not inactivity, is seen to be the cause, yet muscular action in such forms as the expulsion of insects with a fly-flapper from places of resort for the sake of inactivity in regard to injury, is observed. There is, therefore no want of proof that inactivity is a motive of muscular actions.[3] V.

1 इदानीं हेत्वाभासविवेचनस्य फलमाह। आत्मेन्द्रियार्थसन्निकषात्तावज्ज्ञानमुत्पद्यते तच्चात्मनि लिङ्गम् असिद्धिविरुद्धानैकान्तिकेभ्यो ऽन्यत् अनाभासमित्यर्थः। तथाहि ज्ञानमात्मन्युभयथा लिङ्गम् ज्ञानं क्वचिदाश्रितं कार्यत्वाद्रूपादिवदिति वा प्रत्यभिज्ञारूपतया वा यो ऽहमद्राक्षं सो ऽहं स्पृशामीति तत्र ज्ञानगतं कार्यत्वं नासिद्धं यन्निष्पद्यत इत्यभिधानात् न विरुद्धं सामान्यतो दृष्टे ऽत्र विरोधाभावात् न चानैकान्तिकं तत एव तथा च स्वगतकार्यत्वगुणत्वद्वारा सामान्यतो दृष्टेन ज्ञानमेवात्मनि लिङ्गम् प्रत्यभिज्ञानन्तु भिन्नकर्तृकेभ्यो व्यावर्तमातमेककर्तृकतायां पर्यवस्यति।।

2 आत्मन्यनुमानमभिधाय इदानीं परात्मानुमानमाह। प्रत्यगात्मनीति स्वात्मनीत्यर्थः इच्छाद्वेषजनिते प्रवृत्तिनिवृत्ती प्रयत्नविशेषौ ताभ्याञ्च हिताहितप्राप्तिपरिहारफलके शरीरकर्मणी चेष्टालक्षणे जन्येते तथा च परशरीरे चेष्टां दृष्टवा इयं चेष्टा प्रयत्नजन्या चेष्टात्वात् मदीयचेष्टावत् न च प्रयत्न आत्मजन्यः आत्मनिष्ठो वा प्रयत्नत्वात् मदीयप्रयत्नवदिति परात्मानुमानम्।।

3 यद्यपि गमनादिक्रियायां प्रवृत्तिरेव हेतुर्दृश्यते न तु निवृत्तिरिति तथापि हिंसादिनिवृत्तितो गन्तव्यदेशावस्थितानां क्षुद्रजन्तूनां व्याजनादिना अप्रसारणादिरूपा चेष्टा ऽपि दृश्यते एवेति नानुपपत्तिः।।

SECOND DAILY LESSON

आत्मेन्द्रियार्थसन्निकर्षे ज्ञानस्य भावोऽभावश्च मनसो लिङ्गम्।। 1।।

Examination of the ternal sensory

Aph. 1. Existence and non-existence of knowledge on contact of the soul with the objects of sense, are the mark of the existence of an internal organ.

Distinction of real and fallacious arguments is the object of the preceding daily lesson. In order now to bring the investigation of soul to a conclusion, by a breach of the order of enunciation (i.e., of the order in which the substances were enumerated), an examination of the internal organ is instituted. It will be shown that movement of this organ is the mark of the existence of the soul. If the interior sensory be examined as being an instrument of cognition, and as having form, then soul is proved to exist as that by which the internal organ is actuated when it is brought into connection with an organ of sense apprehe̅rsive of its proper object in consequence of the other organ. This is the reason of the breach of the order of enumeration. That is the internal organ which being in connection with an organ of sense, when there is contact of the soul and an object of sense, knowledge exists or comes into being, and which not being in connection with an organ of sense knowledge does not exist, or does not come into being. It may be argued that though the internal organ were an all-pervading substance, all cognition would not necessarily be simultaneous, because of its property as an instrument; further, that the internal organ is an all-pervading substance, because, like time, it is a substance void of any peculiar attribute; because, like soul, it is the site of conjunction with the non-coinhesive cause of knowledge; because, like ether, it possesses absolute negation of sound; and so forth. If this argument to prove that it is an all-pervading substance be adduced, we reply that were the linternal sensory an all-pervading substance, then as it would be in contact with all sensual organs, cognition would be one only and composed of all sensation. If it be replied that such is not the case because there is a contrariety among the effects, we deny this, for the instrument is not concerned with contrariety or non-contrariety, so that one should be aprehensive of a contrariety between visibility and sapidity and the rest, or that there should be a variegated form, as there is a variegated colour. If you object that there is a plurality of simultaneous sensations in the case of eating a long ear of corn [which is at once seen and tasted] we deny this, for in that case also distraction is observed. If you ask how it is that you are conscious of synchronous perception of colour, taste, smell, and touch, we reply that neither is this the case, for this is merely a sense of simultaneity in five cognitions represented in memory and produced successively by the rapidly shifting internal organ. If be urged that the distraction depends on the property of the instrument, we deny this, for the answer has been already stated. If it be maintained that the distraction depends on the desire of knowing, we deny this, for on that supposition it would follow that when there was a desire to know all there would be a total presentation of all objects, whereas the only result of a desire to know is connection of the internal organ with the sense organ percipient of its proper object. Inasmuch, therefore, as non-simultaneity of cognition would be otherwise impossible, the internal organ is proved to possess atomic dimension.[1] U.

तस्य द्रव्यत्वनित्यत्वे वायुना व्याख्याते ।। 2 ।।

Aph. 2. Its substantiality and eternity are explained by air.

It may be urged that the internal organ which is proved to exist by

[1] हेतुहेत्वाभासविवेक आह्निकार्थः। इदानीमात्मपरीक्षाशेषं वर्तयिष्यन् उद्देशक्रमलङ्घनेन मनःपरीक्षामवतारयन्नाह। मनोगतिमात्मनो लिङ्गं वक्ष्यति तद् यदि मनो ज्ञानकरणत्वेन मूर्तत्वेन च परीक्षितं भवति तदा यत्प्रेरितं मन इन्द्रियान्तरादभिमतविषयग्राहिणि इन्द्रिये सम्बध्यते स आत्मेति सिद्धं भवतीत्येतदर्थं क्रमलङ्घनम्। आत्मेन्द्रियार्थसन्निकर्षे सति यस्मिन् इन्द्रियसन्निकृष्टे ज्ञानस्य भाव उत्पादः असन्निकृष्टे ज्ञानस्याभावो ऽनुत्पादस्तन्मन् इत्यर्थः ननु मनोवैभवे ऽपि करणधर्मत्वादेव ज्ञानायौगपद्यमुपपद्यते किञ्च मनो विभु विशेषगुणशून्यद्रव्यत्वात् कालवत् ज्ञानासमवायिकारणसंयोगाधारत्वादात्मवत् स्पर्शात्यन्ताभाववत्त्वादाकाशवदित्यादि वैभवसाधकं प्रमाणमिति चेत् मैवं यदि मनो विभु स्यात् तदा सर्वेन्द्रियसन्निकृष्टात् ततः सर्वेन्द्रियसन्निकृष्टात् ततः सर्वेन्द्रियकमेकमेव ज्ञानं स्यात् कार्यविरोधान्नैवमिति चेन्न न हि सामग्री विरोधाविरोधमाकलयति येन चाक्षुषत्वरासनत्वादिविरो-धाय बिभ्येत् चित्ररूपवत् चित्राकारमेव वा स्यात् भवत्येव दीर्घशष्कुलीभक्षणस्थले इति चेन्न तत्रापि व्यासङ्गदर्शनात् तर्हि रूपरसगन्धस्पर्शान् युगपत् प्रत्येमीति कथमनुव्यवसाय इति चेन्न शीघ्रसञ्चारिमनोजनितेषु पञ्चसु स्मृत्युपनीतज्ञानेषु यौगपद्याभिमानात् व्यासङ्गो ऽपि करणधर्माधीन इति चेन्न उक्तोत्तरत्वात् बुभुत्साधीनो व्यासङ्ग इति चेन्न सर्वबुभुत्सायां सर्वविषयकसर्वोदयप्रसङ्गात् बुभुत्सावा अपि अभिमतार्थग्राहीन्द्रियमनः सम्बन्ध-मात्रफलकत्वात् तस्माज्ज्ञानायौगपद्यान्यथानुपपत्त्या सिध्यति अणु मनः।।

the inference that a sense of pleasure etc.. is effected by an instrument because it is an action, like the sense of colour etc., or because simultaneous cognition is impossible, is proved to exist as an instrument: whence, than, its substantiality and eternity? It is therefore stated that, as an aerial atom inferred to exist by reason of the compound substance air, is a substance because it possesses qualities and actions, so the internal sensory inferred from impossibility of simultaneous cognitions is a substance because it possesses qualities. For without conjunction with the organs of sense it would not be productive of cognition, so that there would be no possession of qualities. Moreover presentation of pleasure etc., must have a sensitive organ as its instrument, because, like the presentation of colour etc., it is a presentation. Therefore the internal sensory is proved to exist as an organ. The nature of an organ is to be a site of conjunction of the internal sensory with the cause of a cognition. It is therefore established without any difficulty that the internal organ is a substance. Its eternity is proved by its having no substratum; and that it has no substratum follows from the absence of any warrant in imagining portions constituent of it.[1] U.

As there is an aerial atom substantiality, inasmuch as it possesses originative conjunction and other attributes; and eternity, inasmuch as there is no warrant for assuming that it has constituent parts; so the substantiality and eternity of the internal organ follow from its possession of conjunction productive of cognition, and its possession of other attributes, and from absence of proof of its production and destruction.[2] V.

प्रयत्नायौगपद्याज्ज्ञानायौगपद्याच्चैकम् ।। 3 ।।

Aph. 3. Because of non-simultaneity of volitions, and non-simultaneity of cognitions it is one [in each body].

[1] ननु सुखाद्युपलब्धिः करणसाध्या क्रियात्वात् रूपोपलब्धिवदित्याद्यनुमानात् युगपज्ज्ञानानुपपत्त्या च यन्मनः सिद्धं तत्करणतया तथा च तस्य द्रव्यत्वं नित्यत्वञ्च कुत इत्यत आह। यथा ऽवयविद्रव्यानुमितो वायुपरमाणुर्गुणवत्त्वात् क्रियावत्त्वाच्च द्रव्यम् तथा युगपज्ज्ञानानुपपत्त्या ऽनुमितं मनो गुणवत्त्वाद्द्रव्यं न हि तस्य इन्द्रियसंयोगान्तरेण ज्ञानोत्पादकत्वं येन गुणवत्त्वं न स्यात् किञ्च सुखादिसाक्षात्कार इन्द्रियकरणकः साक्षात्कारत्वात् रूपादिसाक्षात्कारवदितीन्द्रयत्वेन मनः सिद्धम् इन्द्रियत्वं ज्ञानकारणमनःसंयोगाश्रयत्वमित्ययत्रसिद्धमेव मनसो द्रव्यत्वम् नित्यत्वञ्च तस्यानाश्रिततत्वात् तस्यावयवकल्पनायां प्रमाणाभावादनाश्रितत्वमिति।।

[2] यथा वायवीयपरमाणौ आरम्भकसंयोगादिरूपगुणवत्त्वाद् द्रव्यत्वं तदवयवकल्पनायां प्रमाणभावान्नित्यत्वं तथा ज्ञानजनकसंयोगादिरूपगुणवत्त्वात् तदुत्पदिविनाशयोः प्रमाणभावाच्च मनस्यपि द्रव्यत्वं नित्यत्वञ्चेत्यर्थः।।

A decision is stated with reference to the doubt whether internal organ be one in individual bodies or more than one. The words internal organs and in each body are to be supplied. If there were in each single body many internal organs or common sensories there would be simultaneity of cognitions and volitions.The opinion that many volitions are simultaneously exerted, since we see simultaneous action in the arms, legs, fingers and toes of a dancer, is erroneous, for this arises merely from the rapid transition of the internal organ.[1] U.

The unity of the internal organ in individual bodies is established. When there is conjunction between the mind and any member of the body a volition is exerted in restriction to that member, and not in restriction to other members. It must not, therefore, be said that there being a plurality of internal sensories two volitions may be simultaneously exerted, because conjunction between the mind and each of two members at the same time is possible; and that as determined by the ten fingers and ten toes twenty acts of volition are produced at the same time [for otherwise how would the corresponding actions be produced?]; for the feeling of simultaneity in those actions, as of that in the scattering of the hundred petals of a lotus, is illusory inasmuch as they are produced in successive moments merely by the rapid transition of the internal sensory. So, if the internal organ were manifold, then since each internal organ might be in conjunction with synchronous sensations of smell, taste etc. simultaneous production of cognitions derived from the organs of smell, taste etc. would be possible. The internal sensory therefore, is in each individual body one only and not manifold. If it be objected that the internal organ must necessarily be manifold since we observe action in the two parts of a scorpion and the like when cut in two, we reply that this is not the case, for such action is possible through the mere accession of a new internal organ by the influence of requitative efficacy; and because a plurality of internal organs cannot be allowed, as is evidenced by the non-simultaneity of volition, and non-simultaneity of cognitions. Some have held that simultaneity and non-simultaniety of volitions to cognitions are the result of the contraction and expansion of the inner organ after the manner of a tortoise and an elephant's trunk. This is not satisfactory, for the hypothesis of endless particles, of their previous

[1] तत् किं प्रतिशरीरमेकमनेकं वेति सन्देहे निर्णायकमाह। मनः प्रतिशरीरमिति शेषः यद्येकैकस्मिन्नपि शरीरे बहूनि मनांसि स्युस्तदां ज्ञानप्रयत्नानां यौगपद्यं स्यात् यत्तु नर्तकीकरचरणाङ्गुलीषु युगपत् कर्मदर्शनाद्युगपदेव बहवः प्रयत्ना उत्पद्यन्ते इति मतं तदयुक्तं मनसः शीघ्रसञ्चारादेव तदुपपत्तेः।।

and subsequent non-existences, and of their endless atoms is too operose.[1] V.

प्राणापाननिमेषोन्मेषजीवनमनोगतीन्द्रियान्तरविकाराः सुखदुःखेच्छाद्वेषप्रयत्नाश्च चात्मनो लिङ्गानि।। 4।।

Existence of soul proved.

Aph. 4. The ascending and descending vital airs, the opening and closing of the eyes, life, motions of the internal organ, affections of the other organs of sense, pleasure ans pain, desire and aversion, and volition, are marks of the existence of soul.

The completion of the remainder of the inquiry into the soul is commenced; showing the purpose of the transgression of the order in which the substances were enumerated. It is not to be supposed that consciousness or knowledge alone is the mark of the existence of the soul. The ascending vital air and the rest also are marks of the existence of the soul. For that is soul in consequence of the volition of which the upward and downward motions in the air moving within the body, and known as the upward and downward vital air, take place, not being produced otherwise than by volition, just as the throwing upwards and downwards of a pestle etc. in a mortar etc., is not produced without volition. For the nature of this air which is to move horizontally could not be thus changed except by volition. Nor can it be objected that two airs with differently directed motion may, like two pieces of confluent water, have an upward motion. Were this the case there would be an upward but not a downward motion, or in exsufflations and the like there would be horizontal motion. There is then a being, who, by his volition, impels the vital air upwards or downwards. It is no valid

[1] प्रतिशरीरं मनस एकत्वं व्यवस्थापयति। यदङ्गेन मनसः संयोगो यदा भवति तदा तदङ्गावच्छेदेन प्रयत्न उत्पद्यते नान्यावच्छेदेन एवञ्च मनसो नानात्वे एकदा ऽङ्गद्वयेनापि एकैकस्य मनसः संयोगसम्भवात् प्रयत्नद्वयमुत्पद्यते न च विंशत्यङ्गुल्यवच्छेदेन एकदैव विंशतिः प्रयत्ना उत्पद्यन्ते कथमन्यथा एकदैव तेषां क्रिया उत्पद्यन्ते वाच्यम् उत्पलपत्रशतव्यतिभेद इव तासु यौगपद्यप्रतीतेर्भ्रमरूपत्वात् मनस आशु सञ्चारादेव भिन्नभिन्नक्षणेषु तामामुत्पादात् एवं मनसो नानात्वे युगपदेव घ्राणरसनादिभिः सह तेषामेकैकस्य संयोगसम्भवात् घ्राणजरासनादीनामपि युगपदुत्पादापत्तिरितः प्रतिशरीरं मन एकमेव न तु नानेत्यर्थः। ननु छिन्नवृश्चिकादिखण्डद्वय एव क्रियादर्शनान्मनसो नानत्वमावश्यकमिति चेन्न तदानीमदृष्टवशेन मनोऽन्तरसन्निवेशादेव तत्सम्भवात् अन्यत्र प्रयत्नयौगपद्यस्य ज्ञानायौगपद्यस्य च प्रामाणिकत्वेन मनसो नानात्वस्वीकारस्य कर्तुमशक्यत्वादिति। कूर्मशुण्डादिवन्मनसः सङ्कोचविकाशाभ्यामेव प्रयत्नानां ज्ञानानाञ्च यौगपद्यायौगपद्ययोर्निवाहः ऐकमेवैकस्मिन् शरीरे मन इति केचित् तदपि न मनोरमम् अनन्तावयवानां तत्प्रागभावानां तत्प्रध्वंसानाम् अनन्ततत्परमाणूनाञ्च कल्पने महागौरवादिति संक्षेपः।।

objection to ask how there could be upward and downward motions of the vital air in a condition of dreamless sleep ; for at that time though volition proper does not exist, there exists another kind of volition, which is called automatic conation. In like manner the opening and closing of the eyes causes us to infer a ruler of the body, for closing the eyes is an action productive of conjunction of the eyelids, and the opening of the eyes is an action productive of disjunction of the eyelids. These to actions being constantly manifested without any visible cause such as motive force, are not produced otherwise than by conation. As the dancing of a doll depends upon the volition of a subject willing, so also does the movement of the eyelids. Therefore a being who exerts volition is inferred. Similarly vitality as a mark of the existence of the soul, for by the word life the effects of vitality such as growth, reparation of muscular lesion etc., are indicated by implication. For as the owner of a house builds up the broken edifice or enlarges a building which is too small, so the ruler of the body effects by food etc., the increase or enlargement of the body which in to him in the stead of a habitation, and with medicine and the like causes what is wounded to grow again, and partially dissevered hands or feet to re-coalesce. Thus like the master of a house is proved a guardian of the body. In a like manner the motions of the internal sensory are also a mark of the existence of the soul. For it has been shown in the foregoing section that the internal organ is possessed of form and of indivisibility. Its appliance to an instrument of sense cognisant of its proper object, depends on desire and effort. the desire and effort which actuate the internal organ are inferred to be identical with the soul. This may be exemplified by a child standing in a corner of a room, who throws a ball or a handful of red powder about the room. It may be objected that the dancer of the doll, the master of the house, and the child are not other than body that they should be examples, and that it is in the body that consciousness resides, inasmuch as the body is an object of self-consciousness the conviction of being pale, stout and the like is produced by the juxta-position of the dody with self-consciousness. Moreover, (it may be urged), that which was experienced in childhood is remembered in youth or in old age, whereas in the case of separate bodies as those of Chaitra and Maitra there would be no act of memory, as it is said, One man remembers not that which another saw. In the latter case there will be no recollection, because Chaitra and Maitra are the offspring of different parents; but though childhood and youth be different, the act of recollection will take place in the order of cause and effect, because there is but one individual.To this we reply that it would follow on the same premisses, that the son would remember what was experienced by the father. If it be rejoined that perception of difference of body prevents this, we reply that an old man, by having a body different from that which he had as a child, through perception of his body would be incapable of remembeing what he experienced as a child. A child that never knew his father has no perception of difference of body. The notion my body as generally in the case of the word my belongs to the self-consciousness. If you reply that so also does the notion my soul, we reply that such is not the case, for the word my is usual tropically, since the genitive may be used where no numerical difference is implied as in the case of Rāhu's head [where Rāhu and Rāhu's head are one and the same thing]. Moreover on your supposition there would result the loss of merits and requital unmerited, for the body is constantly different in the transmigratory state; but it is admitted that the harm done by a conscious subject, connot have its the result unfulfilled. It is also inferred from affections of the other organs that there is a soul, for after experiencing the particular taste which accompanies the particular colour of an orange or *chira-villa* fruit, on again observing such fruit, there arises in one desirous of tasting it a watering in the mouth. This can only take place by an inference respecting the acid flavour, the inference only by recalling the invariable coexistence of the colour and taste, the revocation only by a permanent impression, the permanent impression only by experience of the universal co-existence, and experience only by seeing it repeatedly; and this series of cognitions, in the order, of cause and effect is impossible unless there be one and the same agent in all. Accordingly the aphorism of Gautama, From the affection of other organs of sense. Pleasure and the like are also to be regarded, like knowledge, as arguments of the existence of the soul. For pleasure and the like must inhere in something, that is, reside in some substratum, being products or qualities like colour etc. Hence a general inference accompanied by a residual inference takes for its object inherence in a substance other than eight substances. For the proposition that desire, which does not inhere in earth and seven other substances, inheres in a substance, is incomplete unless it assumes as its object inhesion in a substance other than those eight substances. But if the residual method be not first employed, inhesion in a substance other than eight substances will have to be argued by negative probation and thus the division will be made. It is absurd to say that inference has for its form only that which is essential to universal coexistence, for that is the form of conviction without which the conviction is incomplete. Otherwise there could be no inference having for its object inhesion in what is uncaused, such as that a binary atomic aggregate which does not inhere in anything caused or produced, inheres in something, because it is composite.[1] U.

[1] इदानीं क्रमलङ्घनप्रयोजनमादर्शयन्नेवात्मपरीक्षाशेषं वर्तयिष्यन्नाह प्रसिद्धिर्ज्ञानमेव केवलमात्मनो लिङ्गमिति न मन्तव्यं प्राणादयो ऽपि सन्ति आत्मनो लिङ्गानि तथाहि शरीरान्तश्चारिणि समीरणे ग्राणापानलक्षणे ऊर्ध्वाधोगती उत्क्षेपणावक्षेपणे मुशलादाविव प्रयत्नं विना ऽनुपपद्यमाने यस्य प्रयत्नाद्भवतः स नूनमात्मा न हि तिर्यग्गमनस्वभावस्य वायोरेवं स्वभावविपर्ययो विना प्रयत्नात् न च विरूद्धदिक्क्रियोर्वाय्वोः सलिलयोरिवोर्ध्वगतिः स्यादिति वाच्यम् एवं सत्यूर्ध्वगमनमेव स्यान्न त्वधोगमनं फूत्कारादौ वा तिर्यग्गमनम् तथा चास्ति कश्चित् यः प्रयत्नेन वायुमूर्ध्वमधो वा प्रेरयति सुषुप्तिदशायां कथं प्राणापानयोरूर्ध्वाधोगती इति चेन्न तदानीं योग्यप्रयत्नाभावे ऽपि प्रयत्नान्तरस्य सद्भावात् स एव जीवनयोनिः प्रयत्न इत्युच्यते एवं निमेषोन्मेषावपि शरीर स्याधिष्ठातारमनुमापयतः तथाहि निमेषस्तावत् अक्षिपक्ष्मणोः संयोगजनकं कर्म्मउन्मेषस्तयोरेव विभागजनकं कर्म्म एते च कर्म्मणी नोदलाभिघातादि दृष्टिकारणमन्तरेण निरन्तरमुत्पद्यमाने प्रयत्नं विना नोत्पद्येते यथा दारुपुत्रकनर्त्तनं कस्यचित् प्रयत्नात् तथा ऽक्षिपत्त्मनर्त्तनमपि तेन प्रयत्नवाननुमीयते एवं जीवनमप्यात्मलिङ्गं नथाहि जीवनपदेन लक्षणया जीवनकार्य्यं वृद्धिक्षतभग्नसंरोहणादि लक्षयति तथाच यथा गृहपतिर्भरनस्य गृहस्य निर्म्माणं करोति लघीयो वा गृहं वर्द्धयति तथा देहाधिष्ठाता गृहस्थानीयस्य देहत्याहारादिना वृद्धिमुपचयं करोति क्षतञ्च भेषजादिना प्ररोहयति भग्नञ्च करचरणादि संरोहयति तथा च गृहपतिरिव देहस्याप्यधिष्ठाता सिध्यतीति एवं मनोगतिरप्यात्मलिङ्गं तथाहि मनस्तावन्मूर्त्तमणु चेति पूर्वप्रकरणे साधितम् तस्य चाभिमतविषयग्राहिणि इन्द्रिये निवेशनम् इच्छाप्रणिधानाधीनत् तथा च यस्येच्छाप्रणिधाने मनः प्रेरयतः स आत्मेत्यनुमीयते यथा गृहकोणावस्थितो दारकः कन्दुकं लाक्षागुटकं वा गृहाभ्यन्तर एव इतस्ततः प्रेरयति ननु दारुपुत्रनर्त्तयिता गृहपतिर्दारको वा न शरीरादन्यो यो दृष्टान्तः स्यात् किञ्च शरीरमेव चैतन्याश्रयः अहङ्कारास्पदत्वात् भवति हि गौरोऽहं स्थूलोऽहमित्याद्यहङ्कारसामानाधिकरण्ये न प्रत्ययः यत्तु बाल्येऽनुभूतं यौवने वार्द्धके वा स्मरति तत्र चैत्रमैत्रवच्छरीरभेदेऽपि स्मरणं न स्यात् नान्यदृष्टं स्मरत्यन्य इति तत्र चैत्रमैत्रयोर्भिन्नसन्तानत्वेन प्रतिसन्धानं माऽस्तुबाल्यकौमारभेदेऽपि सन्तानैकत्वात् कार्य्यकारणभावेन प्रतिसन्धानमुपपत्स्यत इति तत्र ब्रूमः पित्राऽनुभूतस्य पुत्रेणापि स्मरणप्रसङ्गः तत्र शरीरभेदग्रहो बाधक इति चेत् वृद्धेन बालशरीराद्भेदेनैव स्वशरीरस्य ग्रहात् प्रतिसन्धानानुपपत्तेः अनुपलब्धपितृकस्य बालस्य शरीरभेदाग्रहस्यापि सत्त्वात् मम शरीरमिति मम कारसामान्येनाहङ्कारस्य भानात् ममात्मेत्यत्रापि तथेति चेन्न तत्र मम कारस्यौपचारिकत्वात् राहोःशिर इतिवदभेदेऽपि षष्ट्युपपत्तेः हिंसादिफलञ्च कर्त्तरिनस्यात् शरीरस्यान्यान्यत्वात् पातकमिच्छतोभूतचैतनिकस्य कृतहानमकृताभ्यागमश्च दोष इति दिक् इन्द्रियान्तरविकारात् खल्वपि दृश्यते हि नारङ्गस्य चिरविल्वस्य वा रूपविशेषसहचरितं रसविशेषमनुभूय पुनस्तादृशं फलमुपलभमानस्य रसगद्धिप्रवर्त्तितो दन्तोदकसंल्पवः स च नाम्लरसानुमितिमन्तरेण अनुमितिर्न व्याप्तिस्मृतिमन्तरेण सा च न संस्कारं विना स च न व्याप्त्यनुभवमन्तरेण स च न भूयोदर्शनमन्तरेणेति इयं ज्ञानपरम्परा नैकं कर्त्तारमन्तरेण कार्य्यकारणभूता सम्भवतीति तथा च गौतमीयं सूत्रम् इन्द्रियान्तरविकारात् इति सुखादयश्च ज्ञानवदेवात्मलिङ्गानि द्रष्टव्याः तथाहि सुखादिकं क्वचिदाश्रितं द्रव्याश्रितं वा कार्य्यवस्तुत्वात् गुणत्वाद्वा रूपादिवदितीतरबाधसहकृतं समान्यतोदृष्टमेव अष्टद्रव्यातिरिक्तद्रव्याश्रितत्वं विषयीकरोति नहि पृथिव्याद्यष्टकानाश्रिता इच्छा द्रव्याश्रितेति प्रतिज्ञा अष्टद्रव्यातिरिक्तद्रव्याश्रितत्वं प्रकारमनादाय पर्य्यवस्यति यत्र तु प्रथमं न बाधावतारस्तत्राष्टद्रव्यातिरिक्तद्रव्या–

तस्य द्रव्यत्वनित्यत्वे वायुना व्याख्याते।। 5।।

Aph. 5. Its substantiality and eternity are explained by air.

It may be said, Granted that the soul is perdurable, why is it eternal, and why a substance? It is therefore stated, that as there is no warrant for assuming that an aerial atom has parts, and therefore it is eternal, so also is soul eternal; and that as an aerial atom is a substance because it possesses attributes, so also is soul a substance.[1] U.

यज्ञदत्त इति सन्निकर्षे प्रत्यक्षाभावाद्दृष्टलिङ्गं न विद्यते।। 6।।

Objections to the preceding arguments

Aph. 6. In the contact [of the organs of sense and the object] from which the judgment This is Yajñadatta is derived, there being no perception, there exists no visible mark.

There being contact, if in the judgment This is Yajñadatta there is no act of perception, there is no visible mark, no mark by which a universal co-existence is ascertained from perception. There is no visible mark establishing the existence of soul, as there is a visible mark in the case of fire, viz., smoke observed concomitant with fire perceived.[2] U.

Though there be contact of the eye and other organs with the body of Yajñadatta, yet, since there is no visual or other perception of the soul which presides over that body, there is no visible mark, i.e., no mark which being invariably attended by a predicate, is an object of perception. How, then, is an inference of the existence of the soul possible? For, there being contact with fire etc., after the perception of it, an inference as to fire etc., meets with no obstacle because universal concomitance therewith has been observed; but this is not the case with the present inference.[1] V.

श्रितत्वं व्यतिरेकिसाध्यमिति विभागः व्यापकतावच्छेदकप्रकारिकैवानुमितिरिति तु तुच्छम् येन विना प्रतीतिर्न पर्य्यवस्यति तस्यैव तत्र प्रकारत्वात् अन्यथाद्व्यणुकं काय्यीनाश्रितं सत् क्वचिदाश्रितम् अवयवित्वादित्यादाव-काय्यीश्रितत्वप्रकारिक्यऽनुमितिर्न स्वात्।।

1 ननु सिध्यतु आत्मा स्थिरः सतु नित्य इति कुतः कुतश्च द्रव्यमित्याह यथा वायुपरिमाणोरवयवकल्पनायां न प्रमाणमतो नित्यत्वं तथा च मनोऽपित यथा गुणवत्त्वाद्वायुपरमाणुद्रव्यं तथात्माऽपीत्यार्थः।।

2 सन्निकर्षे सति अयं यज्ञदत्त इति चेत् प्रत्यक्षं नास्ति तदा दृष्टं प्रत्यक्षतो गृहीतव्याप्तिकं लिङ्गं नास्ति यथा वह्निना प्रत्यक्षेण सहचरितो गृहीतो धूमो वह्नौ दृष्टं लिङ्गं तथात्मसाधकं लिङ्गं दृष्टं नास्तीत्यर्थः।।

3 यज्ञदत्तशरीरे चक्षुरोदिसन्निकर्षे सत्यपि तदधिष्ठातुरात्मनश्चाक्षुषाद्यभावात् दृष्टं व्याप्यत्वेन प्रत्यक्षविषयीभूतं लिङ्गं नास्तीत्यतः कथमात्मानुमानं सुघटम् बह्न्यादौ सन्निकर्षे तत्प्रत्यक्षानन्तरं तद्व्याप्तिप्रत्यक्षाद्वह्न्याद्यनुमानन्तु

सामान्यतो दृष्टाच्चाविशेषः।। 7।।

Aph. 7. Moreover, from that which is observed generally there results no distinction.

Though there is a generally observed mark, yet there is no proof therefrom of the existence of the soul, from its nature as soul, or as a substance over and above eight substances. It would be thereby established only that desires etc.. must inhere in something, but there is nothing to suggest the thought of a soul. Therefore it is stated that there results no distinction.[1] U.

From that which is generally observed, i. e. from observation of inclusion under something determined by a general attribute, there results no distinction, i.e. no inference from a peculiar property, according to the rule that there must be observed in that which determines the character of the subject determination by the predicate under which the middle term is contained.[2] V.

तस्मादागमिकः।। 8।।

Aph. 8. Therefore the soul is proved to exist by revelation.

The existence of the soul etc. rests on revelation, for, inasmuch as there is no mark of an observed universal concomitance any inference of the existence of the soul is impossible. The existence, then, of the soul rests solely on the authority of revelation. Thus this system for cogitation on the soul is useless.[3] V.

अहमिति शब्दस्य व्यतिरेकान्नागमिकम्।। 9।।

Objections answered

Aph. 9. Existence of the soul being the *conditio sine qua non* of the use of the word I, is not evidence only by revelation.

Revelation is not the sole evidence of the existence of the soul; but

निराबाधमवेति भावः।।

1 सामान्यतो दृष्टमपि लिङ्गं भवति न तु तत आत्मत्वेन अष्टद्रव्यातिरिक्तत्वाद्द्रव्यत्वेन वा स्यादात्मसिद्धिः किन्तु तेनेच्छादीनां क्वचिदाश्रितत्वमात्रं सिध्येत् तत्र आत्ममननौपयिकमित्यर्थः तदेतदाह अविशेष इति।।

2 सामान्यतो दृष्टात् सामान्यधर्मावच्छिन्नव्याप्यत्वग्रहात् अविशेषः विशेषधर्मप्रकारेण नानुमितिः व्यापकतावच्छेदकत्वप्रहस्यैवानुमितिविधेवयाच्छेदकत्वे तन्त्रत्वादिर्थकः।।

3 आगमिकि इत्यस्य आत्मेत्यादि यतो गृहीतव्याप्तिकलिङ्गाभावादात्मनो ऽनुमितिर्न सम्भवति अत आत्मा आगममात्रप्रमाणक इत्यर्थः। तथा चात्ममननार्थमेतच्छोस्वं विफलमिति भावः।।

that there is a soul is evinced also by the inference that the word I; or the word soul must denote some object, because it is a term, like the terms water-pot etc. It might be said, Let earth etc., be the objects which it denotes. Hence the words because it is the *conditio sine qua non* of the use of the word I, that is, because the term I is excluded from earth etc., For there never arises any such supposition or assurancc as I am earth, I am water, I am light, I am air, I am ether, I am time, I am space, I am mind. If you object that such assurance airses in relation to the body, we reply that it is not so, for it would be equally applicable to the bodies of other: if, that it arises with respect to one's own body we reply that this is not so, for there is not intended a self different from soul, and because the term my body involves a difference of substrata. If you urge that this also is merely observed gererally, and therefore, not being determined by a peculiar attribute, involves a fallacy; we reply that it is not so, for in the term I egoity or spirituality is the form or essence; and that as an attribute of the subject it is determined that the ego is the cause of activity, and this is not common to other objects, being a proof of a particular object. In like manner there is proof of the particular even from the generally observed, accompanied with the argument from impossibility. Whereas it is said, From merely hearing results presentation of soul what need of this proof? this is wrong; for without reflection the dross of unbelief in wavering minds cannot be purged away; without this purification there can be no aptitude for profound meditation on this object; and without profound meditation there can be no presentation of truth competent to eradicate false knowledge together with its impressions. For it is by consuetude only that the sad lover can represent in imagination his beloved. For knowledge from verbal information or from inference is unable to uproot false knowledge, as is seen in the case of illusion in regard to direction in space, and similar instances, If it be asked, how whereas soul is invisible, a sign of its existence can be apprehended, we rejoin : Who has maintained that the soul is unknowable by perception? But soul is cognised by its juxta-position with conjunctions with the internal organ : else how such assurances as I am happy, I know, I desire, I will, I am in pain? since such assurance is not without object or of doubtful object, for like an assurance of blueness etc., it has a definite object. Nor is it derived from argument, for it arises without any knowledge of an argument. Nor is it derived from verbal communication, for it does not follow upon desire of such knowledge. If it be maintained that it is a mere illusory perception, we reply that there must be some object not merely apparent, for it will be shown in the sequel that that which is not an object of certain knowledge connot be erroneously surmised in another object.[1] U.

यदि दृष्टमन्वत्तमहं देवदत्तो ऽहं यज्ञदत्त इति।। 10।।

Aph 10. If the cognition I am Devadatta, I am Yajñadatta is a visual presentation [what need of any inference ?]

An opponent says, If this be so, what need of an inference? The word *iti* marks the form of the cognition, and the word *dṛshta* ends in the affix *kta* used in a passive sense. Presentation means perception. The sense, therefore, is as follows. If the perception which has for its form I am Devadatta, I am Yajñadatta, is only a perception, what occasion is there for the trouble of making an inference? For on seeing an elephant, those who infer do not infer him to be one from his screaming.[2] *U.*

दृष्टआत्मनि लिङ्गे एक एव दृढत्वात् प्रत्यक्षवत् प्रत्ययः।। 11।।

Aph. 11. If a mark of the existence of the soul were seen, there could be but one assurance, for it would be as evident as a percept.

The anticipated objection is refuted. The sense as a whole is that if

[1] नागममात्रं प्रमणमात्मनि किन्त्वहमिति पदं वा साभिधेयं पदत्वात् घटादिपदवत् इत्यनुमानादप्यात्मसिद्धिः। ननु पृथिव्यादि तदभिधेयं स्यादित्यत आह व्यतिरेकादिति पृथिवीत्यादितो ऽहमिति पदस्य व्यतिरेकाद्व्यावृत्तेरित्यर्थः। न हि भवत्यहं पृथिवी अहमापः अहन्तेजः अहं वायुः अहमाकाशम् अहं कालः अहं दिक् अहं मन इति व्यपदेशः प्रत्ययो वा शरीरे भवतीति चेन्न परशरीरे तत्प्रसङ्गात स्वशरीरे भवतीति चेन्न स्वस्यात्मभिन्नस्यानिरुक्तेः मम शरीरमिति वैयधिकरण्येन प्रत्ययाच्च नन्विदमति सामान्यतो दृष्टमेव तच्च विशेषापर्यवसन्नमिति दूषितमेवेति चेन्न अहम्पदे ऽहन्त्वमात्मत्वमेव प्रकारः तथा च पक्षधर्मताबलादेवाहन्त्वस्य प्रवृत्तिनिमित्तत्वं प्रर्यवसन्नं तच्चानन्यसाधारणमेवेति विशेषसिद्धेः एवं सामान्यतो दृष्टादपि बाधसहकृताद्विशेषसिद्धिः यच्चोक्तं श्रवणादेव साक्षात्कारः किमनेनेति तदयुक्तं न हि मननमन्तरेण सङ्कशुकस्याश्रद्धामलक्षालनम् न च तदन्तरेण तत्र निदि-ध्यासनाधिकारः न च निदिध्यासनमन्तरेण सवासनमिथ्याज्ञानोन्मूलनक्षमस्तत्त्वसाक्षात्कारः न हि शाब्दमानुमानिकं वा ज्ञानं मिथ्याज्ञानोन्मूलनक्षमंभवेदिहादौ दृष्टमिति भावः। ननु तथापि परोक्षे आत्मनि कथं संकेतग्रह इति चेत् क एवमाह नात्मा प्रत्यक्ष इति किन्तु मनसा संयोगप्रत्यासत्त्यात्मग्रहः कथमन्यथाहं सुखी जानामीच्छामि यते दुःखीत्यादिप्रत्ययः न ह्ययमवस्तुकः सन्दिग्धवस्तुको वा नीलादिप्रत्ययवत् अस्यापि निश्चितवस्तुवत्वात् न च लैङ्गिकः लिङ्गज्ञानमन्तरेणापि जायमानत्वात् नापि शाब्दः तदनुसन्धानाननुविधानात् प्रत्यक्षाभासो ऽयमिति चेत् तर्हि क्वचिदनाभासविषयो ऽपि न ह्यप्रमितमारोप्यते इत्यावेदयिष्यते।।

[2] एवञ्चेत् किमनुमानेनेति पूर्वपक्षवादी आह। इति शब्दो ज्ञानप्रकारमाह दृष्ट मिति भावोक्तप्रत्ययन्तिम् अन्वक्षमित्यध्यक्षं तेनायमर्थः अयं देवदत्तः अयं यज्ञदत्तइतिप्रकारकं दृष्टं दर्शनं अध्यक्षमेवास्ति यदि किमनुमानप्रयासेन न हि करिणि दृष्टे चीत्कारेण तमनुमिप्रते ऽनुमातारः।।

a mark of the soul's existence were observed or apprehended by the internal organ, even were there an inference, there would be one and one only primary conviction, as in relation to a percept in the case of perception. Whence its primary nature? The being a primary conviction or being of recognised validity, results from its certitude or power of removing doubts of invalidity. As, for instance, when the distant water of a lake etc., has been seen, there arises a doubt as to the objective value of such a perception, there being a feeling of uncertainty whether it may not be a mirage or the like; and when afterwards there arises the inference from cranes, etc., the mark of its being a lake, the doubt ceases on the recognition of the evidence by means of reflection; so, although the soul is perceived a doubt arises as to the validity of the perception, on account of counter probabilites etc., but afterwards, the soul being inferentially cognised, the certitude of such cognition, is easily demonstrated, such certitude consisting of competency to remove suspicion of invalidity through the recognition in that case of validity by means of argumentation. It has accordingly been declared by the sage: The logicians desire to understand by inference even that which is fully established by perception.[1] V.

देवदत्तो गच्छति यज्ञदत्तो गच्छतीत्युपचाराच्छरीरेप्रत्ययः।। 12।।

Aph. 12. The cognition Devadatta goes, Yajñadatta goes, is applied tropically to the body.

It may be objected that if the cognition I Yajñadatta refers to the soul, a judgment of compatibility with motion. such as Yajñadatta goes is impossible. It is therefore stated that there are such judgments as I am fair-complexioned, I am stout, and there are such complex concepts as my body. Of these in the judgment Devadatta goes, the conception and enouncement of compatibility with movement is secondary; whereas the expression mine is used in its primary application. Although the nature of Devadatta is a universal existing in the body,

[1] आशङ्का निरस्यति। दृष्टे मनसा गृहीते आत्मनि लिङ्गे अनुमाने सति प्रत्यक्षवत् प्रत्यक्षसमानाकारक एक एव मुख्यएव प्रत्ययः भवतीति शेषः मुख्यत्वं कुतः दृढत्वात् अप्रामाण्यशङ्कानिवर्तनक्षमत्वात् मुख्यत्वञ्च गृहीतप्रामाण्यकत्वम् यथा दूरस्थेसरोवरादिसलिले दृष्टे ऽपि मरीचिकादिसनेहात्तादृशप्रत्यक्षे ऽयमाण्यशङ्का उदेति ततो बलाकादिलिङ्गेन तदनुमाने सति तदनुमाने सति संवादेन तत्र प्रामाण्यग्रहात्तादृशशङ्का निवर्तते तथात्मनि दृष्टे ऽपि विपरीतसम्भावनादिना तज्ज्ञानऽप्रामाण्यशङ्का सञ्जायते ततो ऽनुमानेनात्मनि गृहीते संवादेन तत्र प्रामाण्यग्रहादप्रामाण्यशङ्कानिवर्तनक्षमत्वरूपं दृढत्वं तादृशग्रहस्य सुघटमेव तदुक्तं मिश्रैः प्रत्यक्षपरिकलितमप्यनुमानेन बुभुत्सन्ते तर्करसिका इति।।

and accordingly the expression Devadatta moves is correct even in its primary sense, as also the judgment; if the term Devadatta be employed with regard to the soul determined thereby, it is then to be understood in a secondary application.[1] U.

It may be asked how, if such a notion as I Yajñadatta has the soul for its object the judgment Yajñadatta goes can apply to the soul, for the soul has not the power of motion. It is therefore stated that the sense conveyed by the proposition Devadatta goes, arises from the observation that the word Devadatta implies corporeality. Since such propositions as Devadatta knows, wishes, acts, hates etc., are used in their primary sense, the term Devadatta must have the power of denoting a soul appropriated to a determinate body. For, as in the meaning of these propositions there is a manifold application the complication of this hypothesis is inoperative i.e., does not invalidate it; and it may be considered that the primary sense possibly belongs to such application to the pression of volition in the proposition He goes.[2] V.

सन्दिग्धस्तूपचारः।। 13।।

Aph. 13. The secondary application, however, is doubted.

The word however indicates the view of an opponent. The name and notion of the Ego are known to relate both to the soul and the body. The doubt in this case is which is the primary and which the secondary application.[3] U.

अहमिति प्रत्यगात्मनिभावात् परत्राभावादर्थान्तरप्रत्यक्षः।। 14।।

Aph. 14. The cognition of the Ego is a perception of a distinctive

[1] ननु यदि यज्ञदत्तो ऽहमिति प्रत्यय आत्मनि तदा यज्ञदत्तो गच्छतीति गमनसामानाधिकरण्यभानमनुपपन्नमित्यत आह। अस्ति हि अहं गौरः अहं स्थूल इति प्रत्ययः अस्ति च मम शरीरमिति भेदप्रत्ययः तत्र देवदत्तो गच्छतीति गतिसामानाधिकरण्यानुभवो भक्तः ममेति प्रत्ययस्य यथार्थत्वात् यद्यपि देवदत्तत्वं शरीरवृत्तिर्जातिस्तेन देवदत्तो गच्छतीति मुख्य एवं प्रयोगो यथार्थ एव च प्रत्ययः तथापि देवदत्तपदं तदवच्छिनात्मनि प्रयुक्तञ्चेत् तदौपचारिको बोद्धव्यः।।

[2] नन्वहं यज्ञदत्त इत्यादिप्रत्यक्षं यद्यात्मविषयकं तदा यज्ञदत्तो गच्छतीति प्रत्ययः कथं स्यादात्मनि गतिमत्त्वस्याभावादित्यत आह। देवदत्तो गच्छतीति वाक्यजन्यप्रत्ययः देवदत्तादिप्रदस्य शरीरे लक्षणाग्रहाद्भवति देवदत्तो जानाति इच्छति करोति द्वेष्टीत्यादिप्रयोगानां मुख्यतया देवदत्तादिपदस्य विजातीयशरीरावच्छिन्नात्मनि शक्तेरावश्यकत्वात्तदर्थे भूरिप्रयोगसत्त्वेन गौरवस्याऽकिञ्चित्करत्वात् गच्छतीत्यत्राख्यातस्य यत्रार्थकत्वे तादृशप्रयोगस्य मुख्यत्वमपि सम्भवतीत्यपि द्रष्टव्यम्।।

[3] तुशब्दः पूर्वपक्षद्योतकः। आत्मशरीरयोस्तावदहमिति प्रत्ययः प्रयोगश्च दृश्यते तत्र क्व मुख्यः क्व वौपचारिक इति सन्देहः।।

entity, since it applies to self-reflective-soul, and not to aught else.

A presentation is which a distinctive entity of the nature of soul is given, is a perception of a distinctive entity. The meaning is as follows. Since the presentation of the Ego is relative to one's own soul, and not to another's, it is proper to regard the reference to the distinctive entity, i.e., to one's own soul, as primary. If, on the other hand, the primary reference were to the body, the notion would be produced by the external organs of sense, for the body is not an object of internal perception, and the presentation of the Ego is subjective being produced without any operation of the external organs of sense. Such cognitions as I am sorry, I am glad, I know, I will, I wish, arise from the internal sensory viewing as its object the soul accompanied with its perceptible discriminative attributes. Such a cognition is not inferential, being produced without seeking any mark of concomitance. It is not verbally communicated, being produced without reflection on words. It, therefore, belongs to the internal organ, and to the internal organ independent of the external organs, not being concerned with the body, etc., Moreover if it be urged that if it referred to the body it would refer to the bodies of others, and if it be referred to one's own soul it would refer to the souls of other; we deny this, for the soul of one man is beyond the senses of another, since its particular attributes cannot be externally perceived, and the soul itself could be perceived only by apprehension of particular attributes appropriate to the several senses. Nor is this the nature of soul only, but of all substances, for substance becomes perceptible by apprehension of particular attributes appropriate to the several senses. If you rejoin that on this ground ether also should be perceptible by the apprehension of sound, we reply that such would be the case were the organ of hearing capable of apprehending a substance, or if ether possessed colour. If you object that the soul is equally devoid of colour, we reply that it is in the case of external substances only that possession of colour is a requisite with regard to perceptibility.[1] U.

[1] अर्थान्तरात्मस्वरूपं प्रत्यक्षं यत्र प्रत्ययो स प्रत्ययो ऽर्थान्तरप्रत्यक्षः अयमर्थः अहमिति प्रत्ययस्य प्रत्यगात्मनि स्वात्मनि भावात् परत्र परात्मनि अभावात् अर्थान्तरे स्वात्मन्येव मुख्यः कल्पयितुमुचितः यदि तु शरीरे मुख्यः स्यात् तदा बहिरिन्द्रियजः स्यात् न हि शरीरं मानसप्रत्यक्षं मानसश्चायमहमिति प्रत्ययः बहिरिन्द्रियव्यापारमन्तरेणापि जायमानत्वात् अहं दुःखी अहं सुखी जाने यते इच्छाम्यहमिति योग्यविशेषगुणोपहितस्यात्मनो मनसा विषयीकरणात् नायं लैङ्गिको लिङ्गानुसन्धानमन्तरेणापि जायमानत्वात् न शाब्दः शब्दाकलनमन्तरेणापि जायमानत्वात् तस्मान्मानस एव मनसश्च बहिरस्वातन्त्र्येण शरीरादावप्रवृत्तेरिति भावः। किञ्च यदि शरीरे स्यात् परशरीरे स्यात् स्वात्मनि

The cognition of the Ego and the expressions I Yajñadatta am happy etc., are the cognitions of a distinctive object, the perception or presentation of an ulterior objcet, of one different from the body etc., since they produce verbal information the object of which is different from the body. Such is the sense resulting from the aphorism. The application, accordingly, to the soul as to something ulterior to the body is primary, that to the body is secondary. Why so? The answer is because of existence, viz., the existence of pleasure etc., in one's own soul, and because of non existence, viz., the non-existence of pleasure, etc., elsewhere, i.e., in the body. There is not therefore so much as the shade of a doubt that of the diverse applications, since pleasure and the like exists in the soul only, the application to the soul is primary, and that to the body, etc., sencondary.[1] V.

देवदत्तो गच्छतीत्युपचारादभिमानात्तावच्छरीरप्रत्यक्षो ऽहङ्कारः।। 15।।

Aph. 15. From the secondary application, through self-consciousness, of the expression Devadatta goes, it follows that self-consciousness is presentative of the body.

Again a doubt is raised. Self-consciousness is the consciousness of the Ego. This is presentative of the body, and that is presentative of the body, wherein the object of perception is the body. You have concluded that the proposition or judgment Deva-datta goes is enounced in a secondary application : but this secondary application is really relative to the soul for the judgments and propositions I am fair-complexioned, I am fair-complexioned, I am stout, I am thin. I am fortunate, and the notion of repeated births cannot be of secondary application.[2] U.

यदि स्यात् तदा परात्मनि स्यादिति चेन्न परात्मनः परस्यातीन्द्रियत्वात् तद्विशेषगुणानामयोग्यत्वात् योग्यविशेषगुणोपग्रहेण तस्य योग्यत्वात् न केवलमात्मन इदं शीलं किन्तु द्रव्यमात्रस्य द्रव्यं हि योग्यविशेषगुणोपग्रहेणैव प्रत्यक्षं भवति आकाशमपि तर्हि शब्दोपग्रहेण प्रत्यक्षं स्यादिति चेत् स्यादेवं यदि श्रोत्रं द्रव्यग्राहकं भवेत् आकाशं वा रूपवत् स्यात् आत्मनो ऽपि नीरूपत्वं तुल्यमिति चेत् बहिर्द्रव्यमात्र एव प्रत्यक्षतां प्रति रूपवत्त्वस्य तन्त्रत्वात् प्रत्यगित्ययं शब्दो ऽनन्यावृत्तमाह।।

[1] अहमतीति अहं यज्ञदत्तः सुखीत्यादिव्यवहारः अर्थान्तरप्रत्यक्षः अर्थान्तरस्य शरीरादिभिन्नस्य प्रत्यक्षं ज्ञानं यस्मात् शरीरादिभिन्नविषयकशाब्दबोधजनक इति फलितार्थः तथा च शरीरादिभिन्न एवात्मनि तादृशप्रयोगो मुख्यः शरीरे त्वौपचारिकः कुत एवमत आह प्रत्यगात्मनि स्वात्मनि भावात् अर्थात् सुखादेः सत्त्वात् परत्र शरीरे ऽभावात् सुखादेरसत्त्वात् तथा च भूरिप्रयोगस्यात्मन्येव सत्त्वात्तत्रैव तादृशप्रयोगस्य मुख्यत्वं शरीरादावौपचारिकत्वमिति न सन्देहागन्धो ऽपीति।।

[2] पुनः शङ्कते। अहङ्कारो ऽहमिति प्रत्ययः स च शरीरप्रत्ययः शरीरं प्रत्यक्षं विषयो यत्र स शरीरप्रत्यक्षः। देवदत्तो गच्छतीत्युपचारात् तावत् प्रयोगः प्रत्ययो वा त्वया समाहितः स चोपचारः आभिमानिकः यतो ऽहं

सन्दिग्धस्तूपचारः ।। 16 ।।

Aph. 16. The secondary application however, is doubted.

This word however, indicates the real fact. This secondary application may be relative to the soul, but whereas it has been said that this conception of the Ego refer to the body, there is a doubt on this subject. Since, therefore, the notion is on both sides a false witness, we must endeavour to find some special principle of determination. Since on making this endeavour we are conscious of the presentation of the Ego even when the eyes are closed, we must hold that it refers to an object different from the body, and not to an object of the external organs of sense. It it related to the body, it would refer to the bodies of others also, and would not be independent of the body. If it be asked how we should then justify the verbal collocation I who am stout (or thin) am happy, we reply that in this case the body may be cognised as accidentally associated with pleasure, as in the words This forest is resonant with the roar of a lion. The notion of the Ego being in juxta-position with the internal organ is affirmed in a secondary sense of the body, just as the heat resented by the organ of touch in the judgments The water is hot, The body is hot.[1] U.

The secondary application is doubted. It is doubted whether the secondary application be in Yajñadatta goes, or in I Yajñadatta am happy, and because, there being no criterion of the diverse application to the body and the soul, it is impossible to adopt either alternative as final. The word however is intended to point out a fixed principle.[2] V.

नतु शरीरविशेषाद्यज्ञदत्तविष्णुमित्रयोर्ज्ञानं विषयः ।। 17 ।।

Aph. 17. But the knowledge of Yajñadatta and Vishnumitra

गौरः अहं कृशः सौभागिनो ऽहं पुनरूक्तजन्मेत्यादयः प्रत्ययाः प्रयोगाश्चोपचारेण समन्वयितुमशक्शया इत्यर्थः।

1 तु शब्दो ऽयं सिद्धान्तमभिव्यनक्ति उपचारो ऽयमाभिमानिकः किन्तु शरीर एवायमहम्प्रत्यय इति यदुक्तं तत्रापि सन्देह एवेत्यर्थः तथा च प्रत्ययस्योभयत्रापि कूटसाक्षित्वेन विशेषावधारणाय यतितव्यं तत्र यत्रे क्रियमाणे निमीलिताज्ञस्याप्याहमिति प्रत्ययदर्शनात् शरीरभिन्ने बहिरिन्द्रयागोचरे वस्तुनि स मन्तव्यः शरीरे भवन् परशरीरे ऽपि स्यात् चक्षुर्नेरपेक्ष्येण न च स्यात् अहं कृशः स्थूलो वा सुखीति कथं समानाधिकरण्यमिति चेन्न सुखाद्यवच्छेदकत्वेनापि तत्र शरीरभानसम्भवात् सिंहनादवदिदं गहनमितिवत् अहन्त्वमात्रं शरीरे समारोप्यते मानसोपस्थितम् त्वगिन्द्रियोपनीतमौषण्यम् उष्णं जलम उष्णं शरीरमितिवत्।।

2 उपचारः सन्दिग्धः किं यज्ञदत्तो गच्छतीत्यत्रोपचारः उत यज्ञदत्तो ऽहं सुखीत्यत्र शरीरे आत्सनि च भूरिप्रयोगस्याविशिष्टत्वेनैकशेषस्य कर्तुमशक्यात्वादित्यर्थः तु शब्दः सिद्धान्तद्योतनार्थः।।

does not, in consequence of the difference of their bodies, become an object.

The word knowledge tacitly indicates the attributers of soul, sensible pleasure, pain and the like. As the bodies of Yajñadatta and Vishnu-mitra are separate from one another, so are their knowledge, pleasure and the like separate. Accordingly as the cognition This is Yajñadatta's body, is an object, so though no knowledge, pleasure etc., be produced in Yajñadatta, the cognitions I feel pleasure, I know, I will, I wish, will be objects; because, the body being an object to the appropriate senses, its knowledge etc., like its colour etc., may be perceptible. But this is impossible. Therefore there is, such is the meaning, to be maintained a subject of knowledge, pleasure and the like, other than the body.[1] U.

The knowledge of Yajñadatta and Vishṇumitra does not in consequence of the difference of their bodies, in consequence, that is of their bodies being different objects, become an object, during the perception of the body. The word knowledge implies genearlly all the particular senible attributes of the soul. Therefore, as in our presentation of soul etc., knowledge etc., is the object, it being universally allowed that there are such cognitions as I know, I wish, I will, I feel pleasure. I am in pain, I hate etc., so would there be in like manner, were the body denoted by the word I, and did it possess the attributes knowledge etc., cognition of knowledge etc., even in the visual perception of body. But no one has a visual presentative cognition in the form, I, the stout Yajñadatta, know. Therefore the use of the words I etc., in reference to the body is only by a secondary application and accordingly we do not surrender the matter of our thesis.[1] V.

[3] ज्ञानमिति योग्यं सुखदुःखादिकमात्मगुणमुपलक्षयति यथा यज्ञदत्तविष्णुमित्रयोः शरीरं परस्परभिन्नं तथा ज्ञानसुखादिकमपि भिन्नमेव तथा च यथा यज्ञदत्तस्येदं शरीरं तथा यज्ञदत्तस्य ज्ञाने सुखादौ वा ऽनुत्पन्ने ऽहं सुखी जाने यते इच्छामीति ज्ञानादिकं विषयो भवति योग्यशरीरविषयकत्वेन तदीयरूपादिवत्तदीयज्ञानादीनामपि प्रत्यक्षसम्भवात् न च सम्भवति तस्मात् ज्ञानसुखादीनां शरीरादन्य एवाश्रयो वक्तव्य इति भावः।।

[2] न तु न हि शरीरविशेषात् शरीरविशेषविषयकत्वात् यज्ञदत्तविष्णुमित्रयोर्ज्ञानमपि विषयो भवति शरीरसाक्षात्कारे इत्यर्थः ज्ञापपदं योग्यात्मविशेषगुणसामान्यपरम् तथा च यथास्माकमात्मसाक्षात्कारे ज्ञानादिकं विषयो भवति अहं जानामि इच्छामि यते मुखी दुःखी द्वेष्मीत्याद्यनुभवस्य सर्वसिद्धत्वात् तथा शरीरचाक्षुषादावपि ज्ञानादेर्भानं स्यात् यदि शरीरमहम्पदवाच्यं ज्ञानादिगुणकञ्च स्यात् न हि स्थूलो यज्ञदत्तो ऽहं जानामीति चाक्षुषप्रत्यक्षं कस्यचिद्भवति तस्माच्छरीरे ऽहमादिव्यवहार औपचारिक एवेति नास्मकं प्रतिज्ञाहानिरिति भावः।।

अहमिति मुख्योयोग्याभ्यां शब्दवद्व्यमिरेकाव्य-विचाराद्विशेषसिद्धेर्नागमिकः।। 18।।

Aph. 18. The knowledge of the Ego, being individually established, like sound as *a conditio sine qua non* neither too narrowly nor too widely affirmed, by its predominant and sensible attributes, does not depend upon revelation.

The following objection might be raised. The soul is not an object of perception, since, like ether, it is a colourless, or a simple substance. Of the cognition I am thin, or pale, the body must be affirmed to be the object.Whereas there is sometimes the judgment I feel pleasure etc., it is proper to suppose that pleasure and the like, becoming manifest without their substratum, are attributed by metaphor to the body: as in the notion Hot, fragrant water, heat and fragrance appearing without a substratum, are metaphorically attributed to water. But in this case, there being such attribution, in the notion of water there is not another object independent of common water. In the case, therefore, of the Ego, the notion I is real only in reference to the body, but pleasure and the like are sometimes metaphorically attributed to the body. There is, then, with reference to soul, no knowledge of it in the form of perception. That then which we must assume as the substratum of pleasure and the like, must be established by revelation. There is no means of directly cognising it. The reply to this objection is the following. The cognition I feel pleasure, I am in pain, is not by revelation, by verbal communication, or by inference, for it arises independently of any attention to words or arguments. Whereas it has been said that colourlessness, and simplicity are preventive of perception, this holds true only in the case of perception by the external organs, for of this the possession of colour, and the existence of a plurality of substances are the necessary conditions. Internal perception is independent of these conditions. It may be objected that this would be the case were there any proof of the existence of the soul, but there is none. Accordingly the words Being individually established, like sound, as a *conditio sine quā non,* neither too narrowly nor too widely affirmed. As sound, as a *conditio sine quā non,* is not unduly restricted or extended, so as to apply to the substances, earth etc., and is decisive, and there is thereby proof of a particular substance, viz. ether, as excluded from other eight substances, as the substratum of sound ; in like manner, since the exclusive argument from desire does not fail by applicability to earth etc., the substratum of desire must be excluded from other eight substances. Lest it be argued that all this shows that the soul is an object of inference, not an object of perception, the words The knowledge of the Ego from its predominant and sensible attributes are employed. By the particle *iti* the form of the cognition is stated. The knowledge of the Ego therefore, which arises, independently of any attention to words or arguments, in one whose eyes are closed, must be produced by an original attribute of egoity, sensible or established by proof; but is not produced by the body, inasmuch as the exclusive argument from desire does not fail by applicability to it. After the words From its predominant and sensible attributes, the words To be established, are to be supplied. Many proofs of the existence of soul, omitted for fear of encumbering this treatise, should be sought in the Mayūkha.[1] U.

The Vadāntins maintain that soul is nothing but eternal knowledge, according to the sacred text. This imperishable soul is true knowledge, the infinite supreme spirit, and that in the course of things, being divided by the products of illusion, the accidents of the form of the internal organ, it appears manifold, according to such texts as, One only without a second, One moreover, the inmost soul of all beings, became the counterpart of every form. This doctrine is here refuted. After The knowledge of the Ego, the words Is the object of perception, are to be supplied. The object, therefore of such common internal perceptions as I am happy, is not proved by revelation, and

[1] नन्वात्मा न प्रत्यक्षः नीरूपद्रव्यत्वात् निरवयवद्रव्यत्वाद्वा आकाशवत् तथाचाहं कृशो गौर इति बुद्धेः शरीरमेव विषयो वाच्यः क्वचिदहं सुखीत्यादि धीरपि यद्यप्यस्ति तथाप्याश्रयमन्तरेण भासमानानां दुखादीनां शरीरे समारोप इत्येव कल्पयितुमुचितम् यथौष्णं सुरभिजलम् इत्याश्रयमन्तरेण प्रतीयमानयोरौष्ण्यसौरभयोर्जले समारोपः नग्वेतदनुरोधेन जलप्रत्ययस्यापि प्रसिद्धजलमन्तरेणान्यविषयत्वम् तथा ऽहमित्यप्यहन्त्वं शरीर एव वास्तवम् सुखादिकन्तु कदाचित् तत्रारोप्यते तेनात्मनि प्रत्यक्षाकारं ज्ञानं नास्त्येव सुखाद्याधारत्वेन यत्कल्पनीयं तदागमसिद्धं भवतु न तत्रापि ग्रह इत्यत आह। अयमर्थः अहं दुःखीति प्रत्ययो नागमिको न शब्दो नापि लैङ्गिकः शब्दलिङ्गयोरन्तरेणापि जायमानत्वात प्रत्यक्षत्वे च नीरूपत्वं निरवयत्वञ्च, यद्बाधकमुक्तं तद्बहिरिन्द्रियप्रत्यक्षतायां भवति तत्र हि रूपवत्त्वानेकद्रव्यवत्त्वयोः प्रयोजकत्वात् मानसप्रत्यक्षता च तदन्तरेणापि। ननु स्यादेवं यद्यात्मनि प्रमाणं स्यात् तदेव तु नास्तीत्यत आह शब्दवद्व्यतिरेकाव्यभिचाराद्विशेषसिद्धेरिति यथा क्षित्यादिषु द्रव्येषु शब्दस्य व्यतिरेको ऽव्यभिचारी नियतस्तेन तदाश्रयस्याष्टद्रव्यातिरिक्तस्याकाशरूपस्य विशेषस्य सिद्धिः एवमिच्छायाः पृथिव्यादिषु व्यतिरेकस्याव्यभिचारात् तदाश्रयेणापि अष्टद्रव्यातिरिक्तेन भवितव्यम्। नन्वेतावता ऽप्यानुमानिक एव आत्मा न तु प्रत्यक्ष इत्यत आह अहमिति मुख्ययोग्याभ्यामिति अहमितीतिकारेण ज्ञानाकारमाह तेन सिद्धमिति ज्ञानं शब्दलिङ्गानुसन्धानमन्तरेण निमीलिताक्षस्य यदुत्पद्यते तन्मुख्येन अहन्त्ववता योग्येन प्रमाणसिद्धेन उपपादनीयम् न तु शरीरादिना तत्रेच्छाया व्यतिरेकाव्यभिचारात् मुख्ययोग्याभ्यामित्यनन्तरम् उपपादनायमिति पूरणीयम् आत्मनि प्रमाणानि बहूनि ग्रन्थगौरवभिया त्यक्तानि मयूखे ऽन्वेष्टव्यानि।।

inseparable from God who is declared in such texts as, True knowledge, the infinite supreme spirit. The reason of this is stated in the words From its predominant and sensible attributes etc., because of the proof of particularity, i.e., because of the proof of separateness from God, by that which is predominant and sensible, i.e., by pleasure and pain. Pleasure is among objects of desire predominant, because it is the object of desire not dependent on other desires; and pain is predominant among objects of aversion, because it is the object of aversion not dependent on other aversions. Appropriateness is the being an object of perception. This is mentioned to remove doubt as to absence of proof of the argument, and to prevent a fallacious application in case of the assumption of eternal bliss in reference to God: for eternal bliss is not appropriate, and consequently generated pleasure and pain is the proof of the difference between the individual soul and God. This generated pleasure and pain implies something more, and generated knowledge, desire, volition, and aversion are to be regarded as proofs of the separateness of the individual soul and God. It may be urged that in such arguments as The soul, the object of the perception of the Ego is different from God, because it possesses generated pleasure etc., there being no example and consequently no observation of congruity of similar instances with the universal affirmation, the knowledge of a universal concomitance is impossible. Hence the words As a *conditio sine quā non* neither too narrowly nor too widely affirmed, that is because of the universality of the exclusion. The conditions necessary to the proof may be universally affirmed in the proof of the particular. Though, therefore, there be no example of the universal affirmation, since by exclusion God may be the example, an inference with respect to the matter in hand is possible, through observation of a universal exclusion, dependent on observation of concomitance with exclusion. To remove the doubt that the proof by a universally exclusive argument of the separateness from God is not applicable, the words Like sound, are added, meaning As is the case with sound and the like. As ether is proved to exist by its mark, viz., sound, which is known by means of the form of universal exclusion; so the proof of the separateness of the individual soul from God, is from the possession by the soul of generated pleasure, etc.[1] V.

[1] वेदान्तिनस्तु नित्यविज्ञानमेवात्मा अविनाशी वा ऽरे ऽयमात्मा सत्यं ज्ञानमनन्तं ब्रह्म इति श्रुतेः स च वस्तुगत्या एकी ऽपि मायाकार्याणामन्तःकरणरूपोपाधीनां भेदान्नानेव प्रतिभाति एकमेवाद्वितीयम् इति एकस्तथा सर्वभूतान्तरात्मा रूपं रूपं प्रतिरूपो बभूव इत्यादिश्रुतेरित्याहुस्तन्मतं दूषयति। अहमितीति प्रत्ययविषय इति

सुखदुःखज्ञाननिष्पत्त्यविशेषादैकात्म्यम्।। 19।।

Alleged unity of soul

Aph. 19. Because of the indifference of the origin of pleasure, pain, and knowledge, soul is one.

The section treating of the investigation of soul being completed, that treating of the plurality of souls is commenced. This aphorism sets forth an adverse doctrine. There is according to this doctrine but one soul,though the bodies of Chaitra, Maitra, and others be numerically diverse. Why? Because of the indifference of the origin of pleasure, pain, and knowledge; since the origin of pleasure, pain and knowledge, as determined by all bodies, is not particular. If there were another mark probative of the separateness of the soul, its separateness might be proved, but there is not; just as, in the production of sound, as determined in such and such places, its mark, sound, being non-particular, ether is one; as, its mark, the notions of simultaneity etc., being non-particular, time is one; and, and its mark, the notions of posteriority and priority being non-particular, space is one.[1] U.

शेष: तथा चाहं सुखीत्यादिलौकिकमानसप्रत्यक्षविषय: न आगमिक: सत्यं ज्ञानमनन्तं ब्रह्म इत्याद्यागमप्रतिपाद्येश्वराभिन्न: अत्र हेतुमाह मुख्ययोग्याभ्यामित्यादि मुख्यं सत् यद्योग्यं सुखं दुःखञ्च ताभ्यां विशेषसिद्धेरीश्वरभेदसिद्धेः इष्टेषु सुखस्य मुख्यत्वं अन्येच्छानधीनेच्छाविषयत्वात् दुःखस्य तु द्विष्टेषु मुख्यत्वम् अन्यद्वेषानधीनद्वेषविषयत्वात् योग्यत्वञ्च प्रत्यक्षविषत्वम् एतत्कथनञ्च हेत्वसिद्धिशङ्कानिरासार्थम् ईश्वरे नित्यसुखाङ्गीकारपक्षे व्यभिचारवारणार्थञ्च नित्यसुखस्यायोग्यत्वात् तथा च जन्यं सुखं दुःखञ्च जीवस्येश्वरभेदसाधकम्। उपलक्षणञ्चैतत् जन्या ज्ञानेच्छायत्ना द्वेषश्च ईश्वरभेदसाधका द्रष्टव्याः। ननु अहमिति प्रत्यक्षविषय आत्मा ईश्वरभिन्न: जन्यसुखवत्त्वादित्यादौ दृष्टान्ताभावेन अन्वयसहचाराग्रहात् व्याप्तिज्ञानं दुर्घटमत उक्तं व्यतिरेकाव्यभिचारादिति व्यतिरेकव्याप्तेरित्यर्थ: प्रयोज्यत्वं पञ्चम्यर्थस्तस्य च विशेषसिद्धावन्वय: तथाचान्वयदृष्टान्ताभावे ऽपि व्यतिरेकेण ईश्वरस्य दृष्टान्तत्वसम्भवेन व्यतिरेकसहचारग्रहाधीनव्यतिरेकव्याप्तिग्रहादेवोक्तस्थले ऽनुमिति: सम्भवतीति भाव: ननु व्यतिरेकव्याप्त्येश्वरभेदसाधकत्वं न दृष्टचरमित्याशङ्कानिरासायोक्तं शब्दवदिति शब्दादिवेत्यर्थ: आकाशस्य यथा शब्दरूपाद्धेतोर्व्यतिरेकव्याप्तिप्रकारेण ज्ञायमानादीश्वरभेदसिद्धिस्तथात्मनो जन्यसुखादिमत्वात् तत्सिद्धिरित्यर्थ:।।

[1] आत्मपरीक्षाप्रकरणं समाप्य इदानीमात्मनानात्वप्रकरणमारभते तत्र पूर्वपक्षसूत्रम्। एक एव आत्मा चैत्रमैत्रादिदेहभेदे ऽहि कुत: सुखदुःखज्ञानानां निष्पन्ने रुत्पत्तेरविशेषात् सर्वशरीरावच्छेदेन सुखदुःखज्ञानानामुत्पत्तिरविशिष्टैव यत:। यद्यात्मभेदसाधकं लिङ्गान्तरं भवेत् तदा सिद्धेदात्मभेद: न च तदस्ति यथा तत्तत्प्रदेशावच्छेदेन शब्दनिष्पत्तावपि शब्दलिङ्गाविशेषादेक एव काल: पूर्वापरादिप्रत्ययलिङ्गाविशेषादेकैवदिक्।।

[2] सिद्धान्तमाह नाना आत्मान: कुत: व्यवस्थात: व्यवस्था: प्रतिनियम: यथा कश्चिदाढर्य: कश्चिदङ्क: कश्चित् सुखी कश्चिद्दुखी कश्चिदुच्चाभिजन: कश्चिन्नीचाभिजन: कश्चिद्विद्वान कश्चित् जाल्म इतीयं व्यवस्था आत्मभेदमन्तरेणानुत्पद्यमाना साधयत्यात्मनां भेदम् न च जन्मभेदेन बाल्यकौमारवार्धक्यभेदेन वा एकस्याप्यात्मनो यथा व्यवस्था तथा चैत्रमैत्रादिदेहभेदे ऽपि स्यादिति वाच्यं कालभेदेन विरुद्धधर्माध्याससम्भवात्।।

व्यवस्थातो नाना।। 20।।

Plurality of souls

Aph. 20. Because of its circumstances soul is manifold.

The doctrine is stated that souls are manifold. Why? Because of their circumstances. Circumstances are the several conditions, as one is rich, another mean, one is happy, another unhappy, one is of high, another of low, birth, one is learned, another reads badly. These circumstances being impossible without a diversity of souls, evince a plurality of souls. It cannot be maintained that as are the circumstances of one soul, due to various states of being, to childhood, youth, and old age, so are the circumstances of one soul in the divers bodies of Chaitra, Maitra etc., for it is by difference of time only that the existence in one subject of contradictory attributes is possible.[1] U.

शास्त्रसामर्थ्याच्च।। 21।।

Aph. 21. And on the authority of the Śāstra.

The Śāstra means revelation (Śruti) For, in the declaration of diversity of soul, it is revealed, that Two spirits are to be known, etc.[1] U.

[1] शास्त्रं श्रुतिः तयाप्यात्मनो भेदप्रतिपादनात् श्रूयते हि द्वे ब्रह्मणी वेदितव्ये इत्यादि।।

Book IV

FIRST DAILY LESSON

सदकारणवन्नित्यम्। 1।।

Aph. 1. The eternal is existent and uncaused.

Some say that the existent is produced from the non-existent. Their view is as follows. A seed etc. is not productive of a sprout etc., as its effect, for were this the case there would be produced a sprout etc., from a seed etc., in a granary. But inasmuch as the shoot is produced after the destruction of the seed when sown, by the disjunction of its constituent parts, it is the destruction of the seed etc., which is cause of the sprout, etc. Accordingly the aphorism of Gautama enuncjatory of an adverse doctrine, From non-existence is production of existence: for without destruction is no manifestation. In refutation of this doctrine a prefatory discourse is set up, treating of atoms etc. The existent means anything which is; uncaused, unproduced; the eternal, matter which does not by destruction cease to exist. The sense is that the primary cause of integrate wholes is not the non-existent; for were destruction or subsequent non-existence the cause, a sprout would be produced even from a seed which had beeen ground into meal.[1] V.

तस्य कार्यं लिङ्गम्। 2।।

Aph. 2. The effect thereof is the mark of its existence.

Thereof—of an atom-an effect or product, a water-pot or the like, is

[1] असतः सज्जायते इति केचिद्वदन्ति तेषामयमभिप्रायः बीजादिर्नाङ्कुरादिकार्यजनकः तथा सति कुशूलस्थबीजादेरप्यङ्कुराद्युत्पत्तेः किन्तु क्षेत्रादौ स्थितस्य बीजस्यावयवविभागेन प्रध्वंसानन्तरमेवाङ्कुरोत्पादात् बीजादि-प्रध्वंस एवाङ्कुरादेः कारणमिति तथा च गौतमीयं पूर्वपक्षसूत्रम् अभावाद्भावोत्पत्तिर्नानुपमृद्य प्रादुर्भवात् इति तदेतन्मतं निराकुर्वन्नेव परमाण्वादिक्रमेण संवादं द्रढयति। सत् भावरूपं किञ्चित् अकारणवत् अजन्यं नित्यं विनाशाप्रतियोगिवस्तु श्रवयविनां मूलकारणं नासत् इत्यर्थः प्रध्वंसस्य कारणत्वे चूर्णीकृतादपि बीजादङ्कुरापत्तरिति भावः।।

the mark of existence. Accordingly the aphorism of Gautama, From the evolved is the production of the evolved, on the evidence of perception. Thus is the sequence of integrant and integrate wholes. If this series were unlimited there would be no difference in size between mount Meru and a grain of mustard seed, for they would both be indifferently originated by an infinity of parts. Nor can it be argued that the difference depends on an aggregation of extensions, for without a difference of number they would be impossible. If it be said that annihilation may be the limit of the series of integrant and integrate bodies, we object that there existing indivisibility in some ultimate element, annihilation is impossible, for it is only disjunction of its constituent parts or decomposition that can destroy matter. Nor is disjunction the limit, for it is impossible that it should reside in a single object. A substance, therefore, without parts, must be the limit, and this is an atom. A mote is not the limit, for a mote has magnitude and is composed of substances more than one, being a visible substance. For magnitude is a condition of visual perception, only as it presupposes multiplicity of substance. Else magnitude would not exist, and what would be the cause? Nor are the constituent parts of a mote atoms, for we must infer that those constituent parts as originative of a substance possessing magnitude, are composed of parts, like threads, or the halves of water-pots. Therefore whatever is a generated substance is composed of parts, and whatever is composed of parts is a produced substance. In whatever part, then, there ceases to be the nature of a product, there ceases also to be that of containing parts; and this is the proof of the existence of invisible atoms.[1] U.

Thereof means of the primary cause; the effect, a mote or other produced substance; the mark, that which determines an inference. If the series of integrant and integrate wholes were endless, it would follow that Meru and a grain of mustard seed would be equal, inasmuch

1 तस्य परिमाणोः कार्यं घटादि लिङ्गम् तथा च गौतमीयं सूत्रं व्यक्तात् व्यक्तस्य निष्पत्तिः प्रत्यक्षप्रामाण्यात् इति अवयवावयविप्रसङ्गस्तावदनुभूयते स यदि निरवधिः स्यात् तदा मेरुसर्षपयोः परिमाणभेदो न स्यात् अनन्तावयवारब्धत्वाविशेषात् न च परिमाण प्रचयविशेषाधीनो विशेषः स्यादिति वाच्यं संख्याविशेषाभावात तयोरप्यनुपपत्तेः प्रलयावधिः स्यादिति चेत् अन्त्यस्य कस्यचिन्निरवयवत्वे प्रलयस्यैवानुपपत्तेः अवयवविभागविनाशयोरेव द्रव्यनाशकत्वात् विभागश्च नावधिः तस्यैकाश्रयत्वानुपपत्तेः तस्मान्निरवयवं द्रव्यमवधिः स एव परमाणुः। न च त्रसरेणुरेवावधिः तस्य चाक्षुषद्रव्यत्वेन महत्त्वादनेकद्रव्यवत्त्वाच्च महत्त्वस्य चाक्षुष प्रत्यज्ञत्वें कारणत्वम् अनेकद्रव्यवत्त्वमादायैव अन्यथा महत्वमेव न स्यात् कस्य कारणत्वं भवेत् न च त्रसरेणोरवयवा एव परमाणवः महद्द्रव्यारम्भकत्वेन तेषामपि सावयवत्वानुमानात् तन्तुवत् कपालवच्च तस्मात् यत कार्यद्रव्यं तत् सावयवं यच्च सावयवं तत् कार्यं द्रव्यम् तथा च यतो ऽवयवात् कार्यत्स्वं निवर्त्तते तत्र सावयवत्वमपीति निरवयवपरमाणुसिद्धिः।।

as they would both indifferently originate in an infinity of constituent parts. We must, therefore, allow a termination at some point. But the termination cannot be in a mote, inasmuch as it is proved to have parts, viz., binary atomic aggregates according to the inference that a mote has parts, for it is a visible substance like a water-pot. Nor can the series terminate in binary atomic aggregates, for by the inference that the constituent parts of a mote must have parts, because they are parts possessed of magnitude, like the halves of a water-pot, it is proved that of an aggregate of two atoms there is a part, an atom as the primary material cause. It cannot in a like order be proved that this has a series of parts, for the hypothesis is impossible, involving an infinite regression, and wanting confirmatory circumstances.[1] V.

कारणभावात् कार्यभावः।। 3।।

Aph. 3. From existence of the cause is existence of the effect.

From the existence of clour etc., in the cause, results its existence in the effect, for the qualities of the cause are antecedent to those of the effect, as is observed in the case of a water pot, a piece, of cloth and the like.[2] U.

From the existence of the cause, of the primary cause, results the existence or being of the effects, compound substances. Otherwise, as the material cause of earth is earthy, it would in like manner follow that, by having the non-existent for a material cause, no product or complex, whole would exist.[3] V.

अनित्य इति विशेषतः प्रतिषेधभावः।। 4।।

Aph. 4. The negation Non-eternal is of the particular.

The negation Non-eternal is of the particular, relates to particular things, and hence arises the negation. A compound substance is not

[1] तस्य मूलकारणस्य कार्यं त्रसरेण्वादिकार्यद्रव्यम् लिङ्गमनुमापकम् तथाहि अवयवावयविधाराया अनन्तत्वे मेरुसर्षपयोरपि साम्यप्रसङ्गः अनन्तावयवारब्धत्वाविशेषात् अतः क्वचिद्विश्रामो वाच्यः न च त्रसरेणौ विश्रामः त्रसरेणुः सावयवः चाक्षुषद्रव्यत्वात् घटवदित्यनुमानेन द्व्यणुकरूपतदवयवसिद्धेः नापि द्व्यणुक एव विश्रामः त्रसरेणेरवयवाः सावयवा महदवयवत्वात् कपालवदित्यनुमानेन द्व्यणुकावयवस्य परमाणुरूपस्य मूलकारणस्य सिद्धेः न चैवं क्रमेण तदवयव-धारापि सिध्येत अनवस्थाभयेनानुकूलतर्काभावेन च तत्कल्पनाया असम्भवात्।।

[2] रूपादीनां कारणे सद्भावात् कार्ये सदभावः कारणगुणपूर्वका हि कार्यगुणा भवन्ति घटादौ तथा दर्शनादित्यर्थः।

[3] कारणस्य मूलकारणस्य भावात् कार्याणाम् अवर्यावना भावः सत्ता अन्यथा मृदुपादानकस्य मृण्मयत्वात् असदापादानकत्वेन कार्याणामवयविनामसत्त्वप्रसङ्गादित्यर्थः।।

eternal. But a universal negation, Ever thing is not eternal, is impossible.[1] V.

अविद्या।। 5।।

Aph. 5. [The supposition that atoms are non eternal is] nescience.

The following objections may be raised. An atom is not eternal for it is matter, like a water-pot. Similarly the possession of colour, taste etc., may be adduced as arguments. So also, by simultaneous conjunction with six other atoms an atom has six facets or parts; and consequently from its possession of parts, and from its being the substratum of conjunction partially inherent we may infer that atoms are non-eternal. Moreover if there be ether inside an atom, then inasmuch as it has an interior it has parts; but if there be not ether inside an atom, it follows that ether is not omnipresent.... Also the non-eternity of an atom follows from the inference which establishes the doctrine of transitoriness, that whatever is, is momentary. If then, there be such a series of inferences, how can it be maintained that an atom is eternal? The answer is as follows. Every inference having for its object the non-eternity of an atom is nescience in the form of error, since it springs from a fallacy. This fallacy is occasionally prevention of proof including the subject; always absence of proof of inclusion due to want of evidence preventive of contrary instances; sometimes absence of proof as to the predicate. This and other matters may be sought in the Samānatantra.[2] U.

Nescience is want of proof, viz., the inference of non-eternity of sound; for it arises from a fallacy, inasmuch as all the aforesaid arguments are vitiated by plurality of consequents.[3] U.

[1] न नित्य इति प्रतिषेध्यस्य भावो भवनं विशेषतः वस्तुविशेषमाश्रित्य तथाचावयवी न नित्य इति प्रतिषेधो भवति न तु सर्वः पदार्थो न नित्य इति सामान्यतः प्रतिषेधः सम्भवति।।

[2] ननु परमाणुर्न नित्यः मूर्तत्वात् घटवत् एवं रूपवत्त्वरसवत्त्वादयः प्रत्येकं हेतव उन्नेयाः एवं षट्केनु युगद्योगात् परमाणोः षडंशता तथा च सावयवत्वात् अव्याप्यवृत्तिसंयोगाश्रयत्वात्। किञ्च परमाणोर्मध्ये यद्याकाशमस्ति तदा सच्छिद्रत्वेनैव सावयवत्वम् अथ नास्ति तदाकाशस्यासर्वगतत्वप्रसङ्गः। अपि च यत् सत् तत् क्षणिकमित्यादिक्षणिकत्व-साधकानुमानादपि परमाणोरनित्यता तथा चेतावतो चेदनुमानपरम्परा तदा कथमुच्यते परमाणुर्नित्य इत्यत आह। परमाणोरनित्यत्वचविषया सर्वाप्यनुमितिः अविद्या भ्रमरूपा आभासप्रभवत्वात् आपाततो धर्मिग्राहकमानबाधः सर्वत्र विपक्षबाधकप्रमाणशून्यत्वाद्व्याप्यत्वसिद्धिः क्वचित् स्वरूपासिद्धिरित्यादि समानतन्त्रे ऽन्वेष्टव्यम्।।

[3] अविद्या अप्रमा अर्थात् परमाणोरनित्यत्वानुमितिः दुष्टहेतुजन्यत्वात् पूर्वोक्तानां हेतूनामनैकान्तिकत्वादिति भावः।।

महत्यनेकद्रव्यपवत्त्वात् रूपाच्चोपलब्धिः ।। 6 ।।

Conditions of perception

Aph. 6. Perception is of the great, in consequence of its containing substances more than one, and in consequence of colour.

Perception—visual and tactual presentation—takes place (for these words are to be supplied) in relation to the great, that is, in relation to that which has great extension. There is, accordingly, no perception of an atom inasmuch as it has no magnitude. It might be asked why there is no perception of air etc., there being great extension; accordingly the words In consequence of colour,—that is in consequence of appreciable colour, and thus though there be colour in the eye etc., there is no perception of it. It might be asked how there exists magnitude in a mote whereas there is none in an atom; accordingly the words In consequence of its containing substances more than one. Since then containing substances more than one is the positive condition with regard to produced magnitude, and this does not exist in an atom etc., magnitude does not exist in an atom, etc. The containing substances more than one is the being a substratum in which a plurality of substances co-inhere.[1] V.

सत्यपि द्रव्यत्वे महत्त्वे रूपसंस्काराभावाद्वायोरनुपलब्धिः ।। 7 ।।

Aph. 7. The non-perception of air, though there be therein substantiality and magnitude, is in consequence of the non-existence of the impression of colour.

Such being the case there should, it may be urged, also be perception of the light of a torch at midday, or of the light of the eye, in which colour inheres in consequence of the inhesion of touch, and which has magnitude. The answer is as follows:—By the term impression of colour is intended inhesion, or appreciability, or non-obscuration, of colour. Though, therefore the self-same inhesion in air of touch is inhesion of colour, yet it is not qualified by colour, for there

[2] उपलब्धिः चाक्षुषं स्पार्शनञ्च प्रत्यक्षम् महति महत्परिमाणवति भवतीति शेषः तथा च परमाणोर्महत्त्वाभावान्न प्रत्यक्षमिति भावः। ननु वाय्वादेरपि महत्परिमाणसत्त्वात् कथं न प्रत्यक्षमत उक्तं रूपादिति उद्भूतरूपादित्यर्थः तेन चक्षुरादौ रूपसत्त्वे ऽपि न प्रत्यक्षम ननु त्रसरेण्वादावेव कथं महत्त्वं न परमाणावित्यत उक्तम् अनेकद्रव्यवत्त्वादिति तथा च जन्यमहत्त्वं प्रति अनेकद्रव्यवत्त्वस्य प्रयोजकत्वात् परमाण्वादौ च तदभावाच महत्त्वम् अनेकद्रव्यत्त्वञ्च अनेकसमवेतसमवेतत्वमिति।।

is in it absolute non-existence of colour. In the light of the eye there is no impression, that is no appreciability, of colour. In the light of the torch at midday there is no impression, that is no non-obscuration, of colour. Of these, therefore, there is no perceptibility. It like manner impression of colour is to be analogously applied to the hot season, heat or fire within a cooking utensil, gold, etc.[1] U.

Impression of colour, or impressed colour (according to the rule that a past passive participle may be employed adjectively) amounts to appreciable or to unobscured colour. This not existing, or in other words there being non-existence of the nature of a substratum having such colour for its essential property, there is no perception or sensuous presentation of air. Nor can it be objected: Why is there not in air the nature of a substratum of colour, inasmuch as the existence of a connection determines the existence of the connected object? For this is contradictory to the non-existence of colour given in the presentative cognition that in air there is no colour ; and there is nothing to prove that air is a substratum of colour, there being no cognition that air possesses colour. It must be understood that existence of a connection determines the existence of the connected object in such cases only where there is no impossibility and where there is another proof. In fine, to affirm the existence of substantiality is to imply the existence of connection with colour. To affirm the existence of great existence is to imply the existence of a cause of perception. To predicate appreciability is to deny perception of fire within culinary utensils etc., and of the hot weather, heat etc. To predicate inappreciability is to deny perception of the light of a torch at midday and the like.[2] V.

अनेकद्रव्यसमवायात् रूपविशेषाच्च रूपोपलब्धिः ।। 8 ।।

Conditions of perception of colour

Aph. 8. Perception of colour is consequent on co-inhesion of substances more than one, and on particularity of colour.

[1] नन्वेवमपि मध्यन्द्रिनोल्काप्रकाशस्य चाक्षुषस्य रश्मेर्वायोर्वा स्पर्शसमवायेन रूपसमवायिनो महतश्चोपलम्भः स्यात् अत आह। रूपसंस्कारपदेन रूपसमवायो रूपोद्भवो रूपानभिभवश्च विवक्षितः। तेन पद्यपि वायौ य एव स्पर्शसमवायः स एव रूपसमवायः तथापि रूपनिरूपितो नास्ति रूपात्यन्ताभावसत्त्वात् चाक्षुषे च रश्मौ रूपसंस्कारः रूपोद्भवो नास्ति मध्यन्धिनोल्काप्रकाशो च रूपसंस्कारो रूपानभिभवो नास्ति इति न तेषां प्रत्यक्षता एवं ग्रीष्मोश्मभर्जनकपालानलकनकादिषु रूपसंस्कार उन्नेयः।।

[2] रूपसंस्कारः संस्कृतं रूपं कृद्विहित इति न्यायात् उद्भूतानभिभूतरूपमिति यावत् तादृशरूपत्वावच्छिन्नाधिकरणत्वाभावान्न

Particularity of colour is particularity residing in colour. This is appreciability and non-obscuration. On its perception is consequent. The words co-inhesion of substances more than one are added, to meet the possible objection that the colour of an atom and of a binary atomic aggregate would be likewise perceived. The term more than one indicates plurality. Perception therefore, is consequent on the co-inhesion of a plurality of substances from a tertiary atomic aggreagate and upwards, of which, as their substratum, are substances more than one or a plurality of substances. Water-pots and the like, originating in two constituent parts, as viewed in regressive order comprehend of a plurality of substances. Visual perceptibility has no relation to taste, touch etc., inasmuch as there does not exist therein the essence of colours. It has no relation to the light of the eye, in consequence of the absence of appreciability. Appreciability is a kind of universal entity residing in a particular quality of colour etc. and included in the essence of colour.[1] U.

तेन रसगन्धस्पर्शेषु ज्ञानं व्याख्यातम्।। ९।।

Minima sensibilia

Aph. 9. By this is explained cognition in the case of taste, smell, and touch.

Of the senses other than touch co-inhesion in the same substratum with colour is the positive condition of perceptibility to the external organs. For this reason the cnditions of perception of colour thus stated, are here extended to other cases. By this means by knowledge afforded by perception of colour. As perception of colour is consequent on a particular kind of colour, that is on non-obscuration and appreciability in the essence of colour, so perception of taste is

वायो उपलब्धिः प्रत्यक्षमित्यर्थः न च सम्बन्धसत्तायाः सम्बन्धिसत्तानियामकत्वात् कथं न वायौ रूपाधिकरणत्वमिति वाच्यं वायौ रूपं नास्तीति प्रत्यक्षसिद्धेन रूपाभावेन विरोधित्वात् वायू रूपवानिति प्रत्ययासत्त्वेन तदधिकरणतायां साधकाभावाच्च यत्र तु न बाधकं किन्तु साधकान्तरं तत्रैव सम्बन्धसत्तासम्बन्धिसत्तानियामका इत्यभ्युपगमस्यावश्यकत्वात् द्रव्यत्वस्य सत्वकथनन्तु रूपसम्बन्धसत्त्वज्ञापनार्थम् महत्परिमाणसत्त्वाभिधानात्तुप्रत्यक्षकारणसम्येत्यर्थम् उदभूतत्वविशेषणं भर्ज्जनकपालादिस्थवह्निग्रीष्मोष्मचक्षुराद्युपलब्धिवारणार्थम् अनभिभूतत्वविशेषणम् मध्यन्दिनोल्काप्रकाशादि प्रत्यक्षवारणार्थमिति संक्षेपः।।

[1] रूपगतो विशेषो रूपविशेषः तच्चोद्भूतत्वमनभिभूतत्वं रूपत्वञ्च तस्माद्रूपस्योपलब्धिः। नन्वेवं परमाणोर्द्व्यणुकस्य च रूपं गृह्येतेत्यत उक्तमनेकद्रव्यसमवायादिति अनेकपदं भूयस्त्वपरं तेनानेकानि भूयांसि द्रव्याणि आश्रयतया यस्य तदनेकद्रव्यं त्रसरेणुप्रभृति तत्समवायात् घटादयो ऽप्यवयवद्वपारब्धाः परम्परया ऽनेकद्रव्याश्रया एव रसस्पर्शादौ रूपत्वविरहात् उद्भवः रूपादिविशेषगुणगतो जातिविशेष एव रूपत्वादिव्याप्यः।।

contingent upon a particular kind of savour, that is, upon the distinctive qualities of non-obscuration and a appreciability in the essence of taste. This remark is to be applied in the other cases (viz., those of smell, and touch), and co-inhesion of a plurality of substances is to be extended to them. From inappreciability to the organs of smell, taste, and touch, results non-apprehension of smells, tastes and touches. It is from their inappreciability in a stone and the like, that smell and taste are not there perceived; for they are perceived in the ashes of the stone, etc. Some maintain that they are perceived indeed in the stone etc., but not distinctly. From inappreciability of colour in a substance, included in its disjunct elements, results its non-presentation. This is the case likewise with taste. In hot water in consequence of appreciability of light or fire and of its obscuration by touch, is non-perception of light or fire. In comminuted camphor, champaka perfume, etc.in consequence of their inappreciability is non-perception of colour, taste and touch.[1] U.

तस्याभावादव्यभिचारः ।। 10 ।।

Aph. 10. Because of the non-existence of this, there is no deviation.

Gravity also is inherent in a plurality of substances, and has a common substratum with colour and magnitude. Why is it not perceptible? This objection is obviated. Because of the non-existence in gravity of the universal appreciability which is the nature of colour, gravity is not perceptible.

It might be said that granted that the essence of colour etc., does not exist, yet there may be perception. Accordingly the words no deviation are added; for it is a law that there is no deviation (or unduly wide or narrow assertion) of the five universal entities, the essences of colour etc., in relation to apprehensibility by the respective organs of sense. For there only where there is one of the five classes, colour etc., is there apprehensibility by the respective exterior organs,

[1] स्पर्शतिरिक्तानां रूपसामानाधिकरण्यमेव बहिरिंद्रियग्राह्यता प्रयोजकमिति रूपप्रत्यक्षसामग्रीमभिधाय तामन्यत्रातिदिशन्नाह। तेनेति रूपप्रत्यक्षज्ञानेनेत्यर्थः यथा रूपविशेषात् रूपत्वानभिभूतत्वोद्भूतत्वाद्रूपोपलब्धिस्तथा रसविशेषात् रसत्वानभिभूतत्वोद्भूतत्वलक्षणात् रसोपलब्धिः एवमितरत्रापि योज्यम् अनेकद्रव्यसमवायश्चातिदेश्यः घ्राणरसनत्वमिन्द्रियाणामनुद्भवाद्गन्धरसस्पर्शनामग्रहणम् पाषाणादावनुद्भवाद्गन्धरसवोः तद्भस्मनि तयोरूपलम्भात् तयोःपाषाणादावुपलम्भ एव न तु स्पष्ट इत्येके। विभक्तावयवाव्यय्यद्रव्यरूपानुदभवात्तदग्रहणम् एवं रसस्यापि उष्णजले तेजोरूपस्यानुद्भवात् स्पर्शस्य चाभिभवात् विततकर्पूरचम्पकादौ रूपरसस्पर्शनानुद्भवादनुपलम्भः।।

according to the logical form, that whereby absence of the one infers absence of the other. Gravity, by reason of the obscurity of the subject of the aphorism, by Praśastadeva classed among things transcendental, is by Vallabhāchārya said to be perceived by touch. U.

It might be asked why there is no perception of gravity etc., since magnitude and appreciable colour exist there in a relation of juxtaposition in a common substratum. Accordingly the answer is given. In this place by the word this there is reflection upon a number of causes not stated in the text, but which are well known as positive conditions of realisations of the effect. From the non-existence of this complement of causes results non-deviation (i.e., neither excess or defect of predication); that is on the hypothesis of the causal relation of appreciable colour etc., there is deviation of affirmation in relation to gravity etc. By reason therefore of the relation of common objectivity to perception in general, and the necessity of admitting that the nature of gravity etc., is preventive of the presentation of gravity and the like, which are transcendental, and by reason of the non-existence in gravity of the mutually exclusive non-existence of these, there being no instrument, there is no perception of gravity etc. By Vallabhāchārya this aphorism is otherwise, explained and maintained, viz., that of gravity etc., there is tactual perception.[1] V

संख्याः परिमाणानि पृथकत्व संयोगविभागौ परत्वाकरत्वे कर्म च रूपिद्रव्यसमवायात् चाक्षुषाणि।। 11।।

Common sensibles

Aph. 11. Numbers, extensions, separateness, conjunction and disjunction, priority and posteriority, and action, as inhering in coloured substance, are visible.

Things perceptible by one organ of sense having being discussed, those perceptible by two are enumerated. The absence of compounds is to indicate the mutual undependence of these as visible and

[1] ननु गुरुत्वादौः कथं न प्रत्यक्षं महत्त्वस्य उद्भूतरूपस्य च सामानाधिकरण्यसम्बन्धेन तत्र सत्त्वादित्यत आह। अत्र तत्पदेन अपक्रान्तस्यापि कारणकलापस्य परामर्शः कार्य्योत्पत्तियोजकतया तस्य प्रसिद्धत्वात् तथा च तस्य कारणकलापस्य अभावात् असत्त्वात् अव्यभिचारः उद्भूतरूपाभावः कार्य्यकारणभावकल्पनायां गुरुत्त्व दौ नान्वयव्यभिचार इत्यर्थः तथा च लौकिकविषयतासम्बन्धेन प्रत्यक्षसामान्यं प्रत्येवातीन्द्रियाणं गुरुत्वादीनां गुरुत्वत्वादीनां प्रति–बन्धतास्वीकारस्यावश्यकत्वेन तदन्योन्याभावस्य गुरुत्वादावसत्त्वेन सामय्यभावान्न गुरुत्वादेः प्रत्यक्षमिति भावः वल्लभाचार्य्यैस्तु एतत्सूत्रमन्यथैव व्याख्यातं स्वीकृतञ्च गुरुत्वादेः स्पार्शनप्रत्यक्षमिति संक्षेपः।।

tangible. Though magnitude is supposed, it is not by the nature of extension. The word and involves the addition of viscidity, fluidity, and velocity. The term visible implies tangibility, or the particle and may be applicable here after visible. The word numbers in the plural comprehends all numbers from unity upwards. If it be held that unity is a universal entity, and not a quality, then if it exist in substance only, it is existence as of neither less nor greater extent than the nature of substance; if, on the other hand, it exist in qualities and actions also, it is existence as of neither less nor greater extent than real existence. If it be asked how then in the former case there is the nature of unity etc., in quality etc., it may be answered that it is by unity imputed : or that by reason of the notion of co inherence in one substance, the nature of unity is justly affirmed. This unity is eternal in eternal substances, in non-eternal substances it has for its non-coinherent or external cause causal unity. Duality etc., is resultant from relative cognition. Relative cognition is the mental basis of various unities, when two homogeneous or heterogenous substances are in contact with the organ of vision.[1] U.

Things perceptible by two organs of sense are enumerated .After the word visible the preceding particle and is to be construed. The meaning is, then, that these entities, beginning with sound that and ending with action inherent in coloured substance, are visible and tangible. The particle and after the word action, includes by implication viscidity, velocity, fluidity and their universal essences. The word coloured indicates appreciability and consequently there is no incongruity in the fact that these entities, when existent in atoms etc. are not perceptible.[2] V.

1 एवमेकैकेन्द्रियग्राह्यानभिधाय द्वीन्द्रियग्राह्यानाह। एतेषां चाक्षुषत्वे स्पार्शनत्वे वा परस्परानपेक्षत्वसूचनाया समासः यद्यपि महत्वापेक्षा ऽस्ति तथापि न परिमाणत्वेन चकारः स्नेहद्रवत्ववेगानामुपसंग्राहार्थः चाक्षुषाणीति स्पार्शनत्वमप्युपलक्षयति यदा चकार एव चाक्षुषाणि चेत्यत्राऽपि योज्यः सङ्ख्या इति बहुवचनम् एकत्वादिकाः सर्व्वा एव सङ्ख्याः संगृह्णाति एकत्वं सामान्यमेव न तु गुण इति चेत् तद् यदि द्रव्यमात्रवृत्ति तद्द्रव्यत्वेन सहान्यूनातिरिक्तवृतिरिक्तवृत्तित्वम् अथ गुणकर्म्मणोरपि वर्त्तते तदा सत्तया सहान्यूनातिरिक्तवृत्तित्वम् कथं तर्हि गुणादावप्येकत्वादि प्रत्ययइति चेत् आरोपितेनैकत्वेन एकार्थसमवायप्रत्यासत्त्या सम्यगेवैकत्वप्रत्ययो वा तदेतदेकत्वं नित्यद्रव्येषु नित्यम् अनित्येषु चकारणैकत्वासमवायिकारणम्।।

2 द्वीन्द्रियग्राह्यानाह। चाक्षुषाणीत्यत्रापि पूर्वचकारो योजनीयः तेन सङ्ख्यादीनि कर्म्मपर्य्यन्तानि रूपवद्द्रव्यसमवेतानि चाक्षुषाणि स्पार्शनानि चेत्यर्थः कर्म्म चेति चकारात् उद्भूतरूपवद्द्रव्याणां योग्यगतानां स्नेहवेगद्रवत्वानां जातीनाञ्च संग्रहः।।

अरूपिष्वचक्षुषाणि।। 12।।

Aph. 12. In uncoloured substances they are imperceptible to sight.

The invisibility of these when existing in inappropriate, i.e., uncloured, substances, though involved in the preceding aphorism, is stated for the sake of perspicuity. The meaning is that these are invisible and intangible in uncoloured or inappropriate subjects. It is not said that they are imperceptible, because of the arising of an internal perception of the unity of soul.[1] V.

एतेन गुणत्वे भावे च सर्वेन्द्रियं व्याख्यतम्।। 13।।

Aph. 13. By this it is explained that knowledge in regard to quality and existence is of all the senses.

Existence means being; of all the senses, produced by all the senses; knowledge, perception. The sense is, therefore, that these inasmuch as they are appropriate to, are cognised by, all the senses.[2] V.

[1] रूपिपद योग्यपरं तेन परमाण्वादिगतानामेतेषामप्रत्यक्षत्वे ऽपि नासङ्गतिः अयोग्यसमवेतानामेतेषामचाक्षुषत्वमर्थायातमपि स्पष्टार्थमाह। अरूपिषु अयोग्येषु एतानि अचाक्षुषाणि अस्पार्शनानि चेत्यर्थः आत्मैकत्वस्य मानसप्रत्यक्षोदयात् अप्रत्यक्षाणीति नोक्तम्।।

[2] भावः सत्ता सर्व्वेन्द्रियं सर्व्वेन्द्रियजन्यम ज्ञानं प्रत्यक्षं तथा च तयोः सर्व्वेन्द्रिय योग्यवृत्तित्वात् सर्व्वैरेवेन्द्रियैस्ते गृह्येते इति भावः।।

SECOND DAILY LESSON

तत् पुनः पृथिव्यादिकार्यद्रव्यं त्रिविधं शरीरेन्द्रियविषयकसंज्ञम्।। 1।।

Trichotomy of the non-eternal substances

Aph. 1. The aforesaid product substance, earth and the like, is threefold, under the names of body, organ, and object.

Of these corporeity is a kind of universal attribute, an absolute whole possessing action, and having for its non-coinherent cause conjunction with soul endowed with volition, but corporeity is not a universal entity, for terrestriality does not admit of the generic and specific. The nature of an organ is adaptability to the common sensory causative of knowledge other than reminiscence; or susceptibility of conjunction with the internal organ cansative of knowledge, accompanied with insusceptibility of the appreciable particular qualities other than sound. In regard to the light of the eye of animals that prowl at night, another kind of light must be admitted, and in regard to visuality the words insusceptibility or appreciable particular qualities other than sound and colour are to be added. While the nature of an object is to be the means of phenomenal experience, that is to say, to be an object of ordinary presentation, which is common to substance, quality, action, generality, and non-existence; it is, in accordance with the aphorism, product substantiality the object of common internal presentation, for it is stated in the aphorism that earth and other product substances are three-fold. Objectivity also, then, is not a universal entity.[1] U.

[1] तत्र शरीरत्वं प्रयत्नवदात्मसंयोगासमवायिकारणवत्क्रियावदन्त्यावयवित्वम् उपाधिभेदः न तु शरीरत्वं जातिः पृथिवीत्वादीनां परापरभावानुपपत्तेः इन्द्रियत्वञ्च स्मृत्यजनकज्ञानकारणमनःसंयोगाश्रयत्वम् शब्देतरोद्भूतविशेषविशेषगुणानाश्रयत्वे सति ज्ञानकारणमनःसंयोगाश्रयत्वं वा नक्तञ्चरनयरश्मिस्तु तेजोन्तरममेव चक्षुष्टवे तु शब्दरूपेतरोद्भूतविशेषगुणनाश्रयत्वे सतीति देयम् न त्विन्द्रियत्वं जातिः पृथिवीत्वादिनां परापरभावानुपपत्तेः विषयत्वञ्च यद्यपि प्रीतयमानभोगसाधनत्वम् तच्च लौकिकसाक्षात्कारविषयत्वमेव द्रव्यगुणकर्म्मसामान्याभाव-साधारणम् तथापि सूत्रानुरोधात् लौकिकसाक्षात्कारविषयकार्य्यद्रव्यत्वं द्रष्टव्यम् पृथिव्यादिकार्य्यद्रव्यम् त्रिविधिमिति सूत्रम् तथा च विषयत्वमपि न जातिः।।

Of these corporeity is a universal existing in that which possesses muscular action existing only in an absolute whole. In this definition the second existing is intended to exclude existence as in a hand, terrestriality, substantiality, existence etc. The term existing in that which possesses muscular motion, is intended to exclude conjunction of water pots, bodies, etc. The universal, therefore, in the definition is applicable to human and other bodies, by consideration of humanity, the nature of Chaitra, and other universals. There exists in trees etc., organic motion through connection with divine air, otherwise fractures and wounds in them would not close up. From the multiplicity of the man-lion's (Vishṇu's) body, according to the division of aeons, the definition may be applied to it by consideration of the universal nature of the man-lion. But corporeity is not to be defined only as universal, for thus there would be confusion with terrestriality etc.; nor as the substratum of muscular motion, for the definition would be too narrow in relation to body deprived of organic movement. The nature of an organ also, is not to be defined only as universal, for there would thus result a confusion with terrestriality etc., but as the site of conjunction with the common sensory causative of congnitions, and not the site of appreciable particular qualities other than sould. The words not the site etc., are intended to prevent an unduly wide predication in regard to the cuticle, and the soul; the causes of cognitions being conjunction of the common sensory and the external organs of sense, conjunction of the cuticle and the internal organ, and conjunction of the soul and the internal organ. The nature of an object is product substantiality, being the means of experiences in an immediate succession. Though it exists in body and organs, it is separately enumerated to give a more distinct conception to the learner.[1] V.

[1] अत्र शरीरत्वम् अन्त्यावयविमात्रचेष्टावद्वृत्तिजातिमत्त्वं हस्तत्वपृथिवीत्वद्रव्यत्व सत्त्वादिवारणाय प्रथमवृत्त्यन्तम् घटत्वादिवारणाय चेष्टावद्वृत्तीति घटशरीरसंयोगादि वारणाय जातीति मनुष्यत्वचैत्रत्वादिजातिमादाय मानुषादिशरीरे लक्षणसमन्वयः वृक्षादावपि चेष्टा ऽस्त्येव आध्यत्मिकवायुसम्बन्धात् अन्यथा भग्नक्षतसंरोदणादिकं न स्यात् कल्पभेदेन नृसिंहशरीरस्य नानात्वात् नृसिंहत्वजातिमादाय तत्र लक्षणसमन्वयः न तु शरीरत्वं जातिः पृथिवीत्वादिना सङ्करात् नापि चेष्टाश्रयत्वम् निश्चेष्टाशरीरे ऽव्याप्तेः। इन्द्रियत्वमपि न जातिः पृथिवीत्वादिना सङ्कप्रसङ्गात् किन्तु शब्देतरोद्भूतविशेषगुणानाश्रयत्त्वे सति ज्ञानकारणमनःसंयोगाश्रयत्वम् इन्द्रियमनःसंयोगचर्म्ममनःसंयोगात्ममनः-संयोगाज्ञानकारणानीति चर्म्मण्यात्मनि चा तिव्याप्तिवारणाय सत्यन्तम् श्रोत्रे ऽव्याप्तिवारणाय शब्देतरेति व्याघ्रादिनयनरश्मेश्चक्षुष्टवस्वीकारे तु रूपेतरेत्यिति वक्तव्यम् घ्राणादौ गन्धादिसत्त्वादुद्भूतेति शुक्लत्वादिव्याप्यम् अनुद्भूतत्वं जातिर्नानैव तदभावकूटत्वमुद्भूतत्वं तच्च संयोगे ऽप्यस्तीत्यसम्भववारणाय विशेषेति कालदिगादावतिव्याप्तिवारणाय ज्ञानकारणेति चक्षुरवयवविषयसंयोगस्यापि चक्षुर्विषयसंयोगद्वारा ज्ञानजनकत्वस्वीकारात् चक्षरवारवादौ चक्षुः संयुक्तकालविशेषणतायाः कालादौ रूपाभावचाक्षुषस्य जनकतयातदघटकसंयोगस्यापि

प्रत्यक्षाप्रत्यक्षाणां संयोगस्याप्रत्यक्षत्वात् पञ्चात्मकं न विद्यते।। 2।।

Aph. 2. The body is not composed of the five elements, for the conjunction of things perceptible and imperceptible is imperceptible.

The author now proceeds of refute the assertion that the body is composed of three or four elements. Were the body, by reason of its odour, moisture, heat, breath, and compressibility, composed of five elements, the body would be imperceptible in the same manner in which conjunction of wind with trees is imperceptible. The aphorism employs an example. After the word is the word body is to be supplied. Moisture, digestive heat and the other qualities exist only in their respective substances water, fire etc. Such is the case also with regard to four elements. Let it then, it may be urged, consist of three elements, for three elements are perceptible. this is not the case for an integration out of heterogeneous elements is denied. One quality in a whole is not originative of other qualities. If therefore the commencement were from earth and water, that which they originate would be void of odour and taste. In like manner if it originated in earth, and air, it would be destitute of smell, taste, colour and touch. Such and other inferences are obvious.[1] U.

गुणान्तराप्रादुर्भावाच्च न त्र्यात्मकम्।। 3।।

Aph. 3. The body is not composed of three elements, because there is not manifested another quality.

A body originated by quality, perceptible earth, water, and light, might be perceptible, if there were manifested in it another quality having for its antecedent a quality of the cause. This is not the case, for

स्वाश्रयविशेषणतासम्बन्धेन चाक्षुषकारणत्वात् तमादाय कालादौ चातिव्याप्तिवारणाय मनःपदम् विषयत्वञ्च साक्षात् परम्परया वोपभोगसाधनत्वे सति जन्यद्रव्यत्वम् तस्य शरीरेन्द्रियवृत्तित्वेऽपि शिष्यबुद्धिवैतद्यार्थं तयोः पृथगुत्कीर्त्तनमिति संक्षेपः।।

[1] इदानीं शरीरस्य त्रैभौतिकत्वचातुर्भौतिकत्वप्रवाद निराकर्तुमाह। गन्धक्लेदपाकव्यूहावकाशदानेभ्यः पाञ्चभौत्तिकं यदि शरीरं भवेत् तदा अप्रत्यक्षं भवेत् यथा प्रत्यक्षाप्रत्यक्षाणां वायुवनस्पतीनां संयोगी ऽप्रत्यक्षस्तथा शरीरमयप्रत्यक्षं स्यादिति दृष्टान्तद्वारकं सूत्रं पञ्चात्मकं न विद्यत इति शरीरमिति शेषः क्लेदपाकादयस्तु उपष्टम्भकजलानलगता एव चातुर्भौतिकोऽप्येवम् नन्वस्तु त्रैभौतिकम् त्रयणां भूतानां प्रत्यक्षत्वांदिति चेन्न विजातीयारम्भस्य प्रतिषेधात् एकस्य गुणयावयविनि गुणानारम्भकत्वात तद यदि पृथिवीजलाभ्यामारम्भः स्यात्ः तदा तदा रब्धमगन्धमरसञ्चस्यात् एवं पृथिव्यनलाभ्याम् गन्धमरूपमरसञ्च स्यात् पृथिव्यनिलाभ्यामगन्धमरसमरूपमस्पर्शञ्च स्यादित्याद्यूह्यम्।।

it has been already stated that a single odour etc., is not originative. Therefore the body is not composed of three elements nor orginated by three coloured substances.[1] U.

अणुसंयोगस्त्वप्रतिषिद्धः।। 4।।

Aph. 4. A conjunction of atoms is not denied.

How then do we observe digestive heat etc., in one single body? The answer is given in the text. A mutual conjunction of the five elements as receptive of one another is not denied. But it is not affirmed that two heterogeneous atoms are the non-coinherent cause of a substance. It is, therefore, in consequence of the receptivity of those that vital heat etc., is observed in the body. If it be asked then, of what nature the human body is, we cite the aphorism of Gautama:—That the body is terristrial, for the particular quality (of earth) is observed. Odour the particular quality of earth is observed in the human body as not departing from it till its dissoloution. Vital heat etc., is not observed in the decayed body. These qualities, therefore, are accidental, but its odour is essential according to the constitution of terrestriality.[2] U.

तत्र शरीर द्विविधं योनिजमयोनिजञ्च।। 5।।

Aph. 5. Of these, body is twofold uterine and non-uterine.

Of these—among terrestrial, aqueous, and other bodies—the terrestrial body is twofold. What are the two kinds? It is answered in the text that they are uterine and non-uterine. Aqueous, igneous, and aerial bodies, known in the spheres of Varuṇa, the sun, and air,are exclusively non-uterine. The bodies of gods and sages are non-uterine, according to the text of revelation. Manu and others the sensorial sons of Brahmā. If it be asked how there can be an effect without a cause, we reply that the womb is not a cause essential to corporeity; for the affirmation that is was so would be erroneous in regard to the bodies

1 पृथिव्यप्तेजसां प्रत्यक्षाणामेवारब्धं शरीरं प्रत्यक्षंस्यादपि यदि तत्र गुणान्तरं कारणगुणपूर्व्वकं प्रादुर्भवेत् न त्वेतदस्ति एकस्य गन्धादेरनारम्भकत्वस्योक्तत्वात् तथा च न त्र्यात्मकमपि शरीरं न रूपवद्भूतत्रयारब्धमपीत्यर्थः।।

2 कथं तर्ह्येकस्मिन्नैव शरीरे पाकादीनामुपलम्भ इत्यत आह। मिथः पञ्चानां भूतानां परस्परमुपष्टम्भकतया संयोगो न निषिध्यते किन्तु विजातीययोरण्वोर्द्रव्यं प्रत्यसमवायिकारणं संयोगो नेष्यते तथा च तदुपष्टम्भात् पाकादीनां शरीरे भवत्त्युपलम्भ इति तर्हि किम्प्रकृतिकतिदं मानुषशरीरमित्यत्र गौतमीयं सूत्रमुपतिष्ठते पार्थिवं तद्विशेषगुणोपलब्धेः पृथिवीविशेषगुणो गन्धो मानुषशरीरे आनाशमनपायी दृश्यते पाकादयस्तु शुष्कशरीरे नोपलभ्यन्ते इति तेषामौपाधिकत्वं गन्धस्य स्वाभाविकत्वमिति पार्थिवत्वव्यवस्थितेः।

of worms, mosquitoes etc., generated by warmth. No difference of constitution is known, for our bodies are not different in appearance from those of the divine sages. The uterine is twofold, viviparous and oviparous. Viviparous are the bodies of men and animals wild and domestic. The bodies of birds and reptiles are oviparous. Snakes, worms, fishes etc., are called reptiles, because it is their nature to creep about. Though tress etc., are a king of bodies, being subjects of fruition, —for life, death, sleep, waking, the use of medicine, seminal. propagation, desire of the agreeable, aversion from the disagreeable, etc., are impossible without a subject of fruition and growth, and the closing up of fractures are manifest, means of fruition; and there is the sacred text. The Śarala and Arjuna trees which grow on the banks of the Narmadā, from contact with the waters of the river attain to the highest state heareafter etc.; and such as In the burning ground grows a tree haunted by herons and vultures; yet germinant bodies do not evidently possess muscular motion and sensitive organs, and they are not therefore, in common usage called bodies.[1] U.

अनियतदिग्देशपूर्वकत्वात्।। 6।।

Non-uterine bodies exist

Aph. 6. Because (the non-uterine body) has antecedents of indeterminate time and space;—

It might be asked how the non-uterine body of Manu and other is produced, seeing that it is atoms originative of semen and blood that are originative of a particular body, and that these do not there exist. In anticipation of this difficulty the aphorism is stated. Atoms indeterminate in time and space are those which are not astricted to particular time and space. From having these for their antecedents or

[1] तत्र पार्थिवाप्यादिशरीरेषु मध्ये पार्थिवं शरीरं द्विविधम् के ते द्वे विधे इत्यत्राह। योनिजमयोनिजश्चेति आप्यतैजसवायवीयशरीराणां वरुणादित्यवायुलोकेषु प्रसिद्धानामयोनिजत्वमेव अयोनिजत्वं शुक्रशौरिणितसन्निपातानपेक्षत्वम् अयोनिजञ्च देवानामृषीणाञ्च श्रूयते हि ब्रह्मणो मानसा मन्वादय इति कारणमन्तरेण कथं कार्य्यमिति चेत् योनेः शरीरत्वावच्छेदेनाकारणत्वात् उष्मजकृमिमशकादिशरीरे व्यभिचारात् संस्थानविशेषवत्त्वस्य चासिद्धेः देवर्षिशरीरापेक्षया ऽस्मदादिशरीराणामन्यादृशत्वात् योनिजम् द्विविधं जरायुजमण्डजञ्च जरायुजमानुषपशुमृगाणां गर्भाशियस्य जरायुजत्वात् सर्पकीटमत्स्यादयो ऽपि सरीसृपा एव यद्यापि वृक्षादयो ऽपि शरीरभेदा एव भोगाधिष्ठानत्वात् न खलु भोगा-धिष्ठानत्वमन्तरेण जीवनमरणस्वप्रजागरणभेषजप्रयोगबीजसजातीयानुबन्धानुकूलोपगमप्रतिकूलापगमादयः सम्भवति वृद्धिक्षतभग्नसंरोहेण च भोगोपपादके स्फुटे एव आगमो ऽप्यस्ति नर्म्मदातीरसम्भूताः शरलार्ज्जुनपादपाः नर्म्मदातोयसंस्पर्शात् ते यान्ति परमां गतिम् इत्यादिः श्मशाने जायते वृक्षःकङ्कगृध्रादिसेवितः इत्यादिश्च तथापि चेष्टावत्त्वमिन्द्रियवत्त्वञ्च नोद्भिदां स्फुटतरमतो न शरीरव्यवहारः।।

conditions, there exist non-uterine bodies, such being the connection of the four aphorisms succeeding the fifth with the tenth. There exist therefore, in the sphere of Varuṇa etc. non-uterine bodies, aqueous, igneous, aerial, sensorial. To meet the question as to whence come the atoms originative of beings whose production is independent of semen, blood etc., it being seen that in the case of uterine bodies it is only seminal and sanguineous atoms that are originative, the following statement has been made. Atoms terrene, aqueous, igneous, and aerial, exist in all quarters and are in all places, and there being no local determination of these, there is no lack of atoms in the production of non-uterine bodies. For it is not true that no atoms other than seminal or sanguineous are originative of bodies, since, were it so, it would follow that there was no production of the bodies of gnats, mosquitoes, trees, shrubs, etc.[1] V.

धर्मविशेषाच्च ।। 7 ।।

Aph. 7. Also because of peculiar merit.

The sense is that in creation etc., motion arises in the atoms in consequence only of conjunction of soul with the fruits of actions done in a former state of being; and that the atoms having by that-action come together originate, in the order of binary atomic aggregates etc., the non-uterine bodies of divine sages and others. The following implication is also to be considered, that it is in consequence of peculiar demerit that the tortured bodies of mospuitoes and other insects generated by heat are produced.[2] U.

[1] ननु मन्वादीनामयोनिजं शरीरं कथमुत्पद्यते शुक्रशोणितारम्भकपरमाणूनामेव विशिष्टशरीरारम्भकत्वेन तत्र तदभावदित्याशङ्कायामाह। अनियतौ दिग्देशौ येषां ते अनियतदिग्देशाः परमाणवस्तत्पूर्वकत्वात् तदधीनत्वात् सन्त्ययोनिजाः इति दशमसूत्रेण पञ्चमान्तरनां चतुर्णां सूत्राणामन्वयः तथा च वरुणलोकादौ अयोनिजा आप्याः तैजसा वायवीया मानसाश्च देहाः सन्ति तेषां शुक्रशोणिताद्यनपेक्षोत्पत्तिकानामारम्भकाः परमाणवः कुत आगच्छन्ति योनिजेषु शुक्रशोणितपरमाणव एवारम्भका दृष्टा इत्याशकानिरासार्थमुक्तमिदम् पार्थिवा जलीयाः तैजसा वायवीयाश्च परमाणवः सर्व्वासुदिक्षु सर्व्वेषु देशेषु च सन्ति तेषां दिग्देशनियमाभावात् अयोनिजशरीरोत्पत्तौ न परमाणुदुर्भिक्षम् न हि शुक्रशोणितपरमाणुभिन्नाः परमाणवो न देहारम्भकाः दंशमशकतरुगुल्मादि-देहानुपपत्तिप्रसङ्गादित्यर्थः।।

[1] अदृष्टवदात्मसंयोगादेव सर्गादौ परमाणूनां कर्म्म तेन च कर्म्मणा सम्भूय परमाणवो द्व्यणुकक्रमेण अयोनिजं देवर्षीणां शरीरमारभन्ते इत्यर्थः उपलक्षणञ्चैतत् अधर्म्मविशेषाच्च क्षुद्रजन्तूनामुष्मजानां मशकादीनां यातनामयानि शरीराण्युत्पद्यन्ते इत्यपि द्रष्टव्यं।।

समाख्याभावाच्च ।। 8 ।।

Aph. 8. Also because names exist.

Because names or terms are or exist, without an ancestor or father to bestow them, for these words, are to be supplied. For not all names are imposed by a father etc., such terms as water-pot, cloth, not being thus assigned. It is therefore the same God who imposed names on water-pots, cloth, and other inanimate things; that imposed the names Manu, Marīchi etc. on non-uterine bodies.[1] V.

संज्ञाया अनादित्वात् ।। 9 ।।

Aph. 9. Because the name is without beginning.

By means of the primordial name Brahmā etc., which became manifest in creation etc., it is known that non-uterine body exists. For there are not parents of Brahmā, by whom the name Brahmā should be invented.[2] U.

सन्त्ययोनिजाः ।। 10 ।।

Aph. 10. There exist non-uterine bodies.

Here is pointed out that which is established by the four preceding aphorisms. The words peculiar bodies of Manu, Marīchi, and others are to be supplied.[3] V.

वेदलिङ्गाच्च ।। 11 ।।

Aph. 11. (This follows) also from the evidence of the Veda.

It is known from evidence or communication in the form of the Veda, from such texts as The Brāhman was his mouth, He created the Brāhman from his mouth, that there exist particular non-uterine bodies. But aqueous, igneous, and aerial bodies possess a sensitive apparatus, having the support of terrene particles. The terrene organ

1 समाख्या संज्ञा तस्याभावात् सत्त्वात् वीजिपित्रादिकं विनैवेति शेषः न हि सर्व्वाः संज्ञाः पित्रादिनैव निवेशिताः घटपटादिसंज्ञानान्तथात्वाभावात् तथा च येनेश्वरेण घटपटाद्यचेतनेषु संज्ञा निवेशितास्तेनैव मनुमरीच्यादिसंज्ञा अयोनिजेषु शरीरेषु निवेशिता इति भावः।।

2 सर्गादौ या ब्रह्मादिसंज्ञा आदिभूता प्राथमिकीतया क्रियते अस्त्ययोनिजं शरीरमिति न हि तदा ब्रह्मणे मातापितरौ स्तः याभ्यां ब्रह्मादिसंज्ञा कृता स्यादिति भावः।।

3 इदानीं चतुर्णामुक्ताणां सूत्रानां साध्यं निर्दिशति मनुमरीच्यादीनां देहविशेषा इति शेषः।।

is that of smell, and this aprehends odour and the universals contained in odour. The organ of smell is earthy, because in the midst of colours etc., it manifests odour only, in the same manner as clarified butter etc., manifests the scent of saffron, or like the fragrant particles wafted by the wind. The organ of taste is aqueous, because, while it does not manifest extraneous colour etc., it does reveal extraneous taste, in the same manner as water which reveals the flavour of grain fried and ground. This is cognistant of taste and the classes contained under it. Smell and taste have no power to cognise matter. The organ of vision is igneous, for whereas it does not manifest odour etc., it does manifest colour, in the same manner as the light of a lamp. This organ, by contact in the form of conjunction, cognises substances of appreciable colour and possessed of magnitude. It cognises also, by contact in the form of co-inherence in the conjunct, colour, number, extension, individuality, conjunction, disjunction, priority, posteriority, velocity, viscidity, fluidity, motion, and generality existing in such substances. By contact in the form of co-inherence in the co-inherent in the conjunct it cognises universal entities existent in that which exists in the existent (such as the nature of the class cow, such nature existing in the class which exists in its constituent members). By being qualitative of the conjunct, by being qualitative of the co-inherent in the conjunct etc. it cognises universal non-existences (viz., antecedent, subsequent, and absolute non-existence) which are non-existent in the existent and also reciprocal non-existences (such as the non-existence of a water-pot as a piece of cloth) which are non-existent in the non-existent residing in the existent. According to the system of Kaṇāda there is no perception of co-inherence. The organ of touch pervades the body, and is cognisant of appreciable touches and the classes therein contained. It thus cognises the objects cognisable to the eye, with the exception of colour and the univesal entities residing in colour only. According to the moderns it also cognises air. Its contact (with the tactile object) is as described above. The form of inference respecting it is, therefore, as follows:—This organ is aerial, for while it does not manifest colour etc., it does manifest touch, like the wind from a fan which manifests coldness in the perspiration adhering to the limbs. In all the aforesaid inferences the clause beginning with while or whereas is inserted to prevent an undue applicability to soul the internal organ, etc. So also, to prevent undue applicability to contact, we must add the qualification there being substantiality. The organ of hearing is ether limited to the outer part of the ear. This cognises sounds by co-inherence and the universals contained in sounds by co-inherence in the co-inherent. Whetever organ is cognisant of anything, is cognisant also of the universal non-existences in it non-existent, and of the reciprocal non-existences residing in it. So much for the five external organs. The common sensory is an internal organ, and by conjunction cognises soul tinged with its peculiar attributes. By co-inherence in the conjunct it cognises thought, pleasure, pain, desire, aversion; and volition, and a universal viz., the nature of soul. By co-inhesion in co-inherent in the conjunct it cognises the universals existent in thought, etc. A full discussion of the subject may be sought elesewhere.[1] V.

[1] वेदरूपं यल्लिङ्गं ज्ञापकं तस्मात तथा ब्राह्मणो ऽस्य मुखमासीत् स मुखतो ब्राह्मणमसृजत् इत्यादिकेभ्यो वेदेभ्य एव अजोनिजाः शरीरविशेषाः सन्तीति ज्ञायते परन्तु जलीयतैजसवायवीयशरीराणां पार्थिवभागोपष्टम्भादुपभोग-साधनत्वम् पार्थिवं इन्द्रियं घ्राणं तच्च गन्धस्य गन्धगतजातीनाञ्च ग्राहकम् घ्राणेन्द्रियं पार्थिवं रूपादिषु मध्ये गन्धस्यैव व्यञ्जकत्वात् कुङ्कुमगन्धाभिव्यञ्जकघृतादिवत् वायूपनीतसुरभिभागवद्वा रसनेन्द्रियं जलीयं परकीयसपाद्यव्यञ्जकत्वे सति परकीयरसव्यञ्जकत्वात् सक्तुरसाभिव्यञ्जकोदकवत् एतच्च रसस्य तद्गतजातीनाञ्च ग्राहकं द्रव्यग्रहणे घ्राणरसनयोर्न सामर्थ्यम चक्षुरिन्द्रियं तैजसं गन्धाद्यव्यञ्जकत्वे सति रूपव्यञ्जकत्वात् दीपप्रभावत् इदञ्च इन्द्रियं संयोगरूपसन्निकर्षेण उद्भूतरूपवन्ति महत्त्वविशिष्टानि च द्रव्याणि गृह्णाति संयुक्तसमवेतसमवायरूपसन्निकर्षेण तादृशद्रव्यवृत्तीनि रूपसंख्यापरिमितिपृथक्त्वसंयोगविभागपरत्वापरत्ववेगस्नेहद्रवत्वकर्म्मसामान्यानि च गृह्णाति संयुक्तसमवेतसमवायरूपसन्निकर्षेण योग्यवृत्तिवृतीनि सामान्यानि गृह्णाति संयुक्तविशेषणतासंयुक्तसमवेतविशेषण-तादिभिर्योग्यप्रतियोगिकान् संसर्गाभावान् योग्यगतान अयोग्यप्रतियोगिकान् अन्योन्याभावान् गृह्णाति काणादनये समवायस्य प्रत्यक्षं न भवति त्वगिन्द्रियं देहव्यापि उद्भूतस्पर्शग्राहकं तद्गतसामान्यग्राहकञ्च एवं रूपभिन्नान रूपमात्रगतसामान्यभिन्नांश्च चक्षुर्ग्राह्यान् गृह्णाति वायुमपि गृह्णातीति नव्याः सन्निकर्षस्तु पूर्व्ववत् तदेतदिन्द्रियं वायवीयं रूपाव्यञ्जकत्वे सति स्पर्शव्यञ्जकत्वात् अङ्गसङ्गिसलिलशैत्यव्यञ्जकव्यजनवातवदित्यादिरनुमानप्रकारः सर्व्वेषूक्तानुमानेषु आत्मनः प्रभृतिषु व्यभिचारवारणाय सत्यन्तम् एवं सन्निकर्षे व्यभिचारवारणाय द्रव्यत्वे सतीति विशेषणं देयम् कर्णशष्कुल्यवच्छिन्नं नभः श्रोत्रमिन्द्रियम् तच्च ममवायेन शब्दान् समवायेन तद्गतानि सामान्यानि च गृह्णाति यदिन्द्रिवं यद् ग्राहकं तत्प्रतियोगिकसंसर्गाभावानां तद्गतानामन्योन्याभावानाञ्च ग्राहकमपि तदिन्द्रियं भवति इति बाह्येन्द्रियाणि दश मनस्तु अन्तरिन्द्रयं तच्च संयोगेन आत्मानं विशेषगुणोपरक्तमेव गृह्णाति संयुक्तसमवायेन बुद्धिसुखदुखःखेच्छाद्वेषप्रयत्नान् आत्मत्वजातिञ्च गृह्णाति संयुक्तसमवेतसमवायेन बुद्ध्यादिगतानि सामान्यानि गृह्णातीत्यन्यत्र विस्तरः।।

Book V

FIRST DAILY LESSON

आत्मसंयोगप्रयत्नाभ्यां हस्ते कर्म।। 1।।

Action investigated

Aph. 1. Action in the hand is by means of conjunction with, and volition of, soul.

The object of the fifth chapter is the investigation of action. The investigation of action determinable by volition is that of the first daily lesson. In this there are sections treating of (1) throwing upwards, (2) throwing upwards effected without volition, (3) of action which has merit for its cause, (4) of actions good, bad and indifferent. The aphorism is propounded in relation to a particular kind of muscular action. Action in the hand as its co-inherent cause is by means of conjunction with soul, and of volition of soul. Of this action the non-coinherent cause is cojunction with soul possessing volition. Volition is the efficient cause. This is muscular action; for muscular action is action whose non-coinherent cause is conjunction with soul possessing volition, or action produced by volition of a subject other than the tangible which is not coinherent with, or excluded from, self.[1]U.

तथ हस्तसंयोगाच्च मुसले कर्म।। 2।।

Aph. 2. In like manner, from conjunction with the hand, is action in the pestle.

By the particle and gravity is implied as another efficient cause. In

[1] कर्म्मपरीक्षा पञ्चमाध्यायार्थः प्रयत्ननिष्पाद्यकर्म्मपरीक्ष प्रथमाह्निकार्थः तत्राप्युत्क्षेपणप्रकरणम् पुण्यहेतुकर्म्मप्रकरणम् पुण्यपापोदासीनकर्म्मप्रकरणञ्च चेष्टाविशेषमधिकत्याह। संयोगप्रयत्नश्च संयोगप्रयत्नौ आत्मनः संयोगप्रयत्नौ ताभ्यां हस्ते समवायिकारणे कर्म्म तस्य च कर्म्मणः प्रयत्नवदात्मसंयोगो ऽसमवायिकारणम् प्रयत्नश्च निमित्तकारणम् इयमेव चेष्टा प्रयत्नवदात्मसंयोगसमवायिकारणकक्रियायाः चेष्टात्वात् स्वासमवेतस्वातिरिक्त-स्पर्शवदन्यप्रयत्नजन्यक्रियाया वा।

like manner from conjunction with the hand may also mean from conjunction with the hand possessed of upward motion.In this instance the non-coinherent cause is conjunction of the pestle with the hand conjunct with soul possessing volition. The co-inherent cause is the pestle. The efficient causes are volition and gravity.[1] U.

अभिघातजे मुसलादौ कर्मणि व्यतिरेकादकारणं हस्तसंयोगः।। 3।।

Aph. 3. In the action produced in a pestle and the like by impact, conjunction with the hand is not a cause, being excluded from it.

The cause of the sudden upward motion which is produced in the pestle when struck by the mortar, is stated. In this instance though there is conjunction of the hand with the rising pestle, such conjunction is superfluous if regarded as a cause. The impact of the mortar is only the non-coinherent cause.It may be asked why this is the case. It is therefore stated that it is so because of the exclusion, that is, because volition would too widely or too narrowly predicated. If there were volition in this case, there would be no sudden upward motion in the pestle. By a volition to hold the pestle and mortar apart there would be a mere sustention of pestle; or the upward motion of the pestle would depend upon volition.[2] U.

तथात्मसंयोगो हस्तकर्मणि।। 4।।

Aph. 4. In like manner conjunction with soul in relation to action in the hand (is not a cause).

The aphorism is stated with the purpose of specifying a particular cause of the action of the hand as it flies upwards with the pestle, and of disproving the con-coinherent causality of conjunction with soul exercising volition.The meaning is that conjunction with soul, that is

[1] चकारेण गुरुत्वं निमित्तकारणान्तरं समुच्चिनोति तथेति तादृशमुत्क्षेपरूपणमेवेत्यर्थः यद्वा तथा हस्तसंयोगादुत्क्षेपणबद्धस्तसंयोगादित्यर्थः अत्र च प्रयत्नदात्मसंयुक्तेन हस्तेन मुसलस्य संयोगो ऽसमवायिकारणम् मुसलं समवायिकारणम् प्रयत्नगुरुत्वे निमित्तकारणे।।

[2] उदूखलाभिहतस्य मुसलस्याकस्माद् यदुत्पतनं जायते तत्र कारणमाह। अत्र यद्यपि मुसलेन उत्पतता हस्तस्य संयोगो ऽप्यस्ति तथा ऽपि स संयोगो ऽन्यथा सिद्धः किन्तु उदूखलाभिधात एव असमवायिकारणम् कुत एवमित्यत आह। व्यतिरेकादिति प्रयत्नस्य व्यभिचारादित्यर्थः यदि यद प्रयत्नः स्यात् मुसलस्यैवाकस्मिकमुत्पतनं न भवेत् विधारकेण प्रयत्नेन मुसलस्य धारणमेव भवेत् चेष्टाधीनं मुसलय पुनरुत्पतनं वा भवेत इति भावः।।

conjunction with soul exercising volition, is likewise not a cause of action in the hand as it suddenly rises with the pestle. The term not a cause is the preceding aphorism. The words in like manner are used to imply analogy.[1] U.

अभिघातान्मुसलसंयोगाद्धस्ते कर्म।। 5।।

Aph. 5. The action in the hand is from impact, and from conjunction with pestle.

An answer is furnished to the question: Whence then at that time the upward motion of the hand ? The hand rises at that time in the same manner in which the metal at the end of the pestle rises. By the word impact, is elliptically expressed recoil produced by impact. A recoil is produced in the pestle as its substratum by the vigorous action in the pestle accompanied with the impact. The upward motion in the hand also is consequent upon conjunction of the hand and pestle, in relation to the recoil so effected, as its non-coinherent cause. But this upward motion has not for its non-coinherent cause conjunction with soul exercising volition, for the hand rises involuntarily together with the pestle.[2] U.

आत्मकर्म हस्तसंयोगाच्च।। 6।।

Aph. 6. Action of the soul is also from conjunction with the hand.

An answer is furnished to the objection: In the case of the action which is produced in the body or in a of the body, conjunction part with soul exercising volition is the cause, why is it not so in the present instance ? The term soul tropically signifies a portion of the body. The impossibility of literal construction is the germ of tropical interpretation. The action then of the soul, that is of a member of the body, that is of the hand, results from conjunction of the hand and

[1] मुसलेन सहोत्यततो हस्तस्य कर्म्मणि कारणे विशेषमभिधातुं प्रयत्नवदात्मसंयोगस्यासमवायिकारणत्वं निराकर्त्तुमाह। मुसलेन सहोत्पततो हस्तस्य कर्म्मणि आत्मसंयोग: प्रयत्नवदात्मसंयोगस्तथा अकारणमित्यर्थ: अकारणमिति पूर्व्वसूत्रस्थं तथेत्यतिदिश्यते।।

[2] कुतस्तर्हि हस्ते तदोत्पतनमत आह। यथा मुसले उत्पतति मुसलमुखस्थं लोहमुत्पतति तथा हस्तो ऽपि तदोत्पतति अत्राभिघातशब्देन अभिघातजनित: संस्कार उच्यते उपचारात् उत्पततो मुसलस्य पटुतरेण कर्म्मणा अभिघातसहकृतेन स्वाश्रये मुसले संस्कारो जनितस्तत्कृतं संस्कारमपेक्ष्य हस्तमुसलसंयोगादसमवायिकारणाद्धस्ते ऽप्युत्पतनं न तु तदुत्पतनं प्रयत्नवद्यत्मसंयोगासमवायिकारणम् अवशो हि हस्तो मुसलेन सहोत्पततीति भाव:।।

pestle. The word and implies also velocity. In the action of the hand conjunction with the hand is the non-coinherent cause. There is here no unduly wide or narrow predication. This conjunction is at some times conjunction with the soul willing, at others conjunction with the pestle possessed of velocity, as is the case with the limbs of one who has the gout.[1] U.

संयोगाभावे गुरुत्वात् पतनम्।। 7।।

Aph. 7. In the absence of conjunction falling results from gravity.

By the term conjunction impediments of whatever kind are also implied. In the absence, therefore, of impediments, in consequence of gravity as its non-coinherent cause falling, an action resulting in conjunction below, is produced. Here in fruit etc., possessing gravity, the impediment is conjunction; in a bird etc., sustentative volition is the impediment to falling; in an arrow discharaed it is the recoil that is the impediment to falling. The sense is that falling is dependent on gravity in the absence of these obstructives.[2] U.

In the case of a body resting upon a tree or other high place, falling in consequence of the breaking of the bough etc., which supports it, or by accidentally slipping, it is gravity which is the cause, not conjunction with soul exercising volition, for that does not occasion falling but sometimes prevents it. Hence it is that in the case of birds etc., soaring in the sky, in consequence of conjunction with soul possessing volition as an impediment, there is no fall. In like manner it is from conjunction with God possessing volition as an impediment, that the earth and other worlds do not fall.[1] V.

[1] ननु शरीरे शरीरावयवे वा यत्कर्म्मोपद्यते तत्र प्रयत्नवदात्मसंयोगः कारणम् प्रकृते कथं न तथेत्यत आह। आत्मशब्दः शरीरावयवपर उपचारात् अन्वयानुपपत्तिरेवोपचारबीजम् तथा चात्मनः शरीरावयवस्यापि हस्तस्य यत्कर्म्म तत् हस्तमुसलसंयोगात् चकाराच्च वेगसमुच्चयः हस्तकर्म्मणि हस्तसंयोगस्तावदसमवायिकारणं तत्र व्यभिचारो नास्ति स च क्वचित् प्रयत्नवदात्मसंयोगः क्वचिद्वेगवन्मुसलादिस्तसंयोगो यथा वातुलस्य शरीरावयवकर्म्मेति भावः।।

[2] संयोगपदेन प्रतिबन्धकमात्रमुपलक्षयति प्रतिबन्धकाभावे गुरुत्वादसमवायिकारणात् पतनम् अधःसंयोगफलिका क्रिया जायते तत्र गुरुत्ववति फलादौ प्रतिबन्धकसंयोगः विहङ्गमादौ तु विधारकः प्रयत्नः पतनप्रतिबन्धकः काण्डादौ क्षिप्ते संस्कार एवः पतनप्रतिबन्धकः एतेषामभावे गुरुत्वाधीनं पतनमित्यर्थः।।

[3] वृक्षाद्युच्चदेशारूढस्य देहस्य अवलम्बनशाखादिभङ्गेन दैवात् स्खलनादिना यत् पतनं भवति तत्र गुरुत्वमेव कारणं न तु प्रयत्नवदात्मसंयोगः तस्य पतनाप्रयोजकत्वात् क्वचित् प्रतिबन्धकत्वाच्च अत् एव विहायसि विहरतां विहङ्गमादीनां प्रयत्नवदात्म संयोगादेव प्रतिबन्धान्न पतनम् एवं प्रयत्नवदीश्वरसंयोगात् प्रतिबन्धादेव भूरादिलोकानां न पतनम्।।

नोदनविशेषाभावान्नोर्ध्वं न तिर्यग्गमनम्।। 8।।

Aph. 8. No upward or sideward motion takes place without a particular impulse.

The perpendicular or horizontal motion which takes place in a clod of earth, an arrow etc., though they possess gravity, results from a particular, that is a violent, impulse. In the case of the falling, therefore, of a fruit, a bird, an arrow etc., in the absence of conjunction, volition, and recoil, there does not exist a particular impulse, and consequently there is no vertical or lateral motion.[1] U.

प्रयत्नविशेषान्नोदनविशेषः।। 9।।

Aph. 9. Particular impulse results from particular volition.

नोदनविशेषादुदसनविशेषः।। 10।।

*Aph.*10. From particular impulse results particular casting upward.

As for particular impulse, whence is it produced ? This question is answered. Particular impulse is produced by particular volition, of which the cause is the desire to throw sidewards or upwards, far or near. By this impulse etc., perpendicular or horizontal movement is produced in a substance such as a clod of earth. Casting upwards is throwing far upwards.[2] U.

हस्तकर्मणा दारककर्म व्याख्यातम्।। 11।।

Aph. 11. By the action of the hand, the action of a child is explained.

The action which is produced in the hand, together with the pestle by the impact of the mortar, is not preceded by volition, or a cause of merit and demerit. The analogy of this motion to a child's movement of its hands and feet, is pointed out. Though a child's movement of its hands and feet, has volition for its antecedent, it has no good or evil

[1] गुरुत्ववतो ऽपि लोष्ठकाण्डादेर्यदूर्ध्वं तिर्य्यक् च गमनं तन्नोदनविशेषात् तीव्रतरान्नोदनात् तथा च फलपक्षिबाणादौ संयोगप्रयत्नसंस्काराभावे यत् पतनं तन्न नोदनविशेषो नास्ति तेन न तिर्य्यञ् न वोद्ध्वं गमनमिति भावः।।

[2] ननु नोदनविशेष एव कुत उत्पद्यते तत्राह। तिर्य्यक् उद्ध्र्वं दूरम् आस वा क्षिपामीतिच्छाकारणकः प्रयत्नविशेषः तज्जनितो नोदनविशेषस्ततो गुरुत्ववतो द्रव्यस्य लोष्टादेरूद्ध्र्वं तिर्य्यक् च गमनमुपपद्यते उदसनं दूरोत्क्षेपणम्।।

result, and is not a cause of merit or demerit. Such is the meaning of the analogy.[1] U.

तथा दग्धस्य विस्फोटने।। 12।।

Aph. 12. In like manner in the case of the bursting open of one burnt.

In a house which has been set on fire by a felon, when a man has there been burnt, and his body torn open by the fire, the action which is produced in the hand etc., by the will to kill the felon, is neither a cause of merit, nor a cause of demerit; as it has been said, In the slaying of a felon there is no sin in him that slays openly or covertly: wrath encounters wrath. An incendiary, a poisoner, an assasin, a thief, a ravisher of wife or field—these six are felons.[2] U.

प्रयत्नभावे प्रसुप्तस्य चलनम्।। 13।।

Involuntary motion

Aph. 13. Movement of the sleeping takes place in the absence of volition.

Movement, action such as the sideward or upward moving of the limbs takes place in the sleeping, in the body possessing a state of profound slumber, even in the absence of volition generated by such desire as to throw upwards. A particular volition is not, therefore, always the cause of such motion.[3] V.

तृणे कर्म वायुसंयोगात्।। 14।।

Aph. 14. Action takes place in grass from conjunction with wind.

1 उदूखलाभिघातात् मुसलेन सह हस्ते यत्कर्म्म उत्पन्नं तत्तावत् प्रयत्नपूर्व्वकं न भवति नापि पुण्यपापहेतुरतस्तत्तुल्यतां बालकस्य क्रीडाकरचरणादिचालनं यत्त्रातिदिशति बालकस्य यद्यपि करचरणादिचालनं प्रयत्नपूर्व्वकमेव तथापि हिताहितफलप्राप्तिफलकं न भवति न वा पुण्यपापहेतुरित्यतिदेशार्थः।।

2 आततायिना केनाप्यगारे दह्यमाने तत्र दग्धस्य पुरुषस्य विस्फोटेवह्निकृते जाते सति तस्याततायिनो वधानुकूलेन प्रयत्नेन हस्तादौ यत्कर्म्म जनितं तन्न पुण्यहेतुर्न वा पापहेतुः यथाहुः नाततायिवधे दोषो हन्तुर्भवति कश्चन प्रकाशं वा ऽप्रकाशं वा मन्युस्तन्मन्युमृच्छति। अग्निदोगरदश्चैव शस्त्रपाणिर्धनापहा। क्षेत्रदाराग्रहारी च षडेते आततायिनः।।

3 उर्ध्वं क्षिषामीत्यादीच्छाजनितप्रयत्नाभावे ऽपि प्रसुप्तस्य सुषुप्त्यवस्थान्वितस्य शरीरस्य चलनं तिर्य्यगू-र्ध्वाङ्गचालनादिकर्म्म उत्पद्यते इत्यर्थः तथा च प्रयत्नाविशेषो न सर्वत्र हेतुरिति भावः।।

The actions of the body being explained, those of other objects are treated of. All such objects as trees, shrubs, climbing plants, are implied in the term grass.[1] U.

मणिगमनं सूच्यभिसर्पणमदृष्टकारणम्।। 15।।

Aph. 15. The movement of the gem, and the approach of the needle, are caused by destiny.

By the term gem are intended vessels made of gold etc., and filled with water. To such a vessel magicians apply incantations for the recovery of stolen property. The tradition of the ancients is that the vessel is set on the ground, and some other person lays his hand upon it. The vessel accompanied with the hand, in consequence of the efficacy of the incantation, turns towards the spot where the stolen property has been deposited. The reason of the movement of such a vessel is not a particular volition, but the efficient cause is the merit of the former possessor or the demerit of the thief. The non-coinherent cause is conjunction of such a vessel with soul possessing such destiny (or results of actions done in previous states of existence); and the co-inherent cause is such a vessel. In like manner destiny is also the cause is such a vessel. In like manner destiny is also the cause of the attraction towards a loadstone, which takes place in needles or metallic rods when in proximity to the magnet. If it be asked in consequence of whose destiny (or previous merits and demerits) motion takes place in needles etc., the reply is that it is the destiny of him to whom benefit or injury accrues by the motion, that is the cause. The term needle implies other objects, iron in general attracted by the loadstone being intended. It is to be inferred that destiny is the cause of the motion of pieces of grass attracted by amber, of the upward flaming of fire, of the horizontal motion of wind, and of the action of the primordial atoms at creation.[2] V.

[1] शरीरकर्म्माणि व्याख्याय तदितराण्याह। तृणपदेन वृक्षगुल्मलतावतानादिकं सर्व्वमुपलक्षयति।।

[2] मणिपदेन जलपूर्णकाञ्चनादिमयपात्राण्यभिप्रेतानि चौर्य्यधनलब्धये तादृशपात्रे मान्त्रिकैर्मन्त्रप्रयोगः क्रियते तादृशपात्रन्तु भूमौ तिष्ठति तदुपरि अपरेण केनचिद्दक्षिणहस्तः स्थाप्यते मन्त्रसामर्थ्यात्तत्पात्रं तादृशहस्तसहितमेव चौर्य्यधनावस्थानाभिमुखं गच्छति तत्र स्थाने गत्वा स्थिरं भवतीति प्राचा किंवदन्ती तादृशपात्रगमनेन प्रयत्नविशेषो हेतुः किन्तु पूर्वस्वामिनः सुकृतं चौरस्य दुष्कतं वा निमित्तकारणम् तादृशपात्रन्तु समवायिकारणम् एवं अयस्कान्तसन्नि-धाने सति सूचीनां लोहशलाकानां यदयस्कान्ताभिमुखगमनं भवति तत्रापि अदृष्टमेव हेतुः ननु कस्यादृष्टेन सूच्यादीनां गमनमितिचेत् तद्गमनेन यस्य हितमहितं वा भवति तददृष्टस्यैव तत्र हेतुत्वम् सूचीत्युपलक्षणम् अयस्कान्ताकृष्टलोह-मात्रमभिप्रेतम् तृणकान्तमण्याकृष्टानां तृणानां गमने वह्नेरूर्ध्वज्वलने वायोस्तिर्य्यग्गमने सर्गाद्यकालीनपरमाणुकर्म्मणि चादृष्टकारणकत्वमूहनीयमिति संक्षेपः।।

इषावयुगपत्संयोगविशेषाः कर्मान्यत्वे हेतुः।। 16।।

Aph. 16. Particular non-simultaneous conjunctions in an arrow are the cause of the diversity of its action.

The sense of this aphorism is as follows. After conjunction of arrows etc., moving with velocity, with a wall and the like, a cessation of motion is observed, though the arrows etc., continue to exist. In this case it is not destruction of the substratum that is destructive of motion, for the substratum continues to exist. Also no other contrary property is observed. It, therefore, follows that it is a self-produced conjunction that destroys the action of the arrow. This conjunction produced in the fourth moment destroys the action in the fifth moment. The meaning, therefore, is that the production of the action, then disjunction, next the destruction of the prior conjunction, the subsequent conjunction, and the destruction of the action, make known the diversity of the action. Particular conjunctions, means peculiarity in conjunction, of self-production. Otherwise, were conjunction in general destructive of action, action could not abide anywhere.[1] U.

नोदनादाद्यमिषोः कर्म तत्कर्मकारिताच्च संस्कारादुत्तरं तथोत्तरमुत्तरञ्च।। 17।।

Aph. 17. The first action of the arrow is from impulse, the next is from self-reproduction caused by that action, and in like manner the next and the next.

The first action in an arrow when discharged is produced by a bowstring drawn by human volition. In this case the impulse is the non-coinherent cause; the arrow is the co-inherent cause; volition and gravity are the efficent causes. By this first action self-reproduction termed velocity is produced in the same substance. This is established by the perception that it is the arrow moves with velocity. By this self-reproduction action is produced in the arrow. Of this the non-coinherent cause is the self-reproduction; the co-inherent cause is the arrow; and the efficient cause is a particular keen impetus. In like

[1] इदमत्राकूतं वेगेन गच्छतां शरदीनां कुड्यादिसंयोगानन्तरं शरादौ सत्येव गत्युपरमोदृश्यते अन्त्राश्रयनाशस्तावन्नतन्नाशकः आश्रयस्य विद्यमानत्वात् विरोधिगुणान्तरञ्च नोपलभ्यते तेन स्वजन्यः संयोगएव कर्म्मनाशकइत्युन्नीयते स च संयोगश्चतुर्थक्षणे जातः पञ्चमक्षणे कर्म्म नाशयति तथाहि कर्म्मोत्पत्तिरथविभागः अथ पूर्व्वसंयोगनाशः उत्तरसंयोगः कर्म्मनाशः तेनायुगपत् संयोगविशेषाः कर्म्मनानात्वज्ञापकाइत्यर्थः संयोगविशेषा इति संयोगेविशेषः स्वजन्यत्वमेव अन्यथा संयोगमात्रस्य कर्म्मनाशकत्वे कर्म्म क्वचिदपि न तिष्ठेत्।।

manner a succession of actions one after the other is produced by the self-reproduction, which continues until the arrow falls. A single self-reproduction produces a succession of actions, for when an action is destroyed by subsequent conjunction produced by itself, the self-reproduction produces another action. It is not proper to suppose a succession of self-reproductions like the succession of actions, for the hypothesis is unnecessary. To show this the words In like manner the next and the next, are added, and term Self-reproduction caused by that action is in the singular number. In the Nyāya doctrine which affirms a succession of self-reproductions like the succession of actions, there is complexity (or a violation of the law of parcimony). The reason that of two arrows simultaneously discharged the velocity of the one is swift and that of the other slow, is the swiftness or slowness of the impetus.[1] U.

संस्काराभावे गुरुत्वात् पतनम्।। 18।।

Aph. 18. Falling results from gravity in the absence of self-reproduction.

It might be objected that in such a case the arrow would continue in motion and never fall. The answer is as follows it: There being non-existence, that is destruction, of the self-reproduction, the velocity produced by the first action, from gravity as its cause, there results falling in an arrow etc.; that is, the time during which the particular velocity lasts, determined as the final moment, destroys such velocity. In some cases also conjunction with another substance is destructive of velocity. It was in consequence, then, of the existence of a preventive velocity that there was no previous fall of the arrow etc., but a succession of motions. There was in consequence of the destruction of the cause

[1] पुरुषप्रयत्ने नाकृष्टया पतञ्जिकया नुन्नस्येषोराद्यं कर्म्म जायते तत्र नोदनमसमवायिकारणम् इषुः समवायिकारणम् प्रयत्नगुरुत्वे निमित्तकारणे तेन चाद्येन कर्म्मणा समानाधिकरणो वेगाख्यः संस्कारो जन्यते स च वेगेन गच्छतीति प्रत्यक्षसिद्धएव तेन संस्कारेण तत्रेषौ कर्म्म जायते तत्रासमवायिकारणं संस्कारः समवायिकारणमिषुः निमित्तकारणन्तु तीव्रो नोदनविशेषः एवञ्चः यावदिषु पतनमनुवर्त्तमानेन संस्कारेण उत्तरोत्तरः कर्म्मसन्तानो जायते स्वजन्योत्तरसंयोगेन कर्म्मणि नष्टे संस्कारेण कर्म्मान्तरजननात् एकएव संस्कारः कर्म्मसन्तानजनकः नतु कर्म्म संतानवत् संस्कारसन्तानो ऽप्यभ्युपगन्तुमुचितो गौरवादिति दर्शयितुमाह। तथोत्तरमुत्तरञ्चेति तत्कर्म्मकारिताञ्चसंस्कारादित्येकवचनञ्च न्यायनये रूपकर्म्मसत्तानवत् संस्कारसन्तानस्वीकारे गौरवम् यत्तु युगपत् प्रक्षिप्तशरयोरेकस्य तीव्रावेगो ऽपरस्य तु मन्दस्तत्र नोदनतीव्रत्वमन्दत्वे निमित्तम्।।

of the action of moving, no subsequent movement, but falling results from the absence of an obstructive. In this there is no impossibility.[1] V.

[1] नन्वेवं शरश्चिरमेव गच्छेत् कदाचिदपि न पतेदित्यत आह। संस्कारस्याद्यकर्म्मजनितस्य वेगस्य अभावे नाशे सति गुरुत्वात् कारणदेवपतनं शरादौ जायते इत्यर्थः यादृशवेगविशेषो यावन्तं कालन्तिष्ठति तावानेवकालो ऽन्तिमक्षणावच्छिन्नस्तादृश वेगं नाशयति क्वचित्तु द्रव्यान्तरसंयोगो ऽपि वेगनाशकः तथा च प्रतिबन्धकस्य वेगस्य सत्त्वादेव पूर्व्वं शरादेर्न पतनं किन्तु गतिसन्तान एवाभूत् उत्तरकालन्तु गमनकर्म्मणः कारणविनाशान्तगमनं किन्तु प्रतिबन्धकाभावात् पतनमेव भवतीति न किञ्चिदनुपपन्नम्।।

SECOND DAILY LESSON

नोदनापीडनात् संयुक्तसंयोगाच्च पृथिव्यां कर्म।। 1।।

*Aph.*1. Action in earth results from impulse, impact, and conjunction with the conjunct.

In earth, in a bamboo etc., action is sometimes produced by the impulse of fire etc., and sometimes from the impact of an axe etc. Similarly action is produced in a chariot etc., through conjunction with the conjunct, through conjunction with the harness conjunct with the horses as they move. In the first of these instances, that of action in a bamboo etc., the impulse of fire etc., is the non-coinherent cause, the bamboo etc., the co-inherent cause, destiny the efficient cause. In the second, the blow with the hatchet etc., is the non-coinherent cause. In the third, conjunction with the harness conjunct with the horses is the non-coinherent cause.[1] V.

तद्विशेषेणादृष्टकारितम्।। 2।।

Aph. 2. That action which is produced in a different manner from these, is caused by destiny.

That which, as an earthquake etc., is produced in a different manner, to the exclusion of these, of impulse, impact, and conjunction with the conjunct, is caused by destiny, i.e., has for its non-coinherent cause conjunction with soul destined; since it is the destiny of him to whom pleasure or pain results from the earthquake, that is the particular cause of the earthquake.[2] V.

[1] पृथिव्यां वंशादौ कदाचिद्वाह्न्यादिनोदनात् कर्म्म जायते कदाचिच्च कुठाराद्यभिघातात एवं संयुक्तसंयोगात् अश्वादिसंयुक्तरज्जुसंयोगात् रथादौ कर्म्म जायते तत्र प्रथमे वंशादिकर्म्मणि वह्न्यादिनोदनमसमवायिकारणम् वंशादिः समवायिकारणम् अद्रष्टादिकं निमित्तकारणम् द्वितीये कुठाराद्यभिघातो ऽसमवायिकारणम् तृतीये ऽश्वसंयुक्तरज्जुसंयोगो ऽसमवायिकारणमिति।।

[2] तेषां नोदनाभिघातसंयुक्तसंयोगानां विशेषेण व्यतिरेकेण जातं यत् भूकम्पादिकं कर्म्म तत् अदृष्टकारितम् अदृष्टवदात्मसंयोगासमवायिकारणकमित्यर्थः भूकम्पेन यस्य सुखं दुःखं वा भवति तदद्रष्टस्य तत्रासाधारणकरणत्वादिति भावः।।

अपां संयोगाभावे गुरुत्वात् पतनम्।। 3।।

Aph. 3. The falling of water results from gravity in the absence of conjunction.

The section investigative of action co-inherent in fluids is here commenced. In this it is stated that the falling of water, in the form of rain, has gravity for its non-coinherent cause. This takes place when there is absence of conjunction, of conjunction with a cloud. The absence of conjunction is, therefore, the efficient cause.[1] U.

द्रवत्वात् स्यन्दनम्।। 4।।

Aph. 4. Flowing results from fluidity.

It may be asked how there is in drops of rain action productive of mutual conjunction. The answer is therefore given. The flowing or distant progression of the stream or great aqueous whole composed by mutual conjunction of the fallen waters or raindrops, is produced by fluidity as its non-coinherent cause, and by gravity as its efficient cause, in the waters as its co-inherent or material cause.[2] U.

नाड्यो वायुसंयोगादारोहणम्।। 5।।

Aph. 5. The sun's rays cause the ascent of water through conjunction with air.

नोदनापीडनात् संयुक्तसंयोगाच्च।। 6।।

Aph. 6. Through the impress of the impulse, and conjunction with the conjunct.

It may be asked how the sun's rays have such power as to draw up waters situated on the earth. Through the impress, the congress by means of the impulse, the impulse of a strong wind, waters conjunct with the sun's rays conjunct with the wind, fly upwards; as the rays of fire driven by the wind draw up boiling water in a caldron. The particle

[1] इदानीं द्रवद्रव्यसमवेतकर्म्मपरीक्षाप्रकरणम् तत्राह। अपां यत् पतनं वर्षणरूपं तद् गुरुत्वासमवायिकारणकम् तत् संयोगस्य मेघसंयोगस्याभावे सति भवति तेन संयोगाभावस्तन्निमित्तकारणमित्यर्थः।।

[2] क्षितौ पतितानामपां बिन्दूनां परस्परं संयोगेन महज्जलावयविस्त्रोतोरूपं यज्जायते तस्त यत् स्यन्दनं दूरसंसरणम् तत् द्रवत्वादसमवायिकारणादुत्पद्यते गुरुत्वान्निमित्तकारणादसमवायिकारणेषु।।

and means as; and the example of water in a caldron is to be considered.[1] U.

वृक्षाभिसर्पणमित्यदृष्टकारितम्।। 7।।

Aph. 7. The circulation in trees is caused by destiny.

The circulation in tree of waters sprinkled on the root is caused by destiny. The action by which the waters rise and cause the growth of the tree, results from conjunction of destiny with the souls of those in whose souls pleasure or pain is effected by the growth of the leaves, stem, fruit, flowers etc., as its non-coinherent cause; from destiny as its efficient cause; and in water as its coinherent cause.[2] U.

अपां सङ्घातो विलयनञ्च तेजःसंयोगात्।। 8।।

Aph. 8. The freezing and thawing of water results from conjunction with light.

Aqueous atoms originating a binary atomic aggregate, in consequence of being impeded by the light of the sky, do not originate in these aggregate fluidity. Snow, hail etc. void of fluidity, are thus originated by constituent elements void of fluidity, and successively by binary and other aggregates. They are consequently observed to be hard. It might be asked what proof there is that snow, hail etc., are water. The words and thawing from conjunction with light are therefore added. Action is produced in the atoms originative of snow, hail etc., by powerful conjunction with light. From this action results disjunction. Then in the course of destruction of the originative conjunction, results destruction of the larger constituent parts of the snow, hail etc. Next in consequence of the departure of the conjunction with light which prevents fluidity, these same atoms

[1] ननु यदि भूमिष्ठानामपाम् ऊर्ध्वं गमनं भवति तदा गुरूत्वात् पतनंवर्षणं सम्भाव्यते तदेव तु कुतइत्यत आह कारयन्तीति शेषः यदपामूर्ध्वमारोहणं तत् नाड्यः सूर्य्यरश्मयो वायुसंयोगात् कारयन्ति ग्रीष्मे वाय्वभिहताः सूर्य्यरश्मयएव आरोहयन्त्यप इत्यर्थः क्वचित् पाठोनाड्यवायुसंयोगादिति स च नाड्यो नाडीसम्बन्धीयो वायुसंयोग इत्युपपादनीयः।।

ननु सूर्य्यरश्मीनां कथमयं महिमा यत् भूमिष्ठा अपऊर्ध्वं नयन्तीत्यत आह। नोदनेन बलवद्वायुनोदनेन आपीडनादास्कन्दनात् वायुसंयुक्ता रश्मयस्तत्संयुक्ता आपऊर्ध्वं धावन्ति यथा स्थालीस्था अपः क्वथ्यमानाः वायुनुन्नवह्निरश्मय ऊर्ध्वं नयन्ति चकार इवार्थस्तत्र च उपमानं स्थालीयाण्वापो द्रष्टव्याः।।

[2] अभितः सर्पणमभिसर्पणं तदभिसर्पणं मूले निषिक्तानामपां वृक्षे तददृष्टकारितं पत्रकाण्डफलपुष्पादिवृद्धिकृतं सुखं दुःखं वा येषामात्मनां अदृष्टवत्तदात्मसंयोगादसमवायिकारणात् अदृष्टान्निमित्तादप्सु समवायिकारणेषु तत् कर्म्म भवति येन कर्म्मणा आप ऊर्द्धं गत्वा वृक्षं वर्द्धयन्तीत्यर्थः।।

originate fluidity in the binary atomic aggregates, from which results the thawing of the snow, and hail etc. thus endowed with fluidity. Of this the efficient cause is the powereful ingress of light.[1] U.

तत्र विस्फूर्जथुर्लिङ्गम्।। 9।।

Aph. 9. In these the rolling of thunder is a mark.

In these in the waters of the sky—the rolling of thunder is a mark of the ingress of the light of the sky;that is, it is the pealing of thunder which warrants the inference. The excessive brilliance of lightning is perceptible, and after that follows the thunder which also is perceptible. It is therefore inferred that lightning, the light of the sky, has entered into the cloud from which the hailstones appear. In consequence of this is the prevention of fluidity in the water originative of hail.[2] U.

वैदिकश्च।। 10।।

Aph. 10. There is also Vedic [authority establishing this.]

अपां संयोगाद्विभागाच्च स्तनयित्नोः।। 11।।

Aph. 11. [The rolling of thunder results] from conjunction with water and disjunction from a cloud.

It may be asked how thunder is produced, for no impact nor any kind of disjunction causative of sound is observed. The answer is here given. Thunder results from conjunction with water, that is from its being struck by wind, and from disjunction from a cloud.[3] V.

[1] दिव्येन तेजसा प्रतिबन्धादाप्या परमाणवोद्व्यणुकमारभमाणाद्व्यणुकेषु द्रवत्वं नारभन्ते ततो द्रवत्वशून्यैरव-यवैर्द्व्यणुकादिप्रक्रमेण द्रवत्वशून्याहिमकरकादय आरभ्यन्ते तेन तेषां काठिन्यमुपलभ्यते नन्वेवं हिमकरकादीनामाप्यत्वे किं प्रमाणमत उक्तं विलयनञ्च तेजः संयोगादिति तेजः संयोगेन बलवता हिमकरकारम्भकपरमाणूनां क्रिया क्रियातो विभागस्ततआरम्भकसंयोगनाशपरम्पराया हिमकरकादिमहावयविनाशस्तत्र द्रवत्वप्रतिबन्धकतेजः संयोगाविगमात् तण्व परमाणवः द्व्यणुकेषु द्रवत्वमारभन्ते ततो द्रवत्ववतां हिमकराकादिनां विलयनं तत्र च वलवत्तेजोनुप्रवेशो निमित्तम्।।

[2] तत्र दिव्यासु अप्सु दिव्यानां तेजसामनुप्रवेशो विस्फूर्ज्जथुर्लि वज्जनिर्घोष एव लिङ्गमित्यर्थः आत्यन्तिकविद्युत्प्रकाशस्तावत्प्रत्यक्ष एव तदनुप्रदञ्च स्फूर्ज्जथुः सोऽपि प्रत्यक्ष एव तेनानुमीयते यस्मान्मेघात् करकाः प्रादुर्भवन्ति तत्र दिव्यन्तेजो विद्युद्रूपमनुप्रविष्टं तदुपष्टम्भेन करकारम्भकाणामयां द्रवत्वप्रतिबन्ध इति।।

[3] ननु शब्दकारणस्याभिघातस्य विभागविशेषस्य चानुभवात् विस्फूर्ज्जथुः कथमुत्पद्यते इत्यत आह अपां जलानां संयोगात् अर्थाद्वायुना अभिघातात् स्तनयित्नोर्मेघाच्च विभागात् विस्फूर्ज्जथुर्भवतीत्यर्थः।।

पृथिवीकर्मणा तेजःकर्म वायुकर्म च व्याख्यातम्।। 12।।

Aph. 12. The action of light and the action of air, are explained by the action of earth.

Conjunction with soul destined has been pronounced the cause of earthquakes. In like manner in the case of the action which is produced in light which causes a sudden conflagration, and in wind which causes a sudden agitation of trees etc., the non-coinherent cause is conjunction with soul influenced by destiny; air and fire are the co-inherent causes; and destiny is the efficient cause.[1] U.

अग्नेरूर्ध्वज्वलनं वायोस्तिर्यक्पवनमणूनां मनसश्चाद्यकर्मादृष्टकारितम्।। 13।।

Aph. 13. The upward flaming of fire, the sideward blowing of wind, and the first action of atoms and of the internal organ, are caused by destiny.

The word first means existing in the earliest time of creation. There being no impulse, impact etc., at that time, it is conjunction with soul influenced by destiny that is in these the non-coinherent cause. The word first applies also to blazing upwards and blowing sidewards. It is proper to hold that velocity is the cause of other actions of blazing and blowing; for there being a visible cause, there is no occasion for an unseen cause (or destiny as a cause).[2] U.

हस्तकर्मणा मनसः कर्म व्याख्यातम्।। 14।।

Aph. 14. The action of the internal organ is explained by the action of the hand.

As the action of the hand in the throwing upwards of a pestle etc., has for its non-coinherent cause conjunction with soul possessing will; in like manner the action of the mind, which has for its purpose contact

1 भूकम्पं प्रत्यदृष्टवदात्मसंयोगः कारणमुक्तम् तत्रैवाकस्मिकदिग्दाहहेतोस्तेजसः आकस्मिकवृक्षादिक्षोभहेतोश्च प्रभञ्जनस्य कर्म्म यत् संजायते तत्राप्यदृष्टवदात्मसंयोगो समवायिकारणम् वायुतेजसी समवायिकारणम् अदृष्टं निमित्तकारणमित्यर्थः।।

2 आद्यमिति सर्गाद्यकालीनमित्यर्थः तदानोदनाभिघातादीनामभावात् अदृष्टयदात्मसंयोग एव तत्रासमवायिकारणम् आद्यमूर्ध्वज्वलनं आद्यं तिर्य्यक् पवनमिति इतरेषां ज्वलनपवनकर्म्मणां। वेगासमवायिकारणकत्वमेव मन्तुमुचितं दृष्टे कारणे सत्यदृष्टकल्पनानवकाशात्।।

with the organ percipient of the desired objects, also has for its non-coinherent cause conjunction with soul exerting volition. Although the internal sensory as an organ is not an immediate object of volition, it is to be considered that action is produced in the internal sensory by volition acting upon the channel which conveys the internal organ. It must be admitted that this channel is perceptible to the sense of touch, else the transmission of what is eaten and drunk, by means of volition acting upon the channel of breath, whould be impossible.[1] V.

आत्मेन्द्रियमनोऽर्थसन्निकर्षात् सुखदुःखम्।। 15।।

Aph. 15. Pleasure and pain result from contact of soul, sense, mind, and object.

Pleasure and pain imply other states. Cognitions and volitions are also to be considered. The infinity of the internal organ has been previously disproved , and its atomic, minuteness proved. It has been stated that the impossibilty of simultaneous cognitions is the mark of the existence of an internal organ. There can, then, be no pleasure and pain without conjunction with the internal sensory determined to such and such an organ of sense. Were there no action in the internal organ there could be no feeling, such as of pleasure in the foot, of pain in the head etc. Although every particular attribute of the soul depends upon contact with the internal organ, pleasure and pain are alone expressly mentioned, these being in consequence of their producing acute affections, more obtrusive than the others.[2] U.

तदनारम्भ आत्मस्थे मनसि शरीरस्य दुःखभावः संयोगः।। 16।।

Aph. 16. Absence of action in the internal sensory reposing in the soul; non-existence of pain in the body—this is union.

It might be objected that if the internal sensory be of a mobile

[1] मुषलोत्क्षेपणादौ यथा प्रयत्नवदात्मसंयोगासमवायिकारणकं हस्तकर्म्म तथा ऽभिमतविषयग्राहिणीन्द्रिये सन्निकर्षार्थं यन्मनसः कर्म्म तदपि प्रयत्नवदात्मसंयोगसमवायिकारणमेव यद्यपीन्द्रियं मनो न साक्षात् प्रयत्नविषयस्तथापि मनोवहनाडीगोचरेण प्रयत्नेन मनसि कर्म्मोत्पत्तिर्द्रष्टव्या नाड्यास्तुत्वगिन्द्रियग्राह्यत्वमङ्गीकर्त्तव्यम् अन्यथा प्राणवहनाडीगोचरेण प्रयत्नेनाशितप्रीताद्यभ्यव हरणमपि न संभ्भवेत।।

[2] सुखदुःखे इत्युपलक्षणं ज्ञानप्रयत्नाद्यपि द्रष्टव्यं मनसो वैभवं पूर्व्वमेव निराकृतं अणुत्वञ्च साधितम् युगपत् ज्ञानानुपपत्तिञ्च मनसो लिङ्गमित्युक्तं तेन तत्तदिन्द्रियप्रदेशेन मनःसंयोगमन्तरेण सुखदुःखे न स्यातामेव यदि मनसि कर्म्म न भवेत् न भवेच्च णादे मे सुखं शिरसि मे वेदनेत्याद्याकारो ऽनुभवइत्यर्थः यद्यपि मनःसन्निकर्षाधीनः सर्व्वोऽप्यात्मविशेषगुणस्तथापि सुखदुःखे तीव्रसंवेगितया ऽतिस्फुटत्वादुक्ते।।

nature, it must be impossible to restrain it, and consequently a system of meditation must be useless, emancipation being impossible, since a presentation of soul is impossible. To this an answer is furnished. When the internal sensory abides in the soul, when by sixfold union the internal sensory quitting the exterior organs etc., abides in the soul alone, there results the non-commencement or non-production of the action of the internal sensory. The sensory then becomes immovable. In this state there is non-existence of pain in the body; that is, pain is not produced in relation to the body.This is called the conjunction or union with soul of the internal organ excluded from all things external. This is established by the words of the Skanda-purāṇa: The internal organ is smitten by the breath: he should not therefore sigh. He should therefore restrain his breath for the sake of immobility of the interior sensory. That he may restrain his breath, let him practise sixfold union. Sitting, checking the vital airs, abstraction, suspension of the faculties, meditation, and contemplation—these are the six elements of union. After this, then, there being cessation of false cognition by the arising of a presentation of soul, final emancipation is unimpeded; and a system of meditation is not therefore fruitless.[1] V.

अपसर्पणमुपसर्पणमशितपं तसंयोगाः
कार्यान्तरसंयोगाश्चेत्यदृष्टकारितानि।। 17।।

Aph. 17. The egress and ingress (of internal sensories from and into bodies), conjunctions with things eaten and drunk, and conjunctions with other effects—all these things are caused by destiny.

Egress, the issuing forth of the internal organ from the body at the time of death; ingress, the entrance of the internal organ into another body when it is produced; conjunctions with food and water eaten and drunk; and conjunctions of other effects with the body that is, of the

[1] ननु मनश्चेत् चञ्चलस्वभावं तदा तस्य निरोधो न सम्भवति तथा च योगमन्तरेणात्मसाक्षात्कारस्यासम्भवाद-पवर्गस्यासम्भवेन मननशास्त्रं निष्प्रयोजनमापद्येतेत्याशङ्कायामाह। आत्मस्थे मनसि षडङ्गयोगेन इन्द्रियादिकं परित्यज्य मनो यदा आत्ममात्रेतिष्ठति तदा तदनारम्भः तस्य मनः कर्म्मणअनारम्भः अनुत्पादः तदा मनो निश्चलं भवति तदवस्थायां शरीरस्य दुःखाभावः शरीरावच्छेदेन दुःखं न जायते स आत्मना बाह्यव्यावृत्तमनसः संयोगो योग उच्यते तथा च तदनन्तरमात्मसाक्षात्कारोदयेन मिथ्याज्ञानादिनि वृत्तौ सत्यामपवर्गो निष्प्रत्यूह एवेति न मननशास्त्रं निष्फलमिति भावः।।

sensual organs and vital airs; the actions from which these conjunctions arise, for these words are to be supplied,—these actions are caused by destiny, that is, have for their non-coinherent cause conjunction with soul destined.[1] V.

तद्भावे संयोगाभावो ऽप्रादुर्भावश्च मोक्षः।। 18।।

Aph. 18. Where there is non-existence of this (that is, of destiny), there is non-existence of conjunction, and non-existence of manifestation, emancipation.

Where there is non-existence of this, that is of destiny, where there is destruction of other than fructescent results of actions by presentation of soul, and of fructescent results by fruition, there is non-existence of conjunction, a severance from connection with the stream or series of bodies. After this there is non-manifestation, that is to say non-production of pain; and from the absence of the body and of destiny as causes, at that time emancipation or liberation is possible. Emancipation, therefore, is not chimerical like the horns of a hare.[2] V.

द्रव्यगुणकर्मनिष्पत्तिवैधर्म्यादभावस्तमः।। 19।।

Darkness

Aph. 19. Darkness is a non-entity being dissimilar to the production of substance, quality, and action.

It may be objected: The action of a substance is observed also in darkness, there being such cognitions as The shadow moves. In such cases there is no volition, no impulse or impact, and no gravity or fluidity; another efficient cause must therefore be posited, but this does not appear. The reply is here supplied. By this also is confirmed the observation that there are only nine substances. The production of substances is dependent only on tangible substances, and no touch is observed in darkness. Nor is therein darkness a touch, but inappreciable touch; for where colour is appreciable, touch must also

[1] अपसर्पणं मरणवस्थायां देहान्मनस उत्क्रमणम् उपसर्पणं देहान्तरोत्पत्तौ तत्र मनसः प्रवेशः असितपीतयोरन्नजलयोः संयोगाः कार्य्यान्तराणामिनिन्द्रियप्राणानां देहेन सह संयोगाश्च यस्मात् कर्म्मणो भवन्ति इति पूरणीयम् इति एतानि कर्म्माणि अदृष्टकारितानि अदृष्टवदात्मसंयोगासमवायिकारणकाणि।।

[2] तदभावे तस्यादृष्टस्याभावे सति प्रारब्धेतरादृष्टानात्मसाक्षात्कारेण प्रारब्धानाञ्च भोगेन क्षये सतीति यावत् संयोगाभावः देहप्रवाहसम्बन्धस्य विन्छेदस्तन्तरश्च अप्रादुर्भावः अर्थाद्दुःखस्यानुत्पत्तिदेहरूपस्यादृष्टरूपस्य च कारणस्य विरहादिति तदानीमेव मोक्षः अपवर्गः सम्भवतीति नापवर्गस्य शशविषाणसमानतेति भावः।।

needs be appreciable. If it be objected that this is the rule with regard to earth, but darkness is a tenth substance; we reply that this is not the case, for no other substance is a substratum of blue colour, and gravity is inseparable from blue colour, as also are taste and smell. If it be urged that as ether has sound only as its differencing attribute, and darkness may in like manner have blue colour for its peculiar property, we reply that it is not so, for there is contradiction to visibility; for were darkness merely something possessing blue colour, or blue colour, it would not be perceived by the eye without an accompanying perception of external light.[1] U.

तेजसो द्रव्यान्तरेणावरणाच्च ।। 20 ।।

Aph. 20. And because of the obscuration of light by another substance.

It may be asked: What then occasions the notion of motion of darkness? The reply is therefore furnished. Light being obscured by another substance in motion, and non-existence of light not being observed in the east and being observed in the west, and thus resembling a moving substance, an erroneous conception of motion results, but there is no real motion in the case, for this appears from an inclusive and exclusive argument. Darkness is absolute non-existence of all light in that which possesses appreciable colour.[2] U.

दिक्कालावाकाशञ्च क्रियावद्वैधर्म्यान्निष्क्रियाणि ।। 21 ।।

Aph. 21. Space, time, and ether, are also inactive, being dissimilar to that which possesses action.

The collateral section, comprising two aphorisms on darkness,

[1] ननु तमसोऽपि द्रव्यस्य कर्म्म दृश्यते चलति छायेति प्रयत्यात् तत्र न प्रयत्नो न वा नोदनाभिघातौ न वा गुरुत्वद्रवत्वेनवासंस्कारस्तथा च निमित्तान्तरं वक्तव्यं तच्च नानुभूयमानमित्यत आह। एतेन नवैवद्रव्याणीत्य-वधारणमप्युपपादितं द्रव्यनिष्पत्तिस्तावत् स्पर्शवद्‌द्रव्याधीना न च तमसि स्पशा ऽनुभूयते न चानुद्‌भूतएव स्पर्शः रूपोद्‌भवे स्पर्शोद्‌भवस्यावश्यकत्वात् पृथिव्यामयं नियमः मतस्तु दशमं द्रव्यमिति चेन्न द्रव्यान्तरस्य नीलरूपानधि ाकरणत्वात् नीलरुपस्य च गुरूत्वनान्तरीयकत्वात् रसगन्धनान्तरीयकत्वात् यथाकाशं शब्दमात्रविशेषगुणं तथा तमोऽपि नीलरूपमात्रविशेषगुणं स्यादितिचेन्न चाक्षुषत्वविरोधात् यदि हि नीलरूपवन्नीलं रूपमेव वा तमः स्यात् बाह्यलोकप्रग्रहमन्तरेण चक्षुषा न गृह्येत्।।

[2] तर्हि गतिप्रतीतिः किन्निबन्धनेत्यत आह गच्छता द्रव्यान्तरेणावृते तेजसि पूर्व्वदेशानुपलम्भादग्रिमदेशे चोपलम्भात्तेजोऽभावस्य गच्छद्‌द्रव्यसाधर्म्याद् गतिभ्रमो नतु वास्तवी तत्र गतिरित्यर्थः अन्वयव्यतिरेकाभ्यां तथा प्रतीतेः उद्‌भूतरूपवद्यावतेजः संसर्गा भावस्तमः।।

being completed, the section treating of voidness of action is stated. The word also implies the addition of soul. The dissimilarity from that which possesses action, is the illimitation of space etc., for action resides only in the concrete.[1] U.

एतेन कर्माणि गुणाश्च व्याख्याताः ।। 22 ।।

Aph. 22. By this are explained actions and qualities.

The inactivity of qualities and actions is stated. By this mean by dissimilarity from that which possesses action. Illimitation the dissimilarity from that which posseses action, belongs also to qualities and actions, and they also are explained to be inactive.[2] U.

निष्क्रियाणां समवायः कर्मभ्यो निषिद्धः ।। 23 ।।

Aph. 23. The co-inherence of things inactive is excluded from actions.

It might be objected: If qualities and actions are inactive, how can there be any connection between them and substance ? connection by conjunction would be possible, but that depends on action only. Hence it is stated that co-inherence is only connection of qualities and action which are inactive, and that this is excluded from actions. Of this connection there is not even the production, much less dependency upon action.[3] U.

कारणं त्वसमवायिनो गुणाः ।। 24 ।।

Aph. 24. But qualities as a cause are non-coinherent.

It might be objected: If qualities, as being immaterial, are not a co-inherent cause of actions, how are qualities and actions produced by qualities ? For causation in the form of being something over and above a co-inherent cause is not possible. The reply to this is therefore furnished.Qualities are a non-coinherent cause, not a co-inherent cause also, that they should be the sites of actions. Non-coinherent causality sometimes results from co-inherence in the same object with

[1] एवं द्विसूत्रकं प्रासङ्गिकं तमःप्रकरणं समाप्य कर्म्मशून्यताप्रकरणमाह चकारादात्मसंग्रहः क्रियावतां वैधर्म्यं दिगादीनाममूर्त्तत्वं मूर्त्यनुविधानात् क्रियायाः ।।

[2] गुणकर्म्मणोर्निष्क्रियत्वमाह। एतेनेति क्रियावद्वैधर्म्येणेत्यर्थः क्रियावद्वैधर्म्यममूर्त्तत्वं गुणकर्म्मणोरपीतिते अपि निष्क्रियत्वेनव्याख्या इत्यर्थः ।।

[3] ननु गुणकर्म्मणी यदि निष्क्रिये तदा ताभ्यां द्रव्यस्य कथं सम्बन्धः संयोगसम्बन्धः सम्भाव्येत स च कर्म्माधीन एवेत्यत आह निष्क्रियाणां गुणकर्म्मणां समवाय एव सम्बन्धः स च कर्म्मभ्यो निषिद्धः तस्य सम्ब-न्धस्य उत्पत्तिरेव नास्ति दूरे तु कर्म्माधीनतेत्यर्थः ।।

the effect, as that of conjunction with soul in the particular attributes of sounds, or of sound in conjunction and disjunction in sound; in other cases it results from co-inherence in the same object with the cause, as that of the colours etc., of the parts of a water-pot etc., in the colour etc., of a water-pot etc.[1] U.

गुणैर्दिगव्याख्याता ।। 25 ।।

Aph. 25. By qualities space is explained.

An objection might be raised. In virtue of such cognitions as, Action is produced here, Action is produced now, time and space also are co-inherent cause of action. Else how could they be its sites? It is therefore stated that as the qualities gravity etc., being unlimited are not co-inherent causes of action, so it follows also from its illimitation that space is not a co-inherent cause of action. That to be a site does not imply co-inherence is proved by such instances as those of cotton in a bowl, curdled milk in a bowl, the roaring of a lion in a forest.[2] U.

कारणेन कालः ।। 26 ।।

Aph. 26. By cause time [is explained.]

The words Is explained to be inactive are to be supplied according to an altered construction. By the words by cause existence is indicated. Time, then, as an efficient cause is merely the site of action, but not co-inherent with action.[3] U.

[1] ननु यद्यमूर्त्तत्वात् गुणाः कर्म्मसमवायिकारणं भवन्ति तदा गुणैर्गुणाः कर्म्माणि च कथमुत्पद्यन्ते न हि समवायिकारणातिरिक्तत्वरूपेणापि कारणता संभवतीत्यत आह गुणा असमवायिकारणं न तु समवायिकारणमपि येन कर्म्माधाराः स्युः सा चासमवायिकारणता क्वचित् कार्य्यकार्थसमवायात् यथात्ममनःसंयोस्यात्मविशेषगुणेषु संयोगविभागशब्दा न शब्दे क्वचित् कारणैकार्थसमवायात् यथा कपालादिरूपादीनां घटादि रूपादिषु।।

[2] ननु इह कर्म्मोत्पद्यते इदानीं कर्म्मोत्पद्यते इत्यादि प्रतीतिबलात् दिक्कालावपि कर्म्मसमवायिकारणे एव कथमन्यथा तत्र तयोराधारतेत्यत आह। यथा गुरुत्वादयो गुणे न कर्म्मसमवायिकारणममूर्त्तत्वात् तथा दिगपि नकर्म्मसमवायिकारणममूर्त्तत्वादेवेत्यर्थः आधारता तु समवायितामन्तरेणापि कुराडे वदराणि कुराडे दधि वने सिंहनादइत्यादिवदुपपद्यते इति भावः।।

[3] उक्तेनैवाभिवभिप्रायेणाह निष्क्रियत्वेन व्याख्यात इति परिणस्यानुषङ्गः कारणेनेति भावप्रधानो निर्देशः तेन निमित्तकारणत्वेनाधारमात्रं कर्म्मणः कालो न तु समवायीत्यर्थः।।

Book VI

FIRST DAILY LESSON

बुद्धिपूर्वा वाक्यकृतिर्वेदे ।। 1 ।।

Aph. 1. There is in the Veda a composition of sentences consequent upon design.

The object matter of the sixth book is the investigation of merit and demerit the primary causes of transmigration. Merit and demerit may be conceived as existing in virtue of such precepts and prohibitions as Let him that desires paradise offer sacrifices, Let him not eat kalañja, assuming the authoritativeness of such injunctions and prohibitions. Such authoritativeness is established by the prior existence of the distinguishing attribute in the speaker of accurate knowledge of the meaning of the words. Absolute authoritativeness being denied, the author proceeds in the first place to prove the quality determinant of the Veda. Composition of sentences, framing of propositions, is consequent upon intention, preceded by the speaker's accurate knowledge of the meaning of the sentences, because it is a composition of sentences, like the composition by ourselves and others of such sentences as There are five fruits on the river's bank. In the Veda means in the aggregate of sentences. Of this the composition of the aggregated sentences is the subject; and there is no unduly assumed causality in the priority of the intention of ourselves and others. For in such instances as Let him that desires paradise offer sacrifices the means of attaining the desired object or the fact of its being an effect are not objects of the intellect of ourselves or of our fellow-creatures. Therefore there is established in the case of the Veda the prior existence of an absolute author, and the definition of the Veda is words of authority not derived from knowledge of the meaning of propositions composed of words, accompained with the nature of that which is not an object of certain knowledge derived from evidence other than of words and of the evidence upon them dependent.[1] U.

ब्राह्मणे संज्ञाकर्म सिद्धिलिङ्गम्।। 2।।

Aph. 2. The formation of names in the Brāhmaṇa is an evidence of design.

It is stated in another manner that the words of the Veda had intelligence as their antecedent. The Brāhmaṇa here denotes a portion of the Veda. The formation there of terms, or making of names, point to the intention of the derivatist, just as the making in ordinary language of such names as Long-ear, Long-nose, Long-neck.[2] U.

बुद्धिपूर्वो ददातिः।। 3।।

*Aph.*3. The words He gives have intelligence as their antecedent.

The injunction to make gifts in such precepts as, He that desires paradise should give a cow, is derived from the knowledge of the causal efficiency of such gifts. The particular employment of the root in the form He gives, impulies giving, the sense of the root.[3] U.

तथा प्रतिग्रहः।। 4।।

*Aph.*4. Likewise reception.

The sacred texts enjoining reception also imply an intelligent antecedent. The word reception implies a sacred text of which it is the subject. Sacred texts enjoining acceptance of lands etc. indicate its

[1] संसारमूलकारणयोर्धर्म्माधर्म्मयोः परीक्षा षष्टाध्यायार्थः धर्म्माधर्म्मौ च स्वर्गकामो च यजेत न च कलञ्जं भक्षयेत् इत्यादिविधिनिषेधबलकल्पनीयो विधिनिषेधवाक्ययोः प्रामाण्ये सति स्यातां तत्प्रामाण्यञ्च वक्तुर्यथार्थवाक्यार्थज्ञानलक्षणगुणपूर्वकत्वादुपपद्यते स्वतः प्रामाण्यस्य निषेधादतः प्रथमं वेदप्रामाण्य-प्रयोजकगुणसाधनमुपक्रमते वाक्यकृतिर्वाक्यरचना सा बुद्धपूर्व्वा वक्तृयथार्थवाक्यार्थज्ञानपूर्व्वा वाक्यरचना त्वात् नदीतीरे पञ्च फलानि सन्तीत्यस्मदादिवाक्याचनावत् वेद इति वाक्यसमुदायः इत्यर्थः तत्र समुदायिनां वाक्यनांकृतिः पक्षः न चास्मदादिबुद्धिपूर्व्वकत्वेनान्यथा सिद्धिः स्वर्गकामो यजेत इत्यादाविष्टसाधनतायाः कार्य्यताया अस्मदादिबुद्धिगोचरत्वात् तेन स्वतन्त्रपुरुषपूर्वकत्वं वेदे सिद्ध्यति वेदत्वञ्च शब्दतदुपजीविप्रमाणाति-रिक्तप्रमाणजन्यत्वमित्यविषयार्थकत्वे सति शब्दजन्यवाक्यज्ञानाजन्यप्रमाणशब्दत्वम्।।

[2] प्रकारान्तरेण वेदवाक्यानां बुद्धिपूर्व्वकत्वमाह। ब्राह्मणमिह वेदभागस्तत्र यत् संज्ञाकर्म्मनामकारणं तत् व्युत्पादकस्य बुद्धिमाक्षिपति तथा लोके लम्बकर्णदीर्घनासलम्बग्रीवादिनामकरणम्।।

[3] स्वर्गकामो गां दद्यात् इत्यादौ यद्दानप्रतिपादनं तद्दानेष्टसाधनताज्ञानजन्यं ददातिरिति धातुनिर्द्देशो धात्वर्थं दानमुपलक्षयति।।

efficacy to the welfare of the receiver. Sacred texts setting forth the reception of the skin of the black antelope etc., imply efficacy to that which is undesired by the recipient. The efficacy to the desired and the undesired cannot be merely objects in the minds of modern persons.[1] U.

आत्मान्तरगुणानामात्मान्तरे ऽकारणत्वात्।। 5।।

Aph. 5. Because the attributes of one soul are not a cause with regard to another soul.

Because the attributes of one soul, its merits and demerits, such as sacrifices injuries etc., are not a cause of the attributes of pleasure and pain in another soul, pleasure and pain are produced by such merit and demerit only as exist in each several soul, not by merit and demerit inhering in different subjects. Otherwise, inasmuch as one by whom a sacrifice was not offered nor a wrong done would receive its recompense there would result a loss of what was done and requital for what was not done.[2] U.

तद्दुष्टभोजने न विद्यते।। 6।।

*Aph.*6. That does not exist in the case of the eating of the wicked.

That denotes the fruit of a benediction. When evil Brāhmans, unworthy recipients, are fed at the obsequial rites, no fruit accrues from this to the ancestor; or the meaning is simply that the result of the obsequial rites does not accre to the ancestor.[3] U.

दुष्टं हिंसायाम्।। 7।।

Aph. 7. The evil has reference to wrong.

Has reference to wrong implies prohibited actions in general. It

[1] प्रमाणान्तरमाह। प्रतिग्रहप्रतिपादिका अपि श्रुतयी बुद्धिपूर्व्विकाः प्रतिग्रहपदं स्वविषयां श्रुतिमुपलक्षयति तेन भूम्यादिप्रतिग्रहप्रतिपादिन्यः श्रुतयः प्रतिग्रहीतुः श्रेयः साधनतत्पराः कृष्णसारचर्म्मादिप्रतिग्रहप्रतिपादिकाः श्रुतयः प्रतिग्रहीतुरनिष्टसाधनताबोधिकाः न चेष्टानिष्टसाधनते अर्वाचीनपुरुषबुद्धिगोचरौ भवितुमर्हतः।।

[2] आत्मान्तरगुणानां यागहिंसादिपुण्यपापानां आत्मान्तरे यौ सुखदुःखात्मकौ गुणौ तयोरकारणत्वात् एवञ्च प्रत्यात्मनिष्टानामेव धर्म्माधर्म्माभ्यां सुखदुःखेन व्यधिकरणाभ्यामन्यथा येन यागहिंसादिकं न कृतं तस्य तत्फलं स्यादिति कृतहानिरकृताभ्यागमश्च प्रसज्येत।।

[3] तदित्याशीर्दानफलं परामृशति दुष्टब्राह्मणाः पात्रानधिकारिणो यत्र श्राद्धे भोज्यन्ते तत्रापि पितरि तत्फलं न विद्यते न भवतीत्यर्थः श्राद्धफलमेव वा न भवति पितरीत्यर्थः।।

should therefore be understood that a man occupied in forbidden action is the wicked.[1] U.

तस्य समभिव्याहारतो दोषः।। 8।।

Aph. 8. Demerit results from association with him.

It is stated that not only is there absence of fruit in the partaking of an unworthy Brāhman invited to the obsequial rite, but also sin accrues. Demerit or guilt results from association, characterised as eating in the same row, sleeping, reading and the like, togther with him, i.e., with a Brāhman occupied in illicit action.[2] U.

तद्दुष्टे न विद्यते।। 9।।

Aph. 9. This does not exist in the case of one not unworthy.

This guilt does not exist, that is, does not accrues in the case of a Brāhman not unworthy, i.e. one who acts according to sacred precepts, invited to partake in the obsequial rite.[3] U.

पुनर्विशिष्टे प्रवृत्तिः।। 10।।

Aph. 10. Again the procedure should be in relation to that which is excellent.

If exellent persons, those who regulate their conduct according to sacred precepts, are procured at obsequial rites or in receiving gifts, a man should avoid those who are censurable though they may have been invited. The text A man should not reject those who are invited, refers to worthy recipients. But a man should gratify blameable persons, when invited, by giving money etc.[4] U.

समे हीने वा प्रवृत्तिः।। 11।।

Aph. 11. Again the procedure should be in relation to an equal or an inferior.

1 हिंसायामिति निषिद्धकर्म्ममात्रोपलक्षणम् तेन निषिद्धे कर्म्मणि प्रवृत्तं विजानीयादित्यर्थः।।

2 न केवलं दुष्टब्राह्मणस्य श्राद्धे निमन्त्रितस्य भोजनेन फलाभावः किन्तु पापमपि भवतीत्याह तस्य निषिद्धे कर्म्मणि प्रवृत्तस्य ब्राह्मणस्य समभिव्याहारात् एकपङ्क्तिभोजनसहशयनसहाध्ययनादिलक्षणात् दोषः पापमित्यर्थः।।

3 तत् पापमदुष्टे यथाशास्त्रं व्यवहारमाणे ब्राह्मणे श्राद्धे भोजते न विद्यते न भवतीत्यर्थः।।

4 श्राद्धे प्रतिग्रहे वा विशिष्टा यथाशास्त्रमनुवर्तमाना यदि लभ्यन्ते तदा निमन्त्रितानपि निन्द्यान् परिहृत्य तानेव भोजयेत् न निमन्त्रितान् प्रत्याचक्षीत इति तुसत्पात्रपरम् निन्द्यांस्तु निमन्त्रितान् द्रविणदानादिना संन्तोषयेत्।।

Where persons more excellent than oneself are not procured at obsequial rites, it is explained that the procedure in obsequial rites, alms etc., should be in relation to an equal, one like oneself, or an inferior, one less in point of merit etc., than oneself. Persons prohibited are by all means to be avoided, but not the unblemished whether they be equals or inferiors.[1] U.

एतेन हीनसमविशिष्टधार्मिकेभ्यः परस्वादानं व्याख्यातम्।। 12।।

Aph. 12. By this is explained reception of property from another, from inferior, equal, and superior, virtuous persons.

Merit, a serial increase of merit, results in the acquisition of land etc., whether from an inferior, or an equal, or one more excelent than oneself, being virtuous. Acquisition is the reception of property or wealth from another. According to the author of the Vṛtti, by the reception of property from another the taking of property by theft etc., is explained. In conformity with this is the text. From a Śūdra on the seventh day, from a Vaiśya on the tenth, from a Kshatriya on the fifteenth, from a Brāhman in case of danger to life. To save himself or his family when starving a man may steal the food of a Śūdra, when he has been without food for seven days; when he has been without food for ten days, that of a Vaiśya; when he has been fifteen days without food, that of a Kshatriya. When his life is in danger, stealing food from a Brāhman tends not to demerit.[2] U.

तथा विरुद्धानां त्यागः।। 13।।

*Aph.*13. Likewise the making away with those who are contrary.

Not only is the taking of others' property, when in danger to life, not forbidden, but in such circumstances those who do not give anything to take away, should even be put to death. And by all this there is no loss of merit, or manifestation of demerit. In such a case those who are

[1] समे स्वसदृशे हीने स्वापेक्षया गुणादिना न्यूने अदुष्टे पात्रे श्राद्धदानादौ प्रवृत्तिस्तेषामेवाशीर्दानात् पितरि सुखमित्यर्थः निषिद्धानां परं त्यागो नत्वादुष्टानां समहीनानामपीति भावः।।

[2] यथोत्तरं धर्म्मोत्कर्षः हीनादपि भूम्यादिपतिग्रहे समादपि स्वापेक्षया विशिष्टादपि धार्म्मिकात् धर्म्म इत्यर्थः परस्यादानं परस्मात् स्वस्य धनस्यादानं प्रतिग्रहः वृत्तिकारस्तु परस्वादानं चौर्य्यादिना परस्वग्रहणं व्याख्यातं तथा च श्रुतिः शूद्रात् सप्तमे वैश्याद्दशमे क्षत्रियात्पञ्चदशे ब्राह्मणात् प्राणसंशये इति क्षुधापीडितमात्मानं कुटुम्बं रक्षितुं सप्तदिनान्याहारमप्राप्य शूद्रभक्ष्यापहारः कार्य्यः एवं दशदिनान्याहारमप्राप्य वैश्यात् पञ्चदशदिनान्याहारमप्राप्य क्षत्रियात् प्राणसंशये ब्राह्मणत् भक्ष्यापहरणं न दोषायेत्याहुः।।

contrary, those who act in the contrary manner, are to be put to death. Therefore it has been said : Let a man save himself when in despair by whatsoever deed, fair or foul; when he is able let him practise righteousness.[1] U.

हीने परे त्यागः।। 14।।

*Aph.*14. Making away with another has reference to an inferior.

If another who does not give anything to take away is inferior to oneself, he, the Śūdra etc., may be put to death.[2] U.

समे आत्मत्यागः परत्यगो वा।। 15।।

Aph. 15. In the case of an equal, suicide, or the destruction of the other.

If the opposite party be one's equal—but only if he be a Brāhman—in such a case suicide—the destruction of oneself by fasting etc.,—is to be committed. If there appear no means of preserving oneself or one's family, and the opposite party be an equal, he is to be made away with, or destroyed.[3] U.

विशिष्टे आत्मत्याग इति।। 16।।

*Aph.*16. In the case of a superior suicide [is to be committed].

In the case of an opposite party superior to oneself, distinguihed by study of the Veda etc., suicide alone is lawful; though there be danger to life, a man may design only his own death, but must not slay a Brāhman.[4] U.

[1] न केवलं प्राणसंशये परस्वादानं न निषिद्धं किन्तु तस्यां दशायामपहर्त्तुं ये न प्रयच्छन्ति तेषां वधोऽपि कार्य्यो न तावता धर्म्महानिरधर्म्मप्रादुर्भावो वेत्याह तस्यां दशायां विरुद्धानां विपरीतमाचरतां त्यागो वधः कार्य्य इत्यर्थः तदुक्तम् कर्म्मणा येन केनापि मृदुना दारुणेन वा उद्धरेद्दीनमात्मानं समर्थो धर्म्ममाचरेत् इति।।

[2] यदि स्वस्माद्धीनः परो भवति योऽपहर्त्तुं न ददाति तस्य शूद्रादेस्त्यागो वधः।

[3] यदि स्वसदृशे ब्राह्मण एव विरोधी भवति तदात्मन एवोपवासादिना त्यागो ऽवसादः कर्त्तव्यः यदि स्वस्य कुटुम्बस्य वा रक्षाप्रकारो न दृश्यते विरोधी च समो भवति तदा तस्यैव त्यागो वध इत्यर्थः।।

[4] स्वापेक्षया विशिष्टे वेदाध्ययनादिना उत्कृष्टे विरोधिनि आत्मन एव त्यागो विधेयः प्राणसंशये सत्यप्यात्मानमेवाभिप्रेयात् न तु ब्राह्मणं हन्यादित्यर्थः।।

SECOND DAILYLESSON

दृष्टादृष्टप्रयोजनाना दृष्टाभावे प्रयोजनमभ्युदयाय।। 1।।

Aph. 1. Of action of which the motives are seen and unseen, a motive, where there is none seen, tends to exaltation.

Actions where the motives are seen are agriculture, merchandise service of the king, etc. Among where the motives are unseen are sacrifice, charity, chastity, etc. Among these actions where a visible motive is not observed, an invisible motive is to be supposed, and such a motive conduces to exaltation, or knowledge of the truth. Or the dative case to exaltation may be employed in the sense of the nominative, in which case the sense will be that exaltation is the result. An unseen result is a remote consequence. If this be produced by asceticism, the exaltation is presentation of soul; if by sacrifice, almsgiving etc., the exaltation is paradise. In this instance such actions as sacrificing, giving alms, continence etc., do not immediately bear fruit, as such actions as milking, cooking etc., have immediate results, and such actions as sowing, ploughing etc., after a while bear fruit; for there is no such proximate result observed. Nor is gain etc., through being known as virtuous, the result. For those who practise secret continence etc., do not design such results. The result therefore is the remotely future paradise etc., and this does not immediately succeed the action which rapidly ceases to exist. It results therefore that there is in the interim a common site of the action and the fruit, viz., requitative efficacy.[1] U.

[1] दृष्टप्रयोजनानि कृषिवाणिज्यराज्यसेवादीनि अदृष्टप्रयोजनानि यागदानब्रह्मचर्यादीनि एतेषां कर्मणां मध्ये यत्र दृष्टं प्रयोजनं नोपलभ्यते तत्रादृष्टं प्रयोजनं कल्पनीयम् तच्चाभ्युदयाय तत्त्वज्ञानाय यद्वा अभ्युदयायेति चतुर्थी प्रथमार्थे तेन फलाभ्युदयइत्यर्थः अदृष्टं फलमपूर्व्वमेव तद् यदि योगजं तदाऽभ्युदय आत्मसाक्षात्कारः यदि यागदानादिजं तदाऽभ्युदयः स्वर्गः तत्रापि यथा दोग्धि पचतीत्यादिक्रिया सद्यःफलिका वपति कर्षतीत्यादिक्रिया च विलम्बभाविफला तथा जयति ददाति ब्रह्मचर्य्यं चरतीत्यादिक्रिया तावत् सद्यःफलिका न भवति तादृशस्य फलस्यानुपलब्धेः न च धार्मिकतया ज्ञानाल्लाभादिकमेव फलम् प्रच्छन्नं ब्रह्मचर्यादि चरता तत्फलानुद्देशात् तस्माच्चिरभा विस्वर्गादिकमेव फलं तच्चाशुतरविनाशिन्याः क्रियाया साक्षादित्यान्तरालिकं क्रियाफलयोः समानाधिकरणम् पूर्व्वं पर्य्ययस्यति।।

अभिषेचनोपवासब्रह्मचर्यगुरुकुलवासवानप्रस्थयज्ञदानप्रोक्षण दिङ्नक्षत्रमन्त्रकालनियमाश्चादृष्टाय ।। 2।।

Aph. 2. Inaugurations, fasting, continence, residence in the family of a spiritual guide, life in the forest, sacrifice, almsgiving, oblation, the cardinal points, constellations, sacred texts, seasons, and religious observances, conduce to invisible result.

Of these, some of the actions of which the result is unseen, are pointed out. These actions conduce to, that is produce, unseen results. Among these inauguration is the sprinkling of kings; fasting, the abstinence of the Śivarātri; continence, abstinence from sexual intercourse; residence in the house of a spiritual guide that of religious students for the purpose of studying the Veda; living in the forest, the actions of those who set out at the close of life for the forest; sacrifice, the Rājasūya etc.; almsgiving , at the beginning of the mouth Āshādha; oblation, of rice, cattle etc.; the cardinal points, orientation of meals etc.; constellations, the obsequial rites of the tenth lunar asterism Maghā etc.; sacred texts, the holy monosyllable Om, the Gāyatrī etc.; seasons, the Chāturmāsya rites etc. ; religious observances, purifications, contentment, penance, study, and meditation on the Deity. By the word and, are to be understood also those not here enumerated, but which are prescribed by revelation and tradition.[1] V.

चातुराश्रम्यमुपधा अनुपधाश्च।। 3।।

Aph. 3. The duty of the four periods of religious life [has been declared]. Fidelities and infidelities [are causes of merit and demerit].

The duty of the four periods of religious life is the conduct prescribed in these four stages, viz., those of the religious student, householder, hermit, and mendicant. This has been already declared: such are the words to be supplied. Infidities are defects of faith; fidelities

[1] तत्रादृष्टफलकानि कानिचित्कर्म्माणि प्रदर्शयति एतानि कर्म्माणि अदृष्टाय अदृष्टजनकानि तत्र अभिषेचनमभिषेको राज्ञाम् उपवासः शिवरात्र्युपवासादिः ब्रह्मचर्यमष्टविधमैथुनाद्विवर्ज्जनम् गुरुकुलवासो ब्रह्मचारिणां वेदाध्ययनाद्यर्थः वानप्रस्थं वयःशेषे वनप्रस्थितानां पुटपाकादिकर्म्म यज्ञो राजसूयादिः दानमाषाद्यादौ प्रोक्षणं ब्रीहिपश्वादीनाम् दिक् प्राङ्मुखभोजनादि नक्षत्रं मघाशाद्धादिमन्त्रः प्रणवगायत्र्यादिजपः कालः चातुर्मास्यव्रतादिः नियमाः शौचसन्तोषतपःस्वाध्यायेश्वरप्रणिधानानि चकारादनुक्तानि श्रौतस्मार्त्तान्यपि।।

non-deficiencies of faith, efficient causes merit and demerit.[1] V.

भावदोष उपधा ऽदोषो ऽनुपधा।। 4।।

Aph. 4. A deficiency of faith is an infidelity; a non-deficiency a fidelity.

Deficiencies of faith, lust, anger, covetousness, infatuation, intoxication, envy etc., are expressed by the term infidelity; non-deficiencies of faith, freedom from negligence and sloth, tranquillity of mind etc., are to be understood by the term fidelity.[2] V.

यदिष्टरूपरसगन्धस्पर्शं प्रोक्षितमभ्युक्षितञ्च तच्छुचि।। 5।।

Aph. 5. That which is of prescribed colour, taste, smell and touch, the aspersed, and the sprinkled, and pure.

That colour etc., which is enjoined by revelation and tradition is prescribed. The substance to which such colour etc., belongs as such is pure. Of these colour is prescribed in such texts as, He buys the soma for a cow, ruddy, one year old, with tawny eyes; He should take a white goat. The aspersed is that which is sprinkled, with water during the recitation of a sacred text; the sprinkled with which is sprinkled with water without a sacred text. The word and implies that which is lawfully acquired. This is such as is denoted by such precepts as that a Brāhman should acquire wealth by performing sacrifices, by teaching, and by receiving presents.[3] U.

अशुचीति शुचिप्रतिषेधः।। 6।।

Aph. 6. Impure denotes the negation of the pure.

The contrary of such substance as is pure is impure. A substance of wrong colour, taste, smell, or touch, one not aspersed or sprinkled, or sprinkled with forbidden water, or unlawfully acquired, as the property

1 ब्रह्मचारिगृहिवानप्रस्थभिक्षुरूपेषु चतुर्षु आश्रमेषु विहितं यत्वार्म्म तत् चातुराश्रम्यं पूर्वमुक्तमितिशेषः उपधा भवदेषाः अनुषधा भावदोषाश्च धर्म्माधर्म्मसाधनानीत्यर्थः।।

2 कामक्रोधलोभमोहमदमात्सर्य्यादयो भावदोषा उपधाशब्दवाच्याः श्रद्धाऽप्रमादानालस्यलनःप्रसादादयौ दोषा अनुपधाशब्दावाच्या इतयर्थः।।

3 इष्टं श्रुत्या स्मृत्या च यद्रूपादिकं विहितं यस्य द्रव्यस्य तत्तथा तत्र रूपं अरुणाया एकहायन्या पिङ्गाक्ष्या गवा सोमं क्रीणाति श्वेतं छागलमालभेतइत्यादौ प्रोक्षितं मन्त्रेणोदकसित्कम् अभ्युक्षितं विनामन्त्रमुदकसि च कारान्योयतो लव तच्च याजनाध्यापनप्रतिग्रहैर्ब्राह्मणो धनमर्जयेदित्यादिनियमविधिबोधतिम्।।

of a Brāhman acquired by agriculture or merchandise, is impure.[1] U.

अर्थान्तरञ्च।। 7।।

Aph. 7. And something else.

That which is vitiated by speech or by disposition even in that which is of exellent colour, taste, smell, or touch, or in that which is aspersed or sprinkled, or justly acquired, is also impure.[2] U.

अयतस्य शुचिभोजनादभ्युदयो न विद्यते नियमाभावात् विद्यते वा ऽथान्तरत्वाद्यमस्य।। 8।।

Aph. 8. To the unrestrained there accrues no exaltation from eating what is pure, inasmuch as there is an absence of religious observance; or it accrues, because restraint is something else.

To the unrestrained means to one deficient in restraint, or wanting in self-control. The eating of one void of the restraint denoted by such a rule as, A man should eat after washing his hands and feet, and rinsing his mouth, restrained in speech, When food is presented to him, though pure, he should twice rinse his mouth, does not tend to exaltation, but to sin. It may be asked why, the answer accordingly is furnished. Inasmuch as there is an absence of religious observance, in consequence of the non-existence of the religious observance, the secondary cause. That which takes place where the observance is performed is stated. Or it accrues,—exaltation accrues only in the case of eating with the accompaniment of the prescribed restraint. It may be asked why, hence it is stated that it is because restraint is something else, that is, is something else than eating. The sense, therefore, is that without the accessory cause there is no realisation of the result, and that with it there is.[3] U.

1 यद्रव्यं शुचि तद्विपरीतमशुचीत्यर्थः अप्रशस्तरूपरसगन्धस्पर्शमन्त्रप्रोक्षितमनभ्युक्षितं निषिद्धजलाभ्युक्षितं वा अन्यायागतम् कृषिवाणिज्यागतं ब्राह्मणद्रव्यमशुचीत्यर्थः।।

2 अप्रशस्तरूपरसगन्धस्पर्शमपि प्रोक्षितमभ्युक्षितं न्यायार्जितञ्च यत्तत्रापि वाग्दुष्टं भावदुष्टञ्च यत्तदप्यशुचीत्यर्थः।।

3 अयतस्य यमरहितस्यासंयतस्येति यावत् हस्तौ पादौ प्रक्षाल्याचम्य वाग्यतो भुञ्जीत भोक्ष्यमाणः प्रयतोऽपि द्विराचामेत् इत्यादिबोधितयमरहितस्य भोजनं नाभ्युदयाय किन्तु पापाय कुत एवमित्यत आह। नियमाभावात् नियमस्य सहकारिणोऽभावात् नियमे सति यत्तदाह विद्यते वा यथोक्तयमसाहित्येन भोजने भवत्येवाभ्युदयः कुत इत्यत आह। अर्थान्तारत्वाद यमस्य भोजनादर्थान्तरं यतो यमः तथा च सहकारिकारणं विना न न फलसिद्धिस्तस्मिन् सति फलसिद्धिरित्यर्थः।।

असति चाभावात् ।। 9 ।।

Aph. 9. For there is non-existence [of exaltation] where [the eating of pure food] does not exist.

Though there be restraint, where the eating of pure food is not, there is non-existence of exaltation:—such is the completion of the ellipse. Restraint and eating are therefore both causes of merit. The word eating designates secondarily other actions. Restraint and religious observance are accessories also of sacrifice, almsgiving, ablutions, oblations, and other acts prescribed by revelation and tradition.[1] U.

सुखाद्रागः ।। 10 ।।

Aph. 10. From pleasure arises desire.

Restraint having been specified as an accessory with regard to merit and demerit, the origin of defects is stated, with the purpose of specifying defects as accesssories. Desire or wish arises from pleasure generated by attachment to garlands, sandal-wood, women, and other objects of sense, or in the pleasures of those successive kinds, or in the means of those pleasures . It is also to be considered that aversion arises from pain begotten by snakes, thorus etc., in those pains, or in the means of those pains. Desire, aversion, and infatuation, in virtue of being incentives to activity, are called defects. Accordingly the aphorism of Gautama, defects have for their characteristic incitement to activity.[2] U.

तन्मयत्वाच्च ।। 11 ।।

Aph. 11. Also through that being engrained.

The words desire and aversion arise are to be supplied. That which is engrained is a particular powerful reproduction engendered by use of objects of sense, by the influence of which it is that the unhappy lover, who has win his mistress, sees his beloved in every objects; and he

1 यमे सत्यपि शुचिभोजनेऽसति अभावादभ्युदयस्येति शेषः तथा च यमो भोजनञ्च द्वयमेव पुण्यकारणमित्यर्थः भोजनमित्युपलक्षणं यागदानहोमादीनामपि श्रौतस्मार्तकर्मणां यमनियमौ सहकारिणौ।

2 एवं धर्माधर्मप्रादुर्भावं प्रति यमसहकारिणमभिधाय दोषं सहकारिणमभिधातुं दोषनिदानमाह स्रक्चन्दनवनितादिविषयसेवनजन्मनः सुखादुत्तरोत्तरं तज्जातीये सुखे तत्साधने वा राग इच्छा संजायते अहिकण्टकादिजन्मनो दुःखात् तत्र तत्साधने वा द्वेष इत्यपि द्रष्टव्यम् रागद्वेषमोहाः प्रवर्त्तकत्वेन दोषा इत्यभिधीयन्ते तथा च गौतमीयं सूत्रम् प्रवर्तनलक्षणा दोषाः इति।।

who does not been once bitten by a snake, in consequence of the forcible reproduction, sees snake everywhere . It has therefore been said: Habituation to an object is its luminous revelation external or internal.[1] U.

अदृष्टाच्च ।। 12 ।।

Aph. 12. Also through destiny.

The words desire and aversion arise are to be supplied. Though destiny be a universal cause, yet in relation to these it sometimes assumes the nature also of a special cause. Such cases are to be inferred as the desire of a mistress at the commencement of youth, even in one who has not experienced in this birth the pleasures of love; the aversion towards snakes even in those who have not experienced pain from snake-bites, etc.[2] U.

जातिविशेषाच्च ।। 13 ।।

Aph. 13. Also through particularly of race.

Another accessory is stated. Thus on the part of the human race there is desire towards rice etc., on that of deer towards grass etc., on that of camels towards briers etc. In all these cases destiny which determines such and such a race is the cause; but race, or particular birth is only a means. Similarly the desire of pigeons etc., for refuse. So also the aversion of buffaloes towards a horse, of dogs towards a jackal, of ichneumons towards a snake etc., is to be inferred.[3] U.

इच्छाद्वेषपूर्विका धर्माधर्मप्रवृतिः ।। 14 ।।

Aph. 14. Activity in merit or demerit has for its antecedents desire and aversion.

Activity in a lawful action has desire for its condition; in an unlawful action, injury etc., activity has aversion for its condition. Activity

[1] रागद्वेषौ भवत इतिशेषः विषयाभ्यासजनितो दृढतरः संस्कारविशेषस्तन्मयत्वं यद्वशात् कामातुरस्य कामिनीमलभमानस्य सर्व्वत्र कामिनीदर्शनम् एकदा भुजभुजङ्गदष्टस्य तत्र दृढतरसंस्कारतः सर्व्वत्र भुजङ्गदर्शनम् तदुक्तं तन्मवत्वं तत्प्रकशो बाह्याभ्यन्तरतस्तथा इति।।

[2] रागेद्वेषावितिशेषः यद्यप्यदृष्टं साधारणकारणं तथापि क्वचित्तौ प्रति असाधारणतामप्युनुभजति यथा तज्जन्माननुभूतकामिनीसुखस्यापि यौवनोद्भेदे कामिनीरागः अननुभूतभुजङ्गदंशदुःखानामपि भुजङ्गेषु द्वेष इत्याद्युन्नेयम्।।

[3] सहकार्य्यान्तरमाह। तथाहि मनुष्यजातीयानामन्नादौ रागः मृगजातीयानां तृणादौ करभजातीयानां कण्टकादौ तत्रापि तत्तज्जातिनिष्पादकमदृष्टमेव तन्त्रं द्वारमात्रन्तु जातिर्जन्मविशेषः एवं पारावतादीनामुत्करे रागः तथा महिषजातीयानां तुरङ्गद्वेषः सारमेयाणां शृगाले नकुलानां भुजङ्गमे इत्याद्युन्नेयम्।।

determined by desire in sacrifice etc. begets merit; activity determined by aversion in injury etc.,begets demerit. These same desire and aversion cause the series of transmigrations. Accordingly the aphorism of Gautama Activity is energy of word thought and body. Verbal activity is energy of voice: it is meritorious so far forth as it is true, kind, and useful; evil so far forth as untrue, unkind, useless. By thought intelligence, by which we think or know, is intended. Sensorial activity, therefore is compassion towards all creatures, etc. Bodily activity is almsgiving ministration etc., evil in ten ways, and good in ten ways.[1] U.

तत्संयोगो विभागः।। 15।।

Aph. 15. By these are conjunction and disjunction.

Existence in a future state is now declared to be the occasion of merit and demerit. By these—by merit and demerit—conjunction, that is birth, is caused. By conjunction is here intended connection with non-previous pains of bodily organs. Disjunction is the disjunction of body and the internal sensory, characterised as death. The meaning is therefore that this transitory world, a series of birth and deaths, otherwise termed existence in a future state, is caused by merit and demerit.[2] U.

आत्मगुणकर्मसु मोक्षो व्याख्यातः।। 16।।

*Aph.*16. Emancipation is declared as dependent on the actions of the soul.

This it is which is the separation of body and soul. When there exist the actions of the soul, emancipation ansures. The actions of the soul are as follows: hearing, meditation, the practice of devotion, abstraction, a sitting posture, restraining the vital airs, of acquistion of quietism and self-subjugation, the presentation of one's own and

[1] विहिते कर्मणि रागनिबन्धना निषिद्धे कर्मणि हिंसादौ द्वेषनिबन्धना प्रवृत्तिः रागनिबन्धना यागादौ प्रवृत्तिर्धर्मं प्रसूते द्वेषनिबन्धना हिंसादौ प्रवृत्तिधर्मं तावेतौ रागद्वेषौ संसारमनुवर्तयतः तथा च गौतमीयं सूत्रम् प्रवृत्तिर्वाग्बुद्धिशरीरारम्भः इति वागारम्भो वाचिकी प्रवृत्तिः सत्यं प्रियं हितमितिपुण्या असत्यमप्रियमहितमिति पापा बुद्धिः बुध्यते ज्ञायतेऽनेनेति तेन बुध्यते तेन मानसी प्रवृत्तिर्भूतदयादिः शारीरीप्रवृत्तिर्दानं परिचरणमित्यादिका दश-विधा पापा दशविधा पुण्या चेति।।

[2] इदानीं धर्माधर्मयोः प्रयोजनं प्रेत्यभावमाह। ताभ्यां धर्माधर्माभ्यां संयोगो जन्म अपूर्व्वाभिः शरीरेन्द्रियवेदनाभिः सम्बन्धः संयोग इहोच्यते विभागस्तु शरीरमनोविभागो मरणलक्षणः तथा चायं जन्ममरणप्रबन्धः संसारः प्रेत्यभावस्याजरञ्जरीभाव इति वैदिकी संज्ञा।।

others' souls, knowledge of merit and demerit previously acquired, whereof there must be fruition in other bodies and places, the formation of various bodies suitable to the fruition thereof, the destruction of merit and demerit by fruition, and emancipation characterised as removal of pain consequent on the cessation of birth, resulting from the cessation of activity in consequence of the non-production of further merit and demerit, by overcoming the mist of defects characterised as desire and aversion. Of these the primary act of soul is knowledge of the real nature of the six categories.[1] U.

[1] अयमेव शरीरविभागः आत्मकर्मसु सत्सु मोक्षो भवतीत्यर्थः तत्रात्मकर्मणि तावत् श्रवणं मननं योगाभ्यासो निदिध्यासनमासनं प्राणायामः शमदमसम्पत्तिः आत्मपरात्मसाक्षात्कारो देहदेशान्तरोपभाग्यपूर्व्वोत्पन्नधर्माधर्मपरिज्ञानं तद् भोगानुरूपनानादेहनिर्माणं तयोर्भोगेन प्रक्षयो रागद्वेषलक्षणदोषातुषारविगमादग्रिमधर्माधर्मयोरनुत्पादात् प्रवृत्तिरपाये जल्मापायो दुःखापायलक्षणोऽपवर्गस्तत्र षट्पदार्थीतत्वज्ञानमाद्यमात्मकर्म।।

Book VII

FIRST DAILY LESSON

उक्ता गुणाः।। 1।।

Aph. 1. The qualities have been stated.

Desirous of investigating the qualities in the seventh book the author reminds us of their enunciation and definition. The meaning is that the qualities have been stated, that is enunciated, and defined.[1] V.

पृथिव्यादिरूपरसगन्धस्पर्शा द्रव्यानित्यत्वादनित्याश्च।। 2।।

Aph. 2. Also the colour, taste, smell, and touch of the earth etc., inasmuch as substances are non-eternal, are non-eternal.

The colour, taste, smell, and touch of earth; the colour, touch, and taste of water; the colour and touch of light or fire; and the touch of air—these, inhearing in the non-eternal are non-eternal, inasmuch as they cease to be on the cessation of the existence of their substrata. The particle also implies unity, individual unity, extension, gravity, natural fluidity, and viscidity. These also are, in the non-eternal, non-eternal.[2] V.

एतेन नित्येषु नित्यत्वमुक्तम्।। 3।।

Aph. 3. By this is declared their eternity in things eternal.

By this—by the affirmation that their non-eternity is caused by the non-eternity of their substrata, the eternity of colour etc. in the eternal substrata is declared, that is virtually asserted, being involved. The

1 सप्तमे गुणान् परीचिक्षिषुस्तदुद्देशलक्षणे स्मारयति। गुण उक्ता उद्दिष्टा लक्षिताश्चेत्यर्थः।।

2 पृथिव्या रूपरसगंधस्पर्शाः, जलस्य रूपरसस्पर्शाः तेजसोरूपस्पर्शौ, वायोः स्पर्शः, एतेषाम् नित्याश्रितानामनित्यत्वम् आश्रयनाशनाश्यत्वात्, चकारादेकत्वैकपृथक्त्वपरिमितिर्गरुत्त्वसांसिद्धिकद्रवत्वस्नेहानां संग्रहः, तेऽपि अनित्यगता अनित्या एवेत्यर्थः।।

reading adopted by the author of the Vṛtti is Non-eternity in things eternal. In this opinion colour etc., are non-eternal in thing eternal, that is in atoms, inasmuch as colour etc., and the other qualities above mentioned are destructible by conjunction with fire. But it is to be considered that in this reading there is no congruity between the words by this and is declared.[1] V.

अप्सु तेजसि वायौ च नित्या द्रव्यनित्यत्वात्।। 4।।

Aph. 4. They are eternal in water, light, and air, inasmuch as the substances are eternal.

It may be objected: Why, whereas colour and the other qualities residing in terrene atoms are destructible by conjunction with fire, is it universally stated that they are eternal in things eternal ? The things eternal are therefore characterised. The sense is that colour and the other qualities are not eternal when existing in eternal earth, but are stated in the preceding aphorism to be eternal only when residing in eternal water, light and air.[2] V.

अनित्येष्वनित्या द्रव्यानित्यत्वात्।। 5।।

Aph. 5. In things non-eternal they are non-eternal, because the substances are non-eternal.

It may be asked whether qualities other than colour etc., existing in things non-eternal are eternal, in which case conjunction etc., would be eternal. It is therefore stated that all qualities which reside in things non-eternal, are non-eternal, in consequence of this non-eternity of their substratum; and that consequently there are no eternal qualities in things non-eternal.[3] U.

कारणगुणपूर्वकाः पृथिव्यां पाकजाः।। 6।।

Aph. 6. [Colour, taste, smell, and touch] produced by

[1] एतेन आश्रयानित्यत्वहेतुकानित्यत्वकथनेन नित्येषु आश्रयेषु रूपादीनां नित्यत्व मुक्तमुक्तप्रायमथोयातत्वादित्यर्थः नित्येष्वनित्यत्वमिति वृत्तिकारसम्मतः पाठः, तन्मते नित्येषु पार्थिवपरमाणुषु रूपादीनामनित्यत्वमग्नि-संयोगनाश्यत्वादित्यर्थः, किन्तु तादृशपाठे एतेनेति उक्तमिति च सङ्गतं न भवतीति ध्येयम्।।

[2] ननु पार्थिवपरमाणुगतानां रूपादीनामग्निसंयोगनाश्यत्वात कथं नित्येष्विति सामान्यत उक्तमतो नित्यानि विशेषयति। न खलु नित्यपृथिवीगता रूपादयो नित्याः किंतु नित्यजलगेजोवायुगता ते एव नित्याः पूर्वसूत्रे उक्ता इत्यर्थः।।

[3] ननु रूपादिभिन्ना अनित्यगता गुणाः किं नित्यास्तथा च संयोगादिकमपि नित्यं स्यादित्यत आह। अनित्येषु ये गुणा वर्तन्ते ते सर्व एवानित्या आश्रयानित्यत्वात् तथा चानित्येषु नित्या गुणा न सन्त्येवेत्यर्थः।।

combustion in earth, have for their antecedents the qualities of their causes.

It is implied that the colour, taste, smell, and touch residing in wholes, have for their antecedents the qualitites of their cause; that is, that they become manifest from the homogeneous qualities which are attributes of the parts, which are cause of their own substratum. It is thus to be understood that the presentation of colour, taste, smell, touch residing in the parts which are the non-coinherent causes of colour, taste, smell, and touch, existing in the wholes, is by the connection of co-inhesion with the coinherent. In anticipatfon of the question how in a dark water-pot etc., after powerful conjunction with fire there is production of red colour etc., it is stated that in earth those qualities produced by burning also—for the word is to be supplied—colour, taste, smell, and touch in earth, even when produced by burning, have for their antecedents the qualities of their causes. Burning is an extraordinary conjunction with fire resulting in change of colour, etc. This also is a non-coinherent cause of colour, etc. On this subject those who maintain the combustion of atoms hold that it is in the atom that the change of colour etc., consequent on combustion takes place, and not in the whole. According to their doctrine the red colour etc., is produced in the atom, after the dissolution of the whole into binary atomic aggregates by destruction of the originative conjunction consequent upon an extraordinary conjunction with fire; and after this ensues again production beginning with binary aggregates and terminating in the whole possessed of magnitude, in the progressive order of originative conjunction etc. caused by the production of action etc., conformable to originative conjunction in consequence of an extraordinary conjunction with fire. Those who maintain the combustion of wholes such as the pot, teach that, the wholes being porous, it is in them that the change of colour etc., takes place in consequence of conjunction with the particular kind of fire; and that there is in this case no destruction of wholes, for this would be contrary to observation. The order of combustion is here omitted to avoid voluminous prolixity, and may be sought elsewhere. According to the doctrine of those who teach that particular blue colours etc., are only individually eternal, the cognition and expression that blue colour has ceased to exist and dark colour has been produced is improper, inasmuch as connection by co-inherence is eternal, and the production of such a cognition and expression, with connection by co-inhesion as its object, is impossible. Else, were it possible, the eternity and unity of water-pots etc., would follow. There being a cognition of difference in the nature of the colour of a water-pot, there cannot but be a difference in the attribute and then in the subject of the attribute. In a piece of cloth etc. originating in various threads etc. of blue, yellow, and other colours, there is produced a composite colour, for were such cloth colourless etc. its visual presentation would be impossible. In conformity with this, they say, is the verse: That is said to be a blue ox which is ruddy in colour in the face, yellowish in the tail, and white in the horns and hoofs. Taste and smell are never composite, there being no harm if it be but allowed that wholes originated by parts possessing various tastes etc. are tasteless, etc. A composite touch must be allowed according to the analogy of colour.[1] V.

एकद्रव्यत्वात् ।। 7 ।।

Aph. 7. Because there is only one substance.

In reply to the objection: How can the qualities of the cause, as not existing in the effect, be productive of the qualities of the effect, there being a difference of substratum ? it is stated that it is because there

[1] रूपरसगंधस्पर्शाः, अवयविगता इति विवक्षणीयं कारणगुणपूर्व्वकाःस्वाश्रयस्य यानि कारणानि अवयवा इति यावत तेषां ये गुणाः स्वसजातीयगुणाः तेभ्यः प्रादुर्भवन्तीत्यर्थः तथा चावयविवृत्तिरूपरस-गन्धस्पर्शानामसमवायिकारणानि अवयवगता रूपरसगंधस्पर्शास्तेषां समवायिकारणप्रत्यासन्नत्वन्तु स्वसमवदयिसम्बन्धेनेति बोध्यम्, ननु श्यामघटादौ बलवदग्निसंयोगानन्तरं कथं रक्ताद्युत्पत्तिरित्यत उक्तं पृथिव्यां पाकजाइति अपीतिशेषः तथा च पृथिव्यां रूपरसगन्धस्पर्शाः पाकजा अपि पाकस्तु रूपादिपरावृत्तिफलकविजातीयतेजः संयोगः, सोऽपि रूपादेरसमवायिकारणं भवति, तत्र च परमाणावेव पाकाद्रूपादिपरावृत्तिर्नावयविनीति पीलुपाकवादिनः, तन्मते विजातीयाग्निसंयोगादारम्भकसंयोगनाशेन द्व्यणुकपर्य्यन्तावयविनाशे सति परमाणौ रक्ताद्युत्पत्तिस्ततोविजातीयाग्निसंयोगादारम्भकसंयोगानु-गुणक्रियाद्युत्पत्त्यारम्भकसंयोगादिप्रकमेण पुनर्द्व्यणुकादिमहावयविपर्य्यन्तानामुत्पत्तिर्भवतीति। पिठरपाकवादिनस्तु अवयविनां सच्छिद्रतया विजातीयाग्निसंयोगात् तेषामपि रूपादिपरावृत्तिर्भवति न तु तत्रावयविनां नाशः प्रत्यभिज्ञाविरोधादित्याहुः। अत्र च पाकप्रक्रिया ग्रंथगौरवभिया परित्यक्ता ऽन्यत्रानुसन्धेया। ये तु नीलरूपादिव्यक्तय एकैका एव नित्या इत्याहुस्तन्मते नीलरूपं नष्टं श्यामरुपमुत्पन्नमित्यादिप्रतीतिव्यवहारयोरनुपपत्तिः समवाय-सम्बन्धस्य नित्यतया तद्विषयतया रूपोपत्त्यसम्भवात् अन्यथा घटादीनामपि नित्यत्वमेकत्वञ्चापद्येत, घटस्य रूपमिति भेदप्रत्ययात् गुणगुणिनोर्नाभेदः नीलपीतादिनानातन्त्वाद्यारब्धे पटादौ चित्ररूपमेव जायते तादृशपटस्य नीरूपत्वे तच्चाक्षुषानुपपत्तेः, नव्यास्तु तत्र पटे तत्तदवयवावच्छेदेन नानैव रूपाणि भवन्ति। अतएव "लोहितो यस्तु वर्णेन मुखे पुच्छे च पाण्डुरः। श्वेतः खुरविषाणाभ्यां स नीलो वृष उच्यते"।। इत्यादिकं सङ्गच्छते इत्याहुः, रसगन्धयोस्तु न चित्रत्वं नानारसादिमदवयवारब्धानामवयविनां नीरसत्वादिस्वीकारेऽपि क्षत्यभावात् चित्रस्पर्शस्तु रूपस्थलीययुक्त्याा स्वीकरणीय एवेति संक्षेपः।।

exists that whereof there is one substance as the substratum, that is because there is common substratum. Notwithstanding, therefore, that the qualities of the cause do not exist in the relation of immediate co-inherence in the effect, yet inasmuch as, in the relation of community of substratum characterised as co-inherence with the co-inherent, they do exist in the effect, the production by them of the qualities of the effect is not impossible.[1] V.

अणोर्महतश्चोपलब्ध्यनुपलब्धी नित्त्वे व्याख्याते।। ८।।

Aph. 8. The perception and non-perception of the atomic and of that which has magnitude, have been explained to be constant.

The word eternal or constant refers, as to a section to that which contains it, to the fourth book which treats of eternity. The respective application of the words perception and non-perception is according to the rule: That which is connected with another is connected with the more remote. Non-perception of the atomic is thus obtained . In the presentative cognition therefore, determined as a large blue-pot, the extension is just as much an object as the blue colour; and by means of this, extension terminating in the atomic as a minimum is inferred, as also from substantiality. Moreover of the perceptibility of substance the cause is coloured extension, for without magnitude substance cannot be percevied. Accordingly it is decided that, as being a cause of perceptibility of substance, and as being of itself perceptible, extension is a quality. For were the form of a water-pot etc., its extension, a man would bring a water-pot, when he was told to bring the great; and thus there would be a contradiction in the order and the apprehension of it, and likewise by the term water-pot, extension would be conveyed, or by the term extension a water-pot. The notion of magnitude is that of a particular cause of the usage of measurement, or that of a universal quality existing in objects and the cause of the presentation of substance. The usage of measurement is the usage of cubits, spans etc., not the usage of weights, numbers etc. This extension is of four kinds, the great, the small, the long, and the short. Of these, infinite greatness and infinite length exist in the four pervading substances, absolute smallness and absolute shortness exist

[1] ननु कारणगुणानां कार्य्येऽसत्वात् कथं कार्यगुणजनकत्वं वैयधिकरण्यादित्याशङ्कायामाह। एकं द्रव्यमधिकरणं यस्य तत्त्वात् सामानाधिकरण्यादित्यर्थ, तथा च कारणगुणानां साक्षात् समवायसम्बन्धेन कार्य्ये ऽसत्त्वेपि स्वसमवायिसमवायरूपसामानाधिकरण्यसम्बन्धेन कार्य्ये सत्त्वात्तद्गुणजनकत्वं नानुपपन्नमिति भावः।।

in atoms. Intermediate smallness and intermediate shortness exist in binary atomic aggregates. Greatness and length reside in substances, from tertiary atomic upwards to composite wholes. In this manner all substances whatever possess two extensions or dimensions. The notion of smallness in a vilva or āmalaka fruit and of shortness in fuel, sugar-canes etc., is relative. The relativity in this case is the existence or non-existence of greater size. There is non-existence in a jujube of the greater size, of which there is existence in an emblic myrobalan. There does not exist in an emblic myrobalan the greater size which exists in a vilva-fruit. This as containing as parts both the primary and secondary magnitudes, is described by the term relative magnitude.[1] U.

कारणबहुत्वाच्च ।। 9 ।।

Aph. 9. Also in consequence of a plurality of causes, extension is produced.

The particle also implies the addition of magnitude and coalescence. Extension is produced is the ellipse to be supplied in the aphorism. Among these, plurality of causes alone produces greatness and length in a tertiary aggregate, since greatness and accretion do not exist in their cause. The plurality is derived from the relative cognition of the Deity. The influence of particular destiny determines a plurality of objects in the divine cognition. Similarly duality existing in two atoms is productive of extension in a binary atomic aggregate. In a piece of

[1] नित्ये इति विषयेण विषयि नित्यत्वप्रतिपादकं चतुर्थाध्यायमुपलक्षयति उपलब्ध्यनुपलब्धी इति यथायोगमन्वयः "येन यस्याभिसम्बन्धी दूरस्थस्यापि तस्य सः" इतिन्यायेन तथा चाणोरनुपलब्धिरिति लभ्यते तदेवं स्थूलो नीलः कलस इति प्रात्यक्षिकप्रत्यये यथा नीलं रूपं विषयस्तथा परिमाणमपि तेन च परिमाणेन परमाणुपर्यन्तं परिमाणमुन्नीयते द्रव्यत्वाच्च किञ्च द्रव्यप्रत्यक्षतायां रूपवत् परिमाणमपि कारणं नहि महत्त्वमन्तरेण द्रव्यं प्रत्यक्षं भवति तथा च द्रव्यप्रत्यक्षकारणत्वेन स्वयञ्च प्रत्यक्षतया परिमाणं गुणोऽस्तीति निश्चीयते यदि हि घटादिस्वरूपं परिमाणं स्यात् तदा महदानयेत्युक्ते घटमात्रमानयेत् तथा च प्रतीतिसंप्रतिपत्ती विरुद्ध्येयाताम् एवं घटपदात् परिमाणं प्रतीयेत परिमाणपदाद्वा घट इति, मानव्यवहारासाधारणकारणत्वं द्रव्यसाक्षात्कारण-विषयनिष्ठसामान्यगुणत्वं वा महत्त्वं मानव्यवहारो हस्तवितस्त्यादिव्यवहारो न तु पलसङ्ख्यादिव्यवहारः तच्च परिमाणञ्चतुर्व्विधं महञ्वमणुत्त्वं दीर्घत्वं ह्रस्वत्वञ्च तत्र परममहत्त्वपरमदीर्घत्वे विभुचतुष्टयवर्त्तिनी परमाणुत्वपरमह्रस्वत्त्वे परमाणुवर्त्तिनी अवान्तराणुत्वावान्तरह्रस्वत्वे द्व्यणुकवर्त्तिनी त्रसरेणुमारभ्य महावयविपर्यन्तं महावयवत्त्वदीर्घत्वे एवञ्च सर्वाण्यपि द्रव्याणि परिमाणद्वयवन्ति बिल्वामलकादावणुत्वव्यवहारः समिदिक्षुदण्डादिषु च हस्वत्वव्यवहारो भक्तिः भक्तिरश्चात्र प्रकर्षभावाभावः आमलके यः प्रकर्षभावस्तस्या-भावः कुवलेबिल्वे यः प्रकर्षभावस्तस्याभाव आमलके स च गौणमुख्योभयभागित्वाद् भक्तिपदवाच्यः, दीर्घत्वह्रस्वत्वे नित्ये न वर्त्तेते इत्येके परिमाण एव ते न भवत इत्यपरे, महत्सु दीर्घ, मानीयतामितिवत् महत्सु वर्तुलं त्रिकोणञ्चानीयतामिति निर्धारणबलाद्वर्तुलत्वादीनामप्यापत्तेरिति तेषामाशयात्।।

cloth originated by two threads not coalescent, it is magnitude alone which is the non-coinherent cause, inasmuch as plurality and coalesence do not there exist. But where a ball of cotton is originated by two balls of cotton, in the case coalesence is the cause, for there is here observed an increase of extension, and there is no plurality; and magnitude even though is existed, could not be an occasion of increase of extension. Such being the case even were magnitude here a cause, there would be no failure in the argument. Hence it has been said: By two, by one, or by all. Coalesence is an originative conjunction, and is defined as conjunction in an object of some of its constituent parts towards itself, in which object some of the constituent parts are non-conjunct towards itself; for it is said that this conjunction of constituent parts involves a lax conjunction of its own portions, is productive of extension, and is involved in the origination of qualities and actions.[1] U.

अतो विपरीतमणु ।। 10 ।।

Aph. 10. The contrary of this is the minute.

That which is the contrary of this, that is of great extension established by perception, is minute extension. The contrariety arises from imperceptibility, and contrariety of causes; for the causes of magnitude are magnitude, plurality, and coalescence; and the cause of minuteness is duality produced by the relative conception of the Deity residing in the cause. By this is also to be understood shortness the contrary of length, and in this case also the contrariety is as aforesaid.[2] U.

[1] चकारो महत्त्वप्रचयौ समुच्चिनोति, परिमाणमुत्पद्यते इति सूत्रशेष: तत्र कारणबहुत्वं केवलं त्र्यणुके महत्वदीर्घत्वे जनयती महत्वप्रचययोस्तत्कारणेऽभावात् तच्च बहुत्वमीश्वरापेक्षाबुद्धिजन्यं तद्बुद्धेरनेकविषयत्वेप्यदृष्टविशेषोपग्रहो नियामक:, एवं परमाणुद्वयगतं द्वित्वं द्व्यणुके परिमाणोत्पादकं वक्ष्यते द्वाभ्यां तन्तुभ्यामप्रचिताभ्यामारब्धे पढे केवलं महत्त्वमेवासमवायिकारणं बहुत्वप्रचययोस्तत्राभावात् यत्र च द्वाभ्यां तूलकपिण्डाभ्यां तूलकपिण्डारम्भस्तत्र परिमाणोत्कर्षदर्शनात् प्रचय: कारणं बहुत्वस्याभावात् महत्त्वस्य सत्त्वेऽपि परिमाणोत्कर्षप्रत्ययप्रयोजकत्वात् एवञ्च सति यदि महत्त्वं तत्र कारणं तदा न दोष: तदुक्तं "द्वाभ्यामेकेन सर्वैर्वा" इति। प्रचयश्च आरम्भक: संयोग:, सच स्वाभिमुखकिञ्चिदवयवासंयुक्तत्वे सति स्वाभिमुखकिञ्चिदवयवसंयोगलक्षण: सचावयवसंयोग: स्वावयवप्रशिथिलसंयोगापेक्ष: परिमाणजनक: गुणकर्मारम्भे सापेक्षइतिवचनात्।।

[2] अत: प्रत्यक्षसिद्धान्महत: परिमाणाद्यद्विपरीतं तदणुपरिमाणमित्यर्थ:। वैपरीत्यञ्चाप्रत्यक्षत्वात् कारणवैपरीत्याच्च महत्त्वे हि महत्त्वबहुत्वप्रचयानां कारणत्वम्, अणुत्वे च कारणगतस्य द्वित्वस्येश्वरापेक्षाबुद्धिजन्यस्य कारणत्वम्, एतेन दीर्घत्वविपरीतं ह्रस्वत्वमित्यपि द्रष्टव्यम्, वैपरीत्यञ्चात्रापि पूर्ववत्।।

अणु महदिति तस्मिन् विशेषभावात् विशेषाभावाच्च ।। 11।।

Aph. 11. The notions greater and smaller [arise] in this conception [of a relatively great and a relatively small object] from the existence of particularity, and from the non-existence of particularity.

The word *iti* refers to the usage. There is, then, a practical assurance that a jujube is small in relation to a bel-fruit, an emblic myrobalan great in relation to a jujube, and a bel-fruit great in relation to an emblic myrobalan. Among these the principal notion is that of greatness. The reason of this is stated to be that there exist particularity; that is, that there exists particular magnitude, because there is a relation of more and less. But among these the notion of smallness is relative. The reason of this is said to be the non-existence of particularity, that is the non-existence there is of particular smallness. For minuteness as a product resides only in binary atomic aggregates, and as eternal abides only in the ultimate particles. But this does not exist in a jujube, etc. In other words, it is because there exist in the particles of the jujube etc., plurality, magnitude and coalescence of constituent elements, which are a particular cause of magnitude; and because there does not exist in the jujube etc. duality not having a common substratum with magnitude, which duality is the cause of smallness.[1] U

एककालत्वात् ।।12 ।।

Aph. 12. Because the time is one.

The greatness and smallness are both experienced at one time, and these greatness and smallness being contrary to one another cannot exist together in one substratum. Therefore, inasmuch as there exists a cause of greatness, the conception of magnitude is in this instance primary and the notion and usage with regard to smallness are derivative or relative only.[2] U.

[1] इतिशब्दो व्यवहारपरतां दर्शयति, तेन बिल्वापेक्षया कुवलमणु कुवलापेक्षयामलकं महत् आमलकापेक्षया बिल्वं महदिति तावद्व्द्रव्यवहारो ऽस्ति, तत्र महदिति, तेषु व्यवहारो मुख्यः कुत एवमतआह। विशेषभावा– महत्त्वविशेषस्यैव तरतमादिभावेन भावात् अणुव्यवहारस्तु तेषु भाक्तः कुत एवमत आह। विशेषस्य तत्राभावात् अणुत्वविशेषस्य तत्राभावात् अणुत्वं हि कार्यं द्व्यणुकमात्रवृत्ति, नित्यं परमाणुवृत्ति कुवलादौ तदभावात् यद्वा विशेषस्य महत्त्वकारणस्यैवावयवबहुत्वमहत्त्वप्रचयानां कुवलाद्यवयवेषु भावात् सद्भावात् विशेषाभावात् विशेषस्य अणुत्वकारणस्य महत्त्वासमानाधिकरणद्वित्वस्य कुवलाद्यवयवेष्वभावादसदभावादित्यर्थः।।

[2] महत्त्वमणुत्त्वञ्च द्वयमप्येकस्मिन् काले ऽनुभूयेते, ते च महत्त्वाणुत्त्वे परस्परविरोधिनी नेकत्राश्रये सह सम्भवतः, अतो महत्त्वकारणसद्भावान्महत्त्वप्रत्ययस्तत्र मुख्योऽणुत्वप्रत्यययोगौ च भाक्तावित्यर्थः।।

दृष्टान्ताच्च।। 13।।

Aph. 13. Also because of the example.

It is seen likewise that in the natural order of things there must be a partical conception of a great, greater, and greatest, in the jujube, emblic myrobalan, and bel-fruits which possess magnitude, just as in the course of things there is a conventional notion of white, whiter, and whitest, in a piece of cloth, a conch shell, crystal etc., which are white.[1] U.

अणुत्वमहत्त्वयोरणुत्वमहत्त्वाभावः कर्मगुणैर्व्याख्यातः।। 14।।

*Aph.*14. The non-existence of greatness and smallness in greatness and smallness, is explained by greatness and smallness.

It may be objected that in virtue of the practical notion of small and great extension, it is known that in magnitude as an extension there exists magnitude, and in smallness as an extension there exists smallness. How then can these exist in substance alone, or how does not the contradiction emerge of the existence of quality in quality? In the answer to this it is stated that as quality and action do not possess quality and action, so also greatness and smallness do not possess greatness and smallness, and that such a conventional notion is to be regarded as tropical.[2] U.

कर्मभिः कर्माणि गुणैश्च गुणा व्याख्याताः।। 15।।

Aph. 15. Actions are explained to be [void] of actions, and qualities of qualities.

It may be urged that as qualities are possessed of qualities—and how else could there be such conventional notions as a loud sound, one sound, twenty-four qualities etc.—and as actions are possessed of actions—and how else could there be such cognitions as, It goes quickly, It goes rapidly?— so in like manner greatness and smallness must also be possessed of greatness and smallness. In the answer to this it is stated that actions are not possessed of actions, nor are qualities

[1] दृश्यते तथा वस्तुगत्या महत्स्वेव कुवलामलकबिल्वेषु स्थूलस्थूलतरस्थूलतमव्यवहारेण भवितव्यमित्यर्थः यथा वस्तुगत्या शुक्लष्वेव पटशङ्खस्फाटिकादिषु शुक्लशुक्लतरशुक्लतमव्यवहारः।।

[2] नन्वणुमहत्परिमाणुव्यवहारबलान्महत्त्वेऽपि परिमाणे महत्त्वमणुत्त्वेचाणुत्वमस्तीति ज्ञायते तत् कथं द्रव्यमात्रवृत्तित्वभनयोः कथं वा गुणे गुणवृत्तित्वविरोधो नोपपद्यत इत्यत आह। यथा गुणकर्मणी नाणुत्वमहत्त्ववती तथा ऽणुत्वमहत्त्वे ऽपि नाणुत्वमहत्त्ववती इत्यर्थः प्रयोगश्च भाक्तो द्रष्टव्यः।।

possessed of qualities, and that in like manner greatness and smallness are not possessed of greatness and smallness, but the conventional notion is in all these cases tropical.[1] U.

अणुत्वमत्त्वहाभ्यां कर्मगुणाश्च व्याख्याताः।। 16।।

Aph. 16. Actions moreover and qualities are explained to be [void] of smallness and greatness.

It may be urged that in virtue of such conventional notions as small actions, great actions, small qualities, great qualities, the extension greatness and smallness must be concluded to exist in action and quality. It is therefore stated that as the extensions greatness and smallness do not exist in the extensions greatness and smallness, in like manner neither of those extensions exists in action or in qualities; and that the aforesaid conventional notions have as their objects increase and diminution.[2] V.

एतेन दीर्घत्वहस्वत्वे व्याख्याते।। 17।।

Aph. 17. By this length and shortness are explained.

It is stated that shortness and length are similar to smallness and greatness. As smallness and greatness are proved to exist by the conventional notions of great and small, so shortness and length are proved to exist by the conventional notions of long and short. In like manner also the notions and convention that one thing is shorter or is longer than another, have for their object increase and diminution.[3] V.

अनित्ये ऽनित्यम्।। 18।।

Aph. 18. In the non-eternal [extension] is non-eternal.

[1] ननु यथा गुणा गुणवन्तः कथमन्यथा महान् शब्दः द्वौ शब्दौ एकः शब्दः चतुर्विंशतिर्गुणा इत्यादिव्यवहारः कर्माण्यपि च कर्म्मवन्ति प्रतीयन्ते कथमन्यथा शीघ्र गच्छति द्रुतं गच्छतीति व्यवहारः तथाचाणुत्वमहत्त्वे अपि न तद्वती स्यातामित्यत आह। कर्मभिः कर्माणि न तद्वन्ति गुणैश्च गुणा न तद्वन्तस्तथाऽणुत्वमहत्त्वे ऽपि न तद्वती, व्यवहारस्तु सर्वत्र भाक्त इत्यर्थः।।

[2] नन्वणूनि कर्माणि महान्ति कर्माणि अणवो गुणा महान्ता गुणा इत्यादिव्यवहारबलात् कर्मणि गुणे च अणुत्वं महत्त्वञ्च परिमाणं सेत्स्यतीत्त्यत आह। यथा ऽणुत्वमहत्त्वपरिमाणयोर्नाणुत्वमहत्त्वपरिमाणे तथा कर्म्मणि गुणेषु च न तदुभयम् उक्तव्यवहाराश्चापकर्षोत्कर्षविषयका एवेति।।

[3] ह्रस्वत्वदीर्घत्वयोरप्यणुत्वमहत्त्वतुल्यतेत्याह। यथा अणु महादितिव्यवहारसिद्धे अणुत्वमहत्त्वे तथा ह्रस्वं दीर्घमितिव्यवहारसिद्धे ह्रस्वत्वदीर्घत्वे एवमिदमस्माद् ह्रस्वमिदमस्माद्दीर्घमित्यादिप्रत्ययव्यवहारा-वप्यपकर्षोत्कर्षविषयकावेवेत्यर्थः।।

Extension is non-eternal in the non- eternal. It is in consequence of the destruction of its substratum that it ceases to exist. It is not to be maintained that in a water-pot and the like, where there is an increase or diminution by two, three or more atoms, there is another extension recognished by perception, on the ground that there is in this case no destruction of the water-pot etc. inasmuch as there exists in regard to it the recognition that it is the same water-pot. For in the case of a diminution or increase of the atoms there is necessarily a destruction commencing in the tertiary atomic aggregates and terminating in the composite wholes, there being necessarily a destruction of the binary aggregates; for the sum of destroying causes tails not in obtaining its effects through any difficulty with regard to the recognition. In the case of an increase in the body etc. there is necessarily a destruction of the composite whole, in consequence of the necessity of the destruction of the non-coinherent cause. Nor can it be urged : Where there is not destruction of a piece of cloth etc. how can there be an addition of extension resulting from conjunction with other threads ? For in this instance there must needs be destruction of the piece of cloth resulting from the destruction of the conjunction of the threads, which conjunction is the non-coinherent cause; such destruction being caused by the striking of the loom, etc. Moreover if that other threads were a portion of that cloth, the cloth of which it is the thread would not previously exist, since the threads which is its cause would not exist. But if that threads be not a part, there can be thereby no addition to its extension, as is the case with other conjunct substances. It must, therefore, necessarily be admitted that in this case, when conjunction with another threads takes place, there results production of another piece of cloth from destruction of the former piece of cloth. The recognition of the composite whole is caused by the homogeneity of the former and latter wholes, as in the recognition of the continuous identity of the flame of a lamp. Nor is it to be maintained that the former threads, through the subsidiary agency of the other threads, originate a new piece of cloth during the existence of the former piece of cloth, for it would involve the contradiction of two substances at the same time occupying the same space.[1] V.

1 परिमाणमनित्ये अनित्यमाश्रयविनाशादेव तन्नश्यतीत्यर्थः नच घटादौ त्रिचतुरादिपरमाणुविश्लेषे तदुपक्षये वा परिमाणान्तरं प्रत्यक्षसिद्धं स एवायं घट इत्यादिप्रत्यभिज्ञायास्तत्र सत्त्वेन घटादेरत्राविनाशादितिवाच्यं परमाणुविश्लेषे तदुपचये वा द्वयणुकनाशस्यावश्वकत्वेन त्रसरेण्वाद्यन्त्यावयविपर्य्यन्तनाशस्याप्यावश्यकत्वात् नहि विनाशसामग्री प्रत्यभिज्ञाभिया कार्य्यं नाशयिष्यति शरीरादाववयवोपचयेऽसमवायिकारणनाशस्यावश्य-

नित्ये नित्यम्।। 19।।

Aph. 19. In the eternal it is eternal.

The extension which exists in things eternal, that is in ether etc., and in atoms is eternal, for there is nothing to destroy it.[1] U.

नित्यं परिमण्डलम्।। 20।।

Aph. 20. Atomic extension is eternal.

The word *parimaṇḍala* technically designate atomic extension, and an atom characterised by such extension. An atom, that is a substance consisting of an ultimate particle characterised by atomic extension, is eternal: there is therefore no scarcity of eternal substance. The eternity thereof has also previously been declared .[2] V.

अविद्या च विद्यालिङ्गम्।। 21।।

Aph. 21. Ignorance, moreover, is an indication of knowledge.

It may be asked why should we admit substance in the form of atoms, since it cannot be perceived; and may be maintained that only such substance as is cognished by perception, such as tertiary atomic aggregates etc., is to be admitted. To this the reply is furnished: Ignorance, the absence of certain knowledge, that is such cognition as that earth is eternal or that water is eternal, having a composite whole as its object, is a mark or indication of the existence of the science or certain knowledge, the object of which is atomic, that earth is eternal; inasmuch as certain knowledge has always for its antecedent the absence of certain knowledge, for such an error as that earth is eternal cannot arise in one that has no notion of eternity. This mode of proving

कत्वादवयविनाश आवश्यकः नच पटाविनाशेऽपि तन्त्वन्तरसंयोगात् कथं परिमाणाधिक्यमितिवाच्यं तत्रापि वेमाद्यभिघातेनासमवायिकारणतन्तुसंयोगनाशादेव पटनाशस्यावश्यकत्वात् किञ्च तन्त्वन्तरस्य तत्पटावयवत्वे पूर्व्वं तत्पट एव न स्यात् तत्तन्तुरूपकारणाभावात् तत्तन्तोरवयवत्वाभावे च न तेन परिमाणाद्यैक्यं संयुक्तद्रव्यान्तरवत् तस्मात्तत्रतन्त्वान्तरसंयोगे सति पूर्व्वपटनाशात्पटान्तरोत्पत्तिरित्यवश्यं स्वीकार्य्यम् अवयविनः प्रत्यभिज्ञानन्तु साजात्येन सैवेयं दीपकलिकेत्यादिवत्। नच पूर्व्वतन्तवएव तन्त्वन्तरसहकारात् पूर्व्वपटे सत्येव पटान्तरमारभन्त इति वाच्यं मूर्त्तयोः समानदेशताविरोधादितिसंक्षेपः।।

[1] नित्येष्वाकाशादिषु परमाणुषु च यत् परिमाणं तन्नित्यं विनाशकाभावात्।।

[2] परिमण्डलशब्दो परमाणुपरिमाणं तद्विशिष्टं परिमाणञ्च परिभाषया प्रतिपादयति परिमण्डलं पारिमाण्डल्यपरिमाणविशि परमाणुरूपं द्रव्यं नित्यमिति न नित्यद्रव्यस्य दुर्भिक्षतेत्यर्थः। तस्य नित्यत्वञ्च प्रागेव प्रतिपादितम्।।

accidentally but really the existence of atoms, which has been formerly described, merits attention.[1] V.

विभवान्महानाकाशस्तथा चात्मा।। 22।।

Aph. 22. Ether, in consequence of its universal pervasion, is infinitely great; and so likewise is soul.

Ether, as pervading all things, in consequence of conjunction with all finite things is infinitely great, or possesses infinitely great extension. This extension is eternal, since ether is eternal. Did there not exist in ether conjunction with all matter, the production of sound limited to various places would be impossible, for conjunction with ether in respective places is the non-coinherent cause of respective sounds. In like manner soul also is possessed of eternal and infinitely great extension, being all-pervasive. The universal pervasion of soul is proved, inasmuch as conjunction with soul influenced by destiny is the cause of action in the atoms at the time of creation.[2] V.

तदभावादणु मनः।। 23।।

Aph. 23. In consequence of non-existence of that [universal pervasion] the internal organ is absolutely small.

It may be urged: The internal organ is also, like soul, an all-pervading substance, inasmuch as it is the substratum of conjunctions which are the non-coinherent causes of cognitions etc.; why therefore has not its infinite greatness been enounced ? In reply to this it is stated, that in consequence of the non-existence of that universal pervasion, the internal sensory is absolutely small, is not possessed of infinitely great extension. The proof that the internal organ, as determinant of non-simultaneity of cognitions, is absolutely small,

[2] ननु परमाणुरूपं द्रव्यं कथमङ्गीकर्तव्यं तस्याप्रत्यक्षत्वात् त्रसरेण्वादिकन्तु प्रत्यक्षसिद्धं यद् द्रव्यं तदेवाङ्गीकरणीमियित्यत आह। अविद्या अप्रमा पृथिवी नित्या जलं नित्यमित्यादिप्रतीतिरवयविविषयिणी विद्यायाः परमाणविषयिण्यः पृथिवी नित्येति प्रमाया लिङ्गम् सर्व्वत्र प्रमाया अप्रमापूर्व्वकत्वात् नहि कुत्रापि नित्यत्वमजानतः पृथिवी नित्येति भ्रमो भवितुमर्हति एतच्चापाततः वस्तुतः परमाणुसिद्धिप्रकारः प्राक् प्रदर्शित एवादरणीयः।।

[2] विभवात् सर्व्वमूर्त्तसंयोगादाकाशो महान् परममहत्परिमाणवान् तच्च परिमाणं नित्यमाकाशस्य नित्यत्वात् आकाशस्य सर्व्वमूर्त्तसंयोगाभावे नानादेशावच्छेदेन शब्दोत्पत्त्यसम्भवात् तत्तद्देशाकाशसंयोगस्य तत्तच्छब्दासमवायिकारणत्वात् एवमात्माऽपि नित्यपरममहत्परिमाणवान् वैभवात् अदृष्टवदात्मसंयोगस्य सर्गाद्यकालीनपरमाणुकर्म्महेतुत्वादात्मवैभवमप्यावश्यकम्।।

results from the impossibility of evidence cognisant of an object of the forementioned inference probative of universal pervasion.[1] V.

गुणैर्दिग् व्याख्याता।। 24।।

Aph. 24. By its qualities space is explained [to be all-comprehensive.]

By its qualities characterised as priority and posteriority existing in all finite things, and consisting of the common prior, posterior, and other conceptions of beings existent in all divisions of the universe, space also is explained to be all-comprehensive. If it be asked how the notion and expression of ten spaces or quarters of the compass arise, whereas it is to be stated that relative conception, having for its object the more and the less in conjunctions with the conjunct, is the cause of the production of priority and posteriority, and whereas the coception of a plurality of spaces is contravened by the complexity of the conception or needlessness of the hypothesis; to this we reply that this is no valid objection, inasmuch as it has been stated that the conception is determined by the particular accidents of space.[2] U.

कारणे कालः।। 25।।

Aph. 25. Time relates to a cause.

The designation time relates to a substance which is the cause of the cognitions of the prior, posterior, reciprocal, simultaneous, non-simultaneous , slow, and fast. Such a cognition, common to persons in all places, would be impossible unless time were universally pervasive. Its universal pervasion is possession of infinite magnitude. Or (it may be argued) that in virtue of such cognitions as born now etc., time is the occasional cause of all that is produced, and this is dependent on universal pervasion; for an occasional cause is the condition of the apprehension of the co-inherent and non-coinherent cause. Or

[1] नन्वात्मवन्मनोऽपि विभुज्ञानाद्यसमवायिकारणसंयोगाश्रयत्वादिति तस्य महत्परिमाणं कुतो नोक्तमत आह। तस्य विभवस्याभावान्मनोऽणु न परममहत्परिमाणवदित्यर्थः ज्ञानायोगपद्यनियामकतयाऽणुत्ववत एव मनसः सिद्धिर्वैभवसाधकप्रगुक्तानुमानस्य धर्मिकग्राहकप्रमाण निबाधतत्वादिति भावः।।

[2] गुणैः सकलद्वीपवर्तिपपुरुषसाधारणपूर्व्वापरादिप्रत्ययरूपैः सकलमूर्त्तनिष्ठपरत्वापरत्वलक्षणैः दिगपि व्यापकत्वेन व्याख्यातेत्यर्थः परत्वापरत्वयोरुत्पत्तौ संयुक्तसंयोगभूयस्त्वाल्पीयस्त्वविषयापेक्षाबुद्धेः कारणत्वस्य वक्ष्यमाणत्वात् नानादिक्कल्पनस्य कल्पनागो वरप्रतिहतत्वात् कथं तर्हि दश दिश इति प्रतीतिव्यपदेशाविति चेन्न तत्तदुपाधिनिबन्धनत्वादित्युक्तत्वात्।।

another argument might be , that the notion of past, present, and future is applicableyto all objects, and therefore time is existent everywhere. Or that the designation time relates to the conventional divisions of moments, *lavas*, hours, watches, days, days and nights, lunar fortnights, seasons, half-years, years etc., and this conventional division being of universal application, time is everywhere existent, and consequentely infinitly great. It has been explained that the conception of a plurality of times is contravened by the complexity of the hypothesis.[1] U.

[1] परापरव्यतिकरयौगपद्यागपद्यचिरक्षिप्रप्रत्ययकारणे द्रव्ये काल इतिसमाख्यानं तादृशः प्रत्ययः सर्व्वदेशपुरुष-साधारणः कालस्य व्यायकतामन्तरेण न सम्भवतीति तस्य व्यापकत्वं परमहत्त्वयोग इत्यर्थः। यद्वा इदानीं जातइत्यादिप्रतीतिबलात् सर्वोत्पत्तिमन्निमित्तकारणत्वं कालस्य प्रतीयते तदपिव्यापकत्वाधीनं निमित्तकारणस्य समवाय्यसमवायिकारणप्रत्यासन्ननियमात्। यद्वा अतीतानागतवर्तमानव्यवहारः सार्वत्रिक इति सर्वगत एव कालः। यद्वा क्षणलवमुहूर्तयामदिनाहोरात्रपक्षमासत्त्र्वयनसाम्वत्सरादिव्यवहारकारणे द्रव्ये कालाख्येति व्यवहारस्य सार्वत्रिकत्वात्कालः सार्वत्रिक इति परममहान तस्य नानात्वकल्पना च कल्पनागौरवप्रतिहतेत्युक्तम्।।

SECOND DAILY LESSON

रूपरसगन्धस्पर्शव्यतिरेकार्थन्तरमेकत्वम्।। 1।।

Aph. 1. Because of the exclusion of colour, taste, smell, and touch, unity is a different object.

The investigation of number, and individuality is commenced after that of extension, because magnitude is the cause of the perceptibility of number, etc. Unity is a different object, different from colour etc., not having colour etc. for its form. The term unity implies number and the four succeeding qualities, viz. extension, individuality, conjunction and disjunction. The object of such cognitions as Space is one, Time is one etc., must be allowed to be some quality different from colour etc., because of the exclusion of colour, taste, smell, and touch, that is because of the non-existence of colour etc., in space etc. It cannot be urged: What is the case with such cognitions as one generality, one particularity, one co-inhesion, one non-existence etc.; for we must admit in regard to these independently a notion of unity, constituted by their being the object of a modification of the intellect. [1]V.

तथा पृथक्त्वम्।। 2।।

Aph. 2. Likewise individuality.

The similarity of the quality individuality to number is stated. Individuality also is, like number, another quality. In this quality single individuality is like the number unity, and dual individuality etc. is like the numbers duality, etc. Nor is it to be argued that, there being observed a community of object in the cognitions, The water-pot is

[1] महत्त्वस्य संख्यादिप्रत्यक्षहेतुत्वात् परिमाणनिरूपणानन्तरमेव संख्यापृथक्त्ववोर्निरूपणमारभते। एकत्वम् अर्थान्तरं रूपादिभ्यो भि नतु रूपादिस्वरूपम् एकत्वपदं सङ्खादिपञ्चकोपलक्षकं गगनमेकं काल एक इत्यादिप्रतीतिविषयो रूपादिभिन्नो गुणोऽवश्यमङ्गीकार्य्यः गगनादिषु रूपरसगन्धस्पर्शव्यतिरेकात् रूपादीनामभावादित्यर्थः नचैकं सामान्यमेकोविशेषः एकः समवायः एकोऽभाव इत्यादिप्रतीतेः का गतिरिति वाच्यं तत्रानायत्त्याधीर्नाविशेषविषयत्वरूपरस्यैकत्वस्य भानाङ्गीकारादधिकमन्यत्रानुसन्धेयम्।।

individually apart from the piece of cloth, or other than, or different from it, individuality is only reciprocal non-existence, and not another quality; for did the negative particle signify no difference from the word apart as an adverb, there could be no dissimilarity between the cognitions, This is apart, and This is not.[1] V.

एकत्वैकपृथक्त्वयोरेकत्वैकपृथक्त्वाभावो ऽणुत्वमहत्त्वाभ्यां व्याख्यातः ।। 3 ।।

Aph. 3. The non-existence of unity, and single individuality in unity and single individuality is explained by smallness and greatness.

It may be objected that in virtue of such cognitions as one unity, there exists unity, and in like manner in virtue of such cognitions as that single individuality is individuality apart from dual individuality, single individuality must be admitted to exist in single individuality; and that consequently there is a difficulty involved in their being qualities, inasmuch as they exist in qualities. In answer to this it is stated that as smallness and greatness do not exist in smallness and greatness, so also unity and single individuality do not exist in unity and single individuality, but this cognition is to be shown possible in some other manner.[2] V.

निःसंख्यत्वात् कर्मगुणानां सर्वैकत्वं न विद्यते ।। 4 ।।

Aph. 4. Unity does not exist in all things, for actions and qualities are void of number.

It may be asked as the notion of unity is common to qualities and to actions, what reasons there is to conclude that the unity which exists in substances does not exist in qualities, etc. Unity does not exist in all things. If it be asked why, it is replied that it is because actions and qualities are destitute of number. Numberlessness is the state of those things that transcend number, that is, that are without number.

[1] पृथक्त्वगुणस्य संख्यातुल्यत्वमाह। पृथक्त्वमपि संख्यावद्गुणन्तरमेव तत्रैकपृथक्त्वम् एकत्वसंख्यातुल्यं द्विपृथक्त्वादिकञ्च दित्वादिसंख्यातुल्यमिति नच घटः पटात् पृथगन्यो भिन्न इत्यादिप्रतीतीनां समानविषयकत्वानुभवादन्योन्याभाव एव पृथक्त्वं नतु गुणान्तरमिति वाच्यं नञ्शब्दस्यैव पृथक्शब्दस्याप्यव्ययतयाऽभेदार्थकतयाच अस्मात् पृथक् इदमिदं नेति प्रतीत्यैर्वैलक्षण्यानुपपत्तेः।।

[2] नन्वेकमेकत्वमित्यादिव्यवहारबलादेकत्वेऽप्येकत्वमेवमेकपृथक्त्वंद्विपृथक्त्वातपृथगितिव्यवहारबलादेकपृथक्त्वऽप्येकपृथकत्वमङ्गीकार्य्यमिति तयोर्गुणत्वं दुर्घटं गुणेऽपि सत्त्वादतआह। यथाऽणुत्वमहत्वे नाणुत्वमहत्त्वयोस्तथाएकत्वैकपृथक्त्वयोरपि नेकत्वैकपृथक्त्वे व्यवहारस्तु प्रकारान्तरेणोपपादनीयइत्यर्थः।।

Accordingly actions and qualities are without number. Inasmuch as number is a quality, number does not exist in qualities. Nor does it exist in actions, for qualities are denied of actions, for otherwise it would follow that actions were substances; and it has been demonstrated that number is a quality, and unity a number.[1] U.

भ्रान्तं तत्।। 5।।

Aph. 5. That [notion] is erroneous.

It may be asked: How then the notion of one colour, one taste etc.? It is stated in reply that the notion of unity in relation to qualities and actions is erroneous. In the aphorism there is an ellipse of the word notion, this being the subject previously mentioned. The notion thus applied is derivative and derived from essential inseparability; but this is not unity, for it has been stated to be other than unity.[2] U.

एकत्वाभावाद्भक्तिस्तु न विद्यते।। 6।।

Aph. 6. In consequence of non-existence of unity, secondariness does not exist.

It may be asked: Say that this notion of unity be secondary or derivative in relation to substances also, and the cognition be erroneous in relation to them, then what of unity? To this the reply is as follows. If unity be no where taken in its primary sense, the notion thus applied cannot be secondary, for the secondary has for its antecedent the primary. Nor is the conception erroneous, for error has for its antecedents certain knowledge, it being the certainly known that is erroneously attributed, for imputation of the unreal [as taught by the Vedāntins], is rejected by the establishment of imputation of the elsewhere experienced [as taught by the Vaiśeshikas].[3]

[1] ननु गुणेषु कर्म्मसु च साधारणएवैकत्वव्यवहारः किमत्र विनिगमकं यद्द्व्येष्वे वैकत्वं न गुणादिष्वित्यत्राह। सर्व्वेषामेकत्वं तन्न विद्यते कुत इत्यत आह निःसङ्ख्यत्वात् कर्म्मगुणानामिति सङ्ख्याया निष्क्रान्ताः सिःसङ्ख्यास्तेषां भावो निःसङ्ख्यत्वम् तथा च कर्म्माणि गुणाश्च निःसङ्ख्यानि सङ्ख्याया गुणत्वेन गुणेषु तावत् सङ्ख्या न विद्यते नवा कर्म्मसु गुणानां कर्म्मसु निषेधात् अन्यथा द्रव्यत्वप्रसङ्गात् साधितञ्च सङ्ख्याया गुणत्वमेकत्वस्य च सङ्ख्यात्वमिति भावः।।

[2] तर्हि कथमेकं रूपमेकोरस इत्यादिज्ञानमित्यत आह। गुणकर्म्मसु यदेकत्वज्ञानं तद् भ्रान्तमित्यर्थः सूत्रे च ज्ञानमितिशेषः प्रक्षिप्तपूर्व्वपक्षत्वञ्च प्रयोगस्तु भाक्तः स्वरूपाभेद एवञ्च मुक्तिः नच तदेवैकत्वमुक्तोत्तरत्वात्।।

[3] ननु द्रव्येप्ययमेकत्वयोगोभाक्तोऽस्तु तत्र भ्रान्तः किमेकत्वेनेत्यत आह। यदि पारमार्थिकमेकत्वं क्वचिन्नाभ्युपगन्तथं तदा न प्रयोगो भाक्तः मुख्यपूर्व्वकत्वाद्भक्तेः न वा प्रत्ययोभ्रान्तः प्रमापूर्व्वकत्वाद्भ्रमस्य प्रमितं ह्यारोप्यते नाप्रमितम् असत्ख्यातेर्निरासात् अन्यथाख्यातेः साधनादिति भावः।।

कार्यकारणयोरेकत्वैकपृथक्त्वकाभावादेकत्वैकपृथक्त्वं न विद्यते।। 7।।

Aph. 7. Of cause and effect there is not unity and single individuality, in consequence of the non-existence of unity and single individuality.

With the purpose of parenthetically rejecting the Sāṅkhya doctrine of the unity, and single individuality and indivisibility of integrant parts and integrated wholes, it is stated that there is neither unity nor single individuality in cause and effect, that is, there resides no unity or single individuality in both the cause and its effect. For this the reason assigned is that there do not exist in the cause and its effect unity and single individuality.Unity is indivisibility, single individuality is non-dissimilarity. Since these do not exist in the sum of constituent parts and the constituted whole, the parts and the whole are not identical; for it is allowed on all hands that the thread is cognised as separate from the cloth, and dissimilar to it.[1] V.

एतदनित्ययोर्व्याख्यातम्।। 8।।

Aph. 8. This is explained in relation to non-eternal [cause and effect.]

This—the possession of non-existence of unity and single individuality, by reason of possession of non-existence of indivisibility and non-dissimilarity—is affirmed of non-eternal cause and effect.Accordingly on the hypothesis of the indivisibility of the threads and cloth, it would follow that in the case of the production of the threads the cloth would be cognised and said to be produced; in the case of the production of the cloth, the thread would cognised and said to be produced; in the case of the destruction of the threads, the cloth would be cognised and said to be destroyed; and in the case of the destruction of the cloth, the threads would be congnised and said to be destroyed. Nor can it be maintained that production and destruction are no proofs, because it is possible that the cognition of these is caused merely by appearence and disappearance; for on the hypothesis of an appearance of an appearance there will result a regress

[1] अवयवायविनोरेकत्वमेकपृथक्त्वञ्च नतु तयोर्भेद इति साङ्ख्यमतं प्रसङ्गान्निराकर्त्तुमाह। कार्य्यकारणयोर्नैकत्वं नवैकपृथक्त्वं किमप्येकत्वमेकपृथक्त्वं वा कार्य्यकारणोभयनिष्ठं न भवतीत्यर्थः। अत्र हेतुमाह कार्य्य-कारणयोरेकत्वैकपृथक्त्वाभावात् एकत्वमभेदः एकपृथक्त्वमवैधर्म्यं तयोरभावात् तन्तुः पटाद्भिन्नः पट-विधर्म्मेत्यादिप्रतीतेः सर्व्वसिद्धत्वादिति भावः।।

to infinity. On the hypothesis of their production, therefore, what fallacy is there involved in the production of the cloth etc. ? And if the appearance in appearance be not allowed to be production, it follows that appearance is constant, but the constancy of appearance is not admitted even by the Sāṅkhyas. In fact, the universal experience that the cloth is produced and destroyed and so forth, is proof of production and destruction; for if experience of one object be allowed to have another object for its object, we must deny also the water-pot cloth, etc. This error has been sufficiently discussed.[1] V.

अन्यतरकर्मज उभयकर्मजः संयोगजश्च संयोगः।। 9।।

Conjunction

Aph. 9. Conjunction is produced by the action, of one of the two conjunct objects, by the action of both, and by conjunction.

Uncontradicted cognition of the conjunct, is proof of the existence of conjunction. As results may be inferred substance as proof of conjunction of integrant parts; colour etc., produced by burning as proof of conjunction with fire; particular extension as proof of accretion, sound as proof of the conjunction of a kettledrum and ether, and so forth. Conjunction is not mere contiguour production; as excluding momentary interruption and modification, conjunction is contact having non-contact as its antecedent. This is produced by the action of one of the conjunct objects, as the conjunction of a hawk in motion with a motionless post, or the conjunction of one in motion with one not in motion towards him, as conjunction of a runner with back of another person running. Conjunction is also produced by the action of both conjunct objects, as that of two rams or of two wrestlers, this being produced by both, each having individually acquired the power. The third kind of conjunction or conjunction produced by conjunction is such as conjunction of the hand with a tree resulting from conjunction

[1] एतदभेदावैधर्म्याभाववत्त्वेनैकत्त्वैकपृथक्त्वाभाववत्त्वम् अनित्ययोः कार्यकारणयोः कथितमित्यर्थः तथाच तन्तुपटयोरभेदाङ्गीकारे तन्तूत्पाददशायां पट उत्पद्यते पटोत्पत्तिदशायां तन्तुरुत्पद्यते तन्तुनाशदशायां पटो नश्यति पटनाशदशायां तन्तुर्नश्यतीत्यादिप्रत्ययप्रयोगयोः प्रसङ्गः न चोत्पत्तिविनाशावेवाप्रमाणिकौ आविर्भावतिरोभावा-भ्यामेव तत्प्रतीत्युमपत्तेरिति वाच्यमाविर्भावाङ्गीकारेऽनवस्थाप्रसङ्गात् तदुत्पत्तिस्वीकारे तु किमपराद्धं पटाद्युत्पत्तिभिः आविर्भावे आविर्भावस्योत्पादस्य चानङ्गीकारे आविर्भावस्य सार्व्वादिकत्वप्रसङ्गः नह्याविर्भावस्य सार्व्वदिकत्वं साङ्ख्यैरपि स्वीक्रियते वस्तुतः पटः उत्पद्यते पटो विनश्यतीत्यादिद्य सार्व्वलौकिकोऽनुभव एवोत्पादविनाशसाधकः एकविषयकानुभवस्य विषयान्तरविषयकत्वस्वीकारे घटपटादेरप्यपलापापत्तेरित्य-लमसदावेशेन।।

of a finger with the tree. This moreover results from one conjunction, as the conjunction of a piece of cloth with the grass may result from the conjunction of a thread and the grass. In some cases one conjunction is produced by two conjunctions, as two conjunctions with ether may be produced by two threads, and by these two conjunctions a single conjunction of a piece of cloth made of two threads with the ether. In other cases a single conjunction is originated by a plurality of conjunctions, as when ten conjunctions with ether originated by ten threads. originate a single conjunction between a piece of cloth made of ten threads and the ether. Sometimes on the other hand, two conjunctions are produced from one single conjunction as their non-coinherent cause, as when there having first taken place a non-originative conjunction between two atoms terrene and aqueous, subsequently two conjunctions originative of binary atomic aggregates are produced, a conjunction in the terrene atom with another terrene atom, and in the aqueous atom with another aqueous atom. By these two conjunctions existing in homogeneous objects two binary atomic aggregates are simultaneously produced. In these by the one non-originative conjunction produced in the terrene and aqueous atoms, a single conjunction of the terrene atom with the aqueous binary atomic aggregate and another conjunction of the aqueous atom with the terrene atomic aggregate, are produced simultaneously with the production of colour etc., in the two binary aggregates; for the conjunction of a cause and non-cause must necessarily produce a conjunction of an effect and non-effect. The conjunction of all—pervading entities with limited objects is produced by reciprocal action only. Of two all—pervading substances there is no conjunction, for there is no cause of conjunction. There exists in them no action, therefore there results in them no conjunction of effect and non-effect from conjunction of cause and non-cause. An eternal conjunction is impossible, for conjunction is contact having non-contact as its antecedent, and this is repugnant to the nature of the eternal. Also in this case (were eternal conjunction possible), no disjunction could be therein produced. Nor can it be allowed (as involving no objection, that no disjunction is therein produced); for conjunction and disjunction reciprocally repugnant and of indestructible condition, are impossible. Moreover previous unconnectedness is a necessary condition of conjunction, and this consists in the individual movement of one or other of two objects, or co-inherence in the substratum of the object joined. Destruction results from disjunction in-coexistent with conjunction, or from disintegration of the site of the conjunction in some instances, as when after the conjunction of two threads, action is produced in that portion of a thread which constitutes its extremity; by this action there is effected disjunction from what now becomes the extremity; from this disjunction results destruction of the originant conjunction; from this results destruction of the thread; from destruction of the thread results destruction of the conjunction, where two threads having been long conjoined action is not produced in them. Some have maintained that when by action in the portions of the thread there is effected destruction of the conjunction originant of the thread, the conjunction is destroyed by destruction of the substratum and disjunction simultaneously produced, inasmuch as action is conceived to exist in another thread. This is impossible: for disjunction is impossible at the moment of the destruction of the co-inherent or material cause, it being a law that the co-inherent cause is of equal duration with the effect. This conjunction is absolute in the origination of substances, and relative in the origination of qualities and actions, non-existent in the case of the absolute non-existence of its proper substratum; for it is observed to be so. The conjunction existing between an ape and a great sacred figtree limited to conjunction with the branches only, exists, inas-much as it is obsereved that there exists in the sacred figtree conjunction with the ape. For were it to be accounted for otherwise than by such mere limitation, conjunction might possibly reside in an ultimate particle, and consequently be not cognisable. Locality is an accidental difference of all-pervading substances; and conjunction as determined in position must be less than co-extensive with them. Of conjunction residing in an ultimate particle, space etc., may be regarded as determinant.[1] U.

[1] संयोगे संयुक्तप्रतीतिरबाधिता प्रमाणं कार्याणि च अवयवसंयोगेषु द्रव्यमग्निसंयोगे पाकजरूपादय: प्रचये परिमाणविशेष: भेर्याकाशसंयोगे शब्द इत्याद्यूह्यम्। नचाविरलोत्पत्तिरेव संयोग: क्षणभङ्गपरिणामयोर्निरासात् अप्राप्तिपूर्विका प्राप्ति: संयोग: सचान्यतरकर्मज: क्रियावता श्येनेन निष्क्रियस्य स्थाणोस्तदभिमुखक्रियारहितस्य सक्रियस्यापि धावत: यथा धावता पुरुषान्तरेण पृष्ठदेशसंयोग: उभयकर्मज: मेषयोर्मल्लयोर्वा प्रत्येकं गृहीतसामर्थ्याभ्यामुभाभ्यामेव तज्जननात् तृतीयस्त्वङ्गुलितरुसंयोगाद्धस्ततरुसंयोग: स चैकस्मादपि भवति यथा तन्तुवीरणसंयोगात् पटवीरणसंयोग: क्वचिद्वाभ्यां संयोगाभ्यामेक: संयोग: यथा द्वाभ्यां तन्तुभ्यामाकाशस्य द्वौ संयोगौ ताभ्यामेक एव द्वितन्तुकपटस्याकाशेन संयोग: क्वच्चि बहुभिरपि संयोगैरेक: संयोग आरभ्यते यथा दशभिस्तन्तुभिराकाशस्य दशसंयोगा एकमेव दशतन्तुकपटाकाशसंयोगमारभन्ते क्वचित् पुनरेकस्मादपि संयोगादसमवायिकारणात् संयोगद्वयमुत्पद्यते यथा पार्थिवाप्ययो: परमाण्वो: प्रथममनारम्भके संयोगे जाते पार्थिवे परमाणो: पार्थिवपरमाण्वन्तरेण आप्ये च परमाणावाप्यपरमाण्वन्तरेण च परमाणावाप्यपरमाण्वन्तरेण

ऐतेन विभागो व्याख्यातः।। 10।।

Aph. 10. By this disjunction is explained.

The analogy of conjunction to disjunction is stated. Disjunction also is of three kinds, as divided into that produced by the action of one of the disjunct objects, that produced by the action of both, and that produced by disjunction. Of these the first is instanced in the disjunction of a hawk from a mountain; the second in that of two rams retiring from conflict; the third is of two kinds, being ether produced by the disjunction of causes only, or by the disjunction of causes and non-causes. Of these disjunctions produced by disjunction, the former class is exemplified where firstly action is produced in one of the two halves of a water-pot, thence disjunction of the two halves of the vessel, thence destruction of the conjunction originant of the water-pot, thence destruction of the water-pot, then by disjunction of two halves of the water-pot disjunction of the halves from the cirumjacent ether etc., thence destruction of the conjunction of the halves with ether etc., thence conjunction with another place, thence destruction of the action. Nor is it to be urged in objection: How is it that disjunction of the halves of the water-pot from the ether in which they were situated while component parts of the vessel, is not produced by the primary

द्व्यणुकद्वयारम्भकं संयोगद्वयमुत्पद्यते ताभ्यां संयोगाभ्यां सजातीयनिष्ठाभ्यां द्व्यणुकद्वयं युगपदारभ्यते तत्र यः पार्थिवाप्यरमाण्वोरनारम्भकसंयोग उत्पन्नस्तेनैकेनैव पार्थिवपरमाणुनाप्यद्व्यणुकेनैकः संयोगः आप्यपरमाणुना पार्थिवद्व्यणुकेनापरः संयोगो द्व्यणुकयोरूपाद्युत्पत्तिसमकालमेव जायते कारणाकारणसंयोगेन कार्यकार्यासंयोगयोरवश्यं जननात् मूर्त्तैर्विभूनामन्यतरकर्मज एव विभुनोस्तु न संयोगः कारणाभावात् कर्म तावत्तत्र नास्ति नच तेन कारणाकारणसंयोगात् कार्याकार्यसंयोगोऽपि नास्ति नित्यस्तु संयोगो न सम्भवति अप्रप्तिपर्विकायाः प्राप्तेः संयोगत्वात् नित्यत्वे तद्विघातात् एवञ्च सति विभागोप्यजस्तत्र स्यात् नचेष्टापत्तिः संयोगविभागयोर्विरोधिनोरविनश्यदवस्थयोरेकत्रानुपपत्तेः किञ्च संयोगं प्रति प्रयोजिका युतसिद्धिः नच विभुनोस्तत्सम्भवः द्वयोरन्यतरस्य वा पृथग्गतिमात्रं युताश्रयाश्रायत्वं वा विनाशस्तु संयोगस्य समाना-धिकरणाद्विभागादाश्रयनाशादपि क्वचित् यथा तन्तुद्वयसंयोगानन्तरमेकस्य तन्तोरवयवेऽर्शे कर्म जायते तेनांश्वन्तराद्विभागः क्रियते विभागादारम्भकसंयोगनाशस्ततस्तुविनाशस्तन्तुविनाशात् संयोगनाशो यत्र तन्तुद्वयं चिरं संयुक्तं सदनुत्पन्नक्रियं भवति केचित्तु तन्त्ववयवकर्मणा यदा तन्त्वारम्भकसंयोगनाशः क्रियते तदा तन्त्वन्तरे कर्मचिन्तनात् आश्रयनाशविभागाभ्यां युगपदत्पन्नाभ्यां संयोगो नश्यतीत्याहुः। तञ्चानुपपन्नं समवायिकारणनाशक्षणे विभागानुत्पत्तेः समवायिकारणस्य कार्यसमकालस्थायित्वनियमात् सचायं संयोगो द्रव्याारम्भे निरपेक्षो गुणकर्मारम्भे सापेक्षः स्वसमानाधिकरणात्यन्ताभावप्रतीयोगी तथैवानुभवात् शाखामात्रावच्छेदेनापि महत्ति न्यग्रोधतरौ वर्तमानः कपिसंयोगः न्यग्रोधतरौ कपिसंयोग इत्यनुभवात् अवच्छेदमात्रेणान्यथासिद्धौ परमाणुवृत्तिरापद्येत तथाच नोपलभ्येत विभूनामप्युपाधिभेद एव पदेशस्तदवच्छेदेन वर्तमानस्य संयोगस्याव्याप्यवृत्तित्वं परमाणुनिष्ठस्यापि संयोगस्य दिगादयोऽवच्छेदकाश्चिन्तनीयाः।।

action in the halves of the water-pot ? For one action productive of disjunction repugnant to the originative con-junction, is contradictory to production of disjunction repugnant to non-originative conjunction (such as that of the halves of the vessel with the ether circumjacent); since otherwise there would follow the possibility of the breaking of the buds of a full-blown lotus. The action, then, in the halves of the vessel cannot produce disjunction repugnant to the non-originative conjunction of the halves of the water-pot and the ether, inasmuch as such action produces disjunction repugnant to the conjunction originative of the water-pot. Nor can it be objected : Whence is it that disjunction of the halves of the vessel and the ether is not produced by the mere disjunction of the two halves, previously to the destruction of the water-pot ? For disjunction from another place is impossible in an existing substance, in any portion possessed of disjunction repugnant to the originative conjunction. Disjunction produced by disjunction of causes and non-causes is exemplified where by action of the hand disjunction of the hand from a tree is produced , and by this mediately disjunction of the body from the tree. In this disjunction the action of the hand is not the cause, for there is a difference of substratum. But there is not art that time action in the body, for the action of a composite whole is determined as the action of the sum of the constituent parts. In this case, therefore, there is produced by disjunction of cause and non-cause a disjunction of effect and non-effect. This same quality, disjunction, is proved to exist by the presentative cognition that one object is disjoined from another, and is not therefore otherwise accounted for or unnecessarily assumed.[1] V.

[1] विभागे संयोगतुल्यतामाह। विभागोऽपि त्रिविध: एककर्मजोभयकर्मजविभागजभेदात् तत्राद्य: श्येनशैलयो: द्वितीयो मेषयो: तृतीयस्तु त्रिविध: कारणमात्रविभागजन्य: कारणाकारणविभागजन्यश्चेति तत्राद्योयथा प्रथमं कपाले कर्म तत: कपालद्वयविभाग: ततो घटारम्भकसंयोगनाशस्ततो घटनाशस्ततस्तेन कपालद्वयविभागेन कपालस्याकाशादिना विभागो जन्यते तत: कपालाकाशादिसंयोगनाश: तत उत्तरदेशसंयोगस्तत: कर्मनाश इति नच प्राथमिकेन कपालकर्मणा कथं कपालाकाशविभागो न जन्यते इति वाच्यम् एकस्य कर्मण आरम्भकसंयोगप्रतिद्वन्द्विविभागजनकस्यानारम्भकसंयोगप्रतिद्वन्द्विविभगजनकत्वविरोधात् अन्यथा विकसत्कमलकुटमलादिभङ्गप्रसङ्गात् तस्मादनारम्भकाकाशकपालसंयोगप्रतिद्वन्द्विविभागो न कपालकर्म जनयेत् तस्य घटारम्भकसंयोगप्रतिद्वन्द्विविभागजनकत्वात् नच कपालविभागेनैव घटनाशात् पूर्वं कुत: कपालाकाशविभागो न जन्यते इति वाच्यम् आरम्भकसंयोगप्रतिद्वन्द्विविभागवतोऽवयवस्य सति द्रव्ये देशान्तरविभागासम्भवात् कारणाकारणविभागजन्यविभागो यथा यत्र हस्तक्रियया हस्ततरुविभागस्तेन शरीरतरुविभागो जायते तत्र च हस्तक्रिया न कारणं व्यधिकरणत्वात् शरीरे तु तदा क्रिया नास्ति अवयविक्रियाया यावदवयवक्रियानियतत्वात् अतस्तत्रकारणाकारणविभागेन कार्यकार्यविभागे जन्यते इति अयमस्माद्विभज्यते इति प्रत्यक्षसिद्धोऽयं विभागगुण: संयोगनाशेन नान्यथासिद्ध इति संक्षेप:।।

संयोगविभागयोः संयोगविभागाभावो ऽणुत्वमहत्त्वाभ्यां व्याख्यातः।। 11।।

Aph. 11. The non-existence of conjunction and disjunction in conjunction and disjunction is explained by smallness and greatness.

Conjunction and disjunction are not possessed of conjunction and disjunction, as smallness and greatness are not possessed of smallness and greatness, for qualities have no qualities.[1] V.

कर्मभिः कर्माणि गुणैर्गुणा अणुत्वमहत्त्वाभ्यामिति।। 12।।

Aph. 12. Actions [are explained to be void] of actions and qualities by smallness and greatness.

The aphorism Actions etc. is repeated for clearness,or to aid the memory. Its meaning has been already expounded (VII.1.15.)[2] V.

युतसिद्ध्यभावात् कार्यकारणयोः संयोगविभागौ न विद्येते।। 13।।

*Aph.*13. Inasmuch as there is non-existence of unconnectedness, ther exist not conjunction and disjunction in an effect and its cause.

A solution of the difficulty why there should not be conjunction and disjunction in constituent parts and constitutes wholes, is stated. Unconnectedness is the state of two objects void of mutual connection. Conjunction and disjunction do not exist in a cause and its effect, that is in the constituent parts and the constituted whole, inasmuch as there is non-existence of unconnectedness. For a constituted whole, a water-pot and the like does not remain in existence out of connection with its constituent parts, the two halves of the vessel etc., that conjuction and disjunction should be possible in the integrant parts and the integrate whole.[3] V.

गुणत्वात्।। 14।।

Aph. 14. Inasmuch as it is a quality [a word has not conjunction with the object which it denotes].

[1] संयोगविभागौ न संयोगविभागवन्तौ यथाऽणुत्वमहत्त्वे नाणुत्वमहत्त्ववती गुणानां निर्गुणत्वादित्यर्थः।।

[2] कर्मभिरिति सूत्रं स्पष्टार्थं स्मरणार्थं वा पुनरुक्तम् अस्यार्थः प्रागेवाभिहितः।।

[3] ननु अवयवावयविनोः कथं न संयोगविभागावित्याशङ्कायामाह। युतसिद्धिः परस्परसम्बन्धशून्ययोरवस्थानं कार्यकारणयोरवयवावयविनोर्न संयोगविभागौ वर्तेते युतसिद्ध्यभावात् नहि घटाद्यवयवी कपालाद्यवयवा-सम्बन्धः सन् निष्ठिति येन तयोः संयोगविभागौ सम्भाव्येयातामिति।।

A previously supposed view is here stated, with the purpose of establishing that there exists between a term and its designates a connection of power, in obviation of the difficulty:— How can there be a conjunction between a verbal sign and its significate; for a word or sound being a quality cannot possess any quality; nor is it to be replied that there exists not between them any conjunction, for were that the case there might result from such a verbal sign as water-pot the verbal apprehension of a piece of cloth, there being no speciality of connection. The term denotative being a quality, there can exist therein no conjunction with the object denoted, that is, with the water-pot, etc.[1] V.

गुणो ऽपि विभाव्यते।। 15।।

Aph. 15. A quality also is implied.

Moreover the object is sometimes characterised as a colour, taste, etc., and with this conjunction is not possible, no quality being allowed to exist in a quality. Hence it is said that a quality also is an object—; these words having to be supplied—a quality, as colour etc., may be the object of a word, but with this there can be no conjunction or connection. Or the sense may be that a quality also is implied or denoted by a word, and that the word can have no conjunction or connection with this quality.[2]

निष्क्रियत्वात्।। 16।।

*Aph.*16. Inasmuch as there is no action [in the term and the object denoted by it, there exists no conjunction between them].

Similarly connection by conjunction cannot exist in substances such as ether denoted by such words as *sky*; for conjunction which is produced by action is impossible in the term designating and the object designated, these being void of action.[3] V.

[1] ननु शब्दार्थयोः कथं संयोगः सम्भवति शब्दस्य गुणत्वेन गुणवत्त्वासम्भवात् नच नास्त्येव तयोः संयोग इति वाच्यं सम्बद्धत्वाविशेषेण घटादिशब्दात् पटादिशाब्दबोधापत्तेरित्यतः पदपदार्थयोः शक्तिसम्बन्धः- व्यवस्थापयिष्यन् पूर्वपक्षयति। प्रतिपादकस्य शब्दस्य गुणत्वात् तत्र प्रतिपाद्यस्य घटादेः संयोगो न सम्भवतीत्यर्थः।।

[2] किञ्च विषयोऽपि क्वचिद्रूपरसादिलक्षणस्तेन संयोगो न सम्भवति गुणे गुणानङ्गी कारादित्याह। गुणोऽपि विषय इतिशेषः गुणोऽपि रूपादिः शब्दस्य विषयो नतु तेन समं संयोगः सम्बन्ध इत्यर्थः यद्वा गुणोऽपि शब्देन विभाव्यते प्रतिपाद्यते तेन च शब्दस्य न संयोगः सम्बन्ध इत्यर्थः।।

[3] एवं गगनादिशब्दप्रतिपाद्ये आकाशादिद्रव्येऽपि संयोगस्य सम्बन्धता न सम्भवति प्रतिपाद्यप्रतिपादकयोः कर्मशून्यत्वेन क्रियाजनकस्य संयोगस्यासम्भवादित्यर्थः। गगनादिशब्दस्य गगनादेश्च निष्क्रियत्वात् संयोगो

असति नास्तीति च प्रयोगात्।। 17।।

Aph. 17. Inasmuch also as the expression *is not* is used of the non-existent.

Conjunction is impossible inasmuch as the object designated may not exist. It is therefore said: Inasmuch also as it is observed that the expression *is not*—and in virtue of the particle *also* is to be understood *will be*—is used of the non-existence, of that which is not known to be. Thus by reason of the expressions. The past water-pot does not now exist. Tomorrow the water-pot will exist, there results a cognition of a past and a future water-pot, and there can be no conjunction etc., between them and words.[1] V.

शब्दार्थावसम्बन्धौ।। 18।।

Aph. 18. Thw word and its meaning are without connection.

If there be conjunction between the word and its meaning it follows that the word and its meaning are without connection.[2] U.

संयोगिनो दण्डात् समवायिनो विशेषाच्च।। 19।।

Aph. 19. [The cognition] of that which possesses conjunction [results from knowledge of the conjunct as] from a staff; and [the cognition] of that which possesses co-inhesion [results] from the particular.

It is stated that there is no cognition conversant about conjunction and other connections between a word and its meaning. From a staff—being conversant about a staff—results a cognition (for these words are to be supplied) of that which possesses conjunction—of a man possessing conjunction with the staff; and from the particular—being conversant about a particular constituent element—results a cognition of that which possesses co-inherence—of a constituted whole. There is, then, no cognition of the term water-pot as possessing a water-pot, or of a water-pot as possessing the word water-pot, as there is a cognition,

न सम्भवतीत्यर्थः।।

[1] प्रतिपाद्यस्यावर्तमानत्वादपि संयोगो न सम्भवतीत्याह। असति अविद्यमाने नास्तीति चकाराद्भविष्यतीति च प्रयोगदर्शनात् तथाचातीतघट इदानीं नास्ति परदिने घटो भविष्यतीत्यादिप्रयोगेण अतीतानागतघटयोर्बोधो भवति नच ताभ्यां शब्दस्य संयोगादिः सम्भवतीत्यर्थः।।

[2] शब्दार्थयोः संयोगश्चेन्नास्ति तदेतदायातं शब्दार्थावसम्बन्धावित्यर्थः।।

conversant about connection by conjunction, of a man with a staff, and a cognition conversant about connection by co-inherence, of an elephant with a trunk, current among men. Therefore there is no connection of conjunction or of co-inhesion between the denotative term and the object denoted.[1] V.

सामयिकः शब्दादर्थप्रत्ययः।। 20।।

Aph. 20. The recognition of a meaning from a word is conventional.

It may be asked, If there be neither conjunction nor co-inherence between a word and its meaning, by what connection does a term convey a determinate sense ? To this the reply is furnished. It is conventional. Convention is the arbitrary dispensation of the Deity, that by such and such a word such and such a sense is to be understood. Whatever word was arbitrarily assigned by the Supreme Being to any meaning, conveys that meaning: it is the will of God that is the connection between term and its signification. This connection is a convention, that is, it is dependent upon convention, as whatever plant the ichneumon touches with his teeth is an antidote to poison. This convention is sometimes derived from common usage, as for instance when any one gives the order Bring the water-pot, and a child standing by infers the cognition of another who receives the order and brings an object possessing a tubular neck; the child inferring that this activity of the bringer is produced by knowledge, inasmuch as it is an activity like its own activity, and that this knowledge is produced by the words of the person who gives the order, because it is brought into being subsequently to those words. The child's knowledge of the meaning of water-pot, piece of cloth, is by the process of insertion and elimination of words, in that the object of this knowledge is an object possessing a tubular neck denoted by the word water-pot. At other times this convention results from direct testimony, as that this tubular-necked object is designated by the term water-pot. At other times it

[2] शब्दार्थयोः संयोगादिसंसर्गावगाही प्रत्ययोऽपि नास्तीत्याहा। दण्डात् दण्डमवगाह्य संयोगिनः दण्डसंयोगिनः पुरुषस्य विशेषादवयवविशेषमवग्राह्य समवायिनोऽवयविनः प्रतीतिर्भवतीतिशेषः तथाच यथा संयोग-सम्बन्धावगाही दण्डी पुरुष इति प्रत्ययः समवायसम्बन्धावगाही करी कुञ्जइति प्रत्ययश्च स्वारसिको लोकानां तथा घटवान घटशब्दः घटाशब्दवान् घटइत्यादिप्रत्ययो नास्तीति पदपदार्थयोर्न संयोगो नवा समवायः सम्बन्ध इत्यर्थः। करी कुञ्जर इत्यादौ तु स्वानुयोगिकसमवायः संसर्गतया भासते कपालं घटवदित्यादौतु समवाय एवेत्यादिकमूहनीयम्।।

results from comparison or recognition of similarity, as through the judgment of similarity that a gayal is like a cow, mudga -parṇī (a kind of bean) is like mudga, māsha-parṇī (a leguminous plant) is like a bean. At other times it results from opprobrious language, as when after hearing, O the camel with pendulous upper lip and long neck, the eater of hard thorns, the vilest of animals,—on seeing such an object there ensues the verbal knowledge that it is a camel. At other times it results from collocation with terms of known import, as when after hearing the proposition. The bee is sipping sweets in the cloven lotus-blossom, it is inferred that this must be that which is denoted by the word bee, inasmuch as this is the agent in the drinking of nectar in the cleft hollow of the lotus, or as in the common example, The cuckoo sings sweetly in the mango-tree. This is, therefore, an inference or even a mere sound producing etymological knowledge, through the force of collocation with words known import. Or it is a kind of knowledge by comparison, through subsumption of similarity to other individual bees etc., viz., agency in the drinking of nectar. The convention, according to the followers of Tutāta has reference only to the universal, being applied to the individual only by a transference. According to the Prābhākaras the denotative capacity is expressive of both the class and the individual, but is cognised in relation to the universal, and by its essential form determines the cognition of the individual. The ancients teach that the convention is the verbal power, and that objects are universals which are the forms of the individuals. This is the case with terms like cow etc., but the object of words expressive of qualities, actions etc., is both the universal and the particular, as is detailed in the Mayūkha.[1] U.

[1] ननु यदि न संयोगो नवा समवायः शब्दार्थयोस्तर्हि केन सम्बन्धेन शब्दो नियतमर्थं प्रतिपादयतीत्यत आह। सामयिक इति समय ईश्वरसङ्केतः अस्माच्छब्दादयमर्थोबोद्धव्य इत्याकारः यः शब्दोयास्मिन्नर्थे भगवता सङ्केतितः स तमर्थं प्रतिपादयति तथाच शब्दार्थयोरोश्वरेच्छैव सम्बन्धः स एव समयस्तदधीन इत्यर्थः यथा नकुलदंष्ट्राग्रस्पृष्टा या काचिदोषधिः सा सर्वाऽहि सर्पविषं हन्ति सच समयः क्वचिद्व्यवहाराद्गृह्यते यथा प्रयोजकेन घटमानयत्युक्ते प्रयोज्यस्य कम्बुग्रीवावन्तमर्थमानयतीतिज्ञानं तावदनुमिनोति तटस्थोबालः इयमस्य प्रवृत्तिर्ज्ञानजन्या प्रवृत्तित्वात् मत्प्रवृत्तिवत् तच्च ज्ञानमेतद्वाक्यजन्यमेतदनन्तरभावित्वात् एतज्ज्ञानविषयो ऽयं कम्बुग्रीवावानर्थो घटपटवाच्यइत्यावापोद्वाद्वप्रक्रियया बालस्य घटपटादावर्थे व्युत्पत्तिः क्वचिच्च साक्षादाप्तवाक्यादेव यथाऽयं कम्बुग्रीवावानर्थो घटपदवाच्च इति क्वचिदुपमानात् यथा गोसदृशोगवयः यथा मुद्रस्तथा मुद्गपर्णी यथा माषस्तथामाषपर्णीत्यादि सांधर्म्योपमानात् क्वचिन्निन्दाकारादपि वाक्यात् यथा धिक् करभमतिलम्बौष्टं दीर्घग्रीवं कठोरकण्टकाशिनमपसदं पशूनामिति निन्दावाक्यश्रवणानन्तरं तादृशपिण्डमुपलभ्यायमसौ करभ इति व्युत्पतिः क्वचित् प्रसिद्धपदसमानाधिकरण्यात् यथा प्रभिन्नकमलोदरे मधूनि मधुकरः पिवतीति वाक्यश्रवणानन्तमरं भवत्ययमसौ मधुकरपदवाच्यः प्रभिन्नकमलोदरे मधुपानकर्तृत्वात्

That connection between words and objects which produces verbal knowledge, is now pointed out. The knowledge of the meaning of words is conventional, or determined by the connection of convention. It is, therefore, a connection of convention between the term and the object, that determines verbal knowledge. Convention is arbitrary arrangement. This is of two kinds, eternal and modern. Eternal arbitrary arrangement is verbal power; modern arbitrary symbolism is terminology. The arbitrary symbolism takes for its form, that such and such a sense is to be understood by such and such a word, or such and such a term shall convey such and such a signification. It has therefore been said: Arbitrary symbolism has been declared two fold, original and modern. The original is eternal, herein is that which is called power; but the modern is occasional, imposed by scientific writers and others. The apprehension of power is from common usage, etc. It has, therefore, been said: The ancients have declared the apprehension of power to be from grammatical analysis, from knowledge of comparison, from lexicography, from testimony, and from usage, from contiguity to a term of know import, from the context, and from explication. The apprehension of the power of roots, crude forms, and affixes, results from grammatical analysis as the knowledge from such rules as,The second case is used of the object,The transitive verb is of the agent, or that the accusative case etc., is used of the object of the action etc. From knowledge of comparision there results, from knowledge of similarity to a cow etc., the apprehension of the power of the terms gayal etc., in restriction to the classes gayal, etc. According to such lexicographical information as White and other terms connecting qualities, in the masculine denote the subject of the attribute, Cold is a quality, The words chill, cool, and benumbed imply possession of that quality, and Powder is that which is triturated, Routed and panic-striken denote extreme confusion,—according to such information there results apprehension of the power of the words white etc. in reference to the white, etc., Apprehension of the power of the terms *pika* etc. in reference to a cuckoo etc., results from testimony such as, A cuckoo is signified by the word *pika.* From the

यथा वा सहकारतरौ मधुरं पिको रौतीति। तदेतदनुमानं वा शब्द एव वा प्रसिद्धपदसमानाधिकरण्य-सामर्थ्याद्धियत्पादकः उपमानविशेष एव वा मधुपानकर्तृत्वस्य भ्रमरादिव्यक्त्यन्तरसाधर्म्यस्योपनयात्। समयश्च जातिमात्रे व्यक्तेराक्षेपत एवोपस्थितइति तौतातिकाः जातौ व्यक्तौ चोभयशक्तिः किन्तु जात्यंशे ज्ञाता व्यक्त्यंशे स्वरूपसती पयोजिकेति प्राभाकराः। समयः शक्तिरेव व्यक्त्याकृतिजातयः पदार्था इति वृद्धाः। गवादिपदानामियं गतिः गुणकर्मादिवाचकपदानान्तु जातिव्यक्ती एवार्थ इति मयूखे विपञ्चितम्।।

practical relation of one who gives and one who receives an order, results apprehension of the power of the terms cow etc., in refrence to objects possessing the essential characters of a cow, etc. For instance, when an adult giving an order says Bring the cow, and another adult receiving the order brings the cow, a child standing by, observing this, reflects that the bringing of a cow is implied by the words. Bring the cow; and afterwards by substitution of one word and elimination of the other in the phrase, Tie up the cow, Bring the horse, he apprehends the power of the terms cow etc., in reference to cows characterised by a dewlap etc. From collocation with words of known import, in such propositions as Air is colourless and tactile, He who gives a girl in a marriage with due ceremony and fittingly adorned is called *kūkuda,* there results apprehension of the power of the terms air etc. in reference to objects colourless, tangible etc., and of the terms *kūkuda* etc., in relation to those who give girls in marriage etc. Similarly also apprehension of verbal power results from the context of words. Thus since the term barley is employed in the common usage of barbarians to denote panic seed, and in that of civilized men to denote the long-awned cereal, if a doubt arise in regard to the word barley is such sacred texts as *Charu* (a kind of oblation) is made of barley, it being impossible to restrict it to one meaning, and illogical to understand it equivocally; apprehension that the power of the term barley is to denote the long-awned cereal only, arises from the sequel of the sentence which supplies the full sense of the injunction, viz: In spring the leaves of all kinds of grain wither away, and the pleasent, bearded barley still remains. Or for example apprehension of the power of the terms elysium etc., to designate a particular kind of bliss, results from such words as That bliss which is not interrupted by pain, which is not forthwith destroyed, and which is obtained by desire, is the object of the term elysium according to the sense of the context : Let him that desires the lordship of heaven sacrifice an agni-shtoma. Apprehension of the power of terms sometimes also results from explication, as that of the personal terminations of the verb to designate action; as from He performs culinary operations, as a proposition identical with He cooks. According to the Mīmāṁsakas verbal power conveys the universal only, and not the individual, for did it apply to the individual it would be either unduly restricted or infinite in extension. According to the doctrine of the Prābhākaras on this point, in such sentences as Bring the cow, there is a knowledge of the individual, a knowledge of the universal apart from the particular being impossible, the act and object of cognition being equal. According to the doctrine of Bhaṭṭa there is first a knowledge of construction of the cow etc., as the object of the verb, by means of the connection of verbal collocation, and afterwards an inference that it is the cow that is the object of the verb. According to the doctrine of Mandanāchārya the individual is designated by implication. This doctrine of these authorities, that verbal power designates the universal, is not correct, for unless in such instances as Bring the cow, the power had reference to the individual, the fact that the individual is the object of verbal knowledge could not be established as it is by experience. Nor does the knowledge of the individual arise from implication, for if the word be not used in its denotative function, to use it in its implicative function is impossible. Nor is a knowledge of the individual possible by equality of the act and the object of knowledge; for while the being an object of verbal knowledge which is an effect, must have a cause, the equality of the act and object of cognition which is a necessary condition cannot be the cause. We must therefore acquiesce in the doctrine that the power of the terms cow etc., is denotative of an individual characterised by the form of the universal. It has therefore been laid down in the aphorism of Gautama that particulars characterised by the form of the universal, are the object of the term.[1] V.

[1] इदानीं शाब्दबौधौपायिकं पदपदार्थयोः सम्बन्धं प्रदर्शयति। शब्दादर्थप्रत्ययः सामयिकः समयरूप-सम्बन्धप्रयोज्यस्तथाच पदपदार्थयोः समयरूपः सम्बन्ध एव शाब्दबोधनियामकः समयश्च सङ्केतः सच द्विविधो नित्य आधुनिकश्च तत्र नित्यसङ्केतः शक्तिः आधुनिसंकेतः परिभाषा संकेतश्चास्माच्छब्दादयमर्थोबोद्ध-व्यइत्याकारकः अयं शब्द इममर्थं बोधयत्वित्याकारको वा तदुक्तम्। आजानिकश्चाधुनिकः संकेतो-द्विविधः स्मृतः। नित्य आजानिकस्तत्र या शक्तिरिति गीयते। कादाचित्कस्त्वाधुनिकः शास्त्रकारादिभिः कृतः। इति शक्तिग्रहश्च व्यवहारादितो भवति तदुक्तम् शक्तिग्रहं व्याकरणोपमानात् कोषाप्तवाक्याद्व्यवहारतश्च। सान्निध्यतः सिद्धपदस्य वृद्धा वाक्यस्य शेषाद्विवृतेर्वदन्ति इति। धातुप्रकृतिप्रत्ययादीनां शक्तिग्रहो व्याकरणाद्भवति यथा कर्मणि द्वितीया कर्तरि परस्मैपदम् इत्याद्यनुशासनात् कर्मत्वादौ द्वितीयादेः उपमानाद् गवादिसादृश्यज्ञानात् गवयत्वादिजात्यवच्छिन्ने गवयादिपदानां शक्तिग्रहः कोषात् गुणे शुक्लादयः पुंसि गुणिलिङ्गास्तु तद्वति। शीतं गुणे तद्वदर्थाः सुशीतः शिशिरोजडः।। चूर्णे क्षोदः समुतिञ्जपिञ्जलौ भृशमाकुले। इत्यादिकात् श्वेतादौ शुक्लादिशब्दानां शुक्लिग्रहः कोकिलः पिकपदवाच्य इत्याद्याप्तवाक्यात् कोकिलादौ पिकादिपदानां शक्तिगृहः प्रयोज्यप्रयोजकव्यवहारात् गोत्वादिविशिष्टे गवादिपदानां शक्तिग्रहः तथाहि यत्र प्रयोजकवृद्धेन गामानयेत्युक्तम् तच्छ्रुत्वा प्रयोज्यवृद्धेन गौरानीतः तदवधार्य पार्श्वस्थोबालो गवानयनं गामानयेति शब्दप्रयोज्यमवधारयति ततश्च गां वधान अश्वमानयेत्यावापोद्वापाभ्यां गवादिपदानां सास्नाविशिष्टगवादौ शक्तिं गृह्णाति प्रसिद्धरर्थकपदसामानाधिकरण्यात् नीरूपः स्पर्शवान वायुः सत्कृत्यालङ्कृतां कन्यां ददानः कूकुदः स्मृतः इत्यादौ रूपशून्यस्पर्शवदादौ वाय्वादिशब्दस्य कन्यादात्रादौ कूकुदादिशब्दस्य च शक्तिग्रहः एवं वाक्यशेषादपि

एकदिक्काभ्यामेककालाभ्यां सन्निकृष्टविप्रकृष्टाभ्यां परमपरञ्च।। 21।।

Priority and posteriority

Aph. 21. The prior and posterior [are produced] by two objects occupying the same space and time and near and remote.

The term prior and posterior is used in an abstract sense. The words are produced are to be supplied; also the prior and posterior may be an elliptical expression for the convention of the prior and posterior, the particle *iti* having to be supplied. By two objects occupying the same space, that is of which there is the same space, and occupying the same time, that is, synchronous,—by these priority and posteriority are produced, or are cognised and named. It is therefore stated that they are produced by two objects near and remote, that is possessed of contiguity or paucity of conjunctions with the conjunct, and of remotness, that is of plurality of conjunctions with the conjunct. Hereby the co-inherent cause is stated. The non-coinherent cause is the conjunction of the object with space. For example, there are produced in a man standing with his face to the east priority and posteriority in relation to the plurality of conjunct conjunctions in one of two bodies situated in the east, and to paucity of conjunct conjunctions in another. The non-coinherent cause has thus been stated. In the words near and remote, there is by the object an indication of the subjective cognition. It is accordingly stated that the efficient cause is the cognition of relativity. Priority and posteriority are produced only between objects

यथा यवपदस्य कङ्गुप्रभृतौ ग्लेच्छानां दीर्घशूके च शिष्टानां व्यवहारात् व्यवहारादेकमात्रशक्तेः परिच्छेतुमशक्यत्वान् नानार्थत्वस्य वान्याय्यत्वात् यवमयश्चरुर्भवति इति श्रुतौ यवपदस्यार्थसन्देहे वसन्ते सर्वशस्यानां जायते पत्रशातनम। मोदमानाश्च तिष्ठन्ति यवाः कणिशशालिनः।। इति विध्यर्थाकाङ्क्षया प्रवर्तमानाद्वाक्यशेषाद्दीर्घशूक एव यवपदस्य शक्तिग्रहः यथा वा स्वाराज्यकामोऽग्निष्टोमेन यजेत इत्यादिविधिशेषीभूतेभ्यः। यन्न दुःखेन सम्भिन्नं न च ग्रस्तमनन्तरम्। अभिलाषोपनीतञ्च तत् सुखं स्वः पदास्पदम्।। इत्यादिवाक्येभ्यः स्वरादिपदस्य विजातीयसुखादौ शक्तिग्रहः। क्वचिद्विवरणादपि यथा पचति पाकं करोतीति तुल्यार्थकवाक्यात् कृत्यादौ तिङादेः शक्तिग्रह इति। तत्र जातावेव शक्तिर्नतु व्यक्तौ व्यभिचारादानन्त्याच्चेति मीमांसकाः तत्रापि प्राभाकरमते व्यक्तिं विना जातिभानस्यासम्भवात्तुल्यवित्तिवेद्यत्वादेव गामानयेत्यादौ व्यक्तेर्भानम् भट्टमते च सामा-नाधिकरण्यसम्बन्धेन कर्मत्वादौ गोत्वादेः प्रथममन्वयबोधः पश्चात्तु कर्मतायां गोवृत्तित्वस्यानुमानं भवतीति। मण्डनाचार्यमते व्यक्तेर्लक्षणय भाषनं भवतीति। तदेतज्जातिशक्तिमतं न समीचीनं गामानयेत्यादौ व्यक्तेः शाब्दबोधविषयत्वस्यानुभवसिद्धस्य विना शक्तिमनुपपत्तेः न च लक्षणया व्यक्तेर्भानम् मुख्यप्रयोगस्यासत्त्वे लाक्षणिकप्रयोगस्यम्भवात् न च तुल्यवित्तिवेद्यतयाऽपि व्यक्तेर्भानं सम्भवति कार्यीभूतशाब्दबोधविषयतायाः कारणप्रयोज्यत्वस्यावश्यकत्वेन नियमरूपस्य तुल्यवित्तिवेद्यत्वस्य तत्राप्रयोजकत्वादिति तस्माज्जात्या-कृतिविशिष्टव्यक्तावेवगवादिपदानां शक्तिरितिमतमेवादरणीयम् तदुक्तं गौतमीये जात्याकृतिव्यक्तयस्तु पदार्थः इति।।

situated in the same space; they do not therefore arise everywhere. The relative conception belongs to only one observer; therefore they do not appear everywhere, for as determined by relative conception they are not everywhere produced. It being evinced by perception that they are produced in consequence of the power of their causes, they are not reciprocally dependent: otherwise they would not be produced or would not appear, for there could be no genesis or cognition of two objects each supposing the other as a pre-requisite whereas priority and posteriority do appear, and this appearance without their production would be impossible. The words by two objects occupying the same time, have reference to priority and posteriority in time. This priority and posteriority is produced by two objects one young and the other old, in which there is existence at the same time. Their contiguity is the being born at an interval of fewer revolutions of the sun, their remoteness is the being born at an interval of fewer revolutions of the sun, their remoteness is the being born at an interval of more revolutions of the sun. There is in this case also indicated by the object a subjective intellection. The two objects young and old are, therefore the co-inherent cause. The conjunction between time and these objects is the non-coinherent cause. The conception of the being born at an interval of fever revolutions of the sun is the efficient cause of priority, and the conception of the being born at an interval of more revolutions of the sun is the efficient cause of posteriority. This priority and this posteriority arise also in objects of determinate position in space. Of these there is a seven-fold destruction of priority and posteriority in space, but the production of the two is simultaneous, else there would be a regress to infinity. Their destruction results from destruction of the relative conception, from destruction of the non-coinherent cause of the conjunction, from destruction of the substance which is the co-inherent cause, from destruction of the efficient, and non-coinherent causes, from destruction of the efficient and co-inherent causes, and from the destructions of the efficient, non-coinherent, and co-inherent causes. From destruction of the relative conception, thus:—the destruction of the cognition of relativity is from the production of posteriority, that is from the general knowledge of posteriority; from the destruction of the relative conception there results destruction of the posteriority in cognising a substance qualified by posteriority; and the whole process may be inferred according to the analogy of the destruction of duality. From destruction of the non-coinherent cause as when first there is a cognition of relativity, then action in the object which is the substratum of posteriority, thence disjunction of the object and space when posteriority is produced, thence destruction of the conjunction between space and the object, thence in consequence of the simple cognition destruction of the cognition of relativity, then from the destruction of the conjunction of the object with space, destruction of the priority and posteriority. In this instance the conception of relativity, though synchronous with the destruction of posteriority, is not destructive of it. If it be urged that there is much confusion involved in the supposition of the destruction of reproduction, necessity etc., consequent on destruction of the conjunction of the soul and the internal organ in the destruction of qualities resulting from the destruction of the non-coinherent cause, we reply that it is not so; for inasmuch as posteriority is prevaded by remoteness, there must needs be a cessation of posteriority consequent on non-existence of remoteness on the removal of the substratum of posteriority. Nor is there at that time another agent of destruction, for it is the destruction of conjunction which is conceived as the agent of destruction, such destruction being otherwise impossible. Inasmuch as we observe long afterwards memory, pleasure etc., the effect of reproduction, necessity etc., we cannot suppose these to be destroyed. This also implies the percipient as a limit, and posteriority and priority are destroyed by the destruction of the conjunction between the percipient and space, this being equally efficient. Destruction of posteriority sometimes also results from destruction of the co-inherent cause, as for instance when by action produced in a portion of a body there is produced disjunction from another portion, then a conception of relativity; from this disjunction results destruction of the conjunction originative of the body and production of posteriority; in the succeeding moment from destruction of the conjunction there results destruction of the substance, and the universal conception of posteriority; from the destruction of the substance there results destruction of posteriority and destruction of the cognition of relativity results from the simple cognition. Destruction of posteriority, therefore, does not result from destruction of the cognition of relativity, for they are simultaneous. Destruction of posteriority is sometimes by destruction of the substance and of the cognition of relativity, as for instance when there arises in the portion of a body a relative cognition of action; thence disjunction from other constituent parts and production of posteriorty; thence destruction of the originative conjunction and a simple cognition; thence destruction of the substance and of the relative cognition thence destruction of posteriority. Sometimes destruction of posteriority is by destruction of the substance and of conjunction, as when there arises disjunction of the constituent parts of a substance; then production of action in the body and of a relative cognition; next the production of destruction of the conjunction of the parts, of the disjunction between the body and space, and of posteriority; thence destruction of the substance, destruction of the conjunction of the body, a universal cognition of posteriority; thence destruction of posteriority by destruction of cognition of the body and space and destruction of the substance, according to the rule that a simple cognition destroys a relative cognition. Destruction of posteriority is sometimes by destruction of conjunction and of the relative cognition, as when there successively ensue production of posteriority and action in the body, a simple cognition and disjunction, destruction of the relative cognition and of the conjunction of the body with space, and thence destruction of posteriority. Destruction of posteriority at other times results from destruction of the co-inherent, non-coinherent, and efficient causes, as when there simultaneously arise production of posteriority, disjunction of the parts of the body, and action in the body; next a universal cognition of posteriority, destruction of the conjunction of constituent parts, and disjunction of the body from space; next from simultaneously produced destruction of the relative cognition, of the substance, and of the conjunction of the body with space, there results destruction of priority or posteriority in space. Of priority and posteriority in time there is no destruction dependent upon destruction of the non-coinherent cause, nor is there destruction of contiguity and remoteness in temporal priority and posteriority, as there is destruction of contiguity and remoteness in priority and posteriority in space, where there is destruction of the conjunction of the body with space. The three cases, therefore, of destruction of temporal priority and posteriority, from destruction of the co-inherent cause, from destruction of the relative cognition, and by both conjointly, are to be inferred according to the analogy of the preceding.[1] U.

[1] परमपरञ्चेति भावप्रधानो निर्देशः उत्पद्यत इति शेषः यद्वा परमपरञ्चेति व्यवहार इति शेषः इतिरध्याहार्यम् एका दिग् ययोस्तावेकदिक्कौ ताभ्यामेकदिक्काभ्यां पिण्डाभ्यामित्यर्थः तुल्यदेशावप्येकदिक्कौ भवतः नतु ताभ्यां परत्वापरत्वे उत्पद्येते व्यवह्रियेते वेत्यत उक्तं सन्निकृष्टविप्रकृष्टाभ्यामिति सन्निकर्षः

The notion and expression of prior and posterior is produced by two bodies occupying the same space, that is, having the same space as their site, and contiguous or remote, that is objects of a cognition of inherence in a substratum of more or less conjunction with the sun. The efficient cause, therefore, of posteriority in space is the cognition of the substratum of more numerous conjunctions with the sun; the non-coinherent cause is conjunction of space in the body which is the substratum of this quality of posteriority, and the co-inherent cause is the matter which is the object of such cognition. The efficient cause of priority in space is the cognition of a substratum of fewer

संयुक्तसंयोगाल्पत्वम् विप्रकर्षस्तद्भूयस्त्वम् तद्वद्भ्यामित्यर्थः एतेन समवायिकारणमुक्तम् दिक्पिण्ड-संयोगस्त्वसमवायिकारणम् तथाहि प्राङ्मुखस्य पुरुषस्यप्राच्यवस्थितयोः पिण्डयोरेकस्मिन् संयुक्तसंयोगभूयस्त्वमपरस्मिन् संयुक्तसंयोगाल्पतरत्वञ्चापेक्ष्य परत्वमपरत्वञ्चोत्पद्यते असमवायिकारणमुक्तम् सन्निकृष्टविप्रकृष्टाभ्यामिति विषयेण विषयिणं प्रत्ययमुपलक्षयति तथाचापेक्षाबुद्धेः निमित्तकारणत्वमुक्तम् एकदिगवस्थितयोरेवपरत्वापरत्वे उत्पद्येते इति न सर्वत्रोत्पत्तिः एकस्यैव द्रष्टुरपेक्षाबुद्धिः समुत्पद्यते इति न सर्वथोत्पत्तिः अपेक्षाबुद्धिनियमान्न सर्वदोत्पत्तिः कारणशक्तेरुत्पन्नयोः प्रत्यक्षसिद्धत्वान्न परस्पराश्रयत्वम् अन्यथाहि नोत्पद्येयातां नवा प्रतीयेयाता परस्परापेक्षायां हि द्वयोरनुत्पत्तिरप्रतीतिश्च स्यात् प्रतीयते च परत्वापरत्वे प्रतीतिश्च तयोर्नोत्पत्तिमन्तरेणेति एककालाभ्यामिति कालिकपरत्वापरत्वे अभिप्रेत्य तत्रैककालाभ्यामिति एको वर्तमानः कालो पयोर्युवस्थविरपिण्डयोः तावेककालौ ताभ्यामेककालाभ्यामित्यर्थः सन्निकर्षोऽल्पतरतप्रनपरिस्पन्दान्त-रितजन्मत्वं विप्रकर्षश्च बहुतरतप्रनपरिस्पन्दान्तरितजन्मत्वम् अत्रापि विषयेण विषयिणीं बुद्धिमुपलक्षयति तेन युवस्थविरपिण्डौ समवायिकारणे कालपिण्डसंयोगश्चासमवायिकारणम् अल्पतरतपनपरिस्पन्दान्तरितजन्म-त्वबुद्धिरपरत्वे बहुतरतपनपरिस्पन्दान्तरितजन्मत्वबुद्धिः परत्वे निमित्तकारणम् एतेच परत्वापरत्वे अनियतदिग्देशयोरपि पिण्डियोरुत्पद्येते तत्र दैशिकपरत्वापरत्वयोः सप्तधा विनाशः उत्पादस्तु युगपदेव द्वयोरन्यथाऽन्योन्याश्रयः स्यात् अपेक्षाबुद्धिनाशात् संयोगस्यासमवायिकारणस्य नाशात् द्रव्यस्य च समवायिकारणस्य नाशात् निमित्तासमवायिकारणयोर्नाशात् निमित्तसमवायिकारणयोर्नाशात् निमित्तना-शासमवायिकारणनाशसमेवायिकारणनाशेभ्यः। तत्रापेक्षाबुद्धिनाशात् तावत् परत्वोत्पत्तिः परत्वसामान्यज्ञानं ततोऽपेक्षाबुद्धिविनाशस्तद्विनाशात् परत्वविशिष्टद्रव्यज्ञानकाले परत्वनाशः द्वित्वनाशवदेव सर्वमूहनीयम्। असमवायिकारणनाशादपि तद्यथा यदैवापेक्षाबुद्धिस्तदैव परत्वाधारे पिण्डे कर्म ततो यदैव परत्वोत्पत्तिस्तदैव दिक्पिण्डविभागस्ततो यदा परत्वसामान्यज्ञानं तदा दिक्पिण्डसंयोगनाशः ततः सामान्यज्ञानादपेक्षाबुद्धिनाशस्तदैव दिक्पिण्डसंयोगनाशात् परत्वापरत्वयोर्नाशः तत्र चापेक्षाबुद्धिनाशस्य परत्वनाशसमकालत्वान्न तन्नाशकत्वम् नन्वसमवायिकारणनाशादपि गुणनाशे आत्ममनःसंयोगनाशादपि संस्कारदृष्टादीनां विनाशे बहु व्याकुलं स्यादिति चेन्न विप्रकृष्टत्वेन परत्वस्य व्यापनात् परत्वाधारस्यान्यत्र गमने विप्रकर्षाभावात् परत्वनिवृत्तिरावश्यकी नच तदा नाशकान्तरमस्तीत्यन्यथाऽनुपपत्त्या संयोगनाश एव नाशकः कल्प्यते संस्कारादृष्टादेः कार्यस्य स्मृतिसुखादेश्चिरेणापि दर्शनान्न तन्नाशकल्पना उपलक्षणञ्चैतत् अवधेर्द्रष्टुश्च तद्देशसंयोगनाशादपि परत्वापरत्वे विनाशयतः युक्तेस्तुल्यत्वात् समवायिकारणनाशादपि क्वचित् परत्वनाशः तथाहि यदा पिण्डावयवे समुत्पन्नेन कर्मणाऽवयान्तराद्विभागस्तदैवापेक्षाबुद्धिः विभागात् पिण्डारम्भाकसंयोगनाशः परत्वसामान्यज्ञानं द्रव्यनाशात् परत्वनाशोऽपेक्षाबुद्धिनाशश्च सामान्यज्ञानात् तथाच यौगपद्यान्नापेक्षाबुद्धिनाशात् परत्वनाशइतिक्वचिद्द्व्यनाशापेक्षाबुद्धि नशाभ्यां परत्वनाशः तद्यथा पिण्डावयवे कर्मापेक्षाबुद्धेरुत्पाद-स्ततोऽवयवान्तरविभागः परत्वोत्पतिः तत आरम्भकसंयोगनाशसामान्यज्ञाने ततो द्रव्यनाशापेक्षाबुद्धिनाशौ

conjunctions of the sun; its co-inherent cause is the body which is the object of such a cognition; the non-coinherent cause is conjunction of space in such matter. For there is such a practical assurance as that to one living at Pāṭaliputra, Kaśi is nearer than Prayāga, and Prayāga further than than Kāśi. The object of this cognition, posteriority, arises in refrence to Prayāga, because Prayāga is there cognised as the site of more numerous conjunctions with the sun; and the priority in reference to Kāśi arises from its being known that Kāśi is the site of less numerous conjunctions with the sun. The notion and expression of prior and posterior is produced by two bodies occupying the same time, that is, by two bodies which have one time to conjoin them, contiguous and remote, that is cognised as substrata of more or less numerous revolutions of the sun. For there arise such cognitions and expressions as that an old man is posterior in relation to a young man, and a young man prior in relation to an old man. The old man is the co-inherent cause of the posteriority which is the object of this cognition; the non-coinherent cause is conjunction with a greater time; the efficient cause is the cognition of the substratum of more numerous revolutions of the sun. The young man is the co-inherent cause of priority; the non-coinherent cause is the conjunction of the body of the young man with a great time; the efficient cause is the cognition of the young man as the substratum of less numerous revolutions of the sun than those inherent in the old man. Although bodies differ according to childhood, youth, and old age, and there is consequently possible therein the contrariety of the revolutions of the sun existent in the old man and the young; yet it is the cognition of heterogeneity in the common substratum of more numerous conjunctions with the sun, that is the cause of temporal posteriority in the old man; and the cognition of heterogeneity in the substratum of less numerous conjunctions with

ततश्च परत्वनाशः क्वचिद्द्रवस्य संयोगस्य च नाशाभ्यां परत्वनाशः तद्यथा यदा द्रव्यावयवविभागस्तदैव पिण्डकर्मापेक्षाबुद्ध्योरुत्पादस्तदनन्तरमवयवसंयोगनाशदिक्पिण्डविभागपरत्वोत्पत्तयः ततो द्रव्यनाशदिक्पिण्डसंयोगनाशपरत्वसामान्यबुद्धयः ततो द्रव्यनाशदिक्पिण्डसंयोगनाशाभ्यां परत्वनाशः सामान्य-बुद्धेरपेक्षाबुद्धिनाश इति क्वचित् संयोगनाशापेक्षाबुद्धिनाशाभ्यां परत्वनाशः तद्यथा परत्वोत्पतिपिण्डकर्मणी सामान्यज्ञानविभागौ अपेक्षाबुद्धिनाशदिक्पिण्डसंयोगनाशौ ततः परत्वनाशः क्वचित् समवाय्यसमवायिनिमित्तना-शेभ्यः तद्यथा परत्वोत्पत्तिपिण्डावयवविभागपिण्डकर्माणि युगपत् तदनन्तरं परत्वसामान्यज्ञानावयवसंयोग-नाशदिक्पिण्डविभागाः तदनन्तरमपेक्षाबुद्धिनाशद्रव्यनाशदिक्पिण्डसंयोगनाशेभ्यो युगपदुत्पन्नेभ्यः परत्वस्या-परत्वस्य वा दैशिकस्य नाशः कालकृतयोस्तु परत्वापरत्वयोरसमवायिकारणनाशाधीनो नाशो नास्ति दैशिक-योर्दिकपिण्डसंयोगनाशे सन्निकर्षविप्रकर्षनाशो यथा न यथा कालिकयोरिति तयोः समवायिकारणनाशादपेक्षा-बुद्धिनाशात् द्वाभ्याञ्चेति त्रयः पक्षाः पूर्ववदूहनीयाः।।

the sun, that is the cause of priority in the youth. It cannot, therefore, be asked in objection, why posteriority is not produced in an atom, as compared with a water-pot etc., inasmuch as there is cognised in the atom the possession of the universal nature terrestriality etc., the common substratum of more numerous movements of the sun. For by this is meant possession of a universal nature non-existent in two contemporaneous common substrata of more numerous movements of the sun. Such a universal nature is the being Chaitra, etc., The solar motion is also to be characterised as other than that which is subsequent to that time. Hence it is that there is not produced posteriority in Maitra as a youth a hundred years old, as compared with Chaitra an old man of eighty. Or remoteness may be defined as production prior to revolutions of the sun, and contiguity as production subsequent thereto. Production prior to the revolution of the sun which was the substratum of the production (i.e. year of the birth) of Chaitra the young man etc., exists in the old man Maitra etc. and therefore there is priority in the senior. Production subsequent to the revolution of the sun which was the substratum of the production of Maitra the senior, exists in Chaitra the junior etc., and posteriority is therefore produced in him. Inasmuch as there is in the unsentient, non-existence of the cognition of priority and posteriority in time, we must add to the definition the condition of there being sentiency. Undue width in the definition,when we consider such and such a particular body, is to be prevented by the addition of a certain universality. It is to be observed that the author of the Muktāvalī states that the destruction of the cognition of relativity is destructive of priority and posteriority in both their forms, that is, of both local and temporal priority and posteriority; while in the Upaskāra it is laid down that it is the destruction of their three-fold causes that is destructive of priority and posteriority.[1] V.

[1] एका दिक् आधारतया ययोस्तावेकदिक्कौ मूर्तौ ताभ्यां मूर्ताभ्यां सन्निकृष्टविप्रकृष्टाभ्यां बहुतरसूर्यसंयोगाश्रयत्वाल्पतरसूर्यसंयोगाश्रयत्वज्ञानविषयाभ्यां परमपरञ्चेति व्यवहारो जायते इत्यर्थः। तथाच दैशिकपरत्वं प्रति बहुतरसूर्यसंयोगाश्रयत्वज्ञानं निमित्तकारणं तदाश्रये मूर्ते दिक्संयोगोऽसमवायिकारणं तादृशज्ञानविषयो मूर्तः समवायिकारणम् दैशिकापरत्वस्याल्पतरसूर्यसंयोगाश्रयत्वज्ञानं निमित्तकारणं तद्विषयो मूर्तः समवायिकारणं तादृशमूर्ते दिक्संयोगोऽसमवायिकारणमिति भवति हि पाटलिपुत्रस्थस्य काशीमपेक्ष्य प्रयागः परः प्रयागमपेक्ष्य काश्यपरेतिव्यवहारः तद्विषयः परत्वं प्रयागे उत्पद्यते तत्र बहुतरसूर्यसंयोगाश्रयत्वेन तस्य ज्ञातत्वात्। काश्याञ्चापरत्वं जायते अल्पतरसूर्यसंयोगाश्रयत्वेन तस्या ज्ञातत्वात् एककालाभ्यामिति एकः कालः संयोगितया ययोः पिण्डयोस्ताभ्यामेककालाभ्यां पिण्डाभ्यां सन्निकृष्टविप्रकृष्टाभ्याम्। अल्पतरतपनपरिस्पन्दबहुतरतपनपरिस्पन्दाश्रयतया ज्ञाताभ्यां परमपरञ्चेति व्यवहारो भवति भवति हि युवानमपेक्ष्य स्थविरः परः स्थविरमपेक्ष्य युवाऽपर इत्यादिको व्यवहारस्तद्विषयत्वं परत्वस्य समवायिकारणं स्थविरः

कारणपरत्वात् कारणापरत्वाच्च।। 22।।

Aph. 22. [Priority and posteriority result] from posteriority of the cause, and from priority of the cause.

Time is the cause of priority and posteriority. There is here stated by indication conjunction with time as the non-coinherent cause of posteriority, and conjunction with time as the non-coinherent cause of priority, in relation to the priority and posteriority of the time. Otherwise there would be no connection between the words of the aphorism; for priority and posteriority could not be produced merely by priority and posteriority. The terms priority and posteriority have, therefore, by implication, the meaning of conjunction with time productive thereof.[1] U.

परत्वापरत्वयोः परत्वापरत्वाभावो ऽणुत्वमहत्त्वाभ्यां व्याख्यातः।। 23।।

Aph. 23. The non-existence of priority and posteriority in priority and posteriority, is explained by minuteness and greatness.

कर्मभिः कर्माणि।। 24।।

Aph. 24. Actions [are void] of actions.

तत्र महाकालस्य संयोगोऽसमवायिकारणम्। बहुतरसूर्यक्रियाश्रयत्वज्ञानं निमित्तकारणम् अपरत्वस्य च युवा समवायिकारणम् युवशरीरमहाकालयोः संयोगोऽसमवायिकारणम् स्थविराश्रिततपनस्पन्दापेक्षया-ऽल्पतरतपनस्पन्दाश्रयत्वेन यूनो ज्ञानं निमित्तकारणम् यद्यपि शरीराणां बाल्ययौवनवार्द्धक्यभेदेन भिन्नत्वात् युवस्थविरगततपनपरिस्पन्दानां वैपरीत्यमपि सम्भवति तथापि बहुतरतपनपरिस्पन्दसमानाधिकरणवैजात्य-वत्त्वज्ञानमेव स्थविरे कालिकपरत्वस्य कारणम् अल्पतरतपनस्पन्दसमानाधिकरणवैजात्यज्ञानञ्च यून्यपरत्वस्य कारणमिति नच घटाद्यपेक्षया परमाणोरपि बहुतरसूर्यक्रियासमानाधिकरणपृथिवीत्वादिजातिमत्त्वज्ञानात् परत्वं कथं नोत्पद्यते इति वाच्यं बहुतरसूर्यक्रियासमानाधिकरणैककालीनद्वयावृत्तिजातिमत्त्वस्य विवक्षिततत्वात् तादृशजातिञ्च चैत्रत्ववादिः सूर्यक्रियाऽपि तत्कालोत्तरकालीनान्यत्वेन विशेषणीया नातोऽशीतिवर्षजीविस्थ-विरचैत्रापेक्षयो शतवर्षजीवियुवमैत्रे परत्वोत्पत्तिः अथवा सूर्यपरिस्पन्दपूर्वोत्पन्नत्वं विप्रकर्षः तदनन्तरोत्पन्नत्वं सन्निकर्षः युवचैत्राद्युत्पत्त्यधिकरणं यः सूर्यस्पन्दस्तत्पूर्वोत्पन्नत्वं स्थविरमैत्रादौ वर्तते इति स्थविरे परत्वम् स्थविरमैत्राद्युत्पत्त्यधिकरणसूर्यस्पन्दानन्तरोत्पन्नत्वं युवचैत्रादावस्तीति तत्रापरत्वं जायते अचेतने कालिकपरत्वापरत्वव्यवहाराभावे तु प्राणित्वे सतीति विशेषणं देयम् तत्तच्छरीरमादायातिप्रसङ्गस्तु जातिविशेषनिवेशेन वारणीय इति संक्षेपः। द्विविधयोः परत्वापरत्वयोर्नाशकोऽपेक्षाबुद्धिनाश इति मुक्तावलीकारः उपस्कारे तु त्रिविधकारणनाशस्यैव परत्वापरत्वनाशकत्वमुक्तमिति।।

[1] परत्वापरत्वयोः कारणं कालस्तस्य परत्वापरत्वे परत्वासमवायिाकारणकालसंयोगोऽपरत्वासमवायि-कारणकालसंयोगश्च लक्षणयोक्तः अन्यथाऽनन्वयापत्तेः नहि परत्वापरत्वाभ्यामेव परत्वापरत्वे उत्पद्येते तस्मात् परत्वापरत्वपदयोस्तदुत्पादककालसंयोगा क्था विलक्षणया।

गुणैर्गुणाः ।। 25 ।।

Aph. 25. Qualities [are void] of qualities.

इहेदमिति यतः कार्यकारणयोः स समवायः ।। 26 ।।

Aph. 26. That is co-inherence by virtue of which it may be said of cause and effect that the one is in the other.

The investigation of co-inherence is described, though to the neglect of thought which is the next subject in order, in favour of the desire of the student to know what co-inherence is, it having been stated that priority and posteriority co-inhere in objects only, and that knowledge, pleasure etc. co-inhere in the soul. The words cause and effect have an implicative force, and are to be considered to apply also to non-cause and non-effect; as it has been stated in the section entitled the Locality of the Categories, that the relation of unconjoined objects subsistent and inherent is co-inherence. The cause of the cognition of the here, non-unconnectedness, is the non-existence of two unconjoined objects. Inasmuch as the thought of clarified butter here present in the bowl; as that of jujubes here present in the bowl; of cloth here present in the threads; of grass here in the blades; of substance, quality, and action here in substance; of the essence of a cow here in the cow; of cognition here in the soul; of sound here in the ether:—this thought of the here which is thus produced, cannot be produced without some connection, it is inferred that there is some connection. This connection is not mere conjuction, for the actions etc., of one only of the two objects cannot produce it; its existence does not terminate in disjunction; connected objects may be non-conjunctly effected, they must be conceived to have a determinate substratum; it is not perceptible, and it is one, and eternal. If it be objected that if co-inherence be one it follows that there is a confusion with regard to substantiality, inasmuch as the essence of action etc. may co-inhere as well as the essence of substance in substance; we reply that it is not so. According to the relation of subsistence and inherence, there can be no confusion. For though that co-inherence which is the co-inherence of the essence of substance, be the co-inherence of the essences of quality action etc.; yet substance is not the substratum of these latter essences, inasmuch as they are not manifested in substance. The essence of substances, or substantiality, appears only in substances; the essence of qualities, only in qualities; the essence of actions only in actions, and nowhere else; accordingly from the observation of this concomitance and its negation, there results a determination of the relation of subsistence and inherence. As there being an ordinary conjunction between a vessel and clarified butter, it is the vessel which is the substratum or receptacle, not the clarified butter, and therefore there is a determination, the relation of containing and contained; so this limitation is here possible only as a consequence of the difference of the power of manifesting and of being manifested. For the essence of action etc. is not manifested by substance, as the essence of substance is. Hence it has been said, All-powerful consciousness is our resource in the apprehension of things. For there is no contradictory intuition in relation to the nature of substrata, since there arises no intuition that substance becomes action, or that the threads are in the cloth; nor in the case of air does there appear the nature of a substratum because in the co-inherence with colour, colour is in air. It is therefore natural power which in every instance determines the relation between the substratum and that which inheres in it. This same co-inherence is, eternal, since it has no cause; for the co-inherent cause is the condition of the production of existences, and the non-coinherent and efficient causes are subsidiary thereto. If, moreover, there were a co-inherent cause of co-inherence, this must exist in virtue of another co-inherence or of same co-inherence. It is not the former, for there would thus emerge a regress to infinity. It is not the latter, for this same co-inherence could not co-inhere with itself, for thus there would be constantly recurring co-inherence.

If we be asked how there arises the cognition of the co-inherence of the cloth in the threads, and of the colour in the cloth, we reply that it is by an essential connection, for on the hypothesis of a second co-inherence there would be regress to infinty. If it be objected: In that case the cognition of the locally present also, as that there is here the colour of the cloth, must also be by essential connection:—we reply that it is not so, there being a non-existence which renders a further connection impossible. If, then, it be objected : In the cognition that there is here on this spot non-existence of a water-pot, there is a co-inherence or other connection:—we reply that it is not so, for this may be produced by essential connection; for on the contrary supposition there would follow a universality of the absolute and reciprocal non-existences of the water-pot, eternal, and co-inherent in a plurality of objects, and emergent non-existence might be destructive as being a co-inherent effect, and antecedent non-existence might be destructive as being not produced by the co-inherent. The nature of existence is not in this case the condition, for possibility belongs to the nature of existence.

The Bhāṭṭas maintain that there is in non-existence another connection, called possession of attributes or predicates . On this hypothesis did possession of attributes belong to all individual non-existences, it would follow that we should cognise non-existence of a water-pot even where a water-pot existed; and the possession of the character of non-existence as a water-pot, might exist merely in virtue of the possession of the character of non-existence as a piece of cloth. If it be replied that the water-pot in this case prevents the thought of the non-existence of the water-pot, it may be replied, that there is in this case non-existence of the preventive by reason of the connection of possession of the attributes. Nor is the nature of the substratum such that there should not be there a manifestation of the non-existence of the water-pot; for after the water-pot has been removed there appears in this substratum, that is, in the place where the water-pot had stood, the non-existence of the water-pot.

If it be objected: How is it that after the destruction of colour, on your hypothesis, there is not a cognition of the coloured, inasmuch as co-inherence is eternal and one ?—we reply that the non-appearance of the coloured is possible in consequence of the destruction of colour only.[1] U.

[1] परत्वापरत्वादीनां मूर्तमात्रसमवेतत्वमुक्तं ज्ञानसुखादीनाञ्चात्मसमवेतत्वं तत्र समवाय एव कइति शिश्यजिज्ञासामनुरुद्ध्य बुद्धेरुद्देशक्रमप्राप्ताया अपि लङ्घनात् समवायपरीक्षामाह। कार्यकारणयोरित्युपलक्षणम् अकार्यकारणयोरित्यपि द्रष्टव्यं तदुक्तं पदार्थप्रदेशाख्ये प्रकरणे अयुतसिद्धानामाधार्याधारभूतानां यः सम्बन्ध ा इहेति प्रत्युयहेतुः स समवायः इति असम्बद्धयोरविद्यमानत्वमयुतसिद्धिः इह कुण्डे दधि इह कुण्डे बदराणीतिवत् इह तन्तुषु पट इह वीरणेषु कट इह द्रव्ये द्रव्यगुणकर्माणि इह गवि गोत्वम् इहात्मनि ज्ञानम् इहाकाशे शब्द इतीहबुद्धिरुत्पद्यमाना न बिना सम्बन्धमुत्पत्तुमर्हति तेनानुमीयतेऽस्ति कश्चित् सम्बन्धः अपिचासौ संयोग एव अन्यतरकर्मादीनां तदुत्पादकानामभावात् विभागपर्यनमानाभावाच्च सम्बन्धिनामयुतसिद्धत्वाच्च नियताधिकरणतयैवोन्नेयत्वात् अप्रत्यक्षत्तादेकत्वान्नित्यत्वाच्च। नन्वेकश्चेत्समवायस्तदा द्रव्यत्वादीनां सङ्करप्रसङ्गः कर्मत्वादिसमवायस्य द्रव्ये सम्भवात् मैवम् आधाराधेयनियमादेवासङ्करो यद्यपि य एव द्रव्यत्वसमवायः स एव गुणत्वकर्मत्वादीनामपि तथापि तेषां द्रव्यमाधारस्तत्र तेषामप्रतीतेः द्रव्येष्वेव साद्रत्वं प्रतीयते गुणेष्वेव गुणत्वं कर्मस्वे एव कर्म्मत्वं नत्वन्यत्रेत्यन्वयव्यतिरेकमतदर्शनादेव नियमः अन्यथा कुण्ड-दध्नोःसंयोगाविशेषेऽपि कुण्डमेवाधारो न दधीत्याश्रयाश्रयिभावनियमस्तथा व्यङ्गव्यञ्जकशक्तिभेदादेवात्रापि नियम उपपत्स्यते नहि द्रव्येण द्रव्यत्ववत् कर्मत्वाद्यप्यभिव्यज्यते तदुक्तम् संविदेव हि भगवती वस्तूपगमे नः शरणम् इति नह्याधारत्वं प्रति विपरीता सम्विदस्ति नहि भवति द्रव्यं कर्मेति नवा भवति पटे तन्तव इति तेन वायौ रूपसमवायेऽपि वायौ रूपमित्याधारता न वायोः प्रतीयते एतस्मात्स्यभावशक्तिरेव सर्वत्र नियामिका स चायं नित्यअकारणकत्वात् समवायिकारणदुत्पत्तिनियमः तदनुरुद्धे च निमित्तासमवायिनां

The connection of cause and effect, of part and whole, wherefrom there results the cognition that such a thing is in such a place, is co-inherence. For a cognition such as those of the cloth in the threads, the water-pot in its halves, the grass in its blades, has for its object the existence of the threads etc, in the cloth etc. This existence is determined by a special kind of connection, for else it would follow that there might be such cognitions as of the water-pot in the threads, the existence of the threads etc., residing by a temporal connection in the water-pot, etc. Connection, therefore, determining existence in a given mode, is co-inherence; for between whole and part conjuction is impossible. The words cause and effect have an implicative power, and it is therefore to be held that, that also which determines the relation of action and agent, of essence and individual, of eternal substance and particular object, and of containing and contained is co-inherence. The proof of co-inherence is determinate cognition, the object of which is the relation of character and characterised or predicate and subject. From determinate cognition such as of a man with a staff there results an inference. In this inference, conjunction etc., being impossible, there is given a proof of co-inherence. It cannot be maintained that by essential connection we are to understand a distinct entity, there being a complexity involved in the conception of a connection of endless essential forms; and that according to this method there could not be proved a distinct connection of non-existence. For it is impossible that the connection of non-existence should be eternal, as that of co-inherence is, for were this the case, it would follow that after a water-pot had been brought to a spot where one had not previously stood, there would be the cognition of the non-existence of the water-

तथाच समवायस्य समवायिकारणं यत् स्यात् तत् समवायान्तरेण तेनैव समवायेन वा न तावदाद्यः अनवस्थापातात् न द्वितीयः नहि स एव स समवायः स्वेनैव समवायः सम्भवतीत्यात्माश्रयात् तन्तुषु पटसमवायः पटे रूपसमवायइति प्रतीतिः कथमिति चेत् स्वरूपसम्बन्धेन समवायान्तराङ्गीकारेऽनवस्थापातात् तर्हीह पटरूपमित्यपीहप्रत्ययः स्वरूपसम्बन्धेनैव स्यात् किं समवायेनेति चेन्न तत्रातिरिक्तसम्बन्धे बाधकाभावात् तर्हीह भूतले घटाभाव इत्यत्रापि समवायः सम्बन्धान्तरं वा स्यादिति चेन्न स्वरूपसम्बन्धेनैव तदुपपतेः अन्यथा घटात्यन्ताभावान्योन्याभावयोर्नित्ययोरनेकसमवेतयोः सामान्यत्वापत्तेः प्रध्वंसस्य च समवेतकार्यत्वेन विनाशित्वापत्तेः प्रागभावस्य च समवेतानुत्पन्नत्वेनाविनाशित्वापत्तेश्च नच भावत्वं तत्र तन्त्र भावत्वस्यापाद्यत्वात् अभावेऽस्त्येव वैशिष्ट्याख्यं सम्बन्धान्तरमिति भाट्टाः तत्र यदि सर्वाभावव्यक्तीनामेकमेव वैशिष्ट्यं तदा घटवत्यपि घटाभावप्रत्ययप्रसङ्गः घटाभाववैशिष्ट्यनैव घटाभाववैशिष्ट्यवत्त्वात घट एव तत्र घटाभाव-धीप्रतिबन्धक इति चेत् वैशिष्ट्यसम्बन्धेन प्रतिबन्धकाभावस्यव तत्र सत्त्वात् नचाश्रयस्वभाव एव तादृशो येन न तत्र घटाभावाभिव्यक्तिः घटापसारणानन्तरं तत्रैव घटाभावप्रतीतेः तवापिरूपनाशानन्तरं कथं न रूपवत्ताप्रत्ययः समवायस्य नित्यवादेकत्वाच्चेतिचत् रूपनाशादेव तदप्रतीतेरुपपत्तेः समवायप्रतिबन्धः।।

pot, in consequence of the eternity of the non-existence of the water-pot and of its connection. Nor can it be admitted that there belongs another non-eternal connection to non-existence; for we should then have to imagine, in the case of a water-pot being brought and taken away a thousand times to and from a spot, a thousand connections. We must therefore maintain that the connection of non-existence of the water-pot, belongs to the essential form of the spot at the time the water-pot is removed. Inasmuch as the time when the water-pot is there does not effect this connection, at the time the water-pot is there, there is no cognition of the absolute non-existence of the water-pot. Thus it being neccessary to allow an essential connection of non-existence of the water-pot on the ground etc., there must in the case of other non-existence be a connection with the essential form; for it is evinced by experience that the cognitions of non-existences are conversant about one uniform kind of connection.[1] V.

द्रव्यत्वगुणत्वप्रतिषेधो भावेन व्याख्यातः ।। 27 ।।

Aph. 27. The negation of the essence of substance and quality is explained by existence.

It may be urged: Let co-inherence be included in substance, or in quality etc., why should it be assumed to be an additional category ? In reply it is stated that the negation, that is, the non-existence of the essence of substance and quality is explained, that is, is declared by existence or being. As, therefore, existence is void of the essence of

[1] कार्यकारणयोरयवावयविनोर्यतः सम्बन्धात् इहेदमिति प्रत्ययः स समवायः तन्तुषु पटः कपालेषु घटः वीरणेषु कटइत्यादिप्रत्ययोहि पटादौ तन्त्वादिवृत्तित्वं विषयीकरोति तच्च वृत्तित्वं सम्बन्धविशेषनियन्त्रितमेवान्यथा तन्तुषु घट इत्यादिप्रतीतिप्रसङ्गात् कालिकेन तन्त्वादिवृत्तित्वस्य घटादौ सत्त्वात् इत्थञ्च तादृशवृत्तितानियामकः सम्बन्धः समवाय एव अवयवावयविनोः संयोगासम्भवात् कार्यकारणयोरित्युपलक्षणं गुणगुणिनोः क्रियाक्रियावतोर्जातिव्यक्तोर्नित्यद्रव्यविशेषपदार्थयोश्चाधाराधेयभावनियामकोऽपि समवाय एवेति मन्तव्यम्। समवाये प्रमाणन्तु गुणक्रियादिविशिष्ट- बुद्धिर्विशेषणविशेष्यसम्बन्धविषया विशिष्टबुद्धित्वाद्दण्डी पुरुष इति विशिष्टबुद्धिवदित्यनुमानं तत्र च संयोगादि- बाधात् समवायसिद्धिः नच स्वरूपसम्बन्धेनार्थान्तरमनन्तरस्वरूपाणां सम्बन्धत्वाभ्युपगमे गौरवात् नचैवमभावस्याप्यनया रीत्या सम्बन्धान्तरं सिद्ध्येदिति वाच्यं यतोऽभाव-सम्बन्धस्य न नित्यत्वसम्भवस्तथा सति भूतले घटानयनानन्तरमपि घटाभावबुद्धिप्रसङ्गात् घटाभावस्य तत्सम्बन्धस्य च नित्यत्वात् नाप्यभावस्य सम्बन्धान्तरमनित्यमङ्गीकर्तुं शक्यते एकस्मिन्नेव भूतले सहस्रधा घटानयनापसारणादौ सम्बन्धसहस्रकल्पनापत्तेस्तस्माद्घटापसरणकालीनभूतलादिस्वरूप एव घटभाव-सम्बन्धः स्वीकारणीयः घटकालस्य सम्बन्धाघटकतया घटकाले न घटात्यन्ताभावप्रतीतिः इत्थञ्च भूतलादौ घटाद्यभावस्य स्वरूप सम्बन्धस्वीकारस्यावश्यकत्वेनाभावान्तरस्थलेऽपि स्वरूपस्यैव सम्बन्धत्वमभावप्रत्यया-नामेकविधसम्बन्धावगाहित्वस्यानुभवसिद्धत्वादिति ।।

substance and of quality as being the object of a differently characterised cognition; so also co-inherent, as being the object of a differently characterised cognition, does not possess the character of substance, etc. There is here an indication, the negation of the essence of action etc. requiring to be understood.[1] V.

तत्त्वं भावेन ।। 28 ।।

Aph. 28. Its reality [is explained] by existence.

The words is explained are to be supplied. Its reality, that is its unity, is explained by existence, that is by being. For as it is one existence that in all cases excites the cognition of the existent, so is there one co-inherence that in all cases excites the cognition of the co-inherent, inasmuch as there is no difference in the marks or characters by which its existence is inferred, and there is non-existence of a particular mark. For we reckon no particular mark or differentiating character, by which we should apprehend variety of co-inherences. Hence it is eternal, inasmuch as non-eternity is inapplicable to that which is indivisible, though there be a division according to space, time etc., as is the case with existence. It may be objected that if this co-inherence be merely a conjunction, there may be disjunction of threads and cloth or of the cloth and its colour. This is not the case, since in the absence of previous unconjoinedness disunion is impossible, for colour and the object coloured, or the parts and the whole do not exist out of mutual connection, that there should be a disunion between them. If it be replied that such unconjoinedness is possible; we deny this, for its possibility is absured inasmuch as it has never been experienced.[2] U.

[1] ननु समवायो द्रव्ये गुणादिषु वाऽन्तर्भवतु किन्तस्यातिरिक्तपदार्थत्वकल्पनेनेत्यत आह। भावेन सत्तया द्रव्यत्वगुणत्वप्रतिषेधो द्रव्यत्वगुणत्वाभावो व्याख्यातः उक्तः तथाच सत्ता यथा द्रव्यत्वगुणत्वशून्या विलक्षणबुद्धिविषयत्वात् समवायोऽपि विलक्षणबुद्धिविषयत्वान्न द्रव्यत्वादिमानित्यर्थः इदमुपलक्षणं कर्मत्वादिप्रतिषेधोऽपि ज्ञेयः।।

[2] व्याख्यातमितिशेषः तत्त्वमेकत्वं भावेन सत्तया व्याख्यातम् यथैका सत्ता सर्वत्र सद्बुद्धिप्रवर्तिका तथैक एव समवायः सर्वत्र समवेतबुद्धिप्रवर्तकः स्वलिङ्गाविशेषाद्विशेषलिङ्गाभावाच्च नहि समवायस्य विशेष लिङ्गं भेदकं लिङ्गमाकलयामो येन नानात्वमभ्युपगच्छामः अतएव नित्यकालादिभेदेऽप्यभिन्नस्य सत्तावदेवानित्यत्वायोगात् ननु समवायो यद्ययं सम्बन्ध एव तदा तन्तुपटयोः पटरूपयोर्वा विश्लेषः स्यादिति चेन्न युतसिद्धभावाद्विश्लेषानुपपत्तेः नहि रूपरूपवतोरवयवावयविनोर्वाऽसम्बद्धयोर्विद्यमानत्वमस्ति येन विश्लेषः स्यात् युतसिद्धिरेवापाद्यत इति चेन्न कदाचिदपि तथाऽननुभवेनापाद्यबाधात्।

Book VIII

FIRST DAILY LESSON

द्रव्येषु ज्ञानं व्याख्यतम्।। 1।।

Aph. 1. Cognition was explained among substances.

The foregoing digression was intended to gratify the curiosity of the learner. The order of enunciation is again embraced. According to this the examination of intellection is the object of the eight book. Intellection has been previously described. The present aphorism is stated with the purpose of recalling this. By the words Among substances, through the object, the third book which treats of that object, i.e. of substances, is implied. The meaning is that cognition has been explained by the two aphorisms The universal notion of organs and their objects is a mark of an entity other than organs and objects, and , That which is brought into being from contiguity of soul, organ, and object, is other than they. In the common declaration of intellection that intellection, apprehension, cognition, and affection, are synonyms, the equivalent terms are enumerated in order to contravene the Sāṅkhya doctrine. For the Sāṅkhyas maintain a distinction of meaning in the terms intelligence, etc. Thus the plastic principle is a state of equipoise between purity, passion, and darkness. This is one, and one only, while spirits are divided to infinity. These spirits are uniform, constant, unchangeable, characterised by eternal consciousness. These moreover are lame, being incapable of modification, while the plastic principle is blind, being unsentient. When there arises in the plastic principle a desire of the fruition of sense-objects, or the wish to see the difference between the plastic principle and spirit, the plastic principle is modified in virtue of throwing as it were a tint of colour upon spirit. The first modification of the plastic principle is intellection, a kind of internal sense. Intellection it is that is the great principle, wherefore it has been said,

From the plastic principle the great. This intelligence is like a clear mirror, and the particular modification in the form of an object such as a water-pot, a piece of cloth etc., by the channel of the external organs of intelligence, is called the cognition, the function of intelligence. Apprehension is according to them that particular conceit, whereby, in consequence of the non-discrimination of spirit or consciousness by reason of the cognition existing in pure intelligence, it is affirmed I know. Affection is the particular modification of intelligence, in the form of pleasure, pain etc., by the channel of the sense-organs, in consequence of the presence of objects of sense such as garlands, sandal wood, and the like. Hence it is that all the particular modifications of intelligence, cognition, pleasure, pain, desire, aversion, volition, reminiscence, merit, and demerit existing only in the plastic principle in their minute proportions, according to diversity of conditions, appear and disappear; while spirit,like a lotus-leaf free from stain, reflects them externally in intelligence. This doctrine which they hold, is rejected by the evidence indicated in the enumeration of the convertible terms. If, then, the word intelligence be derived from agency, inasmuch as it is the instrument of understanding, it may be concluded that it is identical with the internal sense, and the internal sense is not perceptible. But intelligence is known by the internal perception I understand. Moreover the qualities cognition etc., do not belong to the internal organ, for they are proved to exist only as being qualities of an agent. For the phenomena of personal knowledge, personal sensation, personal apprehension, are manifested only as having personality or egoity as their common substratum. If they reply that this phenomenon is conceit, we rejoin that there is nothing to prove the impossibility of the reality. If they say that spirit is unsusceptible of adventitious modes, and unmodified, and that this shews the impossibility of their reality; we deny this, eternity being compatible with the nature of a substratum of adventitious modes. For substance and attribute are not one single principle, that production and destruction of the attribute should be production and destruction of the subject. He then who is conscious, understands, knows, apprehends, and conceits. The hypothesis, therefore, of a distinct entity is not allowable.[1] U.

[1] शिष्यजिज्ञासानुरोधात् क्रमलङ्घनमिदानीमुद्देशक्रममालम्बते तत्र बुद्धिपरीक्षा अष्टमाध्यायार्थः आत्म-साधनाय पूर्वं बुद्धिरुक्ता तां स्मारयन्नाह। द्रव्येष्यिति विषयेण विषयिणं तृतीयाध्यायमुपलक्षयति। इन्द्रियार्थप्रसिद्धिरिन्द्रियार्थेभ्योऽर्थान्तरस्य हेतुः आत्मेन्द्रियार्थसन्निकर्षाद्यन्निष्पद्यते तदन्यत् इत्येताभ्यां सूत्राभ्यां ज्ञानं व्याख्यातमित्यर्थः। तत्र बुद्धिरुपलब्धिर्ज्ञानं प्रत्ययइति पर्यायाः इति समानतन्त्रे बुद्धिलक्षणे साङ्ख्यमतनिरासार्थं

तत्रात्मा मनश्चाप्रत्यक्षे ।। 2 ।।

Aph. 2. Therein soul and the internal sense are imperceptible.

This cognition moreover is twofold—science and nescience. Science is of four kinds, viz., perception, inference, memory and testimony. Nescience likewise is of four kinds, viz. doubt, uncertainty, sleep, and inattention. Of these kinds of science, that which is inferential is not produced by the sense-organs. Why this is so, is stated in the text. The soul is here either the soul of another or one's own. The imperceptibility of one's own soul has been already declared, inasmuch as such occasional personal cognitions as that of one's own paleness, attenuation, length of arm etc. have been rejected in relation to the soul. The particle and implies the applicability of the predicate to ether, time, space, air, and atoms. Sensible knowledge is of two degrees, omniscient, and non-omniscient. Omniscient is the knowledge of such and such complements of objects, by presentation determined by the merit springing from devotion. Thus atoms fall within its sphere, as demonstrable, nameable, and existent. If it be objected:—Since there is no apparatus of such unbounded sense—knowledge, how can this be the case ? and whereas magnitude is the cause of perception, and atoms possess no magnitude; and whereas possession of colour is the cause of common perception, and space etc. have no colour;—how can this be so? We reply that this objection is

पर्यायाभिधानम्। साङ्ख्याहि बुद्ध्यादिशब्दानामर्थभेदमाचक्षते तथाहि सत्त्वरजस्तमसां साम्यावस्था प्रकृतिः सा चैकैव गुरुषास्तुपरं भिद्यन्ते तेच कूटस्था नित्या अपरिमाणामिनो नित्यचैतन्यस्वभावाः तेच पङ्गवोऽपरिणामित्वात् प्रकृतिस्त्वन्धा जडत्वात् यदा विषयभोगेच्छा प्रकृतिपुरुषभेददिदृक्षा च प्रकृतेर्भवति तदा सा पुरुषोपरागवशात् परिणामते तस्याश्चाद्यः परिणामोबुद्धिरन्तःकरणविशेषः बुद्धिरेव महत्तत्त्वं तदुक्तम् प्रकृतेर्महान् इति साच बुद्धिदर्पणव न्नर्मला तस्याश्च बहिरिन्द्रियप्रणाडिकया विषयाकारो यः परिणतिभेदो घट इति पट इत्याद्याकारस्तज्ज्ञानं वृत्तिरिति चाख्यायते स्वच्छायां बुद्धौ वर्तमानेन ज्ञानेन चैतन्यस्य पुरुषस्य भेदाग्रहादहं जानामीति योऽभिमानविशेषः सैवोपलब्धिः स्त्रक्‌चन्दनादिविषयसन्निकर्षादिन्द्रियप्रणाडिकयैव सुखदुःखाद्याकारो बुद्धेरेव यः परिणामविशेषः स प्रत्ययः अतएव ज्ञानसुखदुःखेच्छाद्वेषप्रयत्नसंस्कारधर्म्मा-धमाः सर्व एव बुद्धेः परिणामविशेषः सूक्ष्ममात्रया प्रकृतावेव वर्तमाना अवस्थाभेदादाविर्भवन्ति तिरोभवन्ति च पुरुषस्तु पुष्करपलाशवन्निर्लेपः प्रतिबिम्बते परं बुद्धाविति यन्मन्यन्ते तदनेन पर्ययाभिधानसूचितप्रमाणेन निराक्रियते तथाहि बुद्धिशब्दो यदि बुध्यतेऽनयेति करणव्युत्पन्नस्तदा मन एव तत्पर्यवस्यति नच मन प्रत्यक्षम् बुद्धिस्त्वहबुध्ये इति प्रत्यक्षवेद्यैव नचान्तःकरणस्य ज्ञानादयोधर्माः कर्तृधर्मत्वेनैव तेषां सिद्धेः भवति हि अहं जाने अहं प्रत्येमि अहमुप्रलभे इत्यहन्त्वसामानाधिकरण्येन प्रतिभासः अभिमानोऽसाविति चेत् तात्त्विकत्वे बाधकाभावात् पुरुषस्यागन्तुकधर्मानाधारत्वं कूटस्थत्वं तदेव बाधकमिति चैन्नागन्तुकधर्माधारत्वेऽपि नित्यत्वसम्भवात् नहि धर्माधर्मश्चेत्येकं तत्त्वं येन धर्मोत्पादविनाशावेव धर्मोत्पादविनाशौ स्यातां तथाच एव चेतयते स एव बुध्यते ज्ञानात्युपलभते प्रत्येति चेति नार्थान्तरकल्पना युक्तेतिदिक्।।

invalid, this omniscience being possible by means of the internal sense auxiliary to the merit produced by devotion; or by means of the eye etc. in consequence of the acquisition thereof; for the merit engendered by devotion being of inconceivable efficacy, requires no other auxiliary. The man in question is not omniscient, being a man like myself:—this and similar propositions are not to the point, there being no argument which would render contrary instances impossible, as is the case with the proposition A follower of Prabhākara is not designated a Mimāṁsaka being a man like myself etc. Non-omniscient presentation is of two kinds, discriminative and non-discriminative. Kīrti-diṅnāga and others maintain that discriminative cognition conveys no evidence, for it is manifested as apparent through connection with names. But there can be no connection of the meaning with the designation or name, that a cognition should be coloured, as it were, by the name water-pot or piece of cloth. Moreover the universal or essential etc., is not really existent, that the being characterised by it should be apprehended in objects by the sense-organ; and the self-characterised existent can have no-connection with the non-existent; and the non-existent is no object of sense. Sight therefore is produced by the organs of sense, and the discriminative cognition (which recognises the class of its object) while in process of being produced by magnitude of vision, is said to be perceptible, and to convey assurance. This is impossible ; the phenomenon must be cognisable by connection with its designation, and the condition that evidence be produced by contiguity of organ and object is doubtful. The being characterised by a name is a possible object of (acquired) visual perception, being possible in the same manner as such a presented cognition as that of cool sandalwood. Or it may be maintained that the being characterised by a term does not appear in perceptive knowledge, and that there is only recollection of the name, the distinctive appellation being recalled only, in like manner as there is recollection of the absent object in the cognition of non-existence. Also it may be maintained the universal etc. has a real existence, and that there is therefore a discriminative perception produced by apposition of object and organ. It may be objected:—Non-discriminative cognition neither excites to activity, nor is an object of activity? what proof therefore is there that exists ? We reply that its proof is found in discriminative cognition, for this is a determinate cognition, and this is not produced without a knowledge of predicates, for it is observed that knowledge of the predicates, apposition to the modified sense-organ, and the non-apprehension of non-connection of such knowledge and such apposition, is the cause of determinate cognition.[1] U.

ज्ञाननिर्देशे ज्ञाननिष्पत्तिविधिरुक्तः।। 3।।

Aph. 3. The mode in which cognition is originated has been stated in the enunciation of cognition.

The mode in which cognition is originated, that is the process by which knowledge is produced, has been explained in the enunciation of cognition, that is, in the third book, where the statement of knowledge was made. The causes of knowledge were stated in the aphorism, That which is produced by contiguity of soul, sense-organ, and object, is other than those. The soul, then, is the co-inherent or material cause of cognition; conjunction of the soul and the internal sense, is the non-coinherent cause; apposition of the object is the occasional or efficient cause. This was declared in that aphorism. It is, therefore, to be understood that the causality of contacts in relation to

[1] तच्च ज्ञानं द्विविधं विद्या चाविद्या च विद्या चतुर्विधा प्रत्यक्षलैङ्गिकस्मृत्यार्पलक्षणा अविद्याऽपि चतुर्विधा संशयविपर्ययस्वमानध्यवसायलक्षणा तत्र यल्लैङ्गिक तदनिन्द्रियजम् कुत एतदित्याह। आत्माऽत्र परात्मा स्वात्मा वा स्वात्मनि मानसस्य क्वाचित्काहम्प्रत्यस्याहं गौरः कृशो महाबाहुरित्यादिप्रत्ययतिरग्कतत्वात् स्वात्मनोऽप्यप्रत्यक्षतोक्ता चकारादाकाशकालदिशां वायोः परमाणूनाच्च द्रव्याणामुपग्रहः। इन्द्रियजमपि द्विविधं सर्वज्ञीयमसर्वज्ञीयञ्च सर्वज्ञीयं योगजधर्मलक्षणया प्रत्यासत्त्या तत्तत्पदार्थसार्थज्ञानं तथाहि परमाणवः प्रसक्ताः प्रमेयत्वादभिधेयत्वात् सत्त्वात् सामग्रीविरहात् कथमेवं महत्त्वस्यापि प्रत्यक्षं प्रति कारणत्वात् नच परमाणवो महान्तः रूपवत्त्वस्यापि चाक्षुषप्रत्यक्षकारणत्वात् नच दिगादयोरूपवन्त इति चेन्न योगजधर्मसहकारिणां मनसैव तत्सम्भवात् तदुपग्रहाच्चक्षुरादिना वा अचिन्त्यप्रभावोहि योगजोधर्मौ न सहकार्यन्तरमपेक्षते। विवादाध्यासितः पुरुषो न सर्वज्ञः पुरुषत्वादहमिवेत्यादि तु प्राभाकरो न मीमांसाभिज्ञः पुरुषत्वादहमिवेत्यादिवद्विपक्षबाधकतर्कशून्यत्वादप्रयोजकम् असर्वज्ञीयञ्च प्रत्यक्षं द्विविधं सविकल्पकं निर्विकल्पकञ्च सविकल्पकं ज्ञानं न प्रमाणमि त कीर्तिदिङ्नादयः तथाहि अभिलापसंसर्गयोग्यप्रतिभासं हि तत् नह्यभिलापेन नाम्ना सम्भवत्यर्थस्य सम्बन्धो येन घट इति पट इति वा नामानुरञ्जितः प्रत्ययः स्यात् नच जात्यादि परमार्थसत् येन तद्वैशिष्ट्यं विषयेषु इन्द्रियेण गृह्येत नच सतः स्वलक्षणस्यासता सम्बन्धः सम्भति नचासत् इन्द्रियगोचरः तस्मादिन्द्रियेणालोचनं जन्यते आलोचनमहिम्नाच सविकल्पकमुत्पद्यमानं तत्रार्थे प्रवर्तयत् प्रत्यक्षमिति प्रमाणमिति चोद्यते इति तच्चैतदनुपपन्नमभिलापसंसर्गयोग्यप्रतिभासञ्च भवेत् प्रमाणञ्चेन्द्रियोर्थसन्निकर्षजन्यं स्यादिति सन्दिग्ध व्यतिरेकित्वं नामवैशिष्ट्यञ्च चाक्षुषज्ञाने सम्भवत्येव सुरभिचन्दनमितिवदुपनीतभानसम्भवात् यद्वा संज्ञावैशिष्ट्यप्रत्यक्षज्ञाने न भासते संज्ञायाः स्मरणमात्रम् स्मृतैव स्मर्थव्यावर्तिका अभावज्ञाने प्रतियोगिस्मरणवत् जात्यादिकञ्च वस्तुभूतं साधितम्वेातः सविकल्पकमपीन्द्रियार्थसन्निकर्षजत्वात् प्रत्यक्षम्। ननु निर्विकल्पकं न व्यवहारप्रवर्तकं नवा व्यवहारविषय इति किन्तत्र साधि प्रमाणमिति चेत् सविकल्पकमेव तद्धि विशिष्टज्ञानम् नच विशेषणज्ञानमन्तरेण तदुत्पद्यते विशिष्टज्ञाने हि विशेषणज्ञानविशेष्येन्द्रियन्निकर्षतदुभयासंसर्गाग्रहस्य कारणत्वावधारणात्।।

perception has already been laid down.[1] V.

गुणकर्मसु सन्निकृष्टेषु ज्ञाननिष्पत्तेर्द्रव्यं कारणम्।। 4।।

Aph. 4. Qualities and actions being brought into contact (with the organs of sense), substance is the cause of production of cognition.

Substance is the cause of the cognition which is produced of qualities, as colour etc., and of actions, as upheaving, etc. These are both apprehended only as situate in present substance; the presence, therefore, of the substance is a requisite of cognition. It is by substance, moreover, that their contact is constituted, they being apprehended as conjunctly co-inherent. Although there is apprehended the odour of dispersed particles of the champaka-flower, and of portions of camphor which are imperceptible, yet it is substance, imperceptible though it be, which effects their contact. Although perceptibility of substance is not a requisite of the apprehension of sound, yet sound is only apprehended as inherent in substance, and this is the requisite. If it be asked, Why assume a contact which is invisible? we reply that the production of knowledge, being an effect, necessitates the hypothesis of a cause.[2] U.

सामान्यविशेषेषु सामान्यविशेषाभांवात्तत एव ज्ञानम्।। 5।।

Aph. 5. Inasmuch as in universals and particulars there exist not universals and particulars, cognition of general and special essences results thence [from contact effected by substance].

Another mode is stated in which cognition originates. The universal is existence, the particulars or species, are the essences of substance, quality, and action. Similarly these being also universals or subaltern

[1] ज्ञाननिर्देशे तृतीयाध्याये यत्र ज्ञानस्य निर्देशः कृतस्तत्रैव तन्निष्पत्तिविधिस्तदुत्पत्तिविधानं उक्तः आत्मेन्द्रियार्थसन्निकर्षाद्यन्निष्पद्यते तदन्यत् इति सूत्रे ज्ञानस्य कारणान्युक्तानीत्यर्थः तथाचात्मा ज्ञानस्य समवायिकारणम् आत्ममनःसंयोगोऽसमवायिकारणम् विषयसन्निर्षो निमित्तकारणमिति तस्मिन् सूत्र एवोक्तामिति प्रत्यक्षमधिकृत्य सन्निकर्षस्य हेतुता कथितेति वेदितव्यम्।।

[2] गुणेषु रूपादिषु कर्मसु चोत्क्षेपणादिषु यज्ज्ञानं निष्पद्यते तत्र द्रव्यं कारणं योग्यद्रव्यनिष्टमेव तदुभयं गृह्यत इति द्रव्ययोग्यतैव तत्र तन्त्रम् सन्निकर्षश्च तेषां द्रव्यघटित एव संयुक्तसमवायेन तेषां ग्रहणात् यद्यपि विषक्तचम्पकावयवकर्पूरभागानामयोग्यनां गन्धो गृह्यते तथापि सन्निकर्षघटकं तत्रायोग्यमपि द्रव्यमेव यद्यपि शब्दगृहे द्रव्ययोग्यता न तन्त्रं तत्रापि तत्रैव समवेतः शब्दो गृह्यत इति तदेव तन्त्रम् नन्वदृष्टसन्निकर्षकल्पना कुतः क्रियते इति चेन्न ज्ञाननिपत्तेः कार्येण हि कारणमवश्यं कल्पनीयमिति भावः।।

genera, their particulars or species are the essences of earth etc., of colour etc., and of upheaving etc. Of these essences residing in substances, there results perception common to all the senses, thence, that is, from the particular perceptible substratum, from their cause, form conjunct co-inherence, from co-inherence in the conjunctly co-inherent, and from co-inherence in the co-inherent. Knowledge common to all the senses, of the essence of qualities, arises from co-inherence in the conjunctly co-inherent; of the essence of sound, and of *ka* and other particular sounds, from co-inherence in the co-inherent; of existence, from conjunct co-inherence, from co-inherence in the conjunctly co-inherent, and from conjunct co-inherence in the co-inherent. Conjunct co-inherence and co-inherence are not presentative of the essence of quality. It may, therefore, be urged that the knowledge of it is impossible through contact with its substratum, since in the universal or highets-essence, existence and in the particulars or subaltern genera, the essence of substance, quality, and action, and in the essences of earth etc., there are universals and particulars. In anticipation of this objection the words Inasmuch as there exist not therein universals and particulars, have been added. For there exist not in universals and particulars other universals and particulars essences that is of the essence of objects; for thus there would result a regression to infinity. The appearence of mutual difference between these essences proceeds from their proper form, or from difference of essential attributes existing, for instance, in all cows, there being non-existence of such attributes in objects other than cows; and similarly with the essence of water-pots and other objects.[1] U.

[1] अपरं ज्ञाननिष्पत्तिविधिमाह। मामान्यं सत्ता तस्य विशेषा द्रव्यत्वगुणत्वकर्मत्वानि एवमेतेषामपि सामान्यानि विशेषाः पृथिवीत्वादिरूपत्वाद्युत्क्षेपणत्वादीनि तत्र द्रव्यगतानां सामान्यानां तत एव योग्याश्रयविशेषादेव तन्नि-बन्धनाच्च संयुक्तसमवायात् संयुक्तसमवेतसमवायात्समवेतसमवान्याच्च सार्वेन्द्रियं ज्ञानं गुणत्वे च संयुक्तसमवेतसमवायात् शब्दत्वकत्वादौ समवेतसमवायात् सत्तायाः संयुक्तसमवायात् संयुक्तसमवेतसमवायात् समवेतसमवायाच्च सार्वेन्द्रियं ज्ञानम् गुणत्वे च संयुक्तसमवायसमवायश्च न प्रत्यामत्तिरिति ननु तत एव स्वाश्रयसन्निकर्षादेवेत्यवधारणानुपपत्तिः यतः सामान्ये विशेषेषु च पृथिवीत्वादिषु सामान्याविशेषान्तरमस्त्येव तत्सन्निकर्षोऽपि कारणमेवात आह। सामान्यविशेषाभावादिति नहि सामान्यविशेषेषु सामान्यविशेषा वर्तन्ते अनवस्थाप्रसङ्गात् तेषां परस्परभेदप्रतीतिः स्वरूपत एव गवेतरावृत्तित्वे सति सकलगोवृत्तित्वलक्षणोपारंधिरभेदाद्वा एवं घटत्वादावपीति।।

सामान्यविशेषापेक्षं द्रव्यगुणकर्मसु।। 6।।

*Aph.*6. [Cognition] of substances, qualities, and actions supposes the universal and particular.

It may be asked whether the cognition of substances, qualities and actions is also absolute, in the same manner as the knowledge of universals and particulars is absolute, inasmuch as there exist not in them universality and particularity. It is stated that it is not. Cognition is produced:—these words are to be supplied. Of substances, and actions there is an apprehension determined by the natures of substances, qustances, qualities, and actions. Now, a determinate cognition is produced by contact of subject, attribute, and sense-organ; the universal and particular are therefore necessarily supposed in it. For there exists such determinate cognition as This is a substance, This is a quality, This is an action.[1] U.

द्रव्ये द्रव्यगुणकर्मापेक्षम्।। 7।।

Aph. 7. [Cognition] of substance supposes substance, quality and action.

In the cognition, The white cow with bells is walking, the bell a substance is an attribution, white is a quality, is walking is an action. There is, therefore, no determinate cognition without a determination apprehended; nor can such exist without connection with a determination. Substances, qualities and actions, are therefore supposed in the cognition of the substance.[2] U.

गुणकर्मसु गुणकर्माभावाद्गुणकर्मापेक्षं न विद्यते।। 8।।

Aph. 8. Inasmuch as there exist no qualities and actions in qualities and actions, there is no cognition thereof which supposes

[1] ननु सामान्यविशेषेषु सामान्यविशेषाभावाद्याथा तन्निरपेक्षमेव ज्ञानं तथा द्रव्यगुणकर्मस्वपि किं तन्निरपेक्षमेव नेत्याह। ज्ञानमुत्पद्यते इति प्रकृतम् द्रव्यगुणकर्मसु द्रव्यत्वगुणत्वकर्मत्वविशिष्टबुद्धिस्तावदस्ति विशिष्टज्ञानञ्च विशेष्यविशेषणेन्द्रियसन्निकर्षादुत्पद्यते इति सामान्यविशेषापेक्षा तत्रावश्यकी भवति हि द्रव्यमिदं गुणोऽयं कर्मेदमिति विशिष्टज्ञानमिति भावः।।

[2] ज्ञानमुत्पद्यते इति प्रकृतं घण्टावान् शुक्लोगौर्गच्छतीति ज्ञानम् तत्र द्रव्यं घण्टा विशेषणम् शुक्ल इति गुणः गच्छतीति कर्म तथाच नागृहीतविशेषणाविशिष्टप्रतीतिर्न वा विशेषणसम्बन्धमन्तरेणेति भवति द्रव्यज्ञाने द्रव्यगुणकर्मापेक्षेति भावः।।

qualities and actions.

The aphorism is given in reply to the question: Why therefore do not quality and actions suppose quality and action? There is an ellipsis of the word cognition. Inasmuch as of quality there is no conception determined by quality, and of action no conception determined by action, there is no conception thereof which supposes qualities and actions. For quality does not exist in quality, or action in action, that it should appear therein as a predicate or determination.[1] U.

समवायिनः श्वैत्याच्छ्वैत्यबुद्धेश्च श्वेते बुद्धिस्ते एते कार्यकारणभूते।। 9।।

Aph. 9. The cognition of a white object results from the whiteness of the substratum, and from the cognition of whiteness; and these same stand in a relation of cause and effect.

From the whiteness or white colour of the substratum, and from the cognition of whiteness or the cognition of an attribute consisting of white colour, there results in relation to a white object, a conch-shell etc. possessed of white colour, a cognition that it is white, that is, a sense-given certainty determined by white colour. The possession, therefore, of white colour, and the cognition of white colour are the causes of an effect, viz., of sense-given certainty the form of which is white colour. The relation, then, of co-inherence affords no conditions of sense-given assurance in the form of white colour, viz., possession of white colour, and cognition of white colour. There is, therefore, in consequence of the absence from qualities and actions of qualities and actions as determinations, no perceptive assurance in the form of qualities and actions.[2] V.

[1] तत किं गुणकर्मणोरपि गुणकर्मापेक्षा नेत्याह। ज्ञानमितिशेषः। गुणे गुणविशिष्टबुद्धेः कर्मसु कर्मविशिष्टबुद्धेरभावात् गुणकर्मापेक्षा न तद्गतबुद्धिः नहि गुणेषु गुणो नवा कर्मसु कर्म येन तत्र विशेषणत्वेन भासेतेति भावः।।

[2] समवायिन इत्यभिधानात् सम्बन्धस्य कारणतामाह। तथाच गुणे गुणसमवायाभावात् कर्मसु कर्मसमवायाभावाच्च न तत्तज्ज्ञाने गुणकर्मापेक्षा विशेषणत्वेन विशेष्यत्वेन त्वस्त्येव एवञ्च श्वेतः शङ्ख इत्यादिप्रतीतौ श्वैत्यगुणस्य श्वैत्यविशेषणज्ञानस्य च कारणत्वमित्युक्तं तथाच विशेषणसम्बन्धविशेषणतज्ज्ञानानां विशिष्टप्रत्यक्षप्रमां प्रति कारणत्वमिति तेन पूर्वोक्तं सर्वं सिद्ध्यति।।

द्रव्येष्वनितरेतरकारणाः।। 10।।

Aph. 10. [Cognitions] of substances are not causes one of the other.

It might be urged that in cases where after the perception, This is a water-pot, there arises the perception, This is a piece of cloth, the knowledge of the water-pot is a cause of the knowledge of the piece of cloth, inasmuch as it is antecedent to it, and that consequently there could be no knowledge of the piece of cloth without a knowledge of the water-pot. This collateral objection is denied. Cognitions—for this word is to be supplied—are not the causes one of the other, that is, the mutual causes, in the case of cognitions of substances not determinant of substances fixed in the relation of prior and posterior among substances. Though, therefore, the knowledge of the water-pot be antecedent to the knowledge of the piece of cloth, it is not its cause, inasmuch as it is not its invariable antecedent.[1] V.

कारणोयौपद्यात् कारणक्रमाच्च घटपटादिबुद्धीनां क्रमो न हेतुफलभावात्।। 11।।

Aph. 11. The sequence of the cognitions of the water-pot, piece of cloth etc., resulting from non-simultaneity of the causes [of the cognitions], and from the sequence of their causes, does not result from a relation of cause and effect.

The sequence, constituted by priority and posteriority, of the cognitions of the water-pot, piece of cloth etc., does not result from the relation of reason and consequent, or of cause and effect, but from the sequence, that is from the priority and posteriority, of the contacts etc. of the water-pot, piece of cloth etc., which are the causes of such cognitions. The particle and implies the addition of an unmentioned non-simultaneity, and this word is to be construed after the term

[1] समवायिनः श्वैत्यसमवायिनः श्वैत्यात् शुक्लरूपात् श्वैत्यबुद्धेः शुक्लरूपात्मकविशेषणबुद्धेश्च श्वेते शुक्लरूपवति शङ्खादौ बुद्धिः शुक्लोः ऽयमिति शुक्लरूपविशेषणिका प्रत्यक्षप्रमितिर्भवति अतस्ते शुक्लरूपवत्त्वशुक्लरूपबुद्धी कार्यस्य शुक्लरूपप्रकारकप्रत्यक्षप्रमात्मकस्य कारणभूते इत्यर्थः तथाच समवायसम्बन्धेन शुक्लरूपपप्रकारकप्रत्यक्षप्रमां प्रति शुक्लरूपवत्त्वं शुक्लरूपज्ञानञ्च द्वयमेव तन्त्रमिति गुणकर्मसु गुणकर्मरूपविशेषणविरहान्न तत्प्रकारज्ञप्रत्यक्षप्रमितिरिति भावः।।

sequence. The meaning is, therefore, that the non-simultaneity of the cognitions of the water-pot, piece of cloth etc., results from the non-simultaneity of the contacts etc. with these that are the causes of those cognitions. But where there is a simultaneity of contacts etc., of water-pots, pieces of cloth etc., there is produced simultaneously a cognition which is a support or basis of an aggregate, and which has for its objects the things in contact so many as they may be. It is, therefore, to be understood that there results from simultaneity of cause simultaneity of effect, and from non-sequence of cause non-sequence of effect. Intelligence is primarily divided into experience, and memory. Experience, according to the doctrine of Kaṇda is of two kinds, being divided into perception and inference. Perception is of six kinds, as derived from smelling etc., [from the five external, and from the internal sense]; and is twofold as discriminative and non-discriminative; and twofold as divided into physical and hyperphysical. Inference is threefold, as produced by illation from only positive conditions, from only negative conditions, and from both positive and negative conditions. For example: This is a proposition inasmuch as it is knowable etc., is an illation from only positive conditions; Earth differs from other substances inasmuch as it is possessed of odours, etc., is an illation from only negative conditions; The mountain is fiery inasmuch as it smokes etc., is an illation from both positive and negative conditions. Memory is uniform, dependent on the reproduction called permanent mental impression, the universal from whereof is dependent on assurance not characterised by inattention. In another point of view also intelligence is twofold, science, and nescience. Science is a cognition in a certain form of that which has that form. Nescience is a cognition in a certain form of that in which there is non-existence of that form. Intelligence is also twofold, accordingly as it is divided into certainty and uncertainty. Uncertainty is a cognition whereof the form is mutually repugnant existence and non-existence in one and the same subject of attributes; certainty in regard to a thing is cognition in the form thereof, and not in the form of the non-existence thereof. According to this doctrine in the case of cognition of similarity. and in that of knowledge of terms, an inference takes place by the production of a judgment respecting a mark or middle term, subsequently thereto. Evidence is of two kinds, perception and inference, and accordingly science is correct experience, as will be explained by the author of the aphorisms himself in the sequel.[1] V.

[1] घटपटादिबुद्धीनां क्रमः पौर्वापर्यरूपः न हेतुफलभावात् न कार्यकारणभावात् किन्तु तादृशबुद्धिकारणानां घटपटादिसन्निकर्षादीनां क्रमात् पौर्वापर्यात् चकारोऽनुक्रमयौगपद्यं समुच्चिनोति अयञ्चकारः क्रम इत्यनन्तरं योजनीयः एवञ्च घटपटादिबुद्धीनामयौगपद्यं तत्कारणानां सन्निकर्षादीनामयौगपद्यादित्यर्थः यत्र तु घटपटसन्निकर्षादीनामस्ति यौगपद्यम् तत्र युगपदेव सन्निकृष्टयावत्पदार्थविषयिणी समूहालम्बनात्मिका बुद्धिरूत्पद्यते इति कारणयौगपद्यात् कार्ययौगपद्यं कारणाक्रमात् कार्याक्रमश्चेत्यपि बोद्धव्यम्। बुद्धिः प्रथमतो द्विविधा अनुभूतिः स्मृतिश्च अनुभूतिरपि कणादमते द्विविधा प्रत्यक्षानुमितिभेदात् प्रत्यक्षमपि घ्राणजादिभेदेन षड्विधं सविकल्पकनिर्विकल्पकभेदेन च द्विविधं लौकिकालौकिकभेदेन द्विविधञ्च अनुमितिरपि केवलान्वयिकेवलव्यतिरेक्यन्वयव्यतिरेकिरूपत्रिविधानुमानजन्यत्वात् त्रिविधा तत्रेदं वा ज्ञेयत्वादित्यादिकं केवलान्वय्यनुमानम् पृथिवीतरेभ्यो भिद्यते गन्धवत्त्वादित्यादिकं केवलव्यतिरेक्यनुमानम् अन्वयव्यतिरेक्यनुमानन्तु पर्वतो वह्निमान धूमादित्यादिकमिति। स्मृतिश्चोपेक्षानात्मकनिश्चयाधीनसमानाकारकाभावनाख्यसंस्काराधीना एकविधैव प्रकारान्तरेणापि बुद्धिर्द्विविधा प्रमाऽप्रमाचेति तद्वति तत्प्रकारिका बुद्धिस्तत्प्रमा तदभाववति तत्प्रकारिका बुद्धिस्तदप्रमा संशयनिश्चयभेदेनापि बुद्धिर्द्विविधा तत्रैकधर्मिणि विरुद्धभावाभावप्रकारकज्ञानं संशयः तदभावाप्रकारकं तत्प्रकारकं ज्ञानं तन्निश्चयः एतन्मते तादृश्यज्ञानस्थले पदज्ञानस्थले च तदुत्तरं लिङ्गपरामर्शोत्पत्त्यैवानुमितिर्भवति प्रमाणं द्विविधं प्रत्यक्षमनुमानञ्चेति यथार्थानुभवश्च प्रमा एतच्चाग्रे सूत्रकृदेववक्ष्यतीति संक्षेपः।।

SECOND DAILY LESSON

अयमेष त्वयाकृतं भोजयैनमिति बुद्ध्यपेक्षम्।। 1।।

Aph. 1.This, That, Done by thee, Feed him,—such expressions are relative to cognition.

It is stated that certain cognitions are determinante of other cognitions. The cogniton This is a water-pot, This is a piece of cloth, is relative to cognition, that is determinant of a cognition. This and that being capable of being made objects of perception, cognition in the form of perception, is a determination of such a cognition. The word Thou being capable of being made the object of the speaker's intention, inasmuch as it is the substratum of a self-manifested knowledge, the cognition produced by the expression Done by thee, is determinant of a cognition. In the behest Feed him, also, the cognition produced by the word him, which has the sense of this one, is determinant of a cognition which is a perception.[1] V.

दृष्टेषु भावाददृष्टेष्वभावात्।। 2।।

Aph. 2. Inasmuch as [such expressions] exist in reference to objects seen, and do not exist in reference to objects unseen.

It is shown that this is inductively proved by concomitance and exclusion. When there exists the contiguous object of the cognition This, and the remote object of the cognition That; when there exists the contiguous agent, the object of the cognition By thee, and the object of the action, the object of the notion, Done; and when there exist the giver and the receives of the order, the objects of the notion Feed, in contiguity; then a cognition of this kind (i. e., one determined by another cognition) is produced. But in the case of unseen objects these cognitions are not manifested. This therefore may be inferred

[1] बुद्धिविशेषणिका अपि कश्चिद्बुद्धयो भवन्तीत्याह। अयमेष इति अयं घटः अयं पट इतिज्ञानं बुद्ध्यपेक्षं बुद्धिविशेषणकम् इदमेतदोः प्रत्यक्षविषये शक्तत्वात् प्रत्यक्षरूपा बुद्धिस्तादृशज्ञाने विशेषणम् युष्मच्छब्दस्य स्वजन्यबोधाश्रयतया वक्तुरभिप्रायविषये शक्तत्वात् त्वयाकृतमितिवाक्यजन्यं ज्ञानं बुद्धिविशेषणकं भोजयैनमिति इदमर्थकेनशब्दजन्यज्ञानमपि प्रत्यक्षात्मकबुद्धिविशेषणकम्।।

by the methods of agreement and disagreement.[1] V.

That these terms are applicable to an object differentiated by a mode constituted by cognition, may be inferred by the methods of agreement and disagreement. These expressions have applicability to an object differentiated by modes constituted by cognition, inasmuch as the use of the words This etc., exists in relation to objects seen, or known, that is essentially determined by modes consisting of cognition; and inasmuch as such use does not exist in relation to objects unseen, or unknown, that is not essentially determined by modes consisting of cognition.[2] V.

अर्थ इति द्रव्यगुणकर्मसु।। 3।।

Aph. 3. The term object applies to substances, qualities and actions.

द्रव्येषु पञ्चात्मकत्वं प्रतिषिद्धम्।। 4।।

The senses and their objects

Aph. 4. Under substances identity with the five elements was denied.

This aphorism is stated as the basis of a treatment of the sense-organs, their nature, and the nature of the objects which they apprehend. Under substances, that is, in the aphorisms describing substances, identity with the five elements, possession of the matter of the five elements, was denied or impugned. No substance, then, whether the body or any other, has the nature of the five elements, but all bodies and organs of sense have the nature of some one or other single element.[3] V.

भूयस्त्वाद्गन्धवत्त्वाच्च पृथिवी गन्धज्ञाने प्रकृतिः।। 5।।

[1] अन्वयव्यतिरेकपरिच्छेद्यमेवैतदित्याह। यदाऽयमितिबुद्धेः सन्निकृष्टो विषयः एष इतिबुद्धेर्विप्रकृष्टोऽपि बुद्ध्यायारूढो विषयः त्वयेतिबुद्धेः सन्निकृष्टः कर्ता विषयः कृतमितिबुद्धेः कर्म विषयः भोजयेतिबुद्धेर्नियोज्यनियोक्तारौ विषयौ एनमितिबुद्धेस्तदुभयव्याप्त्यारोविषयः सन्निकृष्टो भवति तदैतादृशी बुद्धिरुत्पद्यते अदृष्टेषु तु विषयेषु नैता बुद्धयः प्रादुर्भवन्तीन्वयव्यतिरेकगम्यमेवैतदित्यर्थः।।

[2] एतेषां पदानां ज्ञानघटितधर्मावच्छिन्ने शक्तिरन्वयव्यतिरेकगम्येत्याह। दृष्टेषु ज्ञातेषु ज्ञानघटितधर्मावच्छि-न्नेष्वितियावत् भावात् इदमादिशब्दप्रयोगस्य सत्त्वात् अदृष्टेषु अज्ञातेषु ज्ञानघटितधर्मानपरिच्छन्नेष्वितियावत् अभावात् तादृशप्रयोगस्यासत्त्वात् बुद्धिघटितधर्मावच्छिन्न एव तेषां शक्तिरित्यर्थः।।

[3] किमिन्द्रियं किम्प्रकृतिकं किमर्थग्राहकमित्यभिधातुं पीठं रचयति। द्रव्यषु द्रव्यनिरूपणसूत्रेषु पञ्चात्मकत्वं पञ्चभूतप्रकृतिकत्वं प्रतिषिद्धं निराकृतं तथाच शरीरादिकं किञ्चिदपि द्रव्यं न पञ्चभूतप्रकृतिकं किन्त्वेकै-कभूतप्रकृतिकान्येव सर्वाणि शरीराणीन्द्रियाणि चेतिभावः।।

Aph. 5. In the cognition of odour earth is the matter, inasmuch as it possesses plurality and odour.

Accordingly it is stated that the organ of smell apprehends only smell among the qualities, and has the nature of earth only. The cognition of odour means that from which the cognition, or sensation, of smell is derived, that is the organ of smell. Earth the subtile element is the nature or material cause, inasmuch as it has plurality, or is originated by particles not overpowered by water etc., and possesses odour. The olfactory organ is not originated by water etc., inasmuch as it does not apprehend taste etc. Possession of odour exists therein inasmuch as, in its relation as percipient, it apprehends odours. It like manner the organ of smell is terrestrial, inasmuch as it reveals odour only among colour and the other qualities, just as clarified butter, etc. manifests the odour of saffron. By this inference it is established that earth is the material cause of the organ of smell.[1] V.

तथापस्तेजोवायुश्च रसरूपस्पर्शविशेषात्।। 6।।

Aph. 6. In like manner water, light, the air, are [the material causes of the organs of taste, sight, and touch] inasmuch as they have no difference from taste, colour, and touch.

The words Are the material causes of the organs of taste, sight, and touch, are to be supplied. Water etc. are respectively the material causes of the organs of taste etc., inasmuch as they respectively apprehend those determinate objects. In these plurality is the condition of the determination. It has been declared that it is determination by possession of the particular qualities of apprehensible kind that is the proof of the possession of taste etc. by the organs of taste etc. In like manner the organ of hearing is a part of ether essentially determined by the outer ear influenced by particular destiny.[2] U.

[1] एवं घ्राणेन्द्रियं गुणेषु गन्धमात्रग्राहकं पृथिविमात्रप्रकृतिकश्चेत्याह। गन्धस्य ज्ञानं प्रत्यक्षं यस्मात् तद्गन्ध-ज्ञानं घ्राणेन्द्रियं तत्र पृथिवी तन्मात्रं प्रकृतिः समवायिकारणम् भूयस्त्वात् जलाद्यनभिभूतभागारब्धत्वात् गन्धवत्त्वाच्च रसाद्यग्राहकत्वात् घ्राणेन्द्रियं न जलाद्यारब्धम् गन्धवत्त्वञ्चात्र ग्राहकतासम्बन्धेन गन्धग्राहकत्वादिति फलितार्थः तथाच घ्राणेन्द्रियं पार्थिवं रूपादिषु मध्ये गन्धस्यैष व्यञ्जकत्वात् कुङ्कुमगन्धाभिव्यञ्जकतादिवदित्यनुमानेन घ्राणस्य पृथिव्युपादानकत्वं सिध्यतीति भावः।।

[2] रसनचक्षुष्ट्वगिन्द्रियाणां प्रकृतिरितिशेषः तेन यथासंख्यं रसनादीनामबादयः प्रकृतयः तत्तत्प्रतिनियतार्थग्राहकत्वात् अत्रापि नियमे भूयस्त्वमेव तन्त्रम् रसादिमत्त्वे च रसनादीनां ग्राह्यजातीयविशेषगुणवत्त्वनियम एव प्रमाणमित्युक्तम् एवञ्च विशिष्टादृष्टोपगृहीतकर्णशष्कुल्यवच्छिगो नभोदेश एव श्रोत्रम्।।

Book IX

FIRST DAILY LESSON

क्रियागुणव्यपदेशाभावात् प्रागसत्।। 1।।

Aph. 1. [An effect] is antecedently non-existent, inasmuch as there is non-existence of assertion of actions and qualities.

The words an effect are to be supplied. Antecedently, that is, before the production of an effect, an effect or product, such as a water-pot or piece of cloth, is non-existent, that is non-existent by self-determined negation during that time. The reason assigned is the absence of predication of actions and qualities. It the effect, the water-pot etc., were existent during that time, it would be affirmed to possess actions and qualities; as in the case of a water-pot already produced, such affirmations are made as that the water-pot is is at rest, or in motion, or seen to be coloured. There is no such assertion antecedent to its production. It is therefore inferred that it is during that time non-existent. While straws are in course of weaving, or threads of joining, or when clay is placed on the potter's wheel, while the work of the potter etc., is it yet going on, there is a universally experienced sensitive cognition that there will be in that place a mat, or a piece of cloth, or a water-jar, inasmuch as it is producing during the tension of the eyes. Herein a cognition constituted either by conjunction, or by co-inherence, could not be efficient; the presentation is therefore a possession of determinations related to the sense-organs. Such is the condition of such a cognitive act. If it be objected that we are arguing in a circle, inasmuch as the cognition thereof depends or the determination, and the determination on the cognition; we reply that such is not the case, for the determination is the proper form of both the cognition and its object, and is capable of producing a proximate assurance, and this proper form has an existence antecedent to the congnition. It has accordingly been stated in the Nyāya-vārttika that in co-inherence, and in non-existence, there is a relation of cause and effect. This antecedent non-existence produces a non-existent, for when a water-pot has been produced, that self-same water-pot is not then brought into existence, for even if there exist therein another cause, an ensuing defect of the cause must follow the defect of its own anterior non-existence. If this self-same water-pot is what prevents the production of that water-pot, then its causality is inevitable by reason of the non-existence of anything which prevents. It may be urged that if there be in the water-pot non-existence of the same, then it follows that it will emerge when the water-pot is destroyed. This we deny, inasmuch as the very destruction of the water-pot is repugnant thereto. For one of two contradictories cannot be manifested during the existence of the other contradictory. For between these two there is no repugnance effected by space, i.e., no exclusion, that is in the case of the real natures of the cow and the horse, there could be a simultaneity. How then could there be a repugnance effected by time and how could there be a synchronous existence?[1] U.

This aphorism is stated as a basis for a description of perception of non-existence. An effect, as a water-pot and the like is non-existent previous to its production, inasmuch as there is non-existence of the assertion or expression of action and quality. There is antecedently no such expression of qualities and action, as there is after the pot is produced, as that the jar is at rest, or in motion, or that it is dark. Thus the doctrine of the pre-existence of effects in their causes is rejected. Previous, therefore, to the production of the water jar, there is antecedent

[1] कार्यमितिशेष: प्रागिति कार्योत्पत्ते: प्राक् कार्यं घटपटादि असत् तत्कालीनस्वजनकाभावप्रतियोगीत्यर्थ: अत्र हेतुक्रियागुणव्यपदेशाभावात् यदि तदानीमपि कार्ये घटादि सदैव स्यात् तदा क्रियावत्त्वेन गुणवत्त्वेन च व्यपदिश्येत यथोत्पन्ने घटे घटस्तिष्ठति घटश्चलति रूपवानयं दृश्यते घट इत्यादिप्रकारेण व्यपदिश्यते न तथोत्पत्ते: प्रागपि कार्यव्यप्रदेशोऽस्ति तेन गम्यते तदानीमसन्निति सच व्यूह्यमानेषु वीरणेषु योज्यमानेषु तन्तुषु चारूढायां मृदि कुलालादिव्यापारेषु अनुवर्तमानेषु भविष्यत्यत्र कट: पटोघटोवेति सार्वलौकिकी प्रत्यक्षप्रतीति: चक्षुर्विस्फारणानन्तरं जायमानत्वात् नच संयोगसमवायान्यतरघटिता प्रत्यासत्तिरत्र प्रभवति तस्मादिन्द्रिय-सम्बद्धविशेषणता प्रत्यासत्तिरत्र तन्त्रम् ननु चान्योन्याश्रय: सत्यां विशेषणतायां तत्प्रतीति: प्रतीतौ च विशेषणतेति चेन्न विशेषणता हि तदुभयस्वरूपमेव उपश्लिष्टप्रत्ययजननयोग्यं तच्च प्रतीते: पूर्वमपि सदेव तदुक्तं न्यायवातिके समवायेऽभावे च विशेषणविशेष्यभाव: इति सतायं प्रागभाव: प्रतियोगिजनक: नहि घटे जाते स एव घटस्तदानीमेवोत्पद्यते तत्र कारणान्तरसत्त्वेऽपि कारणवैकल्यमनुस्त्रियमाणं स्वप्रागभाववैकल्यमेवानुसर्तुमर्हति तद्घटोत्पत्तौ स एव घट: प्रतिबन्धक इति चेत्तर्हि प्रतिबन्धकाभावत्वेन तस्य कारणत्वमवर्जनीयम् ननु यदि घट एव तस्याभावस्तदा घटे नष्टे तदुन्मज्जनापत्तिरिति चेन्न घटनाशस्यापि तद्विरोधित्वात् नहि विरोधित्वकालेऽपि विरोध्यन्तरप्रादुर्भाव इति नह्यनयोर्देशकृतो विरोधो येन गोत्वाश्वत्ववत् समानकालीनत्वं स्यात् तर्हि कालकृतस्तथाच कथमेककालावस्थायित्वं भवेत्।।

non-existence thereof, and this produces a non-existent. Else how, when there exists another cause could there not be reproduction of the produced? A perception such as that there will presently exist a water-pot in this place, is a proof of antecedent non-existence.[1] V.

सदसत्।। 2।।

Aph. 2. The existent [becomes] non-existent.

It is stated that another non-existence is established by the force of perception. It is proved by perception and inference that an existent product, such as a water-pot, after the operation of a hammer etc. which destroys it, is now non-existent, in like manner as it is proved by perception and inference that an effect is, previous to the operation of its cause, non-existent. This mode of non-existence is commonly called destruction (or subsequent or emergent non-existence); for there are such cognitions as that a water-pot is destroyed, or that the letter *ga* previously heard is now no more.[2] U.

असतः क्रियागुणव्यपदेशाभावादर्थान्तरम्।। 3।।

Aph. 3. [Existence] is a thing distinct from non-existence, inasmuch as actions and qualities are not ascribed [to the non-existent].

It may be objected that it is the water-pot that under particular conditions produces the conventional notion of destruction, but the destruction of the water-pot is nothing else than the water-pot itself. The aphorism is therefore laid down. The word Existence is to be supplied. Existence, then, is a thing distinct from non-existence. If it be asked why, it is stated that it is so because actions and qualities are not ascribed to the non-existent. For there are not employed during subsequent non-existence, such phrases as, The water-pot exists,

[1] अभावप्रत्यक्षमभिधित्सुर्भूमिकामाह। घटादिकार्यं स्वोत्पत्तेः प्रागसत क्रियाया गुणस्य च व्यपदेशस्य व्यवहारस्याभावात् घटे जाते यथा घटस्तिष्ठति घटश्चलति घटः श्याम इत्यादिक्रियागुणव्यवहारो भवति पूर्वन्तु न तथा व्यवहार इत्यर्थः अतः सत्कार्यवादे निरस्त इति घटोत्पत्तेः पूर्वं घटप्रागभावस्तिष्ठतीति सच प्रतियोगिजनकः कथमन्यथा कारणान्तरसत्त्वे उत्पन्नस्य न पुनरुत्पादः इहेदानीं घटो भविष्यतीत्यादि प्रत्यक्षमपि प्रागभावे मानमिति।।

[2] यथा कारणव्यापारात् पूर्वं प्रत्यक्षानुमानाभ्यां कार्यस्यासत्त्वं प्रमीयते तथा विनाशकस्य मुद्गरादेर्व्यापारानन्तरं सदेव कार्यं घटादि इदानीमसदिति प्रत्यक्षानुमानाभ्यामेव प्रमीयते सचायमभावो ध्वंस इति गीयते भवति हि घटो नष्टो ध्वस्त इदानीं श्रुतपूर्वो गकारो नास्तीत्यादिधीरिति भावः।।

There is a water-pot, The water-pot is now possessed of colour, Bring the water-pot. In consequence of this difference, the existent is a thing different from the non-existent.[1] U

सच्चासत्।। 4।।

Aph. 4. The existent also is non-existent.

Antecedent and subsequent non-existence being vindicated, the present aphorism is laid down with the purpose of evincing reciprocal non-existence. When the words Is not are asserted of an existent water-pot, there appears an absence of identity. For there are such cognitions as that a horse is not identical with a cow, a cow is non-existent as a horse, a piece of cloth is non-existent as a water-pot, a piece of cloth is not a water-pot, a cow is not a horse, a horse is not a cow. There appears, then, in such a cognition the fact that a cow possesses reciprocal non-existence with a horse, a water-pot is reciprocally non-existent with a piece of cloth; and this reciprocal non-existence is otherwise designated absence of identity. The identity then in this case is essentially non-existent, and this non-existence is in-coexistent with the non-existent object; for there are such cognitions as that the water pot is not the ground on which it is placed. This nonexistence is eternal, for it is impossible that there could ever be identity between a water-pot and a piece of cloth. [2]U.

यच्चान्यदसदतस्तदसत्।। 5।।

Aph. 5. Whatever else, moreover, than these is non-existent, is [absolutely] non-existent.

The fourth non-existence, called absolute non-existence, is here described. Whatever else then these, that is, than the three fore-mentioned non-existences is non-existent, that is, is absolutely non-

[1] ननु घट एवावस्थाविशेषे ध्वंसव्यवहारं करोति नतु घटादन्यस्तस्य ध्वंस इत्यत आह। सदिति सूत्रशेषः असतः सत् अर्थान्तरं कुत इत्यत आह क्रियागुणव्यपदेशाभावादिति नहि प्रध्वंसभावेऽपि वर्तते घटः अस्ति घटः इदानीं रूपवान् घटः घटमानयेत्यादिव्यपदेशस्तदितो वैधर्म्यादसतः सदर्थान्तरमिति।।

[2] प्रागभावप्रध्वंसौ साधयित्वाऽन्योन्याभावं साधयितुमाह। यत्र सदेव घटादि असदिति व्यवह्रियये तत्र तादात्म्याभावः प्रतीयते भवति हि असन्नश्वो गवात्मना असन् गौरश्वात्मना असन् पटो घटात्मना अघटः पटः अनश्वो गौः अगौरश्वश्च इत्यादिप्रतीतिः तदस्यामश्वान्योन्याभाववान् गौः पटान्योन्याभाववान् घट इत्यन्योन्याभाव एव तादात्म्याभावापरनामा भासते तदत्र तादात्म्यं प्रतियोगितावच्छेदकम् प्रतियोगिसमानाधिकरणाश्चायमभावः भवति हि पटो न भूतलमिति प्रतीतिः नित्यश्च कदाचिदपि घटपटयोस्तादात्म्यासम्भवात्।।

existent. The final and complete sense of the aphorism, therefore, is that the non-existence which is distinct from these three non-existences is absolute non-existence. Of these, antecedent non-existence has a subsequent limit; subsequent non-existence has an anterior limit; reciprocal non-existence in-coexists with that which is non-existent; but absolute non-existence differs from all the three, and is therefore a fourth non-existence.[1] V.

That which is non-existent, repugnant to existence, other than the three forementioned non-existences, is non-existent, absolutely non-existent. That usually refers to the existent. The complete sense is that it is technically designated absolute non-existence. This absolute non-existence is the fourth non-existence, and is eternal. There are three things repugnant to absolute non-existence, the object non-existent, and its prior and posterior non-existences. According to the ancients the cognitions that dark colour does not exist in a red water-pot, and that red colour does not exist in a dark water-pot, are conversant about the subsequent and antecedent non-existences; while the moderns have maintained that the subsquent and antecedent non-existences are not repugnant to absolute non-existence, and that consequently there may be absolute non-existence even during the time of subsequent non-existence. They (the moderns) hold that when a water-pot etc., previously removed is brought back to a place, there is during the existence there of the water-pot no notion the absolute non-existence of the water-pot, inasmuch as the time during which the water-pot is there constitutes no connection with non-existence. Some have taught that when there has formerly stood in any place a water-pot, etc. and this has been removed and brought back again, there appears in this case a fourth kind of universal non-existence characterised by production and destruction, and designated temporary non-existence, and not absolute non-existence.[2] V.

[1] इदानीं चतुर्थमभावमत्यन्ताभावाख्यमाह। अतः पूर्वोक्तादभावत्रयाद् यदन्यदसत् तदसत् तदत्यन्तासत्त्वम् असदित्युभयत्र भावप्रधानोनिर्देशः तत्रैकमसदुद्देश्यमसद्विधेयम् तथाचोक्ताभावत्रयभिन्नो योऽभावः सोऽत्यन्ताभाव इति पर्यवसन्नोऽर्थः तत्र प्रागभावस्य उत्तरावधिकत्वम् प्रध्वंसस्य पूर्वावधिकत्वम् अन्योन्याभावस्य प्रतियोगिसमाना-धिकरणत्वमत्यन्ताभावस्य तु त्रितयवैधर्म्यमतश्चतुर्थोऽयमभावः।।

[2] अत उक्तादभावत्रयादन्यद् यत् असत् भावभिन्नम् तदसत् अत्यन्तासत्त्वं भावप्रभावप्रधाननिर्देशोऽयम् अत्यन्ताभावाख्यमिति तु फलितार्थः अयञ्चात्यन्ताभावस्तुरीयोऽभावः सनातनश्च प्रतियोगितत्प्रागभावत-द्ध्वांसास्त्रय एवात्यन्ताभावस्य विरोधिनः रक्तघटे श्याभं रूपं नास्ति श्यामघटेर रूपं नास्तीतिप्रतीतिश्च ध्वंसप्रागभावाववगाहेते नत्वत्यन्ताभावमिति प्राञ्चः नव्यास्तु ध्वंसप्रागभावयोर्नात्यन्ताभावविरोधित्वमतो

असदिति भूतप्रत्यक्षाभावात् भूतस्मृतेर्विरोधिप्रत्यक्षवत्।। 6।।

Aph. 6. [Perception] that a thing is non-existent results from non-existence of a past perception, and reminiscence of the past, like the perception of a repugnant object.

Another section is here commenced, in which this aphorism is stated enouncing the apparatus of the perception of emergent non-existence. Cognition is the form of perception is implied by the particle *iti.* There is therefore a perceptive cognition that a water-pot, for instance, is non-existent, that a water-pot has been destroyed, or that a water-pot is subsequently non-existent. This is exemplified by perception of the repugnant, there being as clear and distinct a perception of a repugnant (or at present non-existent) water-pot etc., as of its subsequent non-existence. The reason of this is non-existence of a past perception, the absence that is to say of a past, produced and destroyed, water-pot and the like. The experience is thus accounted for. The following hypothetical argument is confirmatory of this: If there were a water-pot here it would be seen as the place is seen, but it is not seen, and consequently there is none. Another subsidiary is stated to be reminiscence of the past, by which is meant recollection of a past, and now non-existent, water-pot and the like, the recollection of a thing non-existent.[1]U.

The four kinds of non-existence being analysed, the perception of subsequent non-existence is analysed. Such perceptions as that a thing is non-existent, a water-pot is non-existent, a water-pot is destroyed, a water-pot has ceased to be, are, like the perception of the repugnant, that is like the perception of a not now existing water-pot, given by experience, or produced by ordinary contact (of subject and object). Of these, perception of an object non-existent is produced by

ध्वंसादिकालावच्छेदेनाप्यत्यन्ताभावो वर्तत एव यत्र भूतले पूर्वमपसारितं घटादिकं पुनरानीतं तत्र घटकालस्याभाव-सम्बन्धाघटकत्वाद्धटसत्त्वकाले न घटात्यन्ताभावबुद्धिरित्याहुः केचित्तु यत्र भूतले पूर्वं घटादिकं स्थितमथापसारितं पुनरानीतञ्च तत्रोत्पाद्विनाशशाली सामयिकानामा चतुर्थः संसर्गाभाव एव प्रतीयते नात्यन्ताभाव इत्याहुः।।

[1] इदानीं प्रकरणान्तरमारभते तत्र प्रध्वंसे तावत् प्रत्यक्षसामग्रीमाह। असदितीतिकारेण प्रत्यक्षाकारं ज्ञानमाह तेनासन् घटः नष्टो घटः ध्वस्त इदानीं घट इति प्रत्यक्षप्रतीतिरस्ति तत्र दृष्टान्तो विरोधिप्रत्यक्षवदिति विरोधिनो घटादेर्यथा स्पष्टं प्रत्यक्षं तथा तत्प्रध्वंसस्यापि तत्र कारणमाह भूतप्रत्यक्षाभावादिति भूतस्य उत्पन्नविनष्टस्य घटादेः प्रत्यक्षाभावात् एतेन योग्यानुपलब्धिमाह तत्र चायं तर्कः सहकारी यद्यत्र घटोऽभविष्यत् भूतलमिवाद्रक्ष्यत नच दृश्यते तस्मान्नास्तीति सहकार्यन्तरमाह भूतस्मृतेरिति भूतस्य प्रतियोगियोगिनोघटादेः स्मृतेरिति प्रतियोगिस्मरणमुक्तम्।।

conjunction with the eye etc., while perception of emergent non-existence is produced by determination related to the eye etc. Such is one difference; another is stated to be that the perception of subsequent non-existence results from non existence of past perception, that is from a cause in the form of possible non-apprehension consequent on non-existence of perception of a past, foregone, now non-existent water-pot, and also from a reminiscence of a past water-pot etc., that is from a cognition, which is a recollection, of a non-existent object. The perception, therefore, of subsequent non-existence is produced by non-apprehension of a non-existent object, and by knowledge of a non-existent object; but the perception of a non-existent object is not so, there being a difference.[1] V.

तथा ऽभावे भावप्रत्यक्षत्वाच्च।। 7।।

Aph. 7. Likewise also from perception of existence in non-existence.

The word non-existence, through expressive of non-existence in general, is ascertained from the context to denote antecedent non-existence or potential existence. There is then a perceptive knowledge of antecedent non-existence, as there is of emergent non-existence. Why? Because there is a perception of existence, a perception of the straws in course of weaving (into a mat, which is potentially existent in them), these being made the object of perception. Or it may mean that the perception of antecedent non-existence results from the perception or perceptibility of existence, that is, of the substratum and the object therein non-existent, since perceptibility of the substratum and of the object non-existent is the condition of apprehension of general non-existence. The particle *also* implies recollection of the absent non-existent object, and the hypothetical reasoning aforeasid. Antecedent non-existence without beginning also, and emergent non-existence with-out end, are

[1] अभावचतुष्टयं व्युत्पाद्य ध्वंसप्रत्यक्षं व्युत्पादयति। असदिति असन् घटः नष्टो घटः ध्वस्तो घट इत्यादिप्रत्यक्षं विरोधिप्रत्यक्षवत् प्रतियोगिघटप्रत्यक्षवत् अनुभवसिद्धं लौकिकसन्निकर्षजन्यश्चैत्यर्थः तत्र च प्रतियोगिप्रत्यक्षं चक्षुरादिसंयोगजन्यं ध्वंसप्रत्यक्षन्तु चक्षुरादिसंयुक्तविशेषणताजन्यमिति विशेषः अपरमपि विशेषमाह भूतप्रत्यक्षाभावादिति भूतस्य अतीतस्य प्रतियोगिनो घटादेः प्रत्यक्षस्याभावाद्योग्यानुपलम्भरूपात् कारणात् भूतस्य अतीतघटादेः स्मृतेः स्मरणात्मकात् प्रतियोगिज्ञानाच्च जायमानमिति पूरणीयम् तथाच ध्वंसप्रत्यक्षं प्रतियोग्यनुपलब्धिजन्यं प्रतियोगिज्ञानजन्यञ्च प्रतियोगिप्रत्यक्षन्तु न तथा इतोऽपि विशेष इतिभावः अत्र स्मृतित्वमविवक्षितं ज्ञानमात्रन्तु विवक्षितमिति मन्तव्यम्। एवञ्च घटादयो यथा प्रत्यक्षसिद्धास्तथा तद्ध्वंसा अपीति भावः।।

perceptible only under particular circumstances.[1] U.

There being a restriction of the general term non-existence to antecedent non-existence, so is there also of perception. There is a perceptive knowledge of antecedent, as of subsequent, non-existence, by means of experience rendered possible by apposition of the sense-organ and its object, and of knowledge of the non-existent. It may be asked: Inasmuch as antecedent non-existence has no beginning, how is it that there is no perception of it long before the production of conjunction of the two halves of a water-jar etc., the forementioned causes of such perception being possible at that time also? It is therefore stated that such perception results from perception of existence. The affix *ghaṅ* (in the word *bhāva,* 'existence') denotes the material cause, the source of being. Existence is the ultimate sum of conditions or causal apparatus, and that only is perceptible which is perceptible thereby, inasmuch as it must be manifested by the ultimate causal apparatus. Such is the resultant meaning of the aphorism. It is to be considered that the particle *also* is added to prevent the supposition of perception of supersensible antecedent non-existence of air etc.; and that perceptibility as an absent object is thereby additionally implied.[2] V.

एतेनाघटोऽ गौरधर्मश्च व्याख्यातः।। ८।।

Aph. 8. Hereby are explained the negations not a water-pot, not a cow, and demerit.

The perceptibility of reciprocal non-existence, is declared. The word Hereby suggests recollection of the absent object, apprehension of the substratum (or site of the absent object), and the forementioned

[1] सामान्यवाच्यप्ययमभावशब्दः प्रकरणात् प्रागभावपरः यथा प्रध्वंसे प्रत्यक्षज्ञानं तथा प्रागभावेऽपि कुतः भावप्रत्यक्षत्वात् भावस्य व्यूह्यमानवीरणादेः प्रत्यक्षत्वात् प्रत्यक्षेण विषयीक्रियमाणत्वात् यद्वा भावस्याधिकरणस्य प्रतियोगिनश्च प्रत्यक्षत्वात् योग्यत्वादित्यर्थः संसर्गाभावग्रहेऽधिकरणयोग्यतायाः प्रतियोगियोग्यतायाश्च तन्त्रत्वात् चकारात् प्रतियोगिस्मरणमुक्तञ्च तर्कं समुच्चिनोति अनादेरपि प्रागभावस्यानन्तस्यापि प्रध्वंसस्यावस्थाविशेषमात्रे प्रत्यक्षत्वम्।।

[2] अभावे प्रागभावे सामान्यवाचकशब्दस्य विशेषपरत्वात् तथा प्रत्यक्षम् यथा ध्वंसे इन्द्रियसन्निकर्षयोग्यनुपलब्धिप्रतियोगिज्ञानैः प्रत्यक्षं जायते तथा प्रागभावेऽपीत्यर्थः।। ननु प्रागभावस्यानादित्वात् कपालादि-संयोगजननादतिपूर्वमपि कथं न प्रागभावस्य प्रत्यक्षमुक्तानां कारणानां तदानीमपि सम्भवादित्यत आह। भावप्रत्यक्षत्वादिति भवत्यस्मादित्युपादाने घञ् भावश्चरमकारणासामग्री तेन प्रत्यक्षं यस्य तत्त्वात् चरमकारणसामग्रीव्यङ्ग्यत्वादितिफलितार्थः तथाचोक्तस्थले चरमकारणसामग्र्यभावान्नप्रागभावप्रत्यक्षमितिभावः अतीन्द्रियस्य वाय्वादेः प्रागभावस्य प्रत्यक्षकारणाय चकारस्तेन च प्रतियोगियोग्यत्वं समच्चितमिति मन्तव्यम्।।

hypothetical reasoning. Non-observation of the perceptible is common to all these cases; the particle *and* implying the aforesaid addition. By the word demerit, while the perceptibility of reciprocal non-existence of merit, though supersensible, in its substratum or site, knowledge, pleasure etc., is affirmed, it is at the same time declared that perceptibility of the absent object is not a condition of the apprehension of reciprocal non-existence, and thus it is suggested that the perceptibility of the substratum (or site of the absent object) is the only requisite of such apprehension. How else could there be apprehended reciprocal negation of a fiend in a post, when it, it is recognised that that a post is not a fiend? For since non-apprehension of the fiend as identical with the post, causes apprehension of their reciprocal non-existence, and since that same non-apprehension is repugnant to the existence of the absent object, it would be impossible were the post identical with a fiend, that there should be such non-apprehension. It may argued: Identity with a fiend is not in this instance the absent object, may it then be the fiend? and supposing him though being in the post, to be, like its gravity, not apprehended, then the non-apprehension of him will not be repugnant to the existence of the absent object. We reply that this argument is invalid, for non-perception of that of which the essential characteristic is the being an absent object is, like non-observation of the absent object, a cause of apprehension of non-existence. If it be urged that reciprocal non-existence depends on the apprehension of the absence of an object; that absence of an object (or the state of an object which is non-existent) is identity with exemption from reciprocal non-existence; we reply that this is not the case, for it is an attribute which is cognised as non-existent in any given substratum that has for its essential characteristic the nature of being an absent object, but the condition of the perception of that attribute is not the having for its essential characteristic the nature of being an absent object.[1] U.

[1] अन्योन्याभावस्य प्रत्यक्षतामाह। एतेनेति प्रतियोगिस्मरणाधिकरणाग्रहणप्रागुक्ततर्कानतिदिशति योग्यानुपलम्भः सर्वत्र समानः चकार उक्तसमुच्चयार्थः अधर्म इत्यतीन्द्रियस्यापि धर्मस्य सुखज्ञानादावधिकरणेऽन्योन्याभावस्य प्रत्याक्षतां वदन् अन्योन्याभावग्रहे प्रतियोगियोग्यता न तन्त्रंकिन्त्वधिकरणयोग्यतामात्रं तन्त्रमित्युपदर्शयति कथमन्यथा स्तम्भः पिशाचो न भवतीति पिशाचान्योन्याभावः स्तम्भे गृह्येत स्तम्भात्मतया पिशाचानुपलम्भस्य तदन्योन्याभवग्राहकत्वात् तस्याप्यनुपलम्भस्य प्रतियोगिसत्त्वविरोधित्वात् स्तम्भे पिशाचतादात्म्ये सत्यनुपलम्भानुपपत्तेः। ननु पिशाचतादात्म्यमिह न प्रतियोगि किन्तर्हि पिशाचः सच स्तम्भे वर्तमानोऽपि गुरुत्ववन्नोपलभ्यते इति तदनुपलम्भः प्रतियोगिसत्त्वविरोधी न भवतीति चेन्न प्रतियोग्यनुपलम्भवत् यति-योगितावच्छेदकानुपलम्भ स्याप्यभावग्रहकारणत्वात् ननु प्रतियोगित्वग्रहाधीनोऽन्योन्याभावग्रहः

The recognition of reciprocal non-existence, the form of which recognition is such as that a piece of cloth is not a water-pot, a horse is not a cow, pleasure is not demerit, has been already explained by the description of the perception of emergent and of antecedent non-existence. Such is the sense of the aphorism as a whole. The causes, then, of the apprehension of reciprocal non-existence, are possession of characters in relation with the sense-organs, non-observation of the absent object, and cognition of the absent object. The greatest difference is that the perceptibility of the absent object is the condition of apprehension of general non-existence, whereas it is the perceptibility of the substratum that is the condition of apprehension of reciprocal non-existence. Thus, though merit be a supersensible thing, there is no impossibility in perceiving its reciprocal non-existence in pleasure etc., its sensible substratum. Whereas some have taught that perceptibility of both the absent object and its substratum or site is requisite to the apprehension of general non-existence, this is untrue, inasmuch as were this the case,the perception of non-existence of fragrance in a stone, of non-existence of bitterness in treacle, of non-existence of colour in air, and of non-existence of touch and sound in ether, would be impossible, since the respective substrata are not perceptible to the several sense-organs. It was from this consideration that Paksha-dhara Miśra maintained the perception of the destruction or cessation of the touch of the air, characterised by time conjunct with the skin (the organ of touch.)[1] V.

अभूतं नास्तीत्यनर्थान्तरम्।। ९।।

Aph. 9. [The negation] *Is not* designates nought else than that which has not been.

प्रतियोगित्वञ्चान्योन्याभावविरहात्मत्वं ततश्चान्योन्याभावग्रहाधीन एवान्योन्याभावग्रह इति चेन्नाधिकरणावृत्तित्वेन ज्ञायमानो धर्म एव प्रतियोगितावच्छेदको नतु प्रतियोगितावच्छेदकत्वेनापि तद्ग्रहस्तन्त्रमित्युक्तत्वात्।।

[1] अघटः पटः अगौरश्वः अधर्मः सुखमित्याद्याकारकोऽन्योन्याभावप्रत्ययोऽपि एतेन प्रध्वंसप्रागभावप्रत्ययकथनेन व्याख्यातः कथित इति समुदितार्थः तथाचान्योन्याभावप्रत्यक्षेऽपि इन्द्रियसम्बद्धविशेषणता प्रतियोग्यनुपलम्भः प्रतियोगिज्ञानञ्चैतानि कारणानि इयान् परं विशेषो यत् संसर्गाभावग्रहे प्रतियोगियोग्यत्वं तन्त्रम् अन्योन्याभावग्रहे त्वधिकरणयोयत्वमिति धर्मस्यातीन्द्रियत्वेऽपि सुखादौ योग्याधिकरणे तदन्योन्याभावस्य प्रत्यक्षं निराबाधमेवेति यत्तु संसर्गाभावग्रहे प्रतियोग्यधिकरणोभययोग्यत्वं तन्त्रमिति कैश्चिदुक्तं तन्न समीचीनं तथा सति पाषाणे सौरभाभावस्य गुडे तिक्ताभावस्य वायौ रूपाभावस्य आकाशे स्पर्शाभावस्य शब्दाभावस्य च प्रत्यक्षानुपपत्तेस्तत्तद-धिकरणानां तत्तदिन्द्रियायोग्यत्वात् अतएव त्वक्संयुक्तकालविशेषणतया वायुस्पर्शनाशप्रत्यक्षं पक्षधरमिश्रैः स्वीकृतमिति संक्षेपः।।

The recognition that what has been no longer is, reposes upon emergent non-existence, and is not conversant about the having been; while the recogniton by perception simply that such and such a thing is not, rests upon absolute non-existence. The expression that which has not been points out independence of production and destruction. Designating nought else means purporting that only. For example: There exists not in water terrestriality, There exists not in earth aqueousness, for if there existed terrestriality in that whereof the particles are aqueous it would be observed, whereas it is not observed, wherefore it is not;—a reference to such arguments is to be observed in this aphorism. Thus we must hold that there is non-existence of an object where such object will never be and has never been. The recognition that an object is not relates to the substratum, and is the support of emergent and antecedent non-existence, of that which has been, and will be therein. Hence it is that this absolute non-existence is designated as of trinal time.[1] U.

नास्ति घटो गेहे इति सतो घटस्य गेहसंसर्गप्रतिषेधः।। 10।।

Aph. 10. [The proposition] that there is not a water-pot in a house, is a negation of connection between an existent water-pot and the house.

It may be urged that non-existence of a water-pot in any given house is not absolute non-existence, inasmuch as a water-pot exists sometimes there; nor is it antecedent or emergent non-existence, inasmuch as these reside only in material causes; nor is it absolute non-existence characterised as production and destruction, since there is a contradiction between the absolute and that which comes into being and ceases to be; nor is this the fourth kind of non-existence, general non-existence, inasmuch as that is repugnant to the threefold division. Accordingly this aphorism is stated.[2] U.

[1] भूतमिदानीं नास्तीतिप्रतीतिर्ध्वंसमालम्बते भूतत्वं नोल्लिखति किन्त्विदं नास्तीतिमात्रोल्लेखिनी प्रत्यक्षप्रतीतिरत्यन्ताभावमालम्बते अभूतमित्युत्पादविनाशानालम्बनत्वं द्योतयति अनर्थान्तरत्वमपि तदभिप्रायकमेव यथा जले पृथिवीत्वं नास्ति पृथिव्यां न जलत्वमिति यदि हि जलावयविनि पृथिवीत्वं स्यात् उपलभ्येत्त नचोपलभ्यते तस्मान्नास्तीतितर्कपुरस्कारोऽत्रापि द्रष्टव्यः। एवञ्च यद्वस्तु यत्र न कदाऽपि भविष्यति नच कदाचिद्भूतं तस्य वस्तुनस्तत्रात्यन्ताभावो मन्तव्यः। भूतभविष्यतोश्च तत्र प्रध्वंसप्रागभावलम्बन एव तन्त्राधिकरणे नास्तीतिप्रत्ययः। अतएवामयात्यन्तिकस्त्रैकालिक इत्यभिधीयते।।

[2] ननु गेहे घटाभावो नात्यन्ताभावः कदाचित्तत्र घटसत्त्वात् नापि प्रागभावप्रध्वंसौ तयोः समवायिकारणमात्रवृत्तित्वात् नाप्युत्पादविनाशशीलोऽत्यन्ताभाव एव आत्यन्तिकश्चोत्पादविनाशशीलश्चेति विरोधात् नापि चतुर्थ एवायं

आत्मन्यात्ममनसोः संयोगविशेषादात्मप्रत्यक्षम्।। 11।।

Aph. 11. Perception of the soul [results] from a particular conjunction between the soul and the internal organ in the soul.

Common perception of existence and non-existence having been described, another section is commenced with the purpose of describing the perception of ascetics. The words cognition is produced, are to be supplied. Ascetics are of two kinds those who have mediated on the internal organ, and are called united, and those who have not mediated on the internal organ, and are called disunited. Of these the united having reverently fixed their mind on the object to be presented to it, are engaged in meditation; and in them cognition of soul, whether of their own soul or of that of others, is produced. Perception of soul is that cognition wherein the soul is the percept or object of presentation. Although there is in ourselves and others occasionally a cognition of spirit, this being obscured by nescience has been declared to be virtually non-existent. From a particular conjunction between the soul and the internal organ, means from that particular contiguity between the soul and the internal organ which is the mental state produced by union [with infinite spirit].[1] U.

तथा द्रव्यान्तरेषु प्रत्यक्षम्।। 12।।

Aph. 12. Likewise perception of other substances.

It might be asked how, if the knowledge of those who are united be of the soul only, they can possess omniscience. Accordingly the aphorism is stated. The words Cognition is produced are implied by the nature of the topic. There is, therefore, by means of the internal organ accompained with the merit acquired by asceticism, perception of other substances, that is, of the four atomic substances, of the internal organ, air, space, time and ether. The term substance comprehends the qualities, actions, and universal entities residing in

संसर्गाभावः तस्य त्रैविध्यविभागव्याघातादित्यत आह।।

[1] तदेवं भावाभावविषयकं लौकिकप्रत्यक्षं निरूप्य योगिप्रत्यक्षं निरूपयितु प्रकरणान्तरमारभते। ज्ञानमुत्प्रद्यते इतिशेषः द्विविधास्तावद्योगिनः समाहितान्तकरणा ये युक्ता इत्यभिधीयन्ते असमाहितान्तःकरणाश्च ये वियुक्ता इत्यभिधीयन्ते तत्र युक्ताः साक्षात् कर्तव्ये वस्तुन्यादरेण मनो निधाय निदिध्यासनवन्तः तेषामात्मनि स्वात्मनि परात्मनि च ज्ञानमुत्पद्यते आत्मप्रत्यक्षमिति आत्मा प्रत्यक्षः साक्षात्कारविषयो तत्र ज्ञाने तत्तथा यद्यप्यम्मदादोनामपि कदाचिदात्मज्ञानमस्ति तथाप्यविद्यातिरस्कृतत्वात् तदसत्कल्पमित्युक्तमात्ममनसोः सन्निकर्षविशेषादिति योगजधर्मानुग्रह आत्ममनसोः सचिकर्षे विशेषस्तस्मादित्यर्थः।।

substance, the category of particularity, co-inherence, gravity, elasticity etc. residing in perception, and spontaneous activity, indiscriminative mental retenta, merit and demerit residing in the soul. For the possession of the merit produced by asceticism is equivalent to a perceptive apparatus; otherwise ominiscience would not be affirmed of those ascetics who are said to be united.[1] U.

असमाहितान्तःकरणा उपसंहृतसमाधयस्तेषाञ्च।। 13।।

Aph. 13. In those also whose internal organ is not meditative, and in those whose meditation is consummated [there is perception of soul etc.]

Those whose internal organ is not meditative, are those whose inner sense is destitute of meditation; and they whose meditation is consummated, perfected, or rendered fruitful, in whom are produced the various perfections which are the fruit of meditation, attain perception of souls and other substances. Such is the sense to be gathered from the aphorism. In fine, the ascetic who is in course of union requires contemplation, while he who is united has no need of meditation which is identical with contemplation.[2] V.

तत्समवायात् कर्मगुणेषु।। 14।।

Aph. 14. [Perception] of actions and qualities [arises] from co-inherence therein.

It might be urged that omniscience is not possible in an as cetic, for though there be perception of substances, there is no such cognition of qualities and actions. To this the reply is furnished. From co-inherence therein, that is, in conjunction with the internal organ assisted by merit acquired by asceticism, there is produced in the ascetic, whether in course of union or united, the perception of

[1] तत् किमात्मन्येव युक्तानां ज्ञानं तत् कुतः सार्वज्ञ्यमित्यत आह। ज्ञानमुत्पद्यत इति प्रकरणायातम् तथेति योगजधर्मानुगृहीनैव मनसा द्रव्यान्तरेषु चतुर्ष्वणुषु मनसि वायुदिक्कालाकाशेषु द्रव्यपदेन तद्गतगुणकर्मसामान्यानां विशेषपदार्थस्य समवायस्य प्रत्यक्षगतस्यापि गुरुत्वस्थितिस्थापकादेरात्मगतस्यापि जीवनयोनियत्न-निर्विकल्पकभावनाधर्माधर्मादेः संग्रहः सामग्री योगजधर्मोपग्रहस्य तुल्यत्वत् अन्यथा सार्वज्ञ्यमुक्तं न भवेत्।।

[2] असमाहितान्तःकरणाः असमाहितं समाधिरहितम् अन्तःकारणं येषां ते तथा उपसंहृतः समापितः सफलीकृतः समाधिर्येस्ते समाधेः फलंविविधाः सिद्धयस्ता येषामुत्पन्नास्तादृशाः ये युक्तास्तेषामपि आत्मनाम् अन्येषां द्रव्याणाञ्च प्रत्यक्षं भवतीति समुदितार्थः युञ्जानस्य प्रत्यक्षे ध्यानापेक्षा युक्तस्य प्रत्यक्षे तु ध्यानात्मकसमा-ध्यपेक्षा नास्तीति भावः।।

qualities and actions. For the efficacy of the merit acquired by asceticism is inconceivable. By the power thereof the sage Agastya drank up the ocean, Saurabhi assumed a multitude of bodies, and Vasishtha discovered the curse of Dilīpa by Surabhi. The production, therefore, by merit acquired by asceticism, of presentation of all the categories is not impossible. The term actions and qualities involves more, and universality etc. is to be understood. In a like manner we are to understand perception effected by supersensual cognition in the form of general implication, and implication of cognition.[1] V.

आत्मसमवायादात्मगुणेषु ।। 15 ।।

Aph. 15. [Perception] of the attributes of the soul [arises] from co-inherence in soul.

This aphorism is stated inasmuch as it might be asked whether ascetics have not also the common perception. The conclusion gathered is that there arises in ascetics also the common perception of the attributes of the soul, that is, of pleasure and the other attributes which reside in the soul from co-inherence in soul, that is, from co-inherence in the soul conjoined with the internal organ, being accomplished by that as its instrument.[2] V.

[1] ननु द्रव्याणां प्रत्यक्षसम्भवेऽपि सर्वज्ञत्वं योगिनोऽनुपपन्नमेव गुणादीनामज्ञानादत आह। तस्य योगजधर्मसहकृतमनःसंयोगस्य समवायात् युक्तयुञ्जानयोः कर्मसु गुणेषु च प्रत्यक्षमुत्पद्यते इत्यर्थः अचिन्त्योऽहि योगजधर्मप्रभावः यद्बलेनागस्त्यमुनिः पारावारं पपौ सौभरिश्च कायव्यूहं परिगृहीतवान् वशिष्ठश्च दिलीपस्य सुरभिशापं ज्ञातवान् तस्य योगजधर्मस्य पदार्थसार्थसाक्षात्कारसम्पादनं नासम्भावनीयमिति कर्मगुणेत्युपलक्षणं सामान्यादिकमपि बोध्यम् एवं सामान्यलक्षणानलक्षणारूपालौकिकप्रत्यासत्तिजन्यं प्रत्यक्षमप्यूहनीयम्।।

[2] तत् किं योगिनां लौकिकप्रत्यक्षं न भवतीत्यत आह। आत्मसमवायात् मनःसंयुक्तात्मसमवायात् आत्मगुणेषु स्वात्मवृत्तिसुखादिगुणेषु योगिनां लौकिकमपि प्रत्यक्षं भवति तत्सामग्र्या वृत्तत्वादिति समुदितनिष्कर्षः।।

SECOND DAILYLESSON

अस्येदं कार्यं कारणं संयोगि विरोधि समवायि चेति लैङ्गिकम्।। 1।।

Aph. 1. Inferential cognition is that one thing is the effect or cause of, conjunct with, repugnant to, or co-inherent in, another.

In the preceding daily lesson the perception of ascetics and of non-ascetics was described according to its cause, its nature, and its characteristic. Assurance having been formerly divided into perceptive and inferential, the description of inferential assurance is here commenced. The term cognition is to be supplied, being the subject treated of. Inferential knowledge is that which is produced from a mark or middle term. The mark is that attribute of the subject of the conclusion, which is characterised by pervasion. Pervasion is said to exist therein. The subject is that wherein there is non-existence of assurance repugnant to that which there is desire to prove. Such assurance is proof and disproof , for the minor term is that wherein there is non-existence of both proof and disproof. For where there exists probative and disprobative assurance, no one feels uncertainity or desire of demonstration. The ancients therefore defined the subject of the question to be an object possessing the attributes of the predicate uncertainly, or an object the possession whereby of the attributes of the major is required to be proved. According to Jīvanātha Miśra the subject is that wherein there is non-existence of probation obstructive to the genesis of doubt terminable by decision of the possible comprehension of the major. Some hold that the subject is that wherein there is non-existence of demonstrative evidence backed by absence of desire of proof. According to this doctrine the nature of a subject would exist even in the case of repugnancy. This, then, may be seen in the Anumāna-mayūkha. The attribute of this subject is called the mark or argument. The mark is that which being seen, inferred, or heard, produces cognition, other than memory, and this cognition is inferential. Hence it has been said: That which is connected with the inferrible, and which is generally known as in the concomitant; but in the absence thereof, there is no illative argument.

It is, therefore, the mark which is the instrument of illation; not the sumption, inasmuch as that not having the function, cannot be an instrument; whereas this function belongs to the mark or argument.

If it be asked how, where smoke etc. the argument is past or future, there can be illation; we reply that this is no valid objection, as in this case we infer that the designate of the predicate of the conclusion also as past or future. If it be asked how there can be illation where, in consequence of an impediment in the case, it is not ascertained whether the smoke etc., be past, future or present; we admit that there can in no wise be such illation, inasmuch as there is uncertainity in such as instance also as to the major. If it be asked how an illation can take place where there is certainity as to a previous and a following day, and uncertainity as to the intermediate day; we reply, that it results from inferring the existence of fire etc., limited to those days from smoke etc., limited to those days, in consequence of observing such causality in the pervasion or invariable concomitance asserted in the sumption. If it be asked how illation results from a column of dust mistaken for smoke; we reply that it is because that which is understood to be pervaded (i.e., the column of dust, supposed to be smoke and therefore pervaded by fire), is the mark or middle term, and because the inference is correct or incorrect according to the correctness or incorrectness of such experience (the logical, not involving the material, truth; else how should your own sumption be the instrument in such a case. If it be asked how in the case of a supersensible mark, the sumption not being producible thereby, the mark can have such a function; we reply that it is because the existence of a practical argument demonstrative of the reality thereof, effects the function in such an instance; else it would not be possible that there should exist in hearing etc., the function of co-inherence.

Inference results from a mark which is an effect, as the inference of fire etc. from smoke, light etc. also from a mark which is a cause, as where a deaf man infers a sound from a particular conjunction of a drum with the drumstick; or where a righteous man infers merit, paradise etc., from the due performance of sacrifice, ablution etc.; or where rain is inferred from the due performance of a sacrifice in which the fruit of the Capparis Aphylla is employed; or where the efflux of water is inferred from a channel which men are digging out from a river full of water; or the inference of the rising of a stream from the observation of rain overhead. This single connection, then, characterised as the relation of cause and effect, has been stated in two ways. Inference from a conjunct object is such as inference of the organ of touch from observation of an animal body. Inference from a repugnant object is such as inference of an ichneumon concealed by bushes etc., from observation of an excited snake. Inference from a co-inherent object is such as the inference of fire connected with water, from the heat of the water.[1] U.

अस्येदं कार्यकारणसम्बन्धश्चावयवाद्भवति।। 2।।

Aph. 2. That one thing belongs to another, the connection of cause and effect, arises from a portion.

This aphorism is stated to meet the objection that this distribution of middle terms is inexhaustive, since it does not include the inference of the heaving of the ocean from the rising of the moon, the rise of Canopus from the tranquillity of the waters, the rising of the moon from the expansion of the Nymphaea, the setting of the fourteen

[1] तदेव पूर्वाह्निके योगिप्रत्यक्षमयोगिप्रत्यक्षञ्च कारणतः स्वरूपतो लक्षणतश्च निरूपितम् प्रमाणं द्विविधं प्रत्यक्षं लैङ्गिकञ्चेति यद्विभ तत्र लैङ्गिकमिदानीं निरूपयितुमुपक्रमते। ज्ञानमिति प्रकृतम् लिङ्गाज्जातं लैङ्गिकं व्याप्तिविशिष्टः पक्षधर्मो लिङ्गम् तत्र व्याप्तिरुक्ता यत्सिषाधयिषाविरोधिप्रमाणाभावो यत्र स तं प्रति पक्षः तदृशं प्रमाणं साधकं बाधकश्च तदुभयाभाववतः पक्षत्वात् नहि साधके बाधके वा प्रमाणे सति कस्यचित् संशयः सिषाधयिषा वा अतएव सन्दिग्धसाध्यधर्मा धर्मी सिषाधयिषिसाध्यधर्मा धर्मो वा पक्ष इति प्राञ्चः उत्पाद्यसाध्यवत्तानिर्णयनिवर्त्यसंशयोत्पत्तिप्रतिबन्धकमानत्वावच्छिन्नाभावो यत्र स पक्ष इति जीवनाथमिश्राः सिषाधयिषाविरहसहकृतसाधकमानाभावो यत्र स पक्ष इति केचित् एतन्मते बाधस्थलेऽपि पक्षता तदेतदनुमानमयूखे द्रष्टव्यम् तदेतस्य पक्षस्य धर्मोलिङ्गमित्युक्तं भवति लिङ्गञ्च दृष्टमनुमितं श्रुतं वा यदनुभवरूपं ज्ञानं जनयति तल्लैङ्गिकं तदुक्तम् अनुमेयेन सम्बद्धं प्रसिद्धञ्च तदन्विते। तदभावे तु नास्त्येव तल्लिङ्गमनुमापकम्। इति एतेन लिङ्गमेवानुमितिकरणं नतु तस्य परामर्शः तस्य निर्व्यापारत्वेनाकरणत्वात् लिङ्गस्य तु एव व्यापारः यत्र धूमादेरतीतत्वमनागतत्वं वा तत्र कथमनु मतिरिति चेन्न साध्यस्याप्यतीतानागतत्वयो-स्तत्रानुमानात् तत्रैव प्रतिबन्धात् अतीतत्वमनागतत्वं वर्तमानत्वञ्च धूमादेर्यत्र न निश्चितं तत्र कथमनुमितिरिति चेत् न कथञ्चित् तत्र साध्यस्यापि सन्देहात् पूर्वापरदिनयोः सत्त्वनिश्चये मध्यदिने तु सन्देहे कथमनुमितिरिति चेत् तद्दिनावच्छिन्नधूमादिना तद्दिनावच्छिन्नवह्न्यादेरनुमानात् तथैव व्याप्तेः कारणत्वावधारणात् धूलीपटलात् कथं धूमभ्रमादनुमितिरिति चेत् व्याप्तत्वेन ज्ञातस्यैव लिङ्गत्वात् ज्ञानस्य च याथार्थ्यायाथार्थ्याभ्यामनुमितेस्तादृूप्यात् अन्यथा तवापि कथं तत्र परामर्शः करणं स्यात् अतीन्द्रियलिङ्गस्थले परामर्शस्य तदजन्यतया कथं तद्व्यापारत्वमिति चेत् तत्सत्तानिर्वाहकत्वरूपक्षैमिकसाधनतायास्तत्र व्यापारत्वघटकत्वात् अन्यथा समवायस्य श्रवणादेर्व्यापारत्वानुपपत्तेरिति कार्याल्लिङ्गात् धूमा लोकादेरग्न्याद्यनुमानं कारणादपि यथा बधिरस्य भेरीदण्डसंयोगविशेषात् शब्दानुमानम् यथा वा धर्मिकस्य यथाविधियागम्नानाद्यनुष्ठानाद्धर्मस्वर्गाद्यनुमानम् यथाविधिकारीर्याद्यनुष्ठानाद्वा वर्षानुमानम् पयः पूर्णनद्यादौ खन्यमानप्रवाहाद्वा जलनिःसरणानुमानम् उपरि वृष्टिदर्शनाद्वा नदीवृद्ध्यनुमानम् सचायं कार्यकारणभावलक्षण एक-सम्बन्धः प्रकारद्वयेनोक्तः संयोगिनः शरीरस्य दर्शनात्त्वगिन्द्रियानुमानम् विरोधिनोविस्फूर्जतोऽहेर्दर्शनाज्झाटाद्यन्तरितनकुलानु-मानम् समवायिना जलौष्णयेन तत्सम्बद्धतेजोऽनुमानम्।।

of the lunar mansions from the rising of the other fourteen, of colour from taste, or of a particular taste from a particular colour. The words That one thing belongs to another express the cause, the meaning being that this fire etc. to be inferred, belongs to this smoke etc. the inferential mark, or that this pervaded smoke etc., belongs to this pervading fire etc. It is therefore, the observation of pervasion generally that is the condition of illation , not the relation of cause and effect etc. The words the connection of cause and effect are added, lest it might be objected that the enumeration in the preceding aphorism is consequently irregular; and by these the other connections also are implied. The term connection has a subjective implication, and therefore means the suggestion of connection. It will be asked whence this suggestion arises. It is therefore stated that it arises from a portion, that is from a particular instance or mere example.

According, then, both to this system and those of the Sāṅkhyas and others, the suggestion of connection, whether the relation of cause and effect or other, arises in conformity with the example. Thus, then, pervasion (or the being pervaded, as the mark by that of which it is the mark) is the possession of a natural connection, the natural being that which is not accidental. This intrinsic nature is known from its being ascertained that certain perceptible objects do not pervade (or are not invariably concomitant with) that which is to be proved (or that which is denoted by the major term), while it is ascertained that certain perceptible objects do pervade the inferential mark. Of supersensible objects established by evidence some are pervasive of both, non-pervasive of both, pervasive only of the inferential mark, or non-pervasive only of that which is to be inferred. Among these the non-accidental nature of the first is to be ascertained from their pervading the inferential mark; of the second from their not pervading that which is to be inferred; and of the fourth also from their pervading the inferential mark ..... This inference is of two kinds, for the sake of oneself (or logical), and for the sake of another (or rhetorical). Of these, inference for the sake of oneself arises from investigating for oneself the pervasion or sumption, and the determination of the minor by the middle ; and inference for the sake of another results from knowledge of the pervasion, and of the qualification of the minor, derived from a syllogism enunciated by another.

A syllogism is a sentence which conveys verbal knowledge which is the cause of the third recognition of the inferential mark.The members thereof are five, viz., the question, argument, instance, application, and conclusion. Of these the question is a proposition, a member of the syllogism, conveying verbal knowledge the object whereof is neither less nor more than the conclusion to be afforded; the argument is a member of the syllogism ending in the fifth or ablative case of the middle term under consideration; the instance or example is a member of the syllogism declaratory that the given major is not absent from the middle; the application or subsumption is a member of the syllogism declaratory that the minor is characterised by the middle thus characterised by non-absence of the major; and the conclusion is that member of the syllogism which declares the minor to be characterised by the given major. The syllogism proceeds as follows: Sound is non-eternal (the question); because it is producible (the argument); whatever is producible is non-eternal (the instance); and sound is characterised by producibleness pervaded by non-eternity (the application); therefore it is non-eternal (the conclusion); The descriptive appellations given by the Vaiśeshikas to these five members, are the question (*pratijñā*), reason (*apadeśa*), example (*nidarśana*), application (*anusandhāna*), and conclusion (*pratyāmnāya*). The mode of procedure in colloquy, disputation, and controversy, and the definitions of misconstruction, futile reply, and failure in argumentation, may be sought in the Vādi-vinoda.[1] U.

[1] नन्वव्यापकमिदं परिसङ्ख्यानम् नहि चन्द्रोदयेन समुद्रनलवृदेः जलप्रसादेनागस्त्योदयस्य कुमुदप्रकाशेन चन्द्रोदयस्य चतुर्दशनक्षत्रोदयेनापरचतुर्दशनक्षत्रास्तमयस्य रसेन रूपस्य रूपविशेषेण वा रसविशेषस्यानुमानमनेन संगृह्यते इत्यत आह। अस्येदमित्येतावदेव प्रयोजकं भवतीति अस्य साधनस्य धूमादेरिदं साध्यं वह्न्यादि यद्वाऽस्य व्यापकस्य वह्न्यादेरिदं व्याप्यं धूमादि तथाच व्याप्यत्वग्रहमात्रं तन्त्रं नतु कार्यकारणभावादिरपि ननु पूर्वसूत्रे तर्हि परिसङ्ख्यानमतन्त्रमत आह कार्यकारणसम्बन्ध इति अनेन चोक्तं सम्बन्धान्तरमप्युपलक्षयति सम्बन्धपदे च विषयिलक्षणा तेन सम्बन्ध इति सम्बन्धोपन्यास इत्यर्थः। कुतस्तदुपन्यासइत्यत आह अवयवात् एकदेशात् उदाहरणमात्रात् ल्यपब्लोपे पञ्चमी तेनोदाहरणमनुरुध्य कार्यकारणभावादेः सम्बन्धस्योपन्यास इह दर्शने साङ्ख्यादिदर्शने च भवतीत्यर्थः। एवञ्च स्वाभाविकसम्बन्धशालित्वं व्याप्यत्वम् स्वाभाविकत्व-ञ्चानौपादिकत्वम् तच्च प्रत्यक्षाणां केषाञ्चित् साध्याव्यापकत्वनिश्चयात् केषाञ्चित् साधनव्यापकत्व-निश्चयादेवानुपाधित्वं ज्ञेयम् अतीन्द्रियाणाञ्च प्रमाणसिद्धानां केषाञ्चिदुभयव्यापकत्वम् उभयाव्यापकत्वं साधनमात्रव्यापकत्वं साध्यमात्राव्यापकत्वं वा तत्राद्ये साधनव्यापकत्वात् द्वितीये साध्याव्यापकत्वात् चतुर्थेऽपि साधनव्यापकत्वादेवानुपाधित्वं निश्चेयम्।। तच्चानुमानं द्विविधं स्वार्थं परार्थञ्च तत्र स्वार्थं स्वयमेव व्याप्तिपक्षधर्मतयोरनु-सन्धानात् परार्थञ्च परोदीरितन्यायजन्यव्याप्तिपक्षधर्मताज्ञानात् न्यायश्च तृतीयलिङ्गपरामर्शप्रयोजकशाब्दज्ञानजनकवाक्यम् तदवयवाश्च पञ्च तत्रावयवत्वं तृतीयलिङ्गपरामर्शप्रयोजकशाब्दज्ञानजनकवाक्यत्वम् तानि च वाक्यानि प्रतिज्ञानहेतूदाहरणोपनयनिगमनानि तत्र प्रतिज्ञा उद्देश्यानुमित्यन्यूनानतिरिक्तविषयकशाब्दज्ञानजनकं न्यायावयववाक्यम् हेतुश्च प्रकृतसाधनगतपञ्चम्यन्तो न्यायावयवः उदाहरणन्तु प्रकृतसाध्यासाधनाविनाभावप्रतिपादको न्यायावयवः उपनयश्चाविनाभावविशिष्टस्य हेतोः पक्षवैशिष्ट्यप्रतिपादको न्यायावयवः निगमनन्तु पक्षे प्रकृत-

एतेन शाब्दं व्याख्यातम्।। 3।।

Aph. 3. By this verbal knowledge is explained.

Another section is commenced with the view of including under inferential knowledge other forms of evidence. That knowledge which under the name of verbal knowledge, knowledge whereof words are the instrument, is approved by the Naiyāyikas and others, is explained by this, by the nature of illation, that is, as derived from an inferential mark. Verbal knowledge, like inferential, requires consideration of pervasion or invariable concomitance, and of the nature of the attributes of the subject of the question. For example, such and such verbal meanings are mutually connected, inasmuch as they are recalled by terms involving an ellipse etc., as in the aggregate of verbal meaning, Drive the cow hither. In this instance a man infers the mutual connection, on recognising that there is something recalled by a plurality or terms requiring others to complete the sense, pervaded by mutual connection of the meaning of the terms.[1]U.

By this, by the explanation of inferential knowledge, verbal knowledge or cognition produced by knowledge, of words, is explained. The Naiyāyikas and others hold that there is a kind of experiential cognition termed apprehension of construction, differing both from perception and inference. In the teaching of the Vaiśeshikas this is not admitted. In the case of verbal knowledge they hold, that what takes place is inference regarding contiguity of the senses of terms. For instance upon hearing the proposition. The cow exists, it is inferred that the cow is characterised by existence inasmuch as this is recalled by the term wherein resides implication of words to be supplied favourable to apprehension of construction characterised by the notion of existence in the proper object qualified, as in the familiar instance of a water-pot; or the inference results from what is

साध्यवैशिष्ट्यप्रतिपादको न्यायावयवः एवञ्च प्रवर्तते न्यायः शब्दोऽनित्यः कृतकत्वात् यद् यत् कृतकं तदनित्यम् अनित्यत्वव्याप्यकृतकत्ववांश्चायम् तस्मादनित्यः। एतेषामेव प्रतिज्ञापदेशनिदर्शनानुसन्धानप्रत्याम्नया इत्यन्वर्था वैशेषिकाणां संज्ञाः अत्र च वादजल्पवितण्डानां प्रवृत्तिप्रकारश्छलजातिनिग्रहस्थानलक्षणानि च वादिविनोदेऽन्वेष्टव्यानि।।

[1] प्रमाणान्तराणि लैङ्गिकेऽन्तर्भावयितुं प्रकरणान्तरमारभते। शाब्दं शब्दकरणकं ज्ञानमिदमिति यन्नैयायिकादीनामभिरातं तदप्येतेन लैङ्गिकत्वेन लिङ्गप्रभवत्वेनैव व्याख्यातं यथा व्याप्तिपक्षधर्मताप्रतिसन्धानापेन्क्षं लैङ्गिकं यथा शाब्दमपि तथाहि एते पदार्थाः मिथःसंसर्गवन्तः आकाङ्क्षादिमद्भिः स्मारितत्वात् गामभ्याजेति पदार्थसार्थवत् तत्रहि आकाङ्क्षादिमत्पदकदम्बस्मारितत्वं पदार्थानां मिथःसंसर्गवत्त्वव्याप्यं गृहीत्वैव संसर्गवत्त्वमनुमिनोति।।

recalled by the term *cow*, this term being uttered together with *exists*, as in the case of the eye; but there is no peculiar kind of cognition produced by words. For according to the doctrine of the Naiyāyikas also, apprehension of construction is impossible unless there be assurance that terms were pronounced consecutively in virtue of their forming a sentence, since such assurance is a pre-requisite.[1] V.

हेतुरपदेशो लिङ्गं प्रमाणं करणमित्यनर्थान्तरम्।। 4।।

Aph. 4. There is no difference of meaning in argument, reason, mark, evidence, and instrument.

Though the term *reason (apadeśa)* applies in technical language to merely apparent argument or fallacy, yet it applies also to a term, according to the derivation, something being reasoned or affirmed thereby. It is of inferential knowledge that a term, in its character of inferential mark, is the cause. A term is also the instrument of illative certainty. Similarly instrumentality resides in a term in its character as inferential mark. There is no difference of meaning, therefore, in argument, reason, mark, evidence, and instrument. These terms denote only the inferential mark, and do not denote only that which is fallacious. There is therefore no impossibility in the fallacious not producing an inference, and the term producing an inference, and great accordingly is the error of the objector.[2] V.

अस्येदं बुद्ध्यपेक्षितत्वात्।। 5।।

Aph. 5. Because they are implicated in the notion of this belonging to that.

[2] एतेन लैङ्गिकज्ञानकथनेन शाब्दं शब्दज्ञानजन्यज्ञानमपि व्याख्यातं कथितमित्यर्थः नैयायिकप्रभृतिभिरन्वय-बोधनामकं प्रत्यक्षामुमितिभिन्नमनुभवरूपं ज्ञानं मन्यते वैशेषिकमते तु न तदङ्गीकारः पदज्ञानस्थले पदार्थसंसर्गस्याऽनुमितिरेव भवति तथाहि गौरस्तीतिवाक्यश्रवणान्तरं गौरस्तितावान् स्वधर्मिकास्तित्वान्वय-बोधानुकूलाकाङ्क्षाश्रयपदस्मारितत्वात् घटवत् अस्तिपदसमभिव्याहृतगौःपदस्मारितत्वाद्वा चक्षुर्वदित्यनुमानमेव नतु शब्दजन्यो विलक्षणोबोधः पदानामेकवाक्यतापन्नत्वरूपसमभिव्याहृतत्वनिश्चयं विना न्यायनयेऽप्यन्व-बोधस्यानुत्पत्त्या पूर्वं तस्यावश्यकत्वात्।।

[2] अपदेशशब्दो यद्यपि परिभाषया हेत्वाभासे वर्तते तथापि अपदिश्यते कथ्यतेऽनेनेतिव्युत्पत्त्या शब्दोऽपि स वर्तते शब्दश्च लिङ्गविधया लैङ्गिकज्ञान एव हेतुरिति अनुमितिप्रमितिकरणञ्च शब्दोऽपि एवं लिङ्गविधया करणत्वमपि शब्दे वर्तते तथाच हेतुरपदेशो लिङ्गं प्रमाणं करणमित्यनर्थान्तरं एते शब्दा एकस्य लिङ्गस्य बोधकाः नतु हेत्वाभासमात्रबोधकाः हेत्वाभासस्याननुमापकत्वेऽपि शब्दस्यानुमापकत्वे न काचिदनुपपत्तिरित्या-शङ्कितुर्भ्रान्तिर्महतीति भावः।।

It is laid down that recognition through similarity *(upamāna)* and other processes are included in inference, because their nature is such that there arises respecting them an implication of the notion that such and such an argument included, belongs to such and such a major inclusive; in fine, because they involve a knowledge of pervasion or universal concomitance. It is to be supplied as an ellipse, that the nature of inference belongs to the cognitions instanced as recognition through similarity, disjunctive reasoning, probability, and traditional teaching. Of these the cognition produced by recognition through similarity is the perceptive cognition of a rustic, after the first conjunction of his eye with a gayal, that it is like a cow. Next ensues recollection of the sentence indicatory of analogy, viz. that by the term gayal an animal like a cow is designated. The cognition that arises that an animal of the present kind is designated by the term gayal, is a recognition through similarity. Thus the followers of the Nyāya doctrine. In the teaching of Kaṇāda this is merely an illation, because there is produced at that time only an inference of the designation of the term gayal by means of similitude to a cow as an inferential mark included under designation by the term gayal; while the notion of the applicability of the term gayal does not so much as come into being under the circumstance of absence of the notion of pervasion. Or else, the term gayal, after perception of a gayal, occasions a sense of the nature of a gayal, it having no other function, since it has been applied to that object by the ancients, just as the term cow is the occasion of a sense of the nature of a cow. Or it may be that the occasion of the sense of the nature of a gayal appears from the force of the attribution concerning the subject of the question, by means of the inference that the term gayal is an occasion of a practical acceptation inasmuch as it is a legitimate term.

The Mīmāṁsakas hold that disjunctive reasoning is another form of evidence. For instance, when it has been ascertained from astrology that Devadatta is to live for a hundred years, and from observation that he has no house to live in, it is next presumed that, inasmuch as his living a hundred years is otherwise impossible, he must live in the open air. This, as being a fact of implication, is not accepted by them as an inference. In this example, inasmuch as the notion of living involves the notion of living either in a house or in the open air, and inasmuch as it is impossible that he should live in a house, the other alternative being established, his living in the open air appears in the process of illation. In like manner in the familiar example Devadatta is stout but does not eat by day (therefore he easts at night), it being settled that he must eat, since stoutness is observed to be pervaded or universally accompanied by eating, and it being contrary to the hypothesis that he should eat by day, it follows that he eats at night. Similarly the Paurāṇikas hold probability and traditional teaching to be other forms of evidence. Probability is a cognition dependent on a plurality of concomitances, as for instance learning is probable in a Brāhman, and a hundred instances are probable among a thousand, while there is no pervasion or universal concomitance necessitated. Such is their view. In like manner traditional teaching, which is delivered in the form Thus indeed they have declared, for this is a proposition derived through a succession of witnesses and having no determinate author. For instance In every sacred fig-tree a Yaksha dwells etc. This in the view of the Paurāṇikas, being ascertained as having been declared by competent authority, is not included under verbal knowledge.

This doctrine of theirs is not correct, for traditional teaching being a kind of verbal knowledge is included under inference. Probability, also, so far as it involves a pervasion is included under inference; and so far as it is irrespective of universal concomitance, is not a form of evidence at all. Accordingly it is declared in the aphorisms of Gautama: Inasmuch as traditional teaching is not a different thing, it is not denied of verbal knowledge, and inasmuch as disjunctive argumentation, probability, and impossibility are not different things, they are not denied of inference.

According to the doctrine of Bhaṭṭa and that of the Vedānta non-observation is also another form of evidence, and apprehension of non-existence takes place thereby. This doctrine also cannot be accepted. In the case of non-observation it is perception that arises by means of a presentation of attribution connected with the organs of sense. We do not controvert the fact that this is the cause of non-observation, but to maintain that non-observation is an independent form of evidence does not belong to the course of propriety.[1] V.

[1] उपमानादेरप्यनुमान एवान्तर्भाव इति प्रतिपादयति। अस्य व्यापकस्य साध्यस्य इदं साधनं व्याप्यमिति बुद्धेर्याऽपेक्षा सा जाता येषां तत्त्वात् व्याप्तिज्ञानसापेक्षत्वादिति तु फलितार्थः उपमानार्थापत्तिसम्भवैतिह्यस्थलीयबुद्धीनां लैङ्गिकत्वमिति शेषः। तत्रोपमानजन्या बुद्धिस्तावत् ग्रामीणस्य प्राथमिकगवयचक्षुःसंयोगानन्तरमयं गोसदृश इति प्रात्यक्षिकं ज्ञानं ततो गोसदृशो गवयपदवाच्य इत्यतिदेशवाक्यार्थस्मरणं तत् एतज्जातीयो गवयपदवाच्य इति या बुद्धिरुदेति सोपमितिरिति न्यायमतानुसारिणः कणादमते तु साऽनुमितिरेव गोसमदृश्यलिङ्गेन गवयपदवाच्यत्वव्याप्यतया गृहीतेन गवयपदवाच्यत्वस्यानुमितेरेव तदानीं जननात् व्याप्तिधीविरहदशायाञ्च न भवत्येव गवयपदवाच्यत्वधीरिति। अथवा गवयप्रत्यक्षानन्तरं गवयपदं गवयत्वप्रवृत्तिनिमित्तकम् असति

आत्ममनसोः संयोगविशेषात् संस्काराच्च स्मृतिः।। 6।।

Aph. 6. Reminiscence results from a particular conjunction of the soul with the internal organ, and from reproduction.

The word results is to be supplied. The particular conjunction is reflection and other attention. From this, as the non-coinherent cause, reminiscence, a kind of knowledge, is produced in the soul, as the co-inherent cause. The instrumental cause is stated in the words from reproduction, and by the particle and the active element of former experience is involved. This recollection or reminiscence simulates the correctness or incorrectness of the previous experience; such being the recollection of one who mistakes a rope for a snake and flees from it. Reminiscence does not take place always in every case, since it depends on the resuscitation of a mental retentum. The knowledge of inspired sages is not separately defined by the author of the aphorisms, being included in the perception of ascetics but it is stated in the section intitled Enunciation of the categories, that the presentative cognition which is declared to belong to inspired sages, the promulgators of revelation, resulting from particular merit, from conjunction of the soul and the internal organ irrespective of inferential marks etc., and conversant about supersensible objects past, present, and to come, about merit etc., and about the contents of books, is called the knowledge of inspired sages. This belongs also at times to ordinary people, as when a

वृत्यन्तरे वृद्धैस्तत्र प्रयुज्यमानत्वात् यथा गोपदं गोत्वप्रवृत्तिनिमित्तकम् यद्वा गवयपदं सप्रवृत्तिनिमित्तकं साधुपदत्वादित्यनुमानेन यक्षधर्मताबलाद्गवयत्वप्रवृत्तिनिमित्तकत्वं भासते इति। मीमांसका अर्थापत्ति प्रमाणान्तरं मन्यन्ते तथाहि यत्र देवदत्तस्य शतवर्षजीवित्वं ज्योतिःशास्त्रादवगतं जीविनो गृहासत्त्वञ्च प्रत्यक्षादवगतं। तत्र शतवर्षजीवित्वान्यथानुपपत्त्या बहिः सत्त्वं कल्प्यते तदनुमानेन गतार्थत्वान्नेष्यते तथाहि जीवित्वस्य बहिः सत्त्वगृसहत्त्वान्यतरव्याप्यत्वं गृहीतं तत्रान्यतरसिद्धौ जायमानायां गृहसत्वबाधात बहिः सत्त्वमनुमिनोतीति भासते एवं पीनो देवदत्तो दिवा न भुङ्क्ते इत्यादौ पीनत्वस्य भोजनव्याप्यत्वावगमाद्भोजनं सिद्ध्यत् दिवाभोजन–बाधे रात्रिभोजनं सिध्यति। एवं सम्भवैतिह्ययोरपि प्रमाणान्तरत्वं मन्यन्ते पौराणिकाः तथाहि सम्भवो भूयः सहचाराधीनज्ञानं यथा सम्भवति ब्राह्मणे विद्या सम्भवति सहस्रे शतमत्र च व्याप्तिर्नापेक्षितेति तेषामाशयः एवमैतिह्यमिति होचुरित्यनेन प्रकारेण यदुच्यते तद्धि अनिद्र्दिष्टप्रवक्तृकं परम्परागतं वाक्यं यथा वटे वटे यक्ष इत्यादि तस्याप्रोक्तत्वानिश्चयान्न शब्देऽन्तर्भाव इति पौराणिकानभिसन्धिः तदेतन्मतं न समीचीनम् ऐतिह्यस्य शब्दरूपतया ऽनुमान एवान्तर्भावात् सम्भावोऽपि व्याप्तिसापेक्षोऽनुमान एवान्तर्भवति तन्निरपेक्षस्तु प्रमाणमेव न तदुक्तं गौतमीये शब्द ऐतिह्यानर्थान्तरभावादनुमानेऽर्थापत्तिसम्भवानामनर्थान्तरभावाच्चाप्रतिषेधः इति भट्टमते वेदान्तमते चानुपलब्धेरपि प्रमाणान्तरत्वमस्ति तथाचाभावग्रहो भवतीति तन्मतमपि न मनोरमम् अनुपलब्धि ास्थले इन्द्रियसम्बद्धविशेषणताप्रत्यासत्त्या प्रत्यक्षमेव भवतीति तत्र चानुपलब्धेः कारणत्वं न विप्रतिपद्यामहे प्रमाणान्तरत्वन्तु तस्या न युक्तिपदवीं स्पृशतीति संक्षेपः।।

young maiden says My heart assures me that my brother will depart tomorrow.[1] U.

Reminiscence arises from a particular conjunction of the soul and the internal organ, that is, from a conjunction of the soul and the internal organ accompained with a desire of recollection, from reproduction in its common form called resuscitation, and from an excitant implied by the particle and. The instrument therein is purpose, not identical with disregard; the operation is reproduction; the excitants are the concomitants (or associated ideas); the non-coinherent cause is conjunction of the soul and the internal organ; and the instrumental cause is reflection etc., consisting of the desire of recollection.[2] V.

तथा स्वप्नः ।। 7 ।।

Aph. 7. So also dreaming.

As reminiscence results from a particular conjunction of the soul and the internal organ, so also does cognition in dreaming. Dreaming consciousness is the intellection of the internal organ, which arises by means of the organs of sense in one whose senses are at rest, and whose internal organ is absorbed. This is of three kinds. It arises partly from intensity of reproduction, whatever object one in love or anger thinks of intently when he goes to sleep, taking with him in that state the form of perceptive cognition, through the influence of mental reproductive power produced by previous hearing of the legendaries (*Purāṇas*) etc., in the form. This is the contest between Karṇa and Arjuna, and the like. It arises partly from derangement of the bodily affections wind, bile and phlegm. Of these, one under disorder of flatulency experiences transit through the air, wandering about on the earth, fleeing with fear from tigers etc., another by the excess of the derangement caused by

[1] उत्पद्यत इतिशेषः संयोगविशेषः प्रणिधानादिसन्निधानम् एतस्मादसमवायिकारणादात्मनि समवायिनि स्मृतिर्विद्याविशेष उत्पद्यते निमित्तकारणमाह संस्कारादिति चकारेण व्यापारी पूर्वानुभवः समुच्चीयते अनुभवयाथार्थ्यायथार्थ्यमियमनुविधत्ते रज्जुभुजङ्गतयोपलभ्य पलायितस्य तथैव स्मृतेः नच सततं स्मृतिप्रसङ्गः संस्कारोद्बोधाधीनत्वात् आर्षं ज्ञानं सूत्रकृता पृथग् लक्षितं योगिप्रत्यक्षान्तर्भावितं पदार्थप्रदेशाख्ये तु प्रकरणे तदुक्तं तद्यथा आम्नायविधातृणामृषीणामतीतानागतवर्तमानेष्वतीन्द्रियेषु धर्मादिषु ग्रन्थोपनिबद्धेषु वा लिङ्गाद्यनपेक्षादात्ममनसोः संयोगाद्धर्मविशेषाच्च प्रातिभं ज्ञानं यदुत्पद्यते तदार्षम् इति तच्च कदाचिल्लौकिकानामपि भवति यथा कन्यका वदति श्वो मे भ्राता गन्तेति हृदयं मे कथयतीति।।

[2] आत्ममनसोः संयोगविशेषात् सुस्मूर्षादिसहितादात्ममनःसंयोगात् संस्कारात् समानाकारकात् भावनाख्यात् चकारादुद्बोधकाच्च स्मृतिर्भवति तत्र च उपेक्षानात्मकनिश्चयः करणं संस्कारो व्यापार उद्बोधकास्तत् सहकारिणः आत्ममनःसंयोगोऽसमवायिकारणं सुस्मूर्षारूपप्रणिधानादिकं निमित्तकारणमित्यर्थः।।

inordinate secretion of bile experiences entrance into fire, the embracing of flames of fire, and sees golden mountains, the corruscations of flashing lightning, the conflagration of the spheres etc.; another through predominance of phlegmatic disorder experiences passages through the sea, immersions in rivers and sprinklings with showers of rain, and sees mountains of silver and the like. Through the influence of merits also, in the cognition which is produced in the internal organ immersed in the experiences of this or former states of being, arises auspicious imagination, due to merit, and having as its objects the riding upon elephants, ascent of mountains, assumption of the princely umbrella, feasting upon rice and milk, interviews with the sovereign, and the like; while through demerit arises dreaming imagination of function with oil, the falling through blindness into a well, riding upon camels, immersion in mire, the sight of one's own nuptials and the like. Herein the three are conjointly causes, and this division is to be considered as reposing on the relation of predominance among the qualities.[1] U.

स्वप्नान्तिकम्।। 8।।

Aph. 8. [So also] consciousness in dreaming.

Some one may say: The cognition which arises during a dream, in the form of recollection of that which is experienced in dreaming cognition, has not the nature of dreaming, inasmuch as it is an experience of dreaming; whence then does it arise? The answer is furnished in the aphorism. The words *So also* are to be taken in from the preceding aphorism. The meaning, therefore, is that as dreaming, so also the consciousness in dreaming, arises from a particular conjunction of the soul with the internal organ, and from reproduction. The difference

[1] यथात्ममनसोः संयोगविशेषात् संस्काराच्च स्मृतिस्तथास्वप्नज्ञानमपीत्यर्थः। उपरतेन्द्रियग्रामस्य प्रलीनमनस्कस्य इन्द्रियद्वारेण यदनुभवनं मानसम् तत स्वप्नज्ञानम् तच्च त्रिविधं किञ्चित् संस्कारपाटवात् कामी क्रुद्धो वा यमर्थमादृतश्चिन्तयन् स्वपिति तस्य तस्यामवस्थायां प्रत्यक्षाकारं ज्ञानं पुराणादिश्रवणजनितसंस्कारवशाज्जायते कर्णार्जुनीयं युद्धमिदमित्याकारम् किञ्चिद्धातूनां वातपित्तश्लेष्मणां दोषात् तत्र वातदोषादाकाशगमन-वसुन्धरापर्यटनव्याघ्रादिभयपलायनादीनि पश्यति पित्तोपचयदोषमहिमा वह्निप्रवेषवह्निज्वालालिङ्गेन कनकपर्वत-विद्युल्लताविस्फुरणदिग्दाहादिकं पश्यति श्लेष्मदोषप्राबल्यात्त् समुद्रसन्तरणनदीमज्जनधारासारवर्षणरजतपर्वतादि पश्यति अदृष्टवशादपि तज्जन्मानुभूतेषु जन्मान्तरानुभूते वा सिद्धोपप्लुतान्तःकरणस्य यजज्ञानमुत्पद्यते तत्र शुभावेदकं धर्मात् गजारोहणपर्वतारोहणछत्रलाभपायसभक्षणराजसन्दर्शनादिविषयकम् अधर्मात्तु तैलाभ्यञ्ज-नान्धकूपपतनोष्ट्रारोहणपङ्कमज्जनस्वविवाहदर्शनादिविषयकं स्वप्नज्ञानमुत्पद्यते त्रयाणां मिलितानामेवात्र कारणत्वं गुणप्रधानभावमाश्रित्यायं विभाग द्रष्टव्यः।।

extends thus far that cognition in dreaming results from reproduction produced by former experience, while consciousness in dreaming results from reproduction produced by experience arising at the very time. It has therefore been stated by Praśastadevāchārya that from looking back upon past cognitions recollection only results; and the author of the Vṛtti says that cognition in dreaming, being a flash of experienced objects, is not a different thing from reminiscence. Some teach that conciousness in dreaming is knowledge amounting to certitude during dreams, such as that one is lying in bed.[1] U.

धर्माच्च।। 9।।

Aph. 9. Also from merit.

A cause of dreams and of consciousness in dreaming is added. The particle *also* implies the addition of demerit. The explanation of this has already been given.[2]

इन्द्रियदोषात् संस्कारदोषाच्चाविद्या।। 10।।

*Aph.*10. Nescience results from derangement of the organs of sense, and from imperfection in reproduction.

Intelligence according to another mode is divided into two kinds, certitude and incertitude. Of these, the cause of incertitude is stated. Derangements of the organs of sense are ophthalmia etc. Imperfection in reproduction is the resulting from erroneous experience. The particle *and* implies the addition of such imperfection as remoteness etc., and as sumption of which the inferential mark is illegitimate. The cause then of nescience or incertitude is imperfection; and imperfection, as consisting of biliousness, remoteness etc., is of various kinds.[3] V.

[1] ननु यज्ज्ञानं स्वप्नमध्ये स्वप्नज्ञानानुभूतस्यैवार्थस्य स्मृतिरूपं जायते तत्र स्वप्नत्वं न वर्तते स्वप्नस्यानुभवरूपत्वात् तथाच कस्मात् कारणात्तदुत्पत्तिरित्यत आह। तथेति पूर्वसूत्रादनुवर्तते तेनात्ममनसोः संयोगविशेषात् संस्काराच्च यथा स्वप्नस्तथा स्वप्नान्तिकमप्रीत्यर्थः। एतावानेव विशेषो यत् स्वप्नज्ञानं पूर्वानुभवजस्वनितात् संस्कारात् स्वप्नान्तिकन्तु तत्कालोत्पन्नानुभवजनितसंस्कारादेव तदुक्तं प्रशस्तदेवाचार्यैः अतीतज्ञानप्रत्यवेक्षणात् स्मृतिरेव इति। उक्तञ्च वृत्तिकारैः अनुभूतस्तु स्फुरणार्थतया न स्मरणादर्थान्तरं स्वप्नज्ञानम् इति। स्वप्नमध्ये प्रमाभूतं यज्ज्ञानं तत् स्वप्नान्तिकमिति केचित् यथा शय्यायां शयानोऽस्मीत्यादि।।

[2] स्वप्नस्वप्नान्तिकयोः कारणं समुच्चिनोति। अधर्मसमुच्चयार्थश्चकारः कृतव्याख्यानमेतत्।

[3] प्रकारान्तरेणापि बुद्धिर्द्विविधा प्रमाऽप्रमाचेति तत्राप्रमायाः कारणमाह। इन्द्रियदोषः काचादिः संस्कारदोषो भ्रमानुभवजातत्वादिः चकाराद्दूरत्वादिरूपाणामसल्लिङ्गपरामर्शादिरूपाणाञ्च दोषाणां सङ्ग्रहः तथाचाविद्यायाम-प्रमायां दोषः कारणै दोषस्तु पित्तदूरत्वादिरूपो नानाविध इत्यर्थः।।

तद्दुष्टज्ञानम्।। 11।।

Aph. 11. This is imperfect cognition.

This, an uninflected word, employed pronominally refers to nescience. This nescience is defective cognition, cognition unduly extended or restricted, cognition determined by a form of which it is not susceptible and asserting that this is in that, a cognition the determination of which does not reside in the thing to be determined. Imperfection is defined as being uncertainty of cognition. Suspense, therefore, though admitting of one valid alternative, is vicious, being identical with inattention. The four forms of nescience, therefore, known as suspence, erroneous assurance, dreaming, and non-apprehension are hearby implied.[1] U.

अदुष्टं विद्या।। 12।।

*Aph.*12. Free from imperfection it is science.

The word cognition is to be supplied from the preceding aphorism. Science is experience of that whereof there is cognition free from imperfection, that is produced by organs of sense which are not deranged; recognition of a character in its proper subject; or experience the form of which resides in a common substratum; or experience such that which is not its form does not reside in its subject; and this is of two kinds intuitive and inferential.[2] U.

आर्षं सिद्धदर्शनञ्च धर्मेभ्यः।।13।।

*Aph.*13. The knowledge of inspired sages, and perfect vision result from merits.

Some might ask therefore the knowledge of ascetics is not nescience, since imperfection of the objects, as remotness etc., is possible in such cognition. To this the answer is furnished in the aphorism. The knowledge of inspired sages, which is produced by merit acquired by

[1] तदित्यव्ययपदं सर्वनामसमानार्थकमविद्यां परामृशति साऽविद्या दुष्टज्ञानं व्यभिचारिज्ञानमेतस्मिंस्तदितिज्ञानं व्यधिकरणप्रकारावच्छिन्नं विशेष्यावृत्तिप्रकारक्रमिति यावत् दोषश्च ज्ञानस्यानिश्चयरूपत्वमपि तेनैककोटिसत्त्वेऽपि संशयो दुष्ट एवानवधारणात्मकत्वात् तदनेन संशयविपर्यस्वप्नाप्रत्यवसायानाञ्चत्तुर्णा-मप्युपसंग्रहः।।

[2] ज्ञानमित्युनुवर्तते अदुष्टमदुष्टेन्द्रियजन्यं यत्र यदस्ति तत्र तदनुभवो वा समानाधिकरणप्रकारानुभवो वा विशेष्यावृत्त्यप्रकारकानुभवो वा विद्येत्यर्थः तच्चाध्यक्षं लैङ्गिकञ्च द्वयमेव।।

asceticism, the perfect vision, the vision of all objects perfect or real, arises from merits. If it be suggested that demerit may be the cause thereof, we deny this, for such knowledge is never erroneous, and demerit is the cause of error. But the knowledge of ascetics, depending solely upon merit, arises solely in the form of certitude, inasmuch as remoteness and the like, the defects of the object, cannot effect erroneousness therein, and we feel assured that defects beget error only by the assistance of demerit. Some maintain that the vision which results by means of a spell, as by means of a particular kind of ball of collyrium over which a sacred text has been recited, results only from merits, like the knowledge of inspired sages. The verse of the Raghuvaṁśa, [ch.3.41.]. The son of Dilīpa acquired the vision of supersensible objects etc., well accords with this exposition. Hence they explain the meaning to be that such knowledge also, as depending only upon merit, arises solely in the form of certitude.[1] V.

[1] ननु योगिनां ज्ञानं कथमविद्या न भवति दूरत्वादिरूपविषयदोषस्य तत्रापि सम्भवादत आह। आर्षमृषीणां योगजधर्मेण जनितं यत् सिद्धदर्शनं सिद्धानां सतां सर्वेषां वस्तूनां दर्शनं तद्धर्मेभ्यो जायते नतु तत्राधर्मकारणमिति न तत् कदाचिदपि भ्रमरूपं भ्रमं प्रति अधर्मस्य हेतुत्वात् योगिनां ज्ञानन्तु धर्ममात्राधीनं प्रमारूपमेव भवति दूरत्वादेर्विषयदोषस्य तत्र भ्रमत्वासम्पादकत्वात् दोषाणां भ्रमजनकत्वधर्मसहकारेणैवेति हृदयम् केचित्तु सिद्धेन मन्त्राद्यभिमन्त्रितेन गुटिकाञ्जनविशेषादिना यद्दर्शनं भवति तदपि आर्षवत् धर्मेभ्य एव भवति अतएव रघुवंशे अतीन्द्रियेष्वप्युपपन्नदर्शनो बभूव भावेषु दिलीपनन्दनः इत्यादिकमपि साधु सङ्गच्छते तथाच तादृशज्ञानमपि धर्ममात्राधीनतया प्रमारूपमेव भवतीति भाव इति व्याचक्षते।।

BOOK X

FIRST DAILY LESSON

दृष्टानिष्टकारणविशेषाद्विरोधाच्च मिथः सुखदुःखयोरर्थान्तरभावः ।। 1 ।।

Aph. 1. Inasmuch as causes desirable and undesirable are different and opposed, the relation of pleasure and pain is that of reciprocally different objects.

The object of the tenth book is the exposition of the division of the attributes of the soul according to their cause. The division of pleasure and pain is first stated among these, with the purpose of rejecting the error that pleasure differs not from pain, which error might arise from the omission of pleasure in the aphorism of Gautama which enumerates the objects of certitude. Soul, body, organ of sense, object of sense, intelli-gence, internal organ, activity, fault transmigration, recompense, pain, and emancipation are the objects of certitude. There exists between pleasure and pain the mutual relation of different objects, difference, or variety. Should it be asked why it is so, it is stated that it is because there is a difference in causes desirable and undesirable, that is, because there is a distinction between a desiralbe causer such as garlands, sandalwood, women etc., and an undesirable cause, such as snakes, thorns etc. Difference of effects necessarily depends upon difference of cause. Another ground of the distinction is laid down in the opposition, for pleasure and pain are never experienced simultaneously in one and the same soul. By the particle *and* the difference of the effects of pleasure and pain is implied also as a ground for distinguishing between them. For instance, complaisance, the embrace, clearness of the eyes etc. are the effects of pleasure, while despondency and a sullied countenance are the effects of pain; wherefore pleasure and pain must differ. It has therefore been stated by Prāsasta-devāchārya: Pleasure has complaisance as its characteristic; and is that which is produced through conjunction of the soul and the internal organ supposing merit etc., or through the contiguity of the organ and the object of sense in the recognition of something desirable produced, where garlands and other desirable objects are at hand; and is productive of complaisance, embraces, clearness of the eyes etc. In the case of past objects, such as garlands, sandal-wood, and the like, pleasure arises from reminiscence; in thc case of future objects, from purpose or resolution. The non-enumeration of pleasure in the aphorism of Gautama is to promote indifference; since indifference would arise in one who should account even pleasure as pain.[1] U.

संशयनिर्णयान्तरभावश्च ज्ञानान्तरत्वे हेतुः।। 2।।

Aph. 2. Non-inclusion in doubt and assurance is a mark that [pleasure and pain] are different from cognition.

The mark that pleasure and pain are different from cognition, distinct from the attribute knowledge, is that they are not included under doubt and assurance, that is, that they do not fall under either certainty or uncertainty. For the attribute knowledge is of two kinds, doubt and assurance; and neither plasure nor pain can be included under either of those kinds. For neither pleasure nor pain has the form of two repugnant alternatives, that it should be probable that they have the nature of doubt, nor has either posssession of a given form together with absence of the negation of that form, that it should be likely that they have the nature of assurance or certainty. The supposition of a third form of cognition is chimerical, and consequently neither pleasure nor pain can come under knowledge.[2] V.

[1] आत्मगुणानां कारणतो भेदव्युत्पादनं दशमाध्यायार्थः तत्र आत्मशरीरेन्द्रियार्थबुद्धिमनःप्रवृत्तिदोषः-प्रेत्यभावफलदुःखापवर्गास्तु प्रमेयम् इति गौतमीये प्रमेयाविभागसूत्रे सुखस्यानभिधानात् दुःखाभिन्नमेव सुखमिति भ्रमनिरासार्थं सुखदुःखयोरेव प्रथमं भेदमाह। सुखदुःखयोर्मिथः परस्परमर्थान्तरभावो भेदो वैजात्यमितियावत् कुत इत्यतआह इष्टानिष्टकारणविशेषात् इष्टं इष्यमाणं स्त्रकचन्दनवनितादि अनिष्टमनिष्यमाणमहिकण्टकादि तद्रूपं यत्कारणं तस्य विशेषाद्भेदात् कारणवैजात्याधीनं कार्यवैजात्यमावश्यकं यतः भेदकान्तरमाह विरोधात् सहानवस्थानलक्षणात् नह्येकस्मिन्नात्मन्येकदा सुखदुःखयोरनुभवः। चाकरादनयोः कार्यभेदं भेदकं समुच्चिनोति तथाहि अनुग्रहाभिव्यङ्गनयनप्रसादादिसुखस्य दैन्यमुखमालिन्यादिदुःखस्य कार्यमिति ततोऽप्यनयोर्भेदः। तदुक्तं प्रशस्ताचार्यैः अनुग्रहलक्षणं सुखं स्त्रगाद्यभिप्रेतविषयसान्निध्ये सति इष्टोत्पन्नधी-न्द्रियार्थसन्निकर्षाद्धर्माद्यपेक्षादात्ममनसोः संयोगाद्यद्यदनुग्रहाभिष्वङ्गनयनादिप्रसादजनकमुत्पद्यते तत् सुखम् इति तदिदमतीतेषु स्त्रक्चन्दनादिषु स्मृतिजमनागतेषु सङ्कल्पअम् गौतमीये सूत्रे सुखापरिगणनं वैराग्याय सुखमपि दुःखत्वेन भावयतो वैराग्यं स्यादेतदर्थमिति।।

[2] सुखदुःखयोर्ज्ञानान्तरत्वे ज्ञानगुणभिन्नत्वे संशयनिर्णयान्तराभावसंशयनिश्चयात्तर्गतत्वाभावो हेतुः। ज्ञानगुणोहि द्विविधा सन्देहो निश्चयश्चेति नहि तयोरन्यतरस्मिन्नपि सुखं दुःखं वाऽन्तर्भवितुमर्हति नहि सुखं दुःखं वा

तयोर्निष्पत्तिः प्रत्यक्षलैङ्गिकाभ्याम्।। 3।।

Aph. 3. The production thereof [i.e. of doubt and assurance] is by means of perception and inference.

The production thereof, that is of doubt and assurance, results from perception, and from an inferential mark. Neither pleasure nor pain is produced by the presentative or inferential apparatus. For pleasure is of four kinds, sensuous, accompanying desire, relating to self-esteem, or resulting from consuetude. Of the last three of these origination from juxtaposition of the object to the organ of sense cannot be predicated. And should it be contended that the first is cognition inasmuch as it is generated by contiguity of the organ and object of sense, we reply that it is not so, for part only of the causal appartus cannot prove homogeneity in the product, else all products would be uniform as having time and space as their common antecedents. Moreover, if pleasure were cognition, the pleasure which is not produced through contiguity of the organ and object of sense, would be either non-discriminative or discriminative; but it cannot be the former, for then it would be supersensible, nor can it be the latter, inasmuch as it does not consist of a judgement respecting two objects in the relation of subject and predicate. Again, as pleasure and pain are necessarily accompained with sensibility were they forms of cognition there would be involved in the notion of a sensibility of cognition a regression to infinity. The inferential means an argument, as the objective means an object. The author of the Vṛtti explains the aphorism thus, that the origin of these, that is of cognition and pleasure, is explained by perception and inference that is, by perceptive and inferential cognition; and that whereas perceptive cognition is produced by the senses, and inferential by arguments, it is otherwise with pleasure, etc.[1] U.

विरुद्धकोटिद्वयप्रकारकं येन तयोः सन्देहत्वं सम्भाव्येत नापि तदभावाप्रकारकं सत्तत् प्रकारकं येन निर्णयत्वं सम्भावनीयमिति ज्ञानस्य तृतीयप्रकारस्तु शशविषाणायमानः नातस्तत्र सुखं दुःखं वा प्रवेष्टुमीष्टे इति।।

[1] तयोः संशयनिर्णययोर्निष्पत्तिरूत्पत्तिः प्रत्यक्षाल्लिङ्गाच्च सुखं दुःखं वा न प्रत्यक्षसामग्रीजन्यं न वा लिङ्गजन्यम् चतुर्विधं हि सुखं वैषयिकं मानोरथिकम् आभिमानिकमाभ्यासिकञ्च तत्र त्रयाणामिन्द्रियसन्निकर्षप्रभवत्वं नास्त्येव प्रथममिन्द्रियार्थसन्निकर्षजत्वात् ज्ञानं स्यादिति चेन्न सामग्र्येयेकदेशस्य कार्यस्य साजात्यानापादकत्वात् अन्यथा दिक्कालसाधारण्येन सकलकार्यैकजात्यापत्तेः किञ्च इन्द्रियार्थसन्निकर्षानुत्पद्यमानं सुखं निर्विकल्पकं वा स्यात् सविकल्पकं वा नाद्यः अतीन्द्रियत्वप्रसङ्गात् न द्वितीयः विशेष्यविशेषणभावेन द्वयोरनाकलनरूपत्वात् किञ्च सुखदुःखयोरावश्यकसंवेद्यत्वात् ज्ञानस्यावश्यसंवेद्यत्वेऽनवस्थाप्रसङ्गात् लैङ्गिकमती लिङ्गमेव वैषयिकवत्। वृत्तिकृतस्तु तयोर्ज्ञानसुखयोर्निष्पत्तिः प्रत्यक्षलैङ्गिकाभ्यां प्रत्यक्षलैङ्गिकज्ञानव्याख्यानाभ्यां व्याख्याता प्रत्यक्षं ज्ञानमिन्द्रियजम् लैङ्गिकन्तुं लिङ्गजम् सुखादिकन्तु नैतादृशमिति व्याचक्षुः।।

अभूदित्यपि।। 4।।

Aph. 4. The notion of the past also [is a difference between cognition and pleasure and pain].

A difference depending upon a difference of form in pleasurc etc., as compared with inferential knowledge is here stated. The word *iti* means the form; and the word also adds another form, that of the future. A form, therefore, past etc., is observed in inferential knowledge, as that fire has been or will be in the mountain; but pleasure or pain produced under this form has never been observed.[1] U.

सति च कार्यादर्शनात्।। 5।।

Aph. 5. Also [pleasure and pain are not forms of cognition] inasmuch as the effect is not [always] observed, where [the antecedents] are.

Another difference is added. Pleasure and pain are not merely perception or merely inference, since the effect, pleasure or pain, is not always observed where the antecedent, contiguity of organ and object of sense, or attention to the universal concomitance and the attribution respecting the subject of the question, exists. The meaning, therefore is as follows. Pleasure and pain are not cognition in general; while particular cognition is either perceptive knowledge, or knowldge, in the form of inference. Pleasure and pain are not the former, inasmuch as there is sometimes no experience of the pleasurable, where there is contiguity of the object and organ of sense, as where there is perception of garlands, sandal-wood etc.; nor are they the latter, since there is sometimes no experience of either the pleasurable or the painful, where there exists an inference respecting sandal-wood etc. or an inference respecting fire etc. Since, therefore, pleasure and pain are not always experienced in the particular perception or in the particular inference, they are not those particular perceptions and inferences.[2] U.

[1] लैङ्गिकज्ञानात्सुखादेः प्रकारभेदाधीनं भेद्रमाह। इतिशब्दः प्रकारे अपिशब्दो भविष्यतीत्याकारान्तरसमुच्चये चतथा पर्वते वह्निरभूद्भविष्यति वेति लैङ्गिके ज्ञानेऽतीतादिः प्रकारो दृश्यते नचैवंप्रकारे सुखं व्याप्तिर्वा उत्पद्यमानमुपलब्धम्।।

[2] भेदकान्तरं समुच्चिनोति। सति इन्द्रियार्थसन्निकर्षे सति च न प्रत्यक्षपक्षधर्मतादिप्रतिसन्धाने कार्यस्य सुखस्य दुःखस्य वाऽदर्शनात् न प्रत्यक्षमात्रं सुखं दुःखं वा न लैङ्गिकमात्रं वा तदयमर्थः ज्ञानसामान्यं तावत् सुखदुःखे न भवत इत्युक्तं ज्ञानविशेषः प्रत्यक्षज्ञानं वा भेवेदनुमितिरूपं वा इन्द्रियार्थसन्निकर्षे स्त्रक्चन्द्रनादिप्रत्यक्षे

एकार्थसमवायिकारणान्तरेषु दृष्टत्वात्।। 6।।

Aph. 6. Because [pleasure and pain] are observed to depend on other causes co-inherent with the same object.

Another differentiating character is described. The words pleasure and pain are to be supplied. In relation to pleasure particular causes co-inherent with the same object are merit, desire of pleasure, wish for the cause of pleasure, volition directed upon the material cause of pleasure, and cognition of garlands, sandal-wood etc. In relation to pain particular causes are demerit, cognition of the undesirable, as thorns etc. The meaning is that pleasure and pain differ from inferential cognition, inasmuch as they are observed in causes co-inherent with the same object. But non-discriminative cognition does not require a cause co-inherent with the same object, and a particular cause; while discriminative cognition supposes a knowledge of attribution or judgment, but this is not another cause, that is, is not a cause of its own peculiar kind. Conjunction with the internal organ, as being a cause common to pleasure and pain with cognition, may be discounted. Though reminiscence supposes mental retenta, yet the difference there from is obvious, inasmuch as on interrogating consciousness, the difference is recognised. Although there are required in inference a recollection of pervasion or invariable concomitance, and knowledge of the nature of the characters of the subject of the question, yet these are excluded by the word other. The conclusive meaning of the aphorism is, therefore, that pleasure and pain differ from cognition, inasmuch as they are derived from a peculiar cause of its own kind, having its own common substratum, as is the case with reminiscence, with the first sound in a series of sounds, and the like.[1] U.

एकदेशे इत्येकस्मिन् शिरः पृष्ठमुदरं मर्माणि तद्विशेषस्तद्विशेषेभ्यः।। 7।।

सुखत्वानुभवाभावात् न द्वितीयः चन्दनाद्यनुमितौ वह्न्याद्यनुमितौ वा सुखत्वदुःखत्वान्यतराननुभवात् एवं प्रत्यक्षविशेषेऽनुमितिविशेषे वा सुखदुःखयोरननुभवान्न तद्विशेषोऽपीति।।

[1] भेदकान्तरमाह। सुखदुःखयोरितिशेषः सुखं प्रति एकार्थसमवेतानि असाधारणकारणानि धर्मः सुखे रागः सुखकारणेच्छा तदुपादानयन्त्नः स्रक्चन्दनादिज्ञानम् दुःखं प्रति तु अधर्मो ऽनिष्टकण्टकादिज्ञानम् एषु एकार्थसमवायिषु कारणेषु दृष्टत्वादित्यर्थः ज्ञानन्तु निर्विकल्पकमेकार्थसमवेतसाधारणकारणं नापेक्षत एव सविकल्पकन्त्वपेक्षते विशेषणत्वज्ञानं तन्न कारणान्तरं स्वविजातीयं कारणं न भवति मनःसंयोगस्तु साधारणदविवक्षितः। यद्यपि स्मृतिः संस्कारमसाधारणमपेक्षते तथापि तद्भेदः स्फुटसिद्धः एवेत्यनुभवमादाय भेदचिन्तनात्। लैङ्गिके यद्यपि व्याप्तिस्मृतिपक्षधर्मतादिज्ञानापेक्षा तथाप्यन्तरशब्देनैव तद्व्युदासः। तदयं प्रमाणार्थः सुखदुःखे अनुभवभि स्वसमानाधिकरणस्वजातीयासाधारणकारणजन्यत्वात् स्मृतिवदाद्यशब्दवच्च।।

Aph. 7. The head, the back, the stomach, and the vitals are in one part, in one [body]; their difference results from the difference thereof [that is, from the difference of their causes].

It may be urged that if the difference between pleasure and pain and cognition depend on a difference in the causes, and if the difference between pleasure and pain be like that between a post and a water-pot and the like, there can be no mutual difference between the body and its parts, as the head, feet, back, stomach, etc., there being in regard to these no difference in the ultimate particles, binary atomic aggregates etc., or the causes of blood and semen. Accordingly the statement of the aphorism. In one part means in one constituent portion; in one, in one body. The head is one part; the stomach, the back, and the vitals, imply the muscles etc. The difference of these, that is, their heterogeneity, results from the difference thereof, that is, from the difference of their causes. For the co-inherent cause of the stomach, the back etc., is not of the same kind as that of the head; just as the heterogenity of a piece of cloth, a water-pot etc. results from heterogeneity in the threads, the half-jars etc., which are their co-inherent causes; the heterogeneity of which threads, half-jars, etc., results again from heterogeneity in the fibres, lime etc. of which they are composed. Heterogeneity is thus to be sought in the successive material causes, for while the atoms may be common, the heterogeneity of the respective material causes invariably gives rise to heterogeneity in the material effects; but homogeneity in respect of substance in the material causes does not cause such heterogeneity. [1]U.

[1] ननु यदि कारणभेदाधीनो ज्ञानात् सुखदुःखयोः सुखाच्च दुःखस्य स्तम्भकुम्भादिवदेव परस्परं भेदः तदा शरीरस्य तदवयवानाञ्च शिरःपादपृष्ठोदरादीनां न परस्परं भेदः स्यात् तत्र हि परमाणुद्व्यणुकादीनां लोहितरेतसोबीजकारणानामविशेषादित्यत आह। एकदेशइति अवयवे इत्यर्थः एमस्मिन्निति शरीरे इत्यर्थः शिर इत्येकदेशः उदरं पृष्ठं मर्माणि च स्नायुप्रभृतीनि तेषां विशेषोवैजात्यम् तद्विशेषेभ्यस्तत्कारणविशेषेभ्यः तत्रापि कारणवैजात्यादेव वैजात्यं नहि जज्जातीयं शिरःसमवायिकरणं तज्जातीयमे वोदरपृष्ठादेरपि तन्तुकपालाद्युपादानवैजात्यात् पटघटादौ वैजात्यवत् तत्रापि वैजात्यसम्भवात् तन्तुकपालादेरपि अंशुशर्करादिवैजात्यात् एवं तत्र तत्राप्यन्वेष्टव्यं परमाणूनां साधारण्येऽपि स्वस्वोपादानवैजात्यस्य सर्वत्र वैजात्यप्रयोजकत्वात् द्रयत्वेन तूपादानसाजात्यं न वैजात्यप्रयोजकमितिदिक्।।

SECOND DAILY LESSON

कारणमिति द्रव्ये कार्यसमवायात्।। 1।।

Aph. 1. The position, with regard to a substance, that it is a cause, results from the co-inherence of its effects.

The discrimination of the three kinds of cause is here collaterally instituted. The cognition and expression, as applicable to a substance, that it is a cause, that is, that it is a co-inherent cause:—whence, it may be asked, are these derived? It is therefore stated that they are derived from the co-inhesion of the effect, inasmuch as there co-inhere therein substances, qualities and actions. [1]U.

संयोगाद्वा।। 2।।

Aph. 2. Or from conjunction.

It might be asked whether only co-inherent causulity pertains to substances. The reply is furnished in the aphorism. As co-inherent causality, so also operative causality, belongs to the threads, in the production of a piece of cloth. Inasmuch as conjunction of the shuttle and the threads is also a cause of the cloth, the shuttle and the thread, are mediately through the conjunction operatively causative of the piece of cloth. The particle *or* is used conjunctively. Through the thread be the co-inherent cause of the conjunction of the shuttle and the thread, it is an operative cause of the piece of cloth, mediately through such conjunction.[2] U.

कारणे समवायात् कर्माणि।। 3।।

Aph. 3. Through co-inherence in the cause actions [are non-coinherent causes.]

[1] इदानीं प्रसङ्गतस्त्रयाणां कारणानां विशेषविवेचनमारभते। कारणं समवायिकारणमिदमिति प्रतीतिप्रयोगौ द्रव्ये द्रष्टव्यौ कुत एवमत आह कार्यसमवायात् कार्याणि दव्यगुणकर्माणि तत्रैव समवयन्ति यतः।।

[2] तत् किं समवायिकारणत्वमात्रं द्रव्याणामत आह। पटोत्पत्तो तन्तूनां समवायिकारणत्ववम् निमित्तकारणत्वमपि तुरीतन्तुसंयोगस्यापि पटकारणत्वात् तत्संयोगद्वारा तुर्यास्तन्तोश्च पटनिमित्तकारणत्वमपि वाकारः समुच्चये तुरीतन्तुसंयोगं प्रति तन्तोः समवायिकारणत्वेऽपि पटं प्रति तद्द्वारा निमित्तकारणत्वात्।।

It is explained that causality resides in action. The words are non-coinherent causes are to be supplied. Non-coinherent causality is causality co-inherent in one object connected with the relation of cause and effect. Such causality results either from co-inherence in the same object with the effect, or from co-inherence in the same object with the cause. Of these the former is called in the terminology of the Vaiśeshikas the lesser, the latter the greater. If it be asked how the non-coinherent causality of action in regard to conjunction, disjunction, and reproduction is recognised; it is here replied that it is through co-inherence in the cause, that is, through co-inherence in the co-inherent cause of conjunction etc. Non-coinherent causality, therefore, resides in action, with respect to conjunction etc., by the lesser relation characterised as co-inherence in the same object with the effect.[1] U.

तथा रूपे कारणैकार्थसमवायाच्च।। 4।।

Aph. 4. Also, likewise, through co-inherence in the same object with the cause in regard to colour.

This aphorism is stated in anticipation of the questions as to what causality pertains to colour and other qualities residing in the parts, in relation to the qualities etc., of the wholes. By the words *In regard to the colour,* taste, smell, touch, number, extent, separateness, gravity, fluidity, viscidity and the like, are also indicated. The word *likewise* extends the application of non-coinherent causality. Colour and the rest in the whole commence by the greater relation, by co-inherence in one object togther with that whole which is the co-inherent cause of the colour etc., of the whole; as, for instance, the colour etc., of the half-jar originates the colour etc., in the jar, and similarly in all other cases. The word *also* adds to these occasionally operative causality.[2] U.

[1] कर्मणि यादृशकारणत्वं तदाह। असमवायिकारणानीतिशेषः असमवायिकारणत्वञ्च कार्यकारणभाव-सम्बन्ध्येकार्थसमवेतकारणत्वं तच्च कार्यैकार्थसमवायात् कारणैकार्थसमवायाद्वा तत्राद्या लघ्वी द्वितीया महतीति वैशेषिकपरिभाषा तत्र कया प्रत्यासत्त्या संयोगविभागसंस्कारान् प्रति कर्मणामसमवायिकारणत्वमित्यत आह। कारणे समवायात् कारणे संयोगादिसमवायिकरणे समवायात् तथाच कार्यैकार्थसमवायलक्षणया लघ्व्या प्रत्यासत्त्या संयोगादौ कर्मणोऽसमवायिकारणत्वमित्यर्थः।।

[2] रूपादीनां गुणानामवयववर्तिनामवयविगुणादिषु कीदृशी कारणतेत्यपेक्षायामाह। रूप इति रूपरस-गन्धस्पर्शसङ्ख्यापरिमाणपृथक्त्वगुरुत्वद्रव्यत्वस्नेहाद्युपलक्षयति तथेत्यसमवायिकारणत्वमतिदिशति कारणैकार्थसमवायादिति अवयविरूपादीनां समवायिकारणं यदवयवि तेन सहैकार्थसमवायेन महत्या प्रत्यासत्त्याऽवयविरूपादिकमारभते तद्यथा कपालरूपादिघटे रूपादिकमारभते इति सर्वत्र द्रष्टव्यम् चकारादमीषां क्वचिन्निमित्तत्वमपि समुच्चिनोति।।

कारणसमवायस्य संयोगः परस्य ।। 5 ।।

Aph. 5. Conjunction through co-inherence in the cause [is the non-coinherent cause] of a piece of cloth.

It is stated that the lesser relation belongs to conjunction which is the non-coinherent cause in the origination of a substance. Conjunction, through co-inherence in the cause, that is, in the co-inherent cause, is the non-coinherent cause of the effect or product by the relation characterised as co-inherence in a same object with effect. By the term piece of cloth product substance generally is indicated. A certain author maintains that if conjunction of part with be a non-coinherent cause of the cloth etc., then co-inherence in the same object with the cause is also a non-coinherent cause.[1] U.

कारणकारणसमवायाच्च ।। 6 ।।

Aph. 6. Also through co-inherence with the cause of the cause.

It is stated that causality by the greater relation sometimes pertains to conjunction. The conjunction technically termed coalition, and residing in the constituent portions of a ball of cotton, originates magnitude in the ball of cotton; and there is therein the relation of co-inherence in the same object as the cause.[2] U.

संयुक्तसमवायादग्नेर्वैशेषिकम् ।। 7 ।।

Aph. 7. The differentiating character of fire [is an operative or efficient cause] through co-inherence with the conjunct.

Operative causality is described. The differentrting character of fire, that is heat which is its peculiar attribute, is through co-inherence with the conjunct, the efficient cause of colour etc. produced by baking. Hot touch, then, is the operative cause of qualities produced by baking, by the relation of conjunction with its own substratum. The general definition of an efficient cause is to be understood to be a cause other

[1] द्रव्यारम्भे संयोगस्यासमवायिकारणस्य लघ्वी प्रत्यासत्तिमाह। कारणे समवायिकारणे समवायात् संयोगोऽपि पटादौ कार्ये कार्यैकार्थसमवायलक्षणया प्रत्यासत्त्याऽसमवायिकारणमित्यर्थः पटपदेन कार्यद्रव्यमात्रमुपलक्षपति यदित्ववयवावयविसंयोगोऽपि पटादेरसमवायिकारणं तदा कारणैकार्थसमवायोऽपीति कश्चित्।।

[2] संयोगस्त क्वचित् महत्या प्रत्यासत्त्या कारणत्वमित्याह। तूलपिण्डावयवेषु वर्तमानः प्रचयाख्यः संयोगस्तूलकपिण्डे महत्वमारभते तत्र कारणैकार्थसमवायः प्रत्यासत्तिरित्यर्थः।।

than the co-inherent and non-coinherent causes.[1] V.

दृष्टानां दृष्टप्रयोजनानां दृष्टाभावे प्रयोगो ऽभ्युदयाय।। ८।।

Aph. 8. The employment of visible observances, the uses whereof are visible, in the absence of visible results tends to exaltation.

The employment, or performance, of observances, such as sacrifice, almsgiving, penance etc. which are visible, that is, which are duly celebrated, and the uses whereof are visible, that is, the utility of which is known by imperative precepts, in the absence of visible results of these respective observances, where such results are impossible in consequence of absence of desire for such and such consequences, tends to exaltation, that is, to resultant desire of knowledge induced by purity of intellect. Observances, therefore, whose utility is determined as elysian bliss etc., enjoined by such precepts as Let him who desires paradise offer the sacrifice of horses, when performed disinterestedly, do not produce elysian bliss etc. as their fruit, but produce as their result purity of intellect and the like, according to the Vedic text. They desire knowledge, and the traditional text When wordly attachment has by observances born its fruits, knowledge is afterwards produced.[2] V.

तद्वचनादाम्नायस्य प्रामाण्यमिति।। ९।।

Aph. 9. [It has been stated that] authoritativeness pertains to revelation because declared by Him.

The word *iti* indicates the conclusion of the system. Authoritativeness pertains to revelation, that is to the Veda, because declared, that is promulgated, by Him, the divine being. For it is proved that the Vedas have a personal author, inasmuch as they are an

[1] निमित्तकारणतां निरूपयति। अग्नेर्वैशेषिकं विशेषगुणात्मकमौष्ण्यं संयुक्तसमवायात् पाकजरूपादौ निमित्तकारणम् तथाच पाकजं प्रति स्वश्रयसंयोगसम्बन्धेन उष्णस्पर्शोनिमित्तकारणम् समवायिकारणासमवायिकारणभिन्नं कारणं निमित्तकारणमिति सामान्यलक्षणं बोध्यम्।।

[2] दृष्टानां विधिदृष्टानां दृष्टप्रयोजनानां दृष्टं विध्यर्थवादादिनां ज्ञातं प्रयोजनं येषां तथाविधानां कर्मणां यज्ञदानतपःप्रभृतीनां प्रयोगोऽनुष्ठानं दृष्टानां तत्तत्कर्मफलानामभावे तत्तत् फलकामनाविरहादसम्भवे अभ्युदयाय चित्तशुद्धिप्रयुक्तविविदिषात्मकफलाय भवति तथाच स्वर्गकामोऽश्वमेधेन यजेत इत्यादिविधिविहितानां स्वर्गाद्यात्मकप्रतिनियतप्रयोजनानां कर्मणां निष्कामेण कृतानां न स्वर्गादिफलजनकत्वं किन्तु चित्तशुद्धाद्यात्मक-फलजनकत्वमेव विविदिषन्ति इत्यादिश्रुतेः कषाये कर्मभिः पक्वे ततोज्ञानं प्रजायते इत्यादिस्मृतेश्चेति भावः।।

enouncement. Nor can beings like us be the enunciators of these, appropriated to a thousand branches. Moreover their objects transcend the senses, and beings of our nature cannot behold objects that transcend the senses. The Vedas, again, are rightly affirmed, inasmuch as they are received by the heighest authorities. That which is not rightly affirmed is not received by the highest authorities, but these being received by such, are rightly affirmed. To be rightly affirmed is to be promulgated by an independent personal author; and to be received by the heighest authorities is to be an object in course of performance by persons attached to all the systems. It has been stated that non-existence of result sometimes accrues from the disparity of the action, the agent, and the means. If it be denied that is so, the agent not being remembered; we refuse such denial it having been already proved that the agent is remembered. The promulgation thereof by him is proved inasmuch as it could be promulgated only by an intelligent personal author, while such independent power to promulgate the Vedas in their thousand branches, is, as has been said, impossible for beings of our nature. Inasmuch, moreover, as certitude has excellence for its condition, the certitude of the Veda must have excellence for its condition, and the excellence must in this case be pronounced to be the enunciator's right knowledge of the matter of the enouncement. The enunciator of the Veda must be one who has an intuition of elysium, requitative efficacy, and the like, and there is none such but God alone.[1] U.

[1] इति शस्त्रपरिसमाप्तौ तद्वचनात्तेनेश्वरेण वचनात् प्रणयनादाम्नायस्य वेदस्य प्रामाण्यं तथाहि वेदास्तावत् पौरुषेया वाक्यत्वादितिसाधितं नचास्मदादयस्तेषां सहस्त्रशाखावच्छिन्नानां वक्तारः सम्भाव्यन्ते अतीन्द्रियार्थत्वात् नचातीन्द्रियार्थदर्थिनोऽस्मदादयः किञ्चाप्तोक्तावेदा महाजनपरिगृहीतत्वात् यन्नाप्तोक्तं नन्तन्महाजनपरिगृहीतं महाजनपरिगृहीतञ्चेदं तस्मादाप्तोक्तम् स्वतन्त्रपुरुषप्रणीतत्वञ्चाप्तोक्तत्वम् महाजनपरिगृहीतत्वञ्च सर्वदर्शनान्तःपातिपुरुषानुष्ठीयमानार्थत्वम् क्वचित् फलाभावः कर्मकर्तृसाधनवैगुण्यादित्युक्तम् कर्तृस्मरणाभावान्नैवमिति चेन्न कर्तृस्मरणस्य पूर्वमेव साधितत्वात् तत्प्रणीतत्वञ्च स्वतन्त्रपुरुषप्रणीतत्वादेव सिद्धम् न त्वस्मदादीनां सहस्त्रशाखवेदप्रणयने स्वातन्त्र्यं संभवतीत्युक्तत्वात्। किञ्च प्रमाया गुणजन्यत्वेन वैदिकप्रमाया अपि गुणजन्यत्वमावश्यकं तत्र च गुणो वक्तृयथार्थवाक्यार्थज्ञानमेव वाच्यस्तथाच तादृश एव वेदे वक्ता यः स्वर्गापूर्वादिविषयकसाक्षात्कारवान् तादृशश्च नेश्वरादन्य इति सुष्ठु।।